Holy the Firm

ANNIE DILLARD

Holy the Firm

G.K.HALL &CO.

 Boston, Massachusetts

1978

248
TBC

Library of Congress Cataloging in Publication Data

Dillard, Annie.
  Holy the firm.

  Large print ed.
  1. Meditations. 2. Large type books.
I. Title.
[BV4832.2.D54 1978] 242 78-85
ISBN 0-8161-6571-8

A portion of this work originally appeared in *Harper's Magazine*.

Published in Large Print by arrangement with Harper & Row, Publishers

Set in Compugraphic 18 pt English Times

for Gary

Holy the Firm

PART ONE

Newborn and Salted

Every day is a god, each day is a god, and
holiness holds forth in time. I worship
each god, I praise each day splintered
down, splintered down and wrapped in
time like a husk, a husk of many colors

5

spreading, at dawn fast over the mountains split.

I wake in a god. I wake in arms holding my quilt, holding me as best they can inside my quilt.

Someone is kissing me — already. I wake, I cry "Oh," I rise from the pillow. Why should I open my eyes?

I open my eyes. The god lifts from the water. His head fills the bay. He is Puget Sound, the Pacific; his breast rises from pastures; his fingers are firs; islands slide wet down his shoulders. Islands slip blue from his shoulders and glide over the water, the empty, lighted water like a stage.

Today's god rises, his long eyes flecked in clouds. He flings his arms, spreading colors; he arches, cupping sky in his belly; he vaults, vaulting and spread, holding all and spread on me like skin.

Under the quilt in my knees' crook is a cat. She wakes; she curls to bite her metal sutures. The day is real; already, I can feel it click, hear it clicking under my knees.

The day is real; the sky clicks securely in place over the mountains, locks round the island, snaps slap on the bay. Air fits flush on farm roofs; it rises inside the doors. of barns and rubs at yellow barn windows. Air clicks up my hand cloven into fingers and wells in my ears' holes, whole and entire. I call it simplicity, the way matter is smooth and alone.

I toss the cat. I stand and smooth the quilt. "Oh," I cry, "Oh!"

I live on northern Puget Sound, in Washington State, alone. I have a gold cat, who sleeps on my legs, named Small. In the morning I joke to her blank face, Do you remember last night? Do you remember? I throw her out before breakfast, so I can eat.

There is a spider, too, in the bathroom, with whom I keep a sort of company. Her little outfit always reminds me of a certain moth I helped to kill. The spider herself is of uncertain lineage, bulbous at the abdomen and drab. Her six-inch mess of a web works, works somehow, works miraculously, to keep her alive and me amazed. The web itself is in a corner behind the toilet, connecting tile wall to tile wall and floor, in a place where there is, I would have thought, scant traffic. Yet under the web are sixteen or so corpses she has tossed to the floor.

The corpses appear to be mostly sow bugs, those little armadillo creatures who live to travel flat out in houses, and die round. There is also a new shred of earwig, three old spider skins crinkled and clenched, and two moth bodies, wingless and huge and empty, moth bodies I drop to my knees to see.

Today the earwig shines darkly and gleams, what there is of him: a dorsal curve of thorax and abdomen, and a smooth pair of cerci by which I knew his name. Next week, if the other bodies are any indication, he will be shrunken and gray, webbed to the floor with dust. The sow bugs beside him are hollow and empty of color, fragile, a breath away from brittle fluff. The spider skins lie on their sides, translucent and ragged, their legs drying in knots. And the moths, the empty moths, stagger against each other, headless, in a confusion of arcing strips of chitin like peeling varnish, like a jumble of buttresses for cathedral domes, like nothing resembling moths, so that I should hesitate to call them moths, except that I have had some experience with the figure Moth reduced to a nub.

Two summers ago I was camping alone in the Blue Ridge Mountains in Virginia. I had hauled myself and gear up there to read, among other things, James Ramsey Ullman's *The Day on Fire,* a novel about Rimbaud that had made me want to be a writer when I was sixteen; I was hoping it would do it again. So I read, lost, every day sitting under a tree by my tent, while warblers swung in the leaves overhead and bristle worms trailed their inches over the twiggy dirt at my feet; and I read every night by candlelight, while barred owls called in the forest and pale moths massed round my head in the clearing, where my light made a ring.

Moths kept flying into the candle. They would hiss and recoil, lost upside down in the shadows among my cooking pans. Or they would singe their wings and fall, and their hot wings, as if melted, would stick to the first thing they touched — a pan, a lid, a spoon — so that the snagged moths could flutter only in tiny arcs, unable to struggle free. These I could release by a quick flip with a stick; in the morning I would find my cooking stuff gilded with torn flecks of moth wings, triangles of shiny dust here and there on the aluminum. So I read, and boiled water, and replenished candles, and read on.

One night a moth flew into the candle, was caught, burnt dry, and held. I must have been staring at the candle, or maybe I looked up when a shadow crossed my page; at any rate, I saw it all. A golden female moth, a biggish one with a two-inch wingspan, flapped into the fire, dropped her abdomen into the wet wax, stuck, flamed frazzled and fried in a second. Her moving wings ignited like tissue paper, enlarging the circle of light in the clearing and creating out of the darkness the sudden blue sleeves of my sweater, the green leaves of jewelweed by my side, the ragged red trunk of a pine. At once the light contracted again and the moth's wings vanished in a fine, foul smoke. At the same time her six legs clawed, curled, blackened, and ceased, disappearing utterly. And her head jerked in spasms, making a spattering noise; her antennae crisped and burned away and her heaving mouth parts crackled like pistol fire. When it was all over, her head was, so far as I could determine, gone, gone the long way of her wings and legs. Had she been new, or old? Had she mated and laid her eggs, had she done her work? All that was left was the glowing horn shell of her abdomen and thorax — a fraying, partially collapsed gold tube jammed upright in the candle's round pool.

And then this moth-essence, this spectacular skeleton, began to act as a wick. She kept burning. The wax rose in the moth's body from her soaking abdomen to her thorax to the jagged hole where her head should be, and widened into flame, a saffron-yellow flame that robed her to the ground like any immolating monk. That candle had two wicks, two flames of identical height, side by side. The moth's head was fire. She burned for two hours, until I blew her out.

She burned for two hours without changing, without bending or leaning — only glowing within, like a building fire glimpsed through silhouetted walls, like a hollow saint, like a flame-faced virgin gone to God, while I read by her light, kindled, while Rimbaud in Paris burnt out his brains in a thousand poems, while night pooled wetly at my feet.

And that is why I believe those hollow crips on the bathroom floor are moths. I think I know moths, and fragments of moths, and chips and tatters of utterly empty moths, in any state. How many of you, I asked the people in my class, which of you want to give your lives and be writers? I was trembling from coffee, or cigarettes, or the closeness of faces all around me. (Is this what we live for? I thought; is this the only final beauty: the color of any skin in any light, and living, human eyes?) All hands rose to the question. (You, Nick? Will you? Margaret? Randy? Why do I want them to mean it?) And then I tried to tell them what the choice must mean: You can't be anything else. You must go at your life with a broadax. . . . They had no idea what I was saying. (I have two hands, don't I? And all this energy, for as long as I can remember. I'll do it in the evenings, after skiing, or on the way home from the bank, or after the children are asleep. . . .) They thought I was raving again. It's just as well.

I have three candles here on the table which I disentangle from the plants and light when visitors come. Small usually avoids them, although once she came too close and her tail caught fire; I rubbed it out before she noticed. The flames move light over everyone's skin, draw light to the surface of the faces of my friends. When the people leave I never blow the candles out, and after I'm asleep they flame and burn.

The Cascade range, in these high latitudes, backs almost into the water. There is only a narrow strip, an afterthought of foothills and farms sixty miles wide, between the snowy mountains and the sea. The mountains wall well. The rest of the country — most of the rest of the planet, in some very real sense, excluding a shred of British Columbia's coastline and the Alaskan islands — is called, and profoundly felt to be, simply "East of the Mountains." I've been there.

I came here to study hard things — rock mountain and salt sea — and to temper my spirit on their edges. "Teach me thy ways, O Lord" is, like all prayers, a rash one, and one I cannot but recommend. These mountains — Mount Baker and the Sisters and Shuksan, the Canadian Coastal Range and the Olympics on the peninsula — are surely the edge of the known and comprehended world. They are high. That they bear their own unimaginable masses and weathers aloft, holding them up in the sky for anyone to see plain, makes them, as Chesterton said of the Eucharist, only the more mysterious by their very visibility and absence of secrecy. They are the western rim of the real, if not considerably beyond it. If the Greeks had looked at Mount Baker all day, their large and honest art would have broken, and they would have gone fishing, as these people do. And as perhaps I one day shall.

But the mountains are, incredibly, east. When I first came here I faced east and watched the mountains, thinking, These are the Ultima Thule, the final westering, the last serrate margin of time. Since they are, incredibly, east, I must be no place at all. But the sun rose over the snowfields and woke me where I lay, and I rose and cast a shadow over someplace, and thought, There is, God help us, more. So gathering my bowls and spoons, and turning my head, as it were, I moved to face west, relinquishing all hope of sanity, for what is more.

And what is more is islands: sea, and unimaginably solid islands, and sea, and a hundred rolling skies. You spill your breath. Nothing holds; the whole show rolls. I can imagine Virginias no less than Pacifics. Inland valley, pool, desert, plain — it's all a falling sheaf of edges, like a quick-flapped deck of cards, like a dory or a day launched all unchristened, lost at sea. Land is a poured thing and time a surface film lapping and fringeing at fastness, at a hundred hollow and receding blues. Breathe fast: we're backing off the rim.

Here is the fringey edge where elements meet and realms mingle, where time and eternity spatter each other with foam. The salt sea and the islands, molding and molding, row upon rolling row, don't quit, nor do winds end nor skies cease from spreading in curves. The actual percentage of land masses to sea in the Sound equals that of the rest of the planet: we have less time than we knew. Time is eternity's pale interlinear, as the islands are the sea's. We have less time than we knew and that time buoyant, and cloven, lucent, and missile, and wild.

The room where I live is plain as a skull, a firm setting for windows. A nun lives in the fires of the spirit, a thinker lives in the bright wick of the mind, an artist lives jammed in the pool of materials. (Or, a nun lives, thoughtful and tough, in the mind, a nun lives, with that special poignancy peculiar to religious, in the exile of material; and a thinker, who would think of something, lives in the clash of materials, and in the world of spirit where all long thoughts must lead; and an artist lives in the mind, that warehouse of forms, and an artist lives, of course, in the spirit. So.) But this room is a skull, a fire tower, wooden, and empty. Of itself it is nothing, but the view, as they say, is good.

Since I live in one room, one long wall of which is glass, I am myself, at everything I do, a backdrop to all the landscape's occasions, to all its weathers, colors and lights. From the kitchen sink, and from my bed, and from the table, the couch, the hearth, and the desk, I see land

17

and water, islands, sky.

The land is complex and shifting: the eye leaves it. There is a white Congregationalist church among Douglas firs; there is a green pasture between two yellow fallow fields; there are sheep bent over beneath some alders, and beside them a yard of running brown hens. But everything in the landscape points to sea. The land's progress of colors leads the eye up a distant hill, a sweeping big farm of a hill whose yellow pastures bounce light all day from a billion stems and blades; and down the hill's rim drops a dark slope of fir forest, a slant your eye rides down to the point, the dark silver of land that holds the bay. From this angle you see the bay cut a crescent; your eye flies up the black beach to the point, or slides down the green firs to the point, and the point is an arrow pointing over and over, with its log-strewn beach, its gray singleness, and its recurved white edging of foam, to sea: to the bright sound, the bluing of water with distance at the world's rim, and on it the far blue islands, and over these lights the light clouds.

You can't picture it, can you? Neither can I. Oh, the desk is yellow, the oak table round, the ferns alive, the mirror cold, and I never have cared. I read. In the Middle Ages, I read, "the idea of a thing which a man framed for himself was always more real to him than the actual thing itself." Of course. I am in my Middle Ages; the world at my feet, the world through the window, is an illuminated manuscript whose leaves the wind takes, one by one, whose painted illuminations and halting words draw me, one by one, and I am dazzled in days and lost.

There is, in short, one country, one room, one enormous window, one cat, one spider, and one person: but I am hollow. And, for now, there are the many gods of mornings and the many things to give them for their work — lungs and heart, muscle, nerve, and bone — and there is the no man's land of many things wherein they dwell, and from which I seek to call them, in work that's mine.

Nothing is going to happen in this book. There is only a little violence here and there in the language, at the corner where eternity clips time.

So I read. Armenians, I read, salt their newborn babies. I check somewhere else: so did the Jews at the time of the prophets. They washed a baby in water, salted him, and wrapped him in cloths. When God promised to Aaron and all the Levites all the offerings Israel made to God, the firstfruits and the firstling livestock, "all the best of the oil, and all the best of the wine," he said of this promise, "It is a covenant of salt forever." In the Roman church baptism, the priest places salt in the infant's mouth.

I salt my breakfast eggs. All day long I feel created. I can see the blown dust on the skin on the back of my hand, the tiny trapezoids of chipped clay, moistened and breathed alive. There are some created sheep in the pasture below me, sheep set down here precisely, just touching their blue shadows hoof to hoof on the grass. Created gulls pock the air, rip great curved seams in the settled air: I greet my created meal, amazed.

I have been drawing a key to the islands I see from my window. Everyone told me a different set of names for them, until one day a sailor came and named them all with such authority that I believed him. So I penciled an outline of the horizon on a sheet of paper and labeled the lobes: Skipjack, Sucia, Saturna, Salt Spring, Bare Island. . . .

Today, November 18 and no wind, today a veil of air has lifted that I didn't know was there. I see a new island, a new wrinkle, the deepening of wonder, behind the blue translucence the sailor said is Salt Spring Island. I have no way of learning its name. I bring the labeled map to the table and pencil a new line. Call that: Unknown Island North; Water-Statue; Sky-Ruck; Newborn and Salted; Waiting for Sailor.

Henry Miller relates that Knut Hamsun once said, in response to a questionnaire, that he wrote to kill time. This is funny in a number of ways. In a number of ways I kill myself laughing, looking out at islands. Startled, the yellow cat on the floor stares over her shoulder. She has carried in a wren, I suddenly see, a wren she had killed, whose dead wings point askew on the circular rug. It is time. Out with you both. I'm busy laughing, to kill time. I shoo the cat from the door, turn the wren over in my palm, unmoved, and drop him from the porch, down to the winterkilled hair grass and sedge, where the cat may find him if she will, or crows, or beetles, or rain.

When I next look up from my coffee, there is a ruckus on the porch. The cat has dragged in a god, scorched. He is alive. I run outside. Save for his wings, he is a perfect, very small man. He is fair, thin-skinned in the cat's mouth, and kicking. His hair is on fire and stinks; his wingtips are blackened and seared. From the two soft flaps of the cat's tiger muzzle his body jerks, naked. One of his miniature hands pushed hard at her nose. He waves his thighs; he beats her face and the air with his smoking wings. I cannot breathe. I run at the cat to scare her; she drops him, casting at me an evil look, and runs from the porch.

The god lies gasping and perfect. He is no longer than my face. Quickly I snuff the smoldering fire in his yellow hair with a finger and thumb. In so doing I accidentally touch his skull, brush against his hot skull, which is the size of a hazelnut, as the saying goes, warm-skinned and alive.

He rolls his colorless eyes toward mine: his long wings catch strength from the sun, and heave.

Later I am walking in the day's last light. The god rides barefoot on my shoulder, or astride it, or tugging or swinging on loops of my hair.

He is whistling at my ear; he is blowing a huge tune in my ear, a myth about November. He is heaping a hot hurricane into my ear, into my hair, an ignorant ditty calling things real, calling island out of the sea, calling solid moss from curling rock, and ducks down the sky for the winter.

I see it! I see it all! Two islands, twelve islands, worlds, gather substance, gather the blue contours of time, and array themselves down distance, mute and hard.

I seem to see a road; I seem to be on a road, walking. I seem to walk on a blacktop road that runs over a hill. The hill creates itself, a powerful suggestion. It creates itself, thickening with apparently solid earth and waving plants, with houses and browsing cattle, unrolling wherever my eyes go, as though my focus were a brush painting in a world. I cannot escape the illusion. The colorful thought persists, this world, a dream forced into my ear and sent round my body on ropes of hot blood. If I throw my eyes past the rim of the hill to see the real — stars, were they? something with wings, or loops? — I elaborate the illusion instead; I rough in a middle ground. I stitch the transparent curtain solid with bright phantom mountains, with thick clouds gliding just so over their shadows on green water, with blank, impenetrable sky. The dream fills in, like wind widening over a bay. Quickly I look to the flat dream's rim for a glimpse of that old deep . . . and, just as quickly, the blue slaps shut, the colors wrap everything out. There is not a chink. The sky is gagging on trees. I seem to be on a road, walking, greeting the hedgerows, the rose hips, apples, and thorn. I seem to be on a road walking, familiar with neighbors, high-handed with cattle, smelling the sea, and alone. Already, I know the names of things. I can kick a stone.

Time is enough, more than enough, and matter multiple and given. The god of today is a child, a baby new and filling the house, remarkably here in the flesh. He is day. He thrives in a cup of wind, landlocked and thrashing. He unrolls, revealing his shape an edge at a time, a smatter of content, footfirst: a word, a friend for coffee, a windshift, the shingling or coincidence of ideas. Today, November 18 and no wind, is clear. Terry Wean — who fishes, and takes my poetry course — could see Mount Rainier. He hauls his reef net gear from the bay; we talk on its deck while he hammers at shrunken knots. The Moores for dinner. In bed, I call to me my sad cat, I read. Like a rug or wrap rolling unformed up a loom, the day discovers itself, like the poem.

The god of today is rampant and drenched. His arms spread, bearing moist pastures; his fingers spread, fingering the shore. He is time's live skin; he burgeons up from day like any tree. His legs spread crossing the heavens, flicking hugely, and flashing and arcing around the earth toward night.

This is the one world, bound to itself

and exultant. If fizzes up in trees, trees heaving up streams of salt to their leaves. This is the one air, bitten by grackles; time is alone and in and out of mind. The god of today is a boy, pagan and fernfoot. His power is enthusiasm; his innocence is mystery. He sockets into everything that is, and that right holy. Loud as music, filling the grasses and skies, his day spreads rising at home in the hundred senses. He rises, new and surrounding; he *is* everything that is, wholly here and emptied — flung, and flowing, sowing, unseen, and flown.

PART TWO

God's Tooth

Into this world falls a plane.

The earth is a mineral speckle planted in trees. The plane snagged its wing on a tree, fluttered in a tiny arc, and struggled down.

I heard it go. The cat looked up. There was no reason: the plane's engine simply stilled after takeoff, and the light plane failed to clear the firs. It fell easily; one wing snagged on a fir top; the metal fell down the air and smashed in the thin woods where cattle browse; the fuel exploded; and Julie Norwich seven years old burnt off her face.

Little Julie mute in some room at St. Joe's now, drugs dissolving into the sheets. Little Julie with her eyes naked and spherical, baffled. Can you scream without lips? Yes. But do children in long pain scream?

It is November 19 and no wind, and no hope of heaven, and no wish for heaven, since the meanest of people show more mercy than hounding and terrorist gods.

The airstrip, a cleared washboard affair on the flat crest of a low hill, is a few long fields distant from my house — up the road and through the woods, or across the sheep pasture and through the woods.

A flight instructor told me once that when his students get cocky, when they think they know how to fly a plane, he takes them out here and makes them land on that field. You go over the wires and down, and along the strip and up before the trees, or vice versa, vice versa, depending on the wind. But the airstrip is not unsafe. Jesse's engine failed. The FAA will cart the wreckage away, bit by bit, picking it out of the tree trunk, and try to discover just why that engine failed. In the meantime, the emergency siren has sounded, causing everyone who didn't see the plane go down to halt — Patty at her weaving, Jonathan slicing apples, Jan washing her baby's face — to halt, in pity and terror, wondering which among us got hit, by what bad accident, and why. The volunteer firemen have mustered; the fire trucks have come — stampeding Shuller's sheep — and gone, bearing burnt Julie and Jesse her father to the emergency room in town, leaving the rest of us to gossip, fight grass fires on the airstrip, and pray, or wander from window to window, fierce.

So she is burnt on her face and neck, Julie Norwich. The one whose teeth are short in a row, Jesse and Ann's oldest, red-kneed, green-socked, carrying cats.

I saw her only once. It was two weeks ago, under an English hawthorn tree, at the farm.

There are many farms in this neck of the woods, but only one we call "the farm" — the old Corcoran place, where Gus grows hay and raises calves: the farm, whose abandoned frame chicken coops ply the fields like longboats, like floating war canoes; whose clay driveway and grass footpaths are a tangle of orange calendula blossoms, ropes, equipment, and seeding grasses; the farm, whose canny heifers and bull calves figure the fences, run amok to the garden, and plant themselves suddenly black and white, up to their necks in green peas.

Between the gray farmhouse and the barn is the green grass farmyard, suitable for all projects. That day, sixteen of us were making cider. It was cold. There were piles of apples everywhere. We had filled our trucks that morning, climbing trees and shaking their boughs, dragging tarps heavy with apples, hauling bushels and boxes and buckets of apples, and loading them all back to the farm. Jesse and Ann, who are in their thirties, with Julie and the baby, whose name I forget, had driven down from the mountains that morning with a truckload of apples, loose, to make cider with us, fill their jugs, and drive back. I had not met them before. We all drank coffee on the farmhouse porch to warm us; we hosed jugs in the yard. Now we were throwing apples into a shredder and wringing the mash through pillowcases, staining our palms and freezing our fingers, and decanting the pails into seventy one-gallon jugs. And all this long day, Julie Norwich chased my cat Small around the farmyard and played with her, manhandled her, next to the porch under the hawthorn tree.

She was a thin child, pointy-chinned, yellow bangs and braids. She squinted, and when you looked at her she sometimes started laughing, as if you had surprised her at using some power she wasn't yet ready to show. I kept my eye on her, wondering if she was cold with her sweater unbuttoned and bony knees bare.

She would hum up a little noise for half-hour stretches. In the intervals, for maybe five minutes each, she was trying, very quietly, to learn to whistle. I think. Or she was practicing a certain concentrated face. But I think she was trying to learn to whistle, because sometimes she would squeak a little falsetto note through an imitation whistle hole in her lips, as if that could fool anyone. And all day she was dressing and undressing the yellow cat, sticking it into a black dress, a black dress long and full as a nun's.

I was amazed at that dress. It must have been some sort of doll clothing she had dragged with her in the truck; I've never seen its kind before or since. A white collar bibbed the yoke of it like a guimpe.

It had great black sleeves like wings. Julie scooped up the cat and rammed her into the cloth. I knew how she felt, exasperated, breaking her heart on a finger curl's width of skinny cat arm. I knew the many feelings she had sticking those furry arms through the sleeves. Small is not large: her limbs feel like bird bones strung in a sock. When Julie had the cat dressed in its curious habit, she would rock it like a baby doll. The cat blinked, upside down.

Once she whistled at it, or tried, blowing in its face; the cat poured from her arms and ran. It leapt across the driveway, lightfoot in its sleeves; its black dress pulled this way and that, dragging dust, bent up in back by its yellow tail. I was squeezing one end of a twisted pillowcase full of apple mash and looking over my shoulder. I watched the cat hurdle the driveway and vanish under the potting shed, cringing; I watched Julie dash after it without hesitation, seize it, hit its face, and drag it back to the tree, carrying it caught fast by either forepaw, so its body hung straight from its arms.

She saw me watching her and we exchanged a look, a very conscious and self-conscious look — because we look a bit alike and we both knew it; because she was still short and I grown; because I was stuck kneeling before the cider pail, looking at her sidewise over my shoulder; because she was carrying the cat so oddly, so that she had to walk with her long legs parted; because it was my cat, and she'd dressed it, and it looked like a nun; and because she knew I'd been watching her, and how fondly, all along. We were laughing.

We *looked* a bit alike. Her face is slaughtered now, and I don't remember mine. It is the best joke there is, that we are here, and fools — that we are sown into time like so much corn, that we are souls sprinkled at random like salt into time and dissolved here, spread into matter, connected by cells right down to our feet, and those feet likely to fell us over a tree root or jam us on a stone. The joke part is that we forget it. Give the mind two seconds alone and it thinks it's Pythagoras. We wake up a hundred times a day and laugh.

The joke of the world is less like a banana peel than a rake, the old rake in the grass, the one you step on, foot to forehead. It all comes together. In a twinkling. You have to admire the gag for its symmetry, accomplishing all with one right angle, the same right angle which accomplishes all philosophy. One step on the rake and it's mind under matter once again. You wake up with a piece of tree in your skull. You wake up with fruit on your hands. You wake up in a clearing and see yourself, ashamed. You see your own face and it's seven years old and there's no knowing why, or where you've been since. We're tossed broadcast into time like so much grass, some ravening god's sweet hay. You wake up and a plane falls out of the sky.

That day was a god, too, the day we made cider and Julie played under the hawthorn tree. He must have been a heyday sort of god, a husbandman. He was spread under gardens, sleeping in time, an innocent old man scratching his head, thinking of pruning the orchard, in love with families.

Has he no power? Can the other gods carry time and its loves upside down like a doll in their blundering arms? As though we the people were playing house — when we are serious and do love — and not the gods? No, that day's god has no power. No gods have power to save. There are only days. The one great god abandoned us to days, to time's tumult of occasions, abandoned us to the gods of days each brute and amok in his hugeness and idiocy.

Jesse her father had grabbed her clear of the plane this morning, and was hauling her off when the fuel blew. A gob of flung ignited vapor hit her face, or something flaming from the plane or fir tree hit her face. No one else was burned, or hurt in any way.

So this is where we are. Ashes, ashes,

all fall down. How could I have forgotten? Didn't I see the heavens wiped shut just yesterday, on the road walking? Didn't I fall from the dark of the stars to these senselit and noisome days? The great ridged granite millstone of time is illusion, for only the good is real; the great ridged granite millstone of space is illusion, for God is spirit and worlds his flimsiest dreams: but the illusions are almost perfect, are apparently perfect for generations on end, and the pain is also, and undeniably, real. The pain within the millstones' pitiless turning is real, for our love for each other — for world and all the products of extension — is real, vaulting, insofar as it is love, beyond the plane of the stones' sickening churn and arcing to the realm of spirit bare. And you can get caught holding one end of a love, when your father drops, and your mother; when a land is lost, or a time, and your friend blotted out, gone, your brother's body spoiled, and cold, your infant dead, and you dying: you reel out love's long line alone, stripped like a live wire loosing its sparks to a cloud, like a live wire loosed in space to longing and grief everlasting.

I sit at the window. It is a fool's lot, this sitting always at windows spoiling little blowy slips of paper and myself in the process. Shall I be old? Here comes Small, old sparrow-mouth, wanting my lap. Done. Do you have any earthly idea how young I am? Where's your dress, kitty? I suppose I'll outlive this wretched cat. Get another. Leave it my silver spoons, like old ladies you hear about. I prefer dogs.

So I read. Angels, I read, belong to nine different orders. Seraphs are the highest; they are aflame with love for God, and stand closer to him than the others. Seraphs love God; cherubs, who are second, possess perfect knowledge of him. So love is greater than knowledge; how could I have forgotten? the seraphs are born of a stream of fire issuing from under God's throne. They are, according to Dionysius the Areopagite, "all wings," having, as Isaiah noted, six wings apiece, two of which they fold over their eyes. Moving perpetually toward God, they perpetually praise him, crying Holy, Holy, Holy. . . . But, according to some rabbinic writings, they can sing only the first "Holy" before the intensity of their love ignites them again and dissolves them again, perpetually, into flames. "Abandon everything," Dionysius told his disciple. "God despises ideas."

God despises everything, apparently. If he abandoned us, slashing creation loose at its base from any roots in the real; and if we in turn abandon everything — all these illusions of time and space and lives — in order to love only the real: then where are we? Thought itself is impossible, for subject can have no guaranteed connection without object, nor any object with God. Knowledge is impossible. We are precisely nowhere, sinking on an entirely imaginary ice floe, into entirely imaginary seas themselves adrift. Then we reel out love's long line alone toward a God less lovable than a grasshead, who treats us less well than we treat our lawns.

Of faith I have nothing, only of truth: that this one God is a brute and traitor, abandoning us to time, to necessity and the engines of matter unhinged. This is no leap; this is evidence of things seen: one Julie, one sorrow, one sensation bewildering the heart, and enraging the mind, and causing me to look at the world stuff appalled, at the blithering rock of trees in a random wind, at my hand like some gibberish sprouted, my first opening and closing, so that I think, Have I once turned my hand in this circus, have I ever called it home?

Faith would be that God is self-limited utterly by his creation — a contraction of the scope of his will; that he bound himself to time and its hazards and haps as a man would lash himself to a tree for love. That God's works are as good as we make them. That God is helpless, our baby to bear, self-abandoned on the doorstep to time, wondered at by cattle and oxen. Faith would be that God moved and moves once and for all and "down," so to speak, like a diver, like a man who eternally gathers himself for a dive and eternally is diving, and eternally splitting the spread of the water, and eternally drowned.

Faith would be, in short, that God has any willful connection with time whatsoever, and with us. For I know it as given that God is all good. And I take it also as given that whatever he touches has meaning, if only in his mysterious terms, the which I readily grant. The question is, then, whether God touches anything. Is anything firm, or is time on the loose? Did Christ descend once and for all to no purpose, in a kind of divine and kenotic suicide, or ascend once and for all, pulling his cross up after him like a rope ladder home? Is there — even if Christ holds the tip of things fast and stretches eternity clear to the dim souls of men — is there no link at the base of things, some kernel or air deep in the matrix of matter from which universe furls like a ribbon twined into time?

Has God a hand in this? Then it is a good hand. But has he a hand at all? Or is he a holy fire burning self-contained for power's sake alone? Then he knows himself blissfully as flame unconsuming, as all brilliance and beauty and power, and the rest of us can go hang. Then the accidental universe spins mute, obedient only to its own gross terms, meaningless, out of mind, and alone. The universe is neither contingent upon nor participant in the holy, in being itself, the real, the power play of fire. The universe is illusion, merely, not one speck of it real, and we are not only its victims, falling always into or smashed by a planet slung by its sun — but also it captives, bound by the mineral-made ropes of our senses.

But how do we know — how could we know — that the real is there? By what freak chance does the skin of illusion ever split, and reveal to us the real, which seems to know us by name, and by what freak chance and why did the capacity to prehend it evolve?

I sit at the window, chewing the bones in my wrist. Pray for them: for Julie, for Jesse her father, for Ann her mother, pray. Who will teach us to pray? The god of today is a glacier. We live in his shifting crevasses, unheard. The god of today is delinquent, a barn-burner, a punk with a pittance of power in a match. It is late, a late time to be living. Now it is afternoon; the sky is appallingly clear. Everything in the landscape points to sea, and the sea is nothing; it is snipped from the real as a stuff without form, rising up the sides of islands and falling, mineral to mineral, salt.

Everything I see — the water, the log-wrecked beach, the farm on the hill, the bluff, the white church in the trees — looks overly distinct and shining. (What is the relationship of color to this sun, of sun to anything else?) It all looks staged. It all looks brittle and unreal, a skin of colors painted on glass, which if you prodded it with a finger would powder and fall. A blank sky, perfectly blended with all other sky, has sealed over the crack in the world where the plane fell, and the air has hushed the matter up.

If days are gods, then gods are dead, and artists pyrotechnic fools. Time is a hurdy-gurdy, a lampoon, and death's a bawd. We're beheaded by the nick of time. We're logrolling on a falling world, on time released from meaning and rolling loose, like one of Atalanta's golden apples, a bauble flung and forgotten, lapsed, and the gods on the lam.

And now outside the window, deep on the horizon, a new thing appears, as if we needed a new thing. It is a new land blue beyond islands, hitherto hidden by haze and now revealed, and as dumb as the rest. I check my chart, my amateur penciled sketch of the skyline. Yes, this land is new, this spread blue spark beyond yesterday's new wrinkled line, beyond the blue veil a sailor said was Salt Spring Island. How long can this go on? But let us by all means extend the scope of our charts.

I draw it as I seem to see it, a blue chunk fitted just so beyond islands, a wag of graphite rising just here above another anonymous line, and here meeting the slope of Salt Spring: though whether this be headland I see or heartland, or the distance-blurred bluffs of a hundred bays, I have no way of knowing, or if it be island or main. I call it Thule, O Julialand, Time's Bad News; I name it Terror, the Farthest Limb of the Day, God's Tooth.

PART THREE

Holy the Firm

I know only enough of God to want to worship him, by any means ready to hand. There is an anomalous specificity to all our experience in space, a scandal of particularity, by which God burgeons up or showers down into the shabbiest of occasions, and leaves his creation's dealing with him in the hands of purblind and clumsy amateurs. This is all we are and all we ever were; God *kann nicht anders*. This process in time is history; in space, at such shocking random, it is mystery.

A blur of romance clings to our notions of "publicans," "sinners," "the poor," "the people in the marketplace," "our neighbors," as though of course God should reveal himself, if at all, to these simple people, these Sunday school watercolor figures, who are so purely themselves in their tattered robes, who are single in themselves, while we now are various, complex, and full at heart. We are busy. So, I see now, were they. Who shall stand in his holy place? There is no one but us. There is no one to send, nor a clean hand, nor a pure heart on the face of the earth, nor in the earth, but only us, a generation comforting ourselves with the notion that we have come at an awkward time, that our innocent fathers are all dead — as if innocence had ever been —

and our children busy and troubled, and we ourselves unfit, not yet ready, having each of us chosen wrongly, made a false start, failed, yielded to impulse and the tangled comfort of pleasures, and grown exhausted, unable to seek the thread, weak, and involved. But there is no one but us. There never has been. There have been generations which remembered, and generations which forgot; there has never been a generation of whole men and women who lived well for even one day. Yet some have imagined well, with honesty and art, the detail of such a life, and have described it with such grace, that we mistake vision for history, dream for description, and fancy that life has devolved. So. You learn this studying any history at all, especially the lives of artists and visionaries; you learn it from Emerson, who noticed that the meanness of our days is itself worth our thought; and you learn it, fitful in your pew, at church.

There is one church here, so I go to it. On Sunday mornings I quit the house and wander down the hill to the white frame church in the firs. On a big Sunday there might be twenty of us there; often I am the only person under sixty, and feel as though I'm on an archaeological tour of Soviet Russia. The members are of mixed denominations; the minister is a Congregationalist, and wears a white shirt. The man knows God. Once, in the middle of the long pastoral prayer of intercession for the whole world — for the gift of wisdom to its leaders, for hope and mercy to the grieving and pained, succor to the oppressed, and God's grace to all — in the middle of this he stopped, and burst out, "Lord, we bring you these same petitions every week." After a shocked pause, he continued reading the prayer. Because of this, I like him very much. "Good morning!" he says after the first hymn and invocation, startling me witless every time, and we all shout back, "Good morning!"

The churchwomen all bring flowers for the altar; they haul in arrangements as big as hedges, of wayside herbs in season, and flowers from their gardens, huge bunches of foliage and blossoms as tall as I am, in vases the size of tubs, and the altar still looks empty, irredeemably linoleum, and beige. We had a wretched singer once, a guest from a Canadian congregation, a hulking blond girl with chopped hair and big shoulders, who wore tinted spectacles and a long lacy dress, and sang, grinning, to faltering accompaniment, an entirely secular song about mountains. Nothing could have been more apparent than that God loved this girl; nothing could more surely convince me of God's unending mercy than the continued existence on earth of the church.

The higher Christian churches — where, if anywhere, I belong — come at God with an unwarranted air of professionalism, with authority and pomp, as though they knew what they were doing, as though people in themselves were an appropriate set of creatures to have dealings with God. I often think of the set pieces of liturgy as certain words which people have successfully addressed to God without their getting killed. In the high churches they saunter through the liturgy like Mohawks along a strand of scaffolding who have long since forgotten their danger. If God were to blast such a service to bits, the congregation would be, I believe, genuinely shocked. But in the low churches you expect it any minute. This is the beginning of wisdom.

Today is Friday, November 20. Julie Norwich is in the hospital, burned; we can get no word of her condition. People released from burn wards, I read once, have a very high suicide rate. They had not realized, before they were burned, that life could include such suffering, nor that they personally could be permitted such pain. No drugs ease the pain of third-degree burns, because burns destroy skin: the drugs simply leak into the sheets. His disciples asked Christ about a roadside beggar who had been blind from birth, "Who did sin, this man or his parents, that he was born blind?" And Christ, who spat on the ground, made a mud of his spittle and clay, plastered the mud over the man's eyes, and gave him sight, answered, "Neither hath this man sinned, nor his parents: but that the works of God should be made manifest in him." Really? If we take this answer to refer to the affliction itself — and not the subsequent cure — as "God's works made manifest," then we have, along with "Not as the world gives do I give unto you," two meager, baffling, and infuriating answers to one of the few questions worth asking, to wit, What in the Sam Hill is going on here?

The works of God made manifest? Do we really need more victims to remind us that we're all victims? Is this some sort of parade for which a conquering army shines up its terrible guns and rolls them up and down the streets for the people to see? Do we need blind men stumbling about, and little flamefaced children, to remind us what God can — and will — do?

I am drinking boiled coffee and watching the bay from the window.

Almost all of the people who reef net have hauled their gears for the winter; the salmon runs are over, days are short. Still, boats come and go on the water — tankers, tugs and barges, rowboats and sails. There are killer whales if you're lucky, rafts of harlequin ducks if you're lucky, and every day the scoter and the solitary grebes. How many tons of sky can I see from the window? It is morning: morning! and the water clobbered with light. Yes, in fact, we do. We do need reminding, not of what God can do, but of what he cannot do, or will not, which is to catch time in its free fall and stick a nickel's worth of sense into our days. And we need reminding of what time can do, must only do; churn out enormity at random and beat it, with God's blessing, into our heads: that we are created, *created,* sojourners in a land we did not make, a land with no meaning of itself and no meaning we can make for it alone. Who are we to demand explanations of God? (And what monsters of perfection should we be if we did not?) We forget ourselves, picnicking; we forget where we are. There is no such thing as a freak accident. "God is at home," says Meister Eckhart. "We are in the far country."

We are most deeply asleep at the switch when we fancy we control any switches at all. We sleep to time's hurdy-gurdy; we wake, if we ever wake, to the silence of God. And then, when we wake to the deep shores of light uncreated, then when the dazzling dark breaks over the far slopes to time, then it's time to toss things, like our reason, and our will; then it's time to break our necks for home.

There are no events but thoughts and the heart's hard turning, the heart's slow learning where to love and whom. The rest is merely gossip, and tales for other times. The god of today is a tree. He is a forest of trees or a desert, or a wedge from wideness down to a scatter of stars, stars like salt low and dumb and abiding. Today's god said: shed. He peels from eternity always, spread; he winds into time like a rind. I am or seem to be on a road walking. The hedges are just where they were. There is a corner, and a long hill, a glimpse of snow on the mountains, a slope planted in apple trees, and a store next to a pasture, where I am going to buy the communion wine.

How can I buy the communion wine? Who am I to buy the communion wine? Someone has to buy the communion wine. Having wine instead of grape juice was my idea, and of course I offered to buy it. Shouldn't I be wearing robes and, especially, a mask? Shouldn't I *make* the communion wine? Are there holy grapes, is there holy ground, is anything here holy? There are no holy grapes, there is no holy ground, nor is there anyone but us. I have an empty knapsack over my parka's shoulders; it is cold, and I'll want my hands in my pockets. According to the Rule of St. Benedict, I should say, Our hands in our pockets. "All things come of thee, O Lord, and of thine own have we given thee." There must be a rule for the purchase of communion wine. "Will that be cash, or charge?" All I know is that when I go to this store — to buy eggs, or

sandpaper, broccoli, wood screws, milk —
I like to tease a bit, if he'll let me, with
the owners' son, two, whose name
happens to be Chandler, and who himself
likes to play in the big bins of nails.

And so, forgetting myself, thank God:
Hullo. Hullo, short and relatively new.
Welcome again to the land of the living,
to time, this hill of beans. Chandler will
have, as usual, none of it. He keeps his
mysterious counsel. And I'm out on the
road again walking, my right hand
forgetting my left. I'm out on the road
again walking, and toting a backload of
God.

Here is a bottle of wine with a label,
Christ with a cork. I bear holiness
splintered into a vessel, very God of very
God, the sempiternal silence personal and
brooding, bright on the back of my ribs. I
start up the hill.

The world is changing. The landscape
begins to respond as a current upwells. It
is starting to clack with itself, though

nothing moves in space and there's no wind. It is starting to utter its infinite particulars, each overlapping and lone, like a hundred hills of hounds all giving tongue. The hedgerows are blackberry brambles, white snowberries, red rose hips, gaunt and clattering broom. Their leafless stems are starting to live visibly deep in their centers, as hidden as banked fires live, and as clearly as recognition, mute, shines forth from eyes. Above me the mountains are raw nerves, sensible and exultant; the trees, the grass, and the asphalt below me are living petals of mind, each sharp and invisible, held in a greeting or glance full perfectly formed. There is something stretched or jostling about the sky which, when I study it, vanishes. Why are there all these apples in the world, and why so wet and transparent? Through all my clothing, through the pack on my back and through the bottle's glass I feel the wine. Walking faster and faster, weightless, I feel the wine. It sheds light in slats through my rib cage, and fills the buttressed vaults of my ribs with light pooled and buoyant. I am moth; I am light. I am prayer and I can hardly see.

Each thing in the world is translucent, even the cattle, and moving, cell by cell. I remember this reality. Where has it been? I sail to the crest of the hill as if blown up the slope of a swell. I see, blasted, the bay transfigured below me, that saltwater bay, far down the hill past the road to my house, past the firs and the church and the sheep in the pasture: the bay and the islands on fire and boundless beyond it, catching alight the unraveling sky. Pieces of the sky are falling down. Everything, everything, is whole, and a parcel of everything else. I myself am falling down, slowly, or slowly lifting up. On the bay's stone shore are people among whom I float, real people, gathering of an afternoon, in the cells of whose skin stream thin colored waters in pieces which give back the general flame.

Christ is being baptized. The one who is Christ is there, and the one who is John, and the dim other people standing on cobbles or sitting on beach logs back from the bay. These are ordinary people — if I am one now, if those are ordinary sheep singing a song in the pasture.

The two men are bare to the waist. The one walks him into the water, and holds him under. His hand is on his neck. Christ is coiled and white under the water, standing on stones.

He lifts from the water. Water beads on his shoulders. I see the water in balls as heavy as planets, a billion beads of water as weighty as worlds, and he lifts them up on his back as he rises. He stands wet in the water. Each one bead is transparent, and each has a world, or the same world, light and alive and apparent inside the drop: it is all there ever could be, moving at once, past and future, and all the people. I can look into any sphere and see people stream past me, and cool my eyes with colors and the sight of the world in spectacle perishing ever, and ever renewed. I do; I deepen into a drop and see all that time contains, all the faces and deeps of the worlds and all the earth's contents, every landscape and room, everything living or made or fashioned, all past and future stars, and especially faces, faces like the cells of everything, faces pouring past me talking, and going, and gone. And I am gone.

For outside it is bright. The surface of things outside the drops has fused. Christ himself and the others, and the brown warm wind, and hair, sky, the beach, the shattered water — all this has fused. It is the one glare of holiness; it is bare and unspeakable. There is no speech nor language; there is nothing, no one thing, nor motion, nor time. There is only this everything. There is only this, and its bright and multiple noise.

I seem to be on a road, standing still. It is the top of the hill. The hedges are here, subsiding. My hands are in my pockets. There is a bottle of wine on my back, a California red. I see my feet. I move down the hill toward home.

You must rest now. I cannot rest you.

For me there is, I am trying to tell you, no time.

There are a thousand new islands today, uncharted. They are salt stones on fire and dimming; I read by their light. Small the cat lies on my neck. In the bathroom the spider is working on yesterday's moth.

Esoteric Christanity, I read, posits a substance. It is a created substance, lower than metals and minerals on a "spiritual scale," and lower than salts and earths, occurring beneath salts and earths in the waxy deepness of planets, but never on the surface of planets where men could discern it; and it is in touch with the Absolute, at base. In touch with the Absolute! At base. The name of this substance is: Holy the Firm.

Holy the Firm: and is Holy the Firm in touch with metals and minerals? With salts and earths? Of course, and straight on up, till "up" ends by curving back. Does something that touched something that touched Holy the Firm in touch with the Absolute at base seep into ground water, into grain; are islands rooted in it, and trees? Of course.

Scholarship has long distinguished between two strains of thought which proceed in the West from human knowledge of God. In one, the ascetic's metaphysic, the world is far from God. Emanating from God, and linked to him by Chirst, the world is yet infinitely other than God, furled away from him like the end of a long banner falling. This notion makes, to my mind, a vertical line of the world, a great chain of burning. The more accessible and universal view, held by Eckhart and by many peoples in various forms, is scarcely different from pantheism: that the world is immanation, that God is in the thing, and eternally present here, if nowhere else. By these lights the world is flattened on a horizontal plane, singular, all here, crammed with heaven, and alone. But I know that it is not alone, nor singular, nor all. The notion of immanence needs a handle, and the two ideas themselves need a link, so that life can mean aught to the one, and Christ to the other.

For to immanence, to the heart, Christ is redundant and all things are one. To emanance, to the mind, Christ touches only the top, skims off only the top, as it were, the souls of men, the wheat grains whole, and lets the chaff fall where? To the world flat and patently unredeemed; to the entire rest of the universe, which is irrelevant and nonparticipant; to time and matter unreal, and so unknowable, an illusory, absurd, accidental, and overelaborate stage.

But if Holy the Firm is "underneath salts," if Holy the Firm is matter at its dullest, Aristotle's *materia prima,* absolute at base, then the circle is unbroken. And it is. Thought advances, and the world creates itself, by the gradual positing of, and belief in, a series of bright ideas. Time and space are in touch with the Absolute at base. Eternity sockets twice into time and space curves, bound and bound by idea. Matter and spirit are of a piece but distinguishable; God has a stake guaranteed in all the world. And the universe is real and not a dream, not a manufacture of the senses; subject may know object, knowledge may proceed, and Holy the Firm is in short the philosopher's stone.

These are only ideas, by the single handful. Lines, lines, and their infinite points! Hold hands and crack the whip, and yank the Absolute out of there and into the light, God pale and astounded, spraying a spiral of salts and earths, God footloose and flung. And cry down the line to his passing white ear, "Old Sir! Do you hold space from buckling by a finger in its hole? O Old! Where is your other hand?" His right hand is clenching, calm, round the exploding left hand of Holy the Firm.

How can people think that artists seek a name? A name, like a face, is something you have when you're not alone. There is no such thing as an artist: there is only the

71

world, lit or unlit as the light allows. When the candle is burning, who looks at the wick? When the candle is out, who needs it? But the world without light is wasteland and chaos, and a life without sacrifice is abomination.

What can any artist set on fire but his world? What can any people bring to the altar but all it has ever owned in the thin towns or over the desolate plains? What can an artist use but materials, such as they are? What can he light but the short string of his gut, and when that's burnt out, any muck ready to hand?

His face is flame like a seraph's, lighting the kingdom of God for the people to see; his life goes up in the works; his feet are waxen and salt. He is holy and he is firm, spanning all the long gap with the length of his love, in flawed imitation of Christ on the cross stretched both ways unbroken and thorned. So must the work be also, in touch with, in touch with, in touch with; spanning the gap, from here to eternity, home.

Hoopla! All that I see arches, and light arches around it. The air churns out forces and lashes the marveling land. A hundred times through the fields and along the deep roads I've cried Holy. I see a hundred insects moving across the air, rising and falling. Chipped notes of birdsong descend from the trees, tuneful and broken; the notes pile about me like leaves. Why do these molded clouds make themselves overhead innocently changing, trailing their flat blue shadows up and down everything, and passing, and gone? Ladies and gentlemen! You are given insects, and birdsong, and a replenishing series of clouds. The air is buoyant and wholly transparent, scoured by grasses. The earth stuck through it is noisome, lighted, and salt. Who shall ascend into the hill of the Lord? or who shall stand in his holy place? "Whom shall I send," heard the first Isaiah, "and who will go for us?" And poor Isaiah, who happened to be standing there — and there was no one else — burst out, "Here am I; send me."

There is Julie Norwich. Julie Norwich is salted with fire. She is preserved like a salted fillet from all evil, baptized at birth into time and now into eternity, into the bladelike arms of God. For who will love her now, without a face, when women with faces abound, and people are so? People are reasoned, while God is mad. They love only beauty; who knows what God loves? Happy birthday, little one and wise: you got there early, the easy way. The world knew you before you knew the world. The gods in their boyish, brutal games bore you like a torch, a firebrand, recklessly over the heavens, to the glance of the one God, fathomless and mild, dissolving you into the sheets.

You might as well be a nun. You might as well be God's chaste bride, chased by plunderers to the high caves of solitude, to the hearthless rooms empty of voices, and of warm limbs hooking your heart to the world. Look how he loves you! Are you bandaged now, or loose in a sterilized room? Wait till they hand you a mirror, if you can hold one, and know what it means. That skinlessness, that black shroud of flesh in strips on your skull, is your veil. There are two kinds of nun, out of the cloister or in. You can serve or you can sing, and wreck your heart in prayer, working the world's hard work. Forget whistling: you have no lips for that, or for kissing the face of a man or a child. Learn Latin, an it please my Lord, learn the foolish downward look called Custody of the Eyes.

And learn power, however sweet they call you, learn power, the smash of the holy once more, and signed by its name. Be victim to abruptness and seizures, events intercalated, swellings of heart. You'll climb trees. You won't be able to sleep, or need to, for the joy of it. Mornings, when light spreads over the pastures like wings, and fans a secret color into everything, and beats the trees senseless with beauty, so that you can't tell whether the beauty is *in* the trees — dazzling in cells like yellow sparks or green flashing waters — or *on* them — a transfiguring silver air charged with the wings' invisible motion; mornings, you won't be able to walk for the power of it: earth's too round. And by long and waking day — Sext, None, Vespers — when the grasses, living or dead, drowse while the sun reels, or lash in any wind, when sparrows hush and tides slack at the ebb, or flood up the beaches and cliffsides tangled with weed, and hay waits, and elsewhere people buy shoes — then you kneel, clattering with thoughts, ill, or some days erupting, some days holding the altar rail, gripping the brass-bolt altar rail, so you won't fly. Do you think I don't believe this? You have no idea, none. And nights? Nights after Compline under the ribs of Orion, nights in rooms at lamps or windows like moths? Nights you see Deneb, one-eyed over the trees; you vanish into the sheets, shrunken, your eyes bright as candles and as sightless, exhausted. Nights Murzim, Arcturus, Aldebaran in the Bull: You cry, My father, my father, the chariots of Israel, and the horsemen thereof! Held, held fast by love in the world like the moth in wax, your life a wick, your head on fire with prayer, held utterly, outside and in, you sleep alone, if you call that alone, you cry God.

Julie Norwich; I know. Surgeons will fix your face. This will all be a dream, an anecdote, something to tell your husband one night: I was burned. Or if you're scarred, you're scarred. People love the good not much less than the beautiful, and the happy as well, or even just the living, for the world of it all, and heart's home. You'll dress your own children, sticking their arms through the sleeves. Mornings you'll whistle, full of the pleasure of days, and afternoons this or that, and nights cry love. So live. I'll be the nun for you. I am now.

ON CALL

ON CALL

A Doctor's Journey
in Public Service

ANTHONY S. FAUCI, M.D.

VIKING

VIKING
An imprint of Penguin Random House LLC
penguinrandomhouse.com

ISBN 9780593657478 (hardcover)
ISBN 9780593657485 (ebook)

Printed in the United States of America
1   3   5   7   9   10   8   6   4   2

Designed by Amanda Dewey

For my wife, Christine Grady, who has been my anchor during difficult times and the wind in my sails when I soar,

and for our three amazing daughters, who inspire me and give me great joy and from whom I continue to learn

CONTENTS

Preface   *xi*

Part One: FROM BENSONHURST TO WASHINGTON   *1*

Brooklyn Boy   *3*
Becoming Dr. Fauci   *18*
Heading South   *24*

Part Two: THE AIDS ERA   *31*

Game Changer   *33*
Up Close and Painful   *44*
The Human Immunodeficiency Virus   *49*
Taking the Reins   *61*
Two Brooklyn Boys   *68*
Building an AIDS Research Program   *75*
AIDS Strikes Close to Home   *82*
A Global Catastrophe   *91*
AIDS Activism   *95*
A President, a Gentleman, and a Friend   *118*
La Famiglia   *129*

The Changing of the Guard   *134*

The Search for an HIV Vaccine   *139*

The Lazarus Effect   *147*

HIV Denialism   *153*

An Unequal World   *158*

Part Three: **THE WARS ON TERROR AND DISEASE**   *161*

Widening the Battle   *163*

The Day the World Changed   *167*

Anthrax   *174*

Going Global with AIDS Relief   *188*

Smallpox and Stockpiles   *213*

Project BioShield   *217*

You Have to Love Yogi   *225*

A Reluctant Congress   *228*

Iraq   *232*

Influenza Meets the Supply Chain   *240*

Legacies   *253*

Part Four: **EXPECTING THE UNEXPECTED**   *259*

Enter Obama   *261*

Moving Toward an HIV-Free World   *273*

Epidemics of Disease and Fear   *287*

Patient X   *318*

Zika and Other Surprises   *330*

Passing the Baton   *341*

Part Five: COVID   *343*

A Disease Like None Other   *345*
He Loves Me, He Loves Me Not   *374*
Illegitimi Non Carborundum   *409*
Epilogue   *451*

Acknowledgments   *457*

Preface

I t was Sunday, November 8, 2020, and my wife, Christine, and I were sitting around the fire pit trying to stay warm on this chilly night, balancing plates of shrimp scampi and glasses of wine. We were in the backyard of our longtime next-door neighbors in Northwest Washington, D.C. Christine and I, together with Ellen and Rob, had formed a "COVID pod," as had so many people throughout the country. We were close friends and felt safe and comfortable together. Regardless of the temperature, we shared outdoor dinners almost every weekend during the pandemic, either on our deck or in their backyard. I had been working fourteen to sixteen hours a day for almost a year since the pandemic crashed down on our country and the world in early 2020. Even when the weather found us trying to eat bundled up with scarves and gloves, this brief respite was a welcome relief. New COVID infections were occurring at a rate of about 150,000 per day. There had already been about 10 million infections in the United States, and more than 230,000 people had died. It seemed that our only hope was in vaccines, and several were currently being tested in clinical trials in tens of thousands of people. We had no idea when the trial results would be available or, more importantly, whether the vaccines would work. We were hoping for a vaccine that was at least as effective as the influenza vaccine in a good year and that it might help in containing the pandemic, but there were no guarantees.

About 8:00 p.m. my cell phone rang. "Tony, this is Albert Bourla." Albert is the CEO of the pharmaceutical company Pfizer, which was conducting one of the two mRNA vaccine trials. "Are you sitting down?" he asked. Uh-oh, I thought. This is going to be bad news.

I stood up and walked out to the pathway that separates our front yards to take the call privately. "What's going on, Albert?" I asked, trying to sound upbeat as my stomach lurched.

"You won't believe it, Tony!" he exclaimed. "The DSMB looked at the phase 3 data from the COVID vaccine trial, and there is more than 90 percent efficacy." He was talking about the Data and Safety Monitoring Board, which independently monitors clinical trials to determine if any issues have arisen during the trial that affect the health or safety of patients. At the same time, if results are so good that it would be unethical to continue to give placebo instead of the vaccine, the DSMB can recommend that the trial be terminated early and the data submitted to the Food and Drug Administration (FDA).

This was the case here. Albert continued, "We are planning to announce the news tomorrow."

After we hung up, tears welled up in my eyes, and I felt as if I had lost my breath. I stood there by myself for a moment trying to regain my composure and comprehend the potential impact of what I had just been told. I had been optimistic about the mRNA vaccines all along, but even so, I was not prepared for such resounding results. Influenza vaccines typically have between 40 and 60 percent effectiveness at best in any given flu season. Often, it is much less. The fact that they were projecting at least 90 percent effectiveness for the COVID vaccine was astonishing.

Nor was I expecting to get a vaccine so quickly. It had been just ten months since my team at the National Institutes of Health together with the Pfizer and Moderna companies began working on the novel mRNA vaccine for COVID.

As promised, Pfizer and its German partner, BioNTech, released the results of the trial the next day. A week after Pfizer's news release, Moderna announced that its mRNA vaccine also had more than 90 percent efficacy, and the two companies put in for emergency use authorization with the FDA. This would be the ultimate game changer for the ordeal that the United States and the rest of the world had been suffering through. Millions of lives would be saved.

As I made my way back to the fire pit and picked up my glass of wine, I thought, It is six weeks from my eightieth birthday. What an amazing trip my life has been.

This book is the story of that trip, whose day one was in Brooklyn, New York.

Part One

FROM BENSONHURST
TO WASHINGTON

Brooklyn Boy

The front page of the late city edition of *The New York Times* on Tuesday, December 24, 1940, included headlines such as EVE OF CHRISTMAS FINDS BUSTLING CITY IN FESTIVE SPIRIT juxtaposed next to CHURCHILL BIDS ITALY OUST MUSSOLINI; GREEKS TAKE ANOTHER COASTAL TOWN; GERMANS RAIN BOMBS ON MANCHESTER. That night at 10:24, Anthony Stephen Fauci was born at Brooklyn Hospital to Stephen Anthony Fauci and Eugenia Abys Fauci. My parents were married in 1929, when my mother was nineteen and my father eighteen, and both had just graduated from New Utrecht High School in the Bensonhurst section of Brooklyn. My sister, Denise, was three years old, and now I had arrived to complete the Fauci family. My father told me that my mother went into labor quickly and her obstetrician, who had been called in from a Christmas Eve party, wound up delivering me with a scrub gown worn over his tuxedo. I hope that he had not been celebrating too much before he was called. Nonetheless, everything seemed to turn out all right.

After my father and mother graduated from high school, my father entered Columbia University College of Pharmacy, and my mother entered Hunter College. After getting his degree in pharmacy, my father worked as a clerk for various pharmacies in Brooklyn, and my mother became a full-time homemaker after the birth of my sister. We lived in a two-bedroom apartment on the third floor of a four-story building across the street from New Utrecht High School on Seventy-ninth Street between New Utrecht and Sixteenth Avenues. At that time, the population of Benson-hurst was more than 90 percent Italian immigrants and first-generation Italian Americans and their families. There were both working-class and middle-class families. Few people were poor and few were wealthy, and virtually every adult male had a job. Most women worked as stay-at-home mothers. People were independent and individualistic, were not intimidated by anyone, and were strongly family oriented.

Both my father and my mother were first-generation Italian Americans, born in the Little Italy section of downtown Manhattan. Their parents had emigrated from Italy at the turn of the twentieth century, my father's parents from Sicily and my mother's parents from Naples. Both families moved from Manhattan to Brooklyn when my parents were children. My grandfather on my mother's side was a bohemian artist who often hung out in Greenwich Village and made a living painting landscapes and designing labels for various products such as those gallon-size Italian olive oil cans. My maternal grandmother was a seamstress whose salary was the major source of income for her family. My grandfather on my father's side was the accountant and financial manager of a stevedore (longshoreman) company working out of New York Harbor that employed mostly Italian immigrants. My paternal grandmother was a homemaker. They were by no means wealthy but lived relatively comfortably. My parents met in elementary school at Public School 163 on Bay Fourteenth Street, and according to them and stories from my grandparents, they fell in love in the eighth grade before going on to attend high school together.

One of my few memories of those early years is the sensual impression of warmth, security, and sunlight on my face as my mother pushed me in my stroller through the streets of Brooklyn while she shopped for the evening meals. I also remember an array of delicious smells that enveloped me as my mother and I went in and out of Italian delicatessens, or salumerias, as they were called. Another impression that stays with me to this day is my lying in bed on a foggy night and hearing the extraordinarily soothing sound of the long, slow foghorn blasts of large vessels coming from the Atlantic Ocean and passing through Gravesend Bay on their way through the Narrows to their destination in New York Harbor. Life in Brooklyn was good, even at that very young age.

Denise and I attended Our Lady of Guadalupe elementary school, which was seven blocks from home. We walked to and from school every day unaccompanied by an adult, even at six or seven years old. The neighborhood was so close-knit and protective that this walk alone by children through several city blocks was considered entirely safe. As we passed by candy stores, grocery stores, and small apartment buildings along the way, there were always a few people sitting or standing in front looking out for children like us going and coming from school.

The nuns of the order of Saint Dominic were in charge of Our Lady of Guadalupe School and introduced me to the experience of tough love. They were strict disciplinarians but taught us excellent work habits. Not that I needed this. My mother was keen on striving for excellence and held high expectations for my performance in school. She constantly bought books for me or borrowed them from the public library for me to read. Although my father was extremely bright, he left the academic pushing to my mother. I soon realized on my own how much I enjoyed school and learning even without outside pressure.

When I was eight years old, my father, with financial help from his father, bought his own pharmacy and the two-story building in which the drugstore was contained. The building was located on Thirteenth Avenue and Eighty-third Street, only eight city blocks away, but it seemed as if we were moving out of the country, so tight was our neighborhood culture. Actually, it did strictly speaking take us out of Bensonhurst and put us into the lower end of Dyker Heights, a slight move up the economic ladder. We now lived in a three-bedroom apartment (Denise and I finally got our own bedrooms) immediately above Fauci Pharmacy. It also took us out of the district of Our Lady of Guadalupe parish, but my new parish, St. Bernadette, did not have its own elementary school at the time. I was the top student in the class (the nuns graded every subject numerically with 100 being the top score and the average of subject scores calculated to one decimal place—talk about pressure). They did not want to lose their 98.8 grade point average student, and so I was allowed to stay at Our Lady of Guadalupe. After all, there would be citywide spelling bees and the like, and they told me years after I had graduated that I was their "ringer," and they did not mind cheating a bit to keep me at Our Lady of Guadalupe. You have to love those nuns!

THE MOVE TO DYKER HEIGHTS and St. Bernadette parish introduced me to a whole new group of friends and, importantly, to the culture of organized sports. My love of basketball and baseball began at age nine and became progressively more intense as I became a teenager. I grew almost obsessed with both sports and soon found out that I was a good athlete. I relished the competitive nature of team sports. Mostly, I just had a lot of fun playing them. The various age brackets of sandlot baseball clubs in Brooklyn served as the breeding grounds for several major-league baseball players including Sandy Koufax, Joe Pepitone, Joe and Frank Torre,

Ken and Bobby Aspromonte, and Jerry Casale. My enduring baseball-playing memory is my lining a double down the left field line off Joe Pepitone, the future New York Yankees first baseman, when he pitched against my St. Bernadette team for his sandlot team sponsored by Nathan's Famous hot dog stand in the fourteen-to-sixteen-year-old category of the Coney Island League.

In between league play, we relished street games like stickball, which we played using a sawed-off broom handle as a bat and a pink Spaldeen ball. You were a wimp if you could not hit the ball the distance of two Brooklyn sewer manhole covers. In the fall, just prior to the beginning of the official basketball season, the half-court pickup games on the outdoor courts of the local public elementary school went on until dark every afternoon. In the neighborhood, you were either an athlete or a tough guy, or hood, who hung around with the wrong people and sometimes got into trouble. No bookworms, or at least no one who admitted to being one. My friends and I were mostly athletes who never deliberately bothered anyone, but were not afraid of anyone. We didn't start trouble, but we did get into fistfights with guys from other neighborhoods when provoked. We were not serious troublemakers.

All was good in Brooklyn.

MY MOTHER WAS physically beautiful, petite, with dark brown hair and bright blue eyes. She was soft-spoken and somewhat reserved. Of all her good qualities, kindness and empathy for the suffering of others stand out. When I was almost five years old, and the first photographs of the mushroom cloud appeared on the front page of the *New York Daily News* following the dropping of the atomic bombs on Hiroshima and Nagasaki, she was sitting on the couch, tears flowing down her cheeks. As a young boy toward the end of World War II who frequently played soldiers with his friends, and whose games consisted of shooting and killing enemy soldiers, I thought that what I saw in the newspaper that day was a good thing. I asked her why she was crying. She just looked at me and said, "Anthony, you do not understand now, but this is one of the worst things that could have happened in this world. So many innocent people killed or maimed." It would be many years before I fully understood why she felt that way.

My father was a shy man who possessed a very strong sense of ethics, integrity, and kindness. Above all, he was a religious man. He was also extremely conscientious and a hard worker. He opened the drugstore at 9:00 a.m. and closed it at 10:00 p.m. six days a week (and half a day on Sundays). During the week he took forty-five minutes off at around 6:30 p.m. to have dinner with the family. The drugstore stayed open, tended by a pharmacy clerk—usually a student from a local pharmacy school. Despite these long hours, we were a close-knit, happy family. We lived right across the street from St. Bernadette's church. My mother, sister, and I helped at the store ringing up sales during the after-Mass rush on Sunday mornings. I delivered prescriptions on my Schwinn bicycle on weekends and during school breaks and summers.

As was the case with many Italian American families, every Sunday afternoon we had a big family dinner—either at our house, where things were quiet and reserved, or at the house of one of our sets of grandparents, who lived nearby, where uncles, aunts, and cousins attended, creating a feeling of organized chaos. These meals started off with a wide variety of antipasti including multiple cuts of salami, mortadella, prosciutto, and provolone cheese. This was followed by a primo piatto (first course) of mounds of pasta topped off by aromatically exquisite and absolutely delicious homemade tomato sauce. Next came a second course of roast chicken or veal scallopini. On the eves of religious holidays (no meat for Catholics) the meat was replaced by fish, usually salt cod (baccala) simmered in a garlic-tinged tomato sauce. Who was the cook depended on which grandparents were the hosts. If we were at my maternal grandparents' house, my grandmother did everything in the kitchen with the aunts (her daughters and daughters-in-law) serving as sous-chefs. My artist grandfather would be upstairs painting until the last minute or reading the Italian newspaper *Il Progresso* in the living room. If we were at my paternal grandparents' house, my grandfather did all the cooking of similar dishes but with a decidedly Sicilian bent (less rich sauces; more olive oil and fish; better pastries), while my grandmother sat in the living room reading *Il Progresso*. In both houses when the children were not supposed to hear what was being said, all of a sudden the language switched to Italian. Our parents probably did not fully realize that even though none of the children could speak Italian, after hearing it so often, we picked up much of what they were saying.

DAD WAS GENEROUS to a fault when it came to accommodating customers who could not afford to pay their pharmacy bills. He kept a running account for them, much to the frustration of the whole family. As children, Denise and I would say, "Dad, why are you giving them the medicines if they don't have the money?" My father simply replied, "They cannot afford it; they are struggling. We will just put it on a tab." Weeks and months might go by before these bills were paid; some never were. The furthest thing from his mind was making money, and in fact, despite the long hours in the drugstore, we got by with the necessities but had little left over for savings or luxuries. Over the years, his drugstore became a combination doctor's office, pharmacy, and psychiatrist's couch. The people in the neighborhood came to talk to him about everything from symptoms for which they were reluctant to see a physician, to consolation over the death of a loved one, to marital problems or how to handle a delinquent child (and there were quite a few of these in our neighborhood). Everything that Denise and I witnessed in our formative years was geared toward the concept of consideration for and taking care of others. Our father taught us early in life that because we were fortunate, it was our responsibility to help people when we could and making money should not be a primary goal in life. If our forty-five-minute dinners when my father came up from the drugstore to join us had a theme, this was usually it.

People often ask physicians what motivated them to go into the field of medicine. Like so many others, I am sure my reasons are complex. But, without engaging in too much self-psychoanalysis, it seems clear to me that growing up in a household where both parents were strongly motivated to care for others had a profound influence on my career choice.

THE NUNS' DECISION to allow me to stay at Our Lady of Guadalupe did not pay off as far as spelling bees were concerned. They rehearsed me relentlessly for the citywide Catholic school eighth-grade spelling bee. I made it to the fourth-to-last round and felt as if I were on a roll. Then the judge asked me to spell "millennium." I thought for a moment and blurted out "millenium." "Sorry, Anthony, two *n*'s, not one." I will never forget this first painful academic failure or how to spell the word "millennium." But I did not fail the nuns in another respect.

In New York City at the time, the most academically elite Catholic high school was Regis High School, run by Jesuit priests and located in Manhattan on East Eighty-fourth Street between Madison and Park Avenues. The entering ninth-grade class was selected based on a written test given to the top male student at every Catholic elementary school in the five boroughs of New York City and parts of New Jersey. The Jesuits then took those students with the highest scores and went down the list until they reached the predetermined number of students to fill the freshman class. They offered those students a full four-year scholarship. Almost no one who makes this competitive cutoff turns the offer down.

I made the cut, but I was at first ambivalent about accepting because I was hesitant to make a daily trip to Manhattan, and all my close friends were attending either public or Catholic high schools in Brooklyn. But after I talked with my parents, I was convinced that this was a unique opportunity. Besides, Regis High School had an excellent basketball team, which I was eager to try out for. Also, the Dominican nuns of Our Lady of Guadalupe would probably have persuaded Pope Pius XII to excommunicate me if I had turned down the offer.

All was still good in Brooklyn, but now my horizons were expanding—at least across the bridge to Manhattan. I had to take three different subway lines to get to school, making the trip sixty minutes each way on a good day.

On the first day of school when we introduced ourselves to Father Michael Flanagan, the assistant principal and dean of discipline, I told him that my name was Anthony Fauci. He shook my hand and said, "Hello, Tony, welcome to Regis." That was the first time anyone had ever called me Tony. I had always been Anthony to my family and Fauch to my friends. There was no way that I was going to correct the dean of discipline in front of my classmates on my first day as a freshman.

From that day onward my name has been Tony Fauci.

REGIS HIGH SCHOOL opened up a whole new world for me; it was going to "the next level." The Jesuits provided an atmosphere steeped in intellectual curiosity and academic excellence. The curriculum was heavily weighted to the classics including four years of classical Latin and Greek, two years of a modern language (I chose French), ancient history, and theology as well as the typical core courses of mathematics, chemistry, and biology, among others. I thoroughly enjoyed the academics and being surrounded by bright peers. The Jesuits expected mature behavior and emphasized respect for others. Discipline was swift when such behavior was breached. It did not matter if you came from a tough neighborhood like Bensonhurst or the South Bronx; being called into Father Flanagan's office even for some minor infraction scared the heck out of you.

Regis used the Jesuit motto "Men for Others," with its emphasis not on personal gain but on service to the public, no matter what profession you chose. This could not have been more of a natural extension of the fundamental philosophy of my family upbringing. I felt very much at home. I studied hard, I learned a lot, and I did very well. I loved everything about the school. Importantly, I was as enamored of the classics and humanities as I was of the sciences. I did not appreciate it at the time, but this double affinity greatly influenced my behavior and choices in my medical career years later.

And then there was basketball. I tried out for the freshman team and became a high-scoring starting point guard and captain. I was ecstatic about playing New York City high school basketball with the overabundance of terrific players as we went up against teams throughout the city's five boroughs. In my sophomore year, I skipped the junior varsity and went straight to the varsity. I played sparingly that year, but was thrilled to even get into the game against teams such as St. Ann's Academy, coached by the legendary Lou Carnesecca, who went on to coach St. John's University and enter the Basketball Hall of Fame. St. Ann's was the breeding ground of New York City high school basketball stars such as All-City player York Larese, who became an All-American at the University of North Carolina and was drafted by the St. Louis Hawks in 1960. I was having a lot of fun. By my senior year I was the starting point guard and captain of the varsity. I had a good year, scored a lot of points, and played against some terrific teams and players. But it soon became apparent to me that my hope of becoming a serious basketball player and playing on a Division I college team was unrealistic. My major assets were sharp reflexes, coordination, and an accurate two-handed set shot popular in the 1950s. Above all, I had speed, speed that allowed me to fast-break or to dribble free from my opponent to get off an open shot and score a bunch of points. I must have inherited this speed from my father, who in his modesty did not talk about it much but was a citywide champion in the 100-yard and 440-yard dash competitions during his junior and senior years in high school thirty years earlier.

Unfortunately, as far as basketball was concerned, I also inherited my father's height. I stopped growing midway through high school at five feet, seven inches, and soon realized that a very fast five-foot, seven-inch point guard who can shoot will always be taken to the cleaners by a very fast six-foot, two-inch point guard who also can shoot. This was brought home to me early in the basketball season of my junior year. Our coach had booked some scrimmage games with the freshman teams of a few New York City colleges so we could get a feel for what it was like to play at the college level. It also gave the college freshman teams the opportunity to scrimmage against a team unfamiliar to them as opposed to intra-squad games. As it turned out, the point guard I was put up against on the St. John's College (of future Big East fame) freshman team was Alan Seiden, a five-foot, ten-inch muscular speed machine. Alan had been New York City High School Player of the Year the year before, and went on to be an All-American, leading St. John's to the 1959 National Invitation Tournament Championship. Alan completely embarrassed me. He scored twenty-three points and I scored six. He outran, outshot, outjumped, outscored, and just plain outplayed me.

I spent the summer between my junior and my senior years at a basketball camp at Riverhead, Long Island. Selected New York City high school basketball players went there to perfect their skills by playing against each other at the same time as they were camp counselors for adolescent boys from the city. Among the players was Donnie Burks from Archbishop Molloy High School (formerly St. Ann's Academy), which went on to an undefeated season the following year. Donnie was a charismatic, cheerful, five-foot, eleven-inch young man from Harlem. He was lightning fast and had a deadly jump shot, and was one of the earliest who could easily dunk the ball backward. At summer camp, we became friends and were often matched up in scrimmage games under the hot sun. Friends or not, he totally dominated me on the court. Donnie ultimately became a college all-star for St. John's. If this is what a future college basketball star played like in high school, it certainly was not me. I could take a hint. My unrealistic dreams of going on to a career in basketball ended.

Yet, to this day, I carry with me the excitement that I felt getting ready for the buzzer to go off at the beginning of a basketball game. The adrenaline rush of playing against a worthy opponent is pure magic. You go one-on-one against somebody who is an excellent player, and you outplay them or, as happens, you get outplayed and say to yourself, "Damn! What did I do wrong?" Then you go on to the next game and play your heart out again.

More than forty years later, Lou Carnesecca and I received Lifetime Achievement Awards from an Italian American group in Washington, D.C.—Lou for sports and I for medicine. We sat at the same table at the gala dinner, and I joked with Lou about my frustration at just not having what it took to be a college basketball star. Lou, known for his wry sense of humor, looked at me, laughed, and said, "Tony, I have taught a lot of young basketball players a lot of basketball skills and tricks, but I know for sure, you cannot teach someone height."

As sure as I was that basketball would not be my profession, I was not sure what my profession would be. I did not know how to reconcile my interest in the classics and humanities and my desire to help people with my aptitude for and love of science. My decision was greatly influenced by a group of young teachers at Regis.

When future Jesuit priests are in training as seminarians, they are referred to as scholastics and addressed as "Mr.," not "Father." These are young men in their early twenties on their way to the priesthood who are devoted to the teaching and counseling of students. Mr. Hinfey and Mr. McCann enthusiastically taught me Latin and Greek and kindled even further my love of the classics. At the same time, Mr. McMahon expressed an equal amount of enthusiasm for chemistry and science. It was Mr. McMahon who solidified for me as we sat talking after class one afternoon in the chemistry laboratory that I could do both. If I became a physician, I could interact directly with people in the context of science—the health sciences. It just felt right. Now that I clarified that, college was the next decision.

At the time, unlike today, the Jesuits at Regis had a major influence on where you went to college. In fact, they "strongly recommended" (code phrase—told you) where you would attend. The College of the Holy Cross, a Jesuit college in Worcester, Massachusetts, was nationally known as one of the top premedical programs among Catholic colleges, or for that matter among any schools in the country. It was "strongly recommended" that I go there. I applied and received a full academic scholarship, and in the fall of 1958 off I went to Holy Cross together with several of my Regis classmates who also were headed for premed.

At Holy Cross, I continued to pursue my dual interests in the humanities and science, enrolling in a hybrid curriculum with the unusual title of "Bachelor of Arts—Greek—Pre-med." It concentrated on the classics with three years each of Latin, Greek, and French, and many courses in philosophy including metaphysics, logic, epistemology, and philosophical psychology, among others. Squeezed in there were enough science courses such as embryology, biology, physics, and inorganic and organic chemistry to allow acceptance into medical school. It was a terrific curriculum, and the Jesuit tradition that I embraced at Regis was in full bloom at Holy Cross. But I was impatient. From the moment I arrived on campus, my overriding purpose was to get through the next four years so that I could get on with what I really wanted to do.

But I did develop some enduring friendships. One in particular was Robert "Bob" Emmett Curran Jr. During the first week on campus as a freshman I ran into someone whom I had last seen as I tried to dribble past him on a fast break toward the basket in a tournament title game between Regis and St. Agnes of Rockville Centre, where Bob was the star forward. Besides being an excellent athlete, he was a top student who stood out because of his complete lack of self-promotion. It did not take long for us to go from archrivals to best buddies, which continued throughout college and well beyond.

DURING SUMMER BREAKS I worked on high-paying construction gangs doing manual labor. I became a card-carrying member of one of the New York local branches of the International Hod Carriers', Building, and Common Laborers' Union of America. I was able to get into the union (I paid my dues) and work almost every day with the help of one of my friends' uncles whose exact occupation I could never figure out and did not ask. I was on various jobs for periods ranging from a couple of weeks to the entire summer, rarely missing a day of work. I enjoyed the physical labor, and I made plenty of money. This was critical for me because my father's drugstore business was not doing too well, and my parents could not help me much financially even though I was on a full scholarship to Holy Cross. The construction gang that I worked on before my final year in college was building the Samuel J. Wood Library at Cornell Medical School on York Avenue between East Sixty-eighth and East Sixty-ninth Streets. I spent an entire summer pushing a wheelbarrow, hauling bricks, and watching the medical students, doctors, and nurses walking in and out of the medical school and the adjacent New York Hospital. One hot August day, I was walking into the building wearing my dirty boots and hard hat to take a look at the Uris Auditorium on the first floor, when the security guard stopped me. I told him that I just wanted to look around because someday I would be a student here. The guard glared at me and said, "Sure, buddy, and someday I am going to be New York City police commissioner, and so get the heck out of here."

Becoming Dr. Fauci

I had wanted to go to Cornell University Medical College since my first year at Holy Cross, when the premed students started to check out the choices we would make a couple of years later. Cornell was in the middle of New York City, it was ranked among the top medical schools in the country, and it had a distinctive reputation of caring for the students within an environment that was highly intellectual, culturally refined, and not at all cutthroat.

I entered the first-year class at Cornell in September 1962 and began one of the happiest, most fulfilling periods of my life— learning how to become, and ultimately becoming, a physician. The coursework in the first year with gross anatomy, histology, physiology, and biochemistry was demanding but exhilarating. The learning curve was steep. The second year challenged us with pathology; pharmacology; microbiology; and, most important, our first exposure to live patients, a course in physical diagnosis taught by the immensely popular Dr. Elliot Hochstein. He was beloved by students and taught us the fine points of history taking and physical examination, the essence of the hands-on doctor. Dr. Hochstein's course cemented in my mind that I had made the right choice in going to medical school. I was champing at the bit in anticipation of rotating on the wards with the "real doctors"—the interns and residents who were just a few years older than I but who were our idols and role models. The attendings were like gods to us, and we were overflowing with enthusiasm about soon learning from them.

The third and fourth years were pure pleasure; we were student doctors and dealing directly with patients every day in every subspecialty including internal medicine, surgery, obstetrics (there is nothing more exciting than delivering your first baby under the watchful eye of an experienced chief resident), pediatrics, psychiatry, and anesthesiology. The first patient that I examined by myself before the intern and resident did a full workup was a woman in her sixties with severe mitral valve stenosis and congestive heart failure. I had read about the complexity of heart murmurs and the crackles in the lungs that I could expect to hear through my brand-new stethoscope, but now these sounds were pinging in my ears. I could not recall ever feeling this type of excitement. I was looking forward to describing what I had heard to the intern and resident as well as the attending, but it also filled me with anxiety because I hoped that I would get it right. One thing I knew I had gotten right was that I remembered what Dr. Hochstein had taught me— that I was dealing with a human being who was in the unfamiliar setting of a hospital and who needed care, compassion, and comfort in addition to the correct description of her heart murmurs. Right from the get-go I felt the importance of this combination of the art and the science of medicine.

My rotations as a third- and fourth-year student through the various subspecialties at The New York Hospital–Cornell Medical Center exposed me to some of the most intense and instructive clinical experiences imaginable. My classmates were some of the finest people that I had ever met, and we developed strong bonds. We were now learning to be what we really wanted to be, and the friendships and relationships we forged ran deep and many would last a lifetime. Foremost among these was my dear friend Bob Curran, who had joined me on the journey from Holy Cross to medical school. We shared a lot of fun together from double-dating to backpacking through Europe between our second and our third years of medical school.

I realized that I loved clinical medicine, and the challenge and excitement of taking care of very ill patients greatly attracted me. I could not wait to graduate and move on to my internship and residency. Soon I would be a "real doctor."

But nothing could have prepared me for the day during my fourth year when my mother came to visit me to bring me some toiletries and changes of clothing that she had washed and pressed. She told me that she felt weak and bloated and had lost her appetite. Having just finished my rotation on the internal medicine ward, I felt a jolt in my gut. I immediately set up an appointment for my mother, who was fifty-six years old, with my attending physician, Dr. David M. Roseman. Dr. Roseman saw her in his office within two days and called me on the ward where I was rotating. "Tony, I am very sorry, but I believe the situation is serious," he said. "Your mother has a massively enlarged liver that is hard upon palpation. It is likely a cancer."

I felt numb, but for the first time I was thinking about my mother both as a son and as a physician. What next? She needed surgery for a definitive diagnosis, so the attending surgeon, Dr. Henry Mannix, did an open biopsy. Again, a call that I kind of expected: "Tony, your mother has a liver full of tumor, and the prognosis is really very bad." The only thing to do for my mother was to keep her comfortable. I was training to be a physician, and here I was, helpless. I took the subway to Brooklyn and told my father. It was one of the most painful moments in my young life. He was crushed.

My mother died eight short weeks later. My father had lost the love of his life, his sweetheart from New Utrecht High School. This loss left a great gap in his life, and very soon he sold the pharmacy and moved to Manhattan, where he worked in the Memorial Hospital pharmacy. Despite his sadness, he continued his theme of kindness and consideration for others punctuated by a legendary sense of humor that over the years had won him many friends.

I did not have the luxury of grieving properly. Unfortunately, back then there were no mental health days. I was in the middle of my surgery rotation in my final year of medical school. We buried my mother in Green-Wood Cemetery in Brooklyn and I had to be back on call on the wards the next night. I stuffed my painful feelings down deep and put my energy into saving the lives that were possible to be saved.

Six months later, I graduated number one in my class at Cornell Medical School. I had my pick of post-medical-school training and decided that I wanted to remain at The New York Hospital–Cornell Medical Center to pursue an internship and medical residency in internal medicine. The code of service to others instilled in me by my parents, followed by the "Men for Others" theme of Regis High School, strengthened by my experience with the Jesuits at Holy Cross, had culminated with the extraordinary medical training at Cornell.

My years of internship and residency training were when I truly found myself. I felt as if I were doing what I was born to do. I was most challenged and comfortable diagnosing and treating the sickest patients who came into the hospital with every possible disease. Even at that early stage in my career, it was obvious to my mentors that I had what they referred to as "instinctively good clinical judgment" where I could analyze with a clear mind all the complexities of a desperately ill patient and map out a well-thought-out strategy to diagnose and treat. I had a natural capability to remain calm and in control even under the most stressful life-and-death circumstances. All of this prepared me for an unprecedented medical and public health challenge that would come several years later and whose dimensions I could not possibly anticipate.

DURING MY YEARS in medical school from 1962 to 1966, our country was involved in the war in Vietnam, and all male physicians in training like me were registered by the Selective Service. In my fourth year, a major in the U.S. Army had gathered my class in the same Uris Auditorium where I had encountered the security guard five years earlier. He told us that every male medical student in the room would, at the end of the year, be committed to three years in one of the uniformed services. We were to submit our preferences in priority order. I listed my choices as (1) U.S. Public Health Service; (2) U.S. Navy; (3) U.S. Army; (4) U.S. Air Force. In medical school I had developed a strong interest in infectious diseases. The idea of dealing with a disease, usually acute and caused by a specific identifiable agent that could be serious enough to kill the patient but that you could prevent, treat, and even totally cure, was particularly attractive to me. A three-year stint as a Public Health Service officer at either the National Institutes of Health (NIH) or the Centers for Disease Control (now the Centers for Disease Control and Prevention, or CDC) seemed like the best fit. I applied to the NIH and was invited for an interview in the fall of 1966 by Dr. Sheldon M. "Shelly" Wolff, clinical director of the National Institute of Allergy and Infectious Diseases (NIAID). I had done my homework for this interview by reading about the accomplishments of his lab. Little did I know that Dr. Wolff had also done some homework on me; one of his close friends was one of my clinical professors at Cornell. Sitting across his desk from Dr. Wolff at noon on the appointed day, I was caught off guard by his first question: "Do you like soft-shell crabs?"

This was not exactly a staple of my medical school diet, and besides, I had never heard of them. But I thought to myself, You are the great Shelly Wolff. If you want me to like soft-shell crabs, I like soft-shell crabs. He then took me down the hall to his conference room, where his technician was cooking up crabs for lunch in a frying pan over a Bunsen burner. We talked about his vision for the lab, and I was hired for a combined fellowship doing research and seeing patients in infectious diseases and clinical immunology that would start a little less than two years later after I completed my internship and residency training. Shelly and I shared many soft-shell crab lunches over the coming years.

Heading South

I packed my three pieces of furniture and my luggage into the rented Ryder trailer attached to my oil-burning, gas-guzzling 1960 white Pontiac Bonneville and headed toward the Lincoln Tunnel and Interstate 95 south. I arrived at the NIH on June 27, 1968, twenty-seven years old, fresh out of my medical residency training, to begin my fellowship in Bethesda, Maryland, a sleepy country town especially in comparison to the hustle and bustle of midtown Manhattan. One person who shared this feeling of culture shock with me was my good friend Bob Curran, who had just completed with me our years of internship and residency at The New York Hospital–Cornell Medical Center and by some quirk of fate also had obtained an NIH fellowship, his at the National Cancer Institute. Counting our rivalry on the basketball court in high school, this was Bob's and my thirteenth year in lockstep.

I had had the honor of being the best man at his recent wedding, and Bob arrived with his new bride, Peggy.

My training over the next three years was under Shelly's tutelage. He was an excellent physician and scientist, a street-smart, self-made, down-to-earth guy from Newark, New Jersey. His major asset was an uncanny ability to sense talent in young physicians and to put them on projects that they could ultimately develop on their own. He would then get out of their way and be available for support and encouragement. Ten years my senior, he not only became my mentor but filled a spot somewhere between an older brother and an uncle. Whenever my emotions got the best of me and I went to him to vent about some perceived academic injustice, such as not getting a scientific paper that I submitted immediately accepted by a journal, he just looked at me, shook his head, said, "Anthony, Anthony," and laughed; Shelly was the only person outside my family who called me by my full first name. Years later, when I got married, he was my best man.

My basic research laboratory project was involved in the newly emerging field of human immunology, the study of the component of the body that protects one against attacks by infectious diseases and cancers. I was fortunate that Shelly assigned me to a clinical project that was just in its earliest stages. It involved the study of a group of diseases characterized by profound inflammation of blood vessels leading to collapse of the function of various organs such as the kidneys and the lungs. They were referred to as the vasculitis syndromes. Most deadly among these was Wegener's granulomatosis (now called granulomatosis with polyangiitis). It had a devastating mortality rate of almost 100 percent. We studied our NIAID patients on the wards of the NIH Clinical Center Hospital. Other NIH institutes such as the National Cancer Institute, the National Heart, Lung, and Blood Institute, and the National Institute of Diabetes and Digestive and Kidney Diseases, among others, also studied their patients there. In addition, the Clinical Center was the hub for the multi-institute research laboratories including the one where I worked. The plan was to treat our patients with drugs such as cyclophosphamide (a drug that kills certain immune cells in the body) and steroids (anti-inflammatory drugs) that were being used by the National Cancer

Institute researchers working two floors up from us. We used these drugs at much lower doses than those used to wipe out cancers, but high enough doses to suppress the out-of-control inflammatory and immunological responses that were harming the patients whom I was personally taking care of. Because our lab was located within yards of the patients' rooms, we drew blood, did bone marrow biopsies, and examined these specimens back in our lab for effects of our therapy as we monitored the patients for improvement in their disease. Shelly put me on that project for the three years of my fellowship, and the preliminary results were striking, resulting in a 93 percent remission rate.

My hands-on experience with patients during the years of my fellowship was not limited to work in the Clinical Center. In the spring of 1971, the anti–Vietnam War movement was at a high pitch. There was a massive demonstration in Washington, D.C., involving tens of thousands of protesters who congregated on the Mall and in a nearby park. Calls went out for physician volunteers to be on hand, and I and a few of my colleagues answered the call. We were stationed at a makeshift clinic inside a small church just north of the Mall. After tending to several people with a variety of medical conditions, from poorly controlled diabetes to heat exhaustion, we heard that a group of demonstrators had been tear-gassed and a guy about my age with severe asthma was in distress. His clothes reeked of tear gas when a pickup truck dropped him off in front of the clinic. I was focused strictly on his breathing, and with tears flowing from my irritated eyes, I brought him inside to treat his asthma. Really bad idea! Within seconds, the tear gas that had permeated his clothing had contaminated the inside of the church, causing us to evacuate for about half an hour. There is always something to learn in clinical medicine. If I ever had to take care of a tear-gassed person again, I would remember to take off their clothes before bringing them inside.

As I approached the end of my fellowship, which is a classic decision point in a young investigator's career, Shelly offered me a highly desirable position at NIAID as a senior tenured investigator, an amazing offer for someone at such an early stage in their career. At the same time, I was offered the position as chief medical resident in the Department of Medicine back at The New York Hospital–Cornell Medical Center, a stepping stone to a lucrative hospital-based or private practice there. Being the resident in charge of the care of internal medicine patients and the training of younger physicians in a globally preeminent hospital was very appealing. Before I came to the NIH, this is exactly what I thought I wanted to do. I still cherished the opportunity to be chief medical resident, although as much as I loved the hands-on care of patients and totally respect and even admire physicians who do this full time, I now did not want to do only clinical work without a research component. I wanted to do both, and I felt that I could do this best at the NIH. I had begun to think about and appreciate more and more the concept of my work having a multiplier effect. As the leader of a research team at the NIH, I felt we could use the information we gathered from the detailed study of our patients to contribute to the medical literature. This knowledge could then inform hundreds of physicians throughout the world who could use that knowledge to benefit many thousands of patients. As good as I was in a one-to-one interaction with an individual patient, the impact of my studies could potentially go well beyond the patient for whom I was caring.

I worked out a deal with Shelly that I would go back to New York, serve the year as chief medical resident, and then resume my work at the NIH as the head of my own laboratory doing basic and clinical research on the interface between infectious diseases and the human immune response.

My year of chief residency was one of the most challenging and exhilarating years of my life. It was clinical medicine at its best. I had about fifty younger physicians under me, and I liked the role of teaching them the art and science of clinical medicine. I was called to see the sickest and most clinically complicated patients in the hospital: diabetic coma, GI bleeds, heart attacks, congestive heart failure, overwhelming infections, patients without a clear diagnosis but who were desperately ill. I was on call every other night and every other weekend. I was single and this was my entire life. I learned an enormous amount and honed my clinical skills to the point that I felt there was no medical problem that I could not handle and handle as well as anyone, and I loved it, every minute of it.

WHEN I RETURNED TO the NIH in July 1972, I picked up where I had left off at the Clinical Center. I continued my basic research studies on the regulation of the human immune response while expanding my clinical studies on patients with the vasculitis syndromes. As with our earlier studies on granulomatosis with polyangiitis, we were now getting equally dramatic results with our therapeutic regimens on other related inflammatory vascular diseases such as polyarteritis nodosa, which often led to death by renal failure, heart attack, and/or stroke.

Five years after I returned, Shelly left the NIH to become chairman of the Department of Medicine at Tufts Medical Center in Boston, and I carried on with the vasculitis program with even greater success over the next several years. Although the diseases were uncommon, our research led to the saving of many lives directly by us, and by physicians throughout the world who were now using our protocols. My upward career trajectory was steep. I was becoming well-known and respected nationally and internationally in this somewhat narrow field (at the time) of the treatment of autoinflammatory diseases. Several years later, a Stanford

University Arthritis Center survey of the American Rheumatism Association membership ranked my work on the treatment of polyarteritis nodosa and Wegener's granulomatosis as one of the most important advances in patient management in rheumatology over the past twenty years.

I had already been elected into several honorific academic societies and was being offered endowed chairs in Departments of Medicine in prestigious medical centers throughout the country. But I felt at home in the intellectual atmosphere of the NIH and had no interest in leaving for an exalted title at another institution.

Despite these professional milestones, for reasons I could not fully understand at the time, part of me felt unfulfilled. For the prior few years, I had the nagging feeling that although I was academically successful and our work was saving lives, something was missing. I had met the main challenge of developing effective therapies for formerly fatal diseases. But we were dealing with unusual diseases that lacked a broad public health impact. Certainly others would come along and improve on what we had done, but what I was doing now seemed to me to be only incremental. I had been on a clear path ever since I had decided as a student at Regis High School twenty-five years earlier to become a physician. Now I was forty years old, and I was starting to feel unchallenged. I was at a crossroads.

Part Two

THE AIDS ERA

Game Changer

I turned away from the view of the beautiful and bucolic NIH campus outside my eleventh-floor window to concentrate on dismissing the mostly junk mail cluttering my desk on this summer Friday afternoon. About halfway through the pile I picked up the June 5, 1981, issue of the CDC's weekly publication, *Morbidity and Mortality Weekly Report* (*MMWR*). *MMWR*, which to a layperson sounds admittedly ominous, serves the extremely useful purpose of alerting the medical and public health community to the emergence of unexpected diseases, most of which are of an infectious nature. For example, the number of cases of influenza each flu season is tracked in *MMWR*. Unexpected outbreaks of new diseases such as Legionnaires' disease in a Philadelphia hotel during the American Legion convention in 1976 were first reported in *MMWR*. The title of one of the articles in the issue in my hand was "*Pneumocystis* Pneumonia—Los Angeles." The article reported the occurrence of an unusual form of pneumonia, called *Pneumocystis carinii* pneumonia, in five men who had been otherwise healthy. I was puzzled because there were a few things about this report that were atypical. First, this type of pneumonia was usually seen only in individuals whose immune system was significantly

compromised, as was the case with people who were receiving chemotherapy for various forms of cancer. I had considerable experience in this area, because as an infectious disease specialist I had
spent the previous decade consulting on patients in the NIH Clinical Center who were being treated with intensive chemotherapy
by my colleagues at the National Cancer Institute for cancers such
as Hodgkin's disease and various lymphomas and leukemias. Often
these patients developed *Pneumocystis* pneumonia. They were treated
by a drug called pentamidine, whose distribution was controlled
by the CDC and so it was easy to track the number of cases of this
disease. The immediate question in my mind was why these men
in Los Angeles would be developing *Pneumocystis* pneumonia if
they had been otherwise healthy? Even more puzzling and difficult to ascribe to coincidence was the fact that the report indicated
that all five men were homosexual. I sat there scratching my head
and assumed that the report did not contain all of the information
needed to explain what was going on. My first thought was that
perhaps these men had taken some powerful and toxic recreational
drug that had markedly suppressed their immune systems and that
was why they contracted this unusual form of pneumonia. Amyl
nitrite, or poppers, were being used as enhancers of sexual performance, particularly among gay men. But these drugs were not
new, and they had never been known to cause clinically significant
suppression of the immune system.

I was not going to figure this out on a Friday afternoon. I finished up the mail and drove home to start what hopefully would be
an enjoyable weekend. The next day, during a hike on the Billy
Goat Trail, which runs along the Potomac River, I remember
thinking for just a moment that the *MMWR* report was really bi-
zarre. I concluded that this was just a curiosity that would never be
resolved and that this report was likely the last that I would hear
about it.

A MONTH WENT by and I had thought very little of the June 5 *MMWR* report. I was caught up in the tide of accelerated activity that characterizes the months of June and July in most academic medical centers. July 1 typically marks the arrival of most new interns, residents, and fellows. The NIH was no exception, and our new fellows were just beginning their three-year commitment to clinical and research training in immunology or infectious diseases. They needed to be oriented and supervised in the care, treatment, and study of patients with unusual diseases, and, importantly, they would begin choosing the research laboratory where they would spend their next three years learning basic and clinical research similar to the situation I was in thirteen years previously.

Because the workload was heavy, I came into my office on Saturday, July 4. I was planning to go to the National Mall to watch the traditional Fourth of July fireworks that evening if the rain let up, and I wanted to take care of some work before then. Again, I wrestled with the paperwork on my desk and picked up the July 3, 1981, issue of *MMWR* that had arrived on Friday afternoon. I must admit that I had almost forgotten the earlier article about the five gay men from Los Angeles. The title of a new article in this issue stunned me: "Kaposi's Sarcoma and *Pneumocystis* Pneumonia Among Homosexual Men—New York City and California." I raced through the article. There it was. Twenty-six men from New York City, Los Angeles, and San Francisco who were seen at various medical facilities with this unusual form of pneumonia. Some also had Kaposi's sarcoma, a rare form of cancer that was seen in certain parts of Africa and in men of Mediterranean background, but otherwise was seen only in individuals with severely compromised immune systems. This was typically a result of receiving chemotherapy for the prevention of rejection of transplanted organs. In addition, several patients in the report had other rare infections, again seen only in individuals with severely weakened immune systems. And then came the punch to my gut. All twenty-six men were homosexual! I thought I had seen it all in the fifteen years since I graduated from medical school, but this was the first time that a clinical report had ever given me goose bumps. What the hell was going on here?

I could no longer pass this off as a curiosity. I had not yet searched the literature, but this had to be a brand-new disease. I could not believe that all of these men had taken some toxic drug that had destroyed their immune systems. It was acting as if it had to be an infectious agent. But why now? Why was this never seen before?

The idea of a totally new infectious agent was beyond my comprehension. I had not heard of such a thing in recent recorded history. Perhaps it was a well-known virus such as cytomegalovirus (commonly seen in gay men with multiple sexual partners) that had mutated toward a highly virulent form. All manner of speculation raced through my mind, but nothing made sense except a totally new and unheard-of infection.

As I sat at my desk completely confounded, I had no idea that the disease this report was foreshadowing would ultimately afflict millions of people throughout the world. It also would have a profound impact on my career and indeed my entire life.

APART FROM THE back-and-forth chatter between my colleagues in New York, California, the CDC, and us at the NIH, as well as a handful of newspaper articles, there was little public attention paid to this disease outside the gay community. The first newspaper story had in fact appeared in the *New York Native*, which then was the most influential gay newspaper in the country, on May 18, 1981, almost three weeks before the first cases were reported in the

June 5 *MMWR*. Another story appeared in the *Los Angeles Times* on June 5, 1981, reporting the five Los Angeles cases of *Pneumocystis* pneumonia. The next day, the *San Francisco Chronicle* ran a short article by the health reporter David Perlman on these unusual cases. And a month later, Dr. Lawrence Altman reported in the July 3 *New York Times* on Kaposi's sarcoma among now forty-one gay men in New York and California. There was speculation and even wild guesses by the reporters as to what caused this syndrome and whether and how it spread from one person to another.

The CDC took the lead in tracking and studying the disease. In this regard, the CDC differs substantially from the NIH. Both are agencies within the Department of Health and Human Services (HHS). Although the CDC does some basic and clinical research, they are predominantly a public health agency. One of their primary responsibilities is that of "disease detective." They stay alert for the appearance or reappearance of new and known diseases, tracking the evolution of outbreaks and implementing measures critical to the public health of the nation. Their mandate is to prevent diseases, injury, and disability. In contrast, the twenty-seven institutes and centers within the NIH are responsible predominantly for conducting and supporting basic and clinical research aimed at understanding, preventing, and treating the particular diseases that fall under a given institute or center. NIAID is responsible for research in the areas of infectious diseases, allergy, and immune-mediated diseases.

From an epidemiological standpoint (the pattern of disease spread), the outbreak looked very much like a sexually transmitted disease given the clustering of cases among sexual partners. Early studies by the CDC looking under a microscope at blood and tissue specimens strongly suggested that the cause was a virus, simply because the microscopic examination of tissues and culturing for bacteria, fungi, and parasites were all negative. My laboratory was not yet involved in specific research studies, but I was practically consumed with curiosity about the disease. I began probing issues related to gay culture. I wondered whether relatively recent behavioral changes might have occurred that could provide some insight into these strange events. Homosexuality has existed since the beginning of humankind, of course, so why this disease now at this time? Reading through old press reports, I quickly learned something that to my embarrassment I had not previously been aware of. Something had indeed changed relatively recently, certainly in the United States.

The gay population in the twentieth century had largely been "in the closet" and was subjected to stigma, severe discrimination, and even persecution, often in the form of unprovoked violence, sometimes on the part of police. A huge disruption in the status quo came on June 28, 1969, at the Stonewall Inn, a popular gay bar on Christopher Street in Manhattan's Greenwich Village. That night police raided the bar (not an uncommon occurrence). However, the results this night were different. Rather than submitting to the police, the gay population fought back. It sparked a series of riots and demands from the men that the violent discrimination against them be stopped. This event triggered a transformation in the gay community's ability and willingness to express their sexuality in the open, uninhibited, without fear of official repercussions. This was all to the good, but it also had the collateral effect of intensifying a bathhouse culture where gay men could easily participate in indiscriminate sexual activity with large numbers of often anonymous partners over a period of a day or a weekend. The problem was that although this behavior was seemingly innocuous in and of itself, it created the perfect environment for the spread of a sexually transmitted infection, were such a pathogen to be introduced into this subset of the population. Only years later would we become fully aware of this catastrophic dynamic.

In the late fall of 1981, just a few months after the initial *MMWR* reports, I made a decision that many of my friends and advisers told me was a serious, potentially career-ending mistake. I decided to transfer to others the highly successful research that I had been conducting on immune-mediated diseases and the basic research that I had been conducting over the previous nine years on the regulation of the normal human immune response and focus my efforts completely on this mysterious new disease seemingly restricted at this point to gay men.

The concept of dealing with a lethal disease, which I was sure was an infection and whose cause was completely unknown, was too much of a challenge for me to walk away from. And then there was the illusion of fate. I was trained for years as an immunologist *and* an infectious disease specialist. Here was a disease that certainly was infectious. It also was destroying the immune system and rendering the patients highly susceptible to opportunistic infections such as *Pneumocystis* pneumonia and many others with strange names like cytomegalovirus, toxoplasmosis, cryptococcosis, and candidiasis. Names that are not generally familiar to those outside the medical profession because they rarely if ever occur in otherwise healthy people. I felt that it was my destiny to get involved in this disease. Also, I felt a strong empathy with these young men whose lives were being wrecked and often ended by this strange illness.

I made my decision. This devastating disease would be my full-time job.

Devoting myself to the study of this mysterious new disease meant we would now begin to proactively admit these patients to the NIH Clinical Center. Because my laboratory was expert in immunology, I would study the immune defects in these patients even though we did not know at the time what was causing these defects. I could not do this alone, because many of these patients were desperately ill and some required intensive care. I needed to put together a small team of committed physicians and other health-care providers.

Two years earlier in 1979, as part of his three-year fellowship, a young physician named H. Clifford Lane had joined my laboratory, having just completed a three-year medical internship and residency at the highly regarded Department of Medicine of the University of Michigan Hospital. Cliff, mostly serious but with a mischievous sense of humor, was a talented clinician who was showing great promise at the research bench doing studies on the regulation of a certain component of the human immune system referred to as the B cell limb of the immune response. He had come to the NIH to learn basic immunology under my tutelage. Because he was the rising young star of my lab and a pleasure to work with, I made him an offer that I hoped he would not refuse. I asked him to join me in studying these dreadfully ill gay men. Without hesitating and to my great relief—and in what turned out to be to the benefit of the entire field of AIDS research—he agreed. We had the first two-thirds of the original AIDS team at NIAID.

The medical intensive care unit at the NIH Clinical Center was already overburdened with acutely ill patients having nothing to do with this mysterious disease, mostly from the National Cancer Institute. These patients had received intensive chemotherapy for a variety of tumors and suffered from the complications of these therapies, such as infections and bleeding. Our soon-to-be-admitted patients would surely overburden the unit. We would need our own intensive care specialist who would be largely responsible for our sickest patients. Enter Dr. Henry Masur.

I had met Henry in 1971 when he was a fourth-year student at my alma mater Cornell University Medical College and I was chief medical resident at The New York Hospital–Cornell Medical Center. When I returned to the NIH in 1972, Henry went on, similar to what I had done in 1966, to a medical residency at The New York Hospital. After a subsequent advanced medical residency at Johns Hopkins, he took a fellowship in infectious diseases at The New York Hospital. There in 1981 as a junior faculty member, he was the lead author who described the first patients from New York City with this new disease in the December 10, 1981, issue of *The New England Journal of Medicine*. He knew as much about the disease as anyone. I pushed hard for Henry to come down to the NIH. He agreed, and now our group was a trio. Henry was not an intensive care specialist, but soon became one.

When word got out about my self-imposed career change, some folks were encouraging, but many were skeptical. Prominent among the skeptics was Shelly Wolff. I will never forget Shelly's words after I explained to him what I was doing and why. He just looked at me with his mischievous grin and said, "Anthony, Anthony, I love you and respect what you are doing, but please don't give up your day job yet. This might all go away." To his credit, a year or so later, as the pandemic evolved, Shelly called me and told me how wrong he had been. Nonetheless, in response to this type of skepticism, and feeling somewhat defensive, I wrote an article in December 1981 that appeared in print in June 1982 in the respected medical journal *Annals of Internal Medicine* titled "The Syndrome of Kaposi's Sarcoma and Opportunistic Infections: An Epidemiologically Restricted Disorder of Immunoregulation." It is noteworthy that at the time the name AIDS had not yet been used and the disease was referred to by names such as gay-related immune deficiency, or GRID. There had been only 290 cases reported to the CDC. In my article, I made the unfortunately prophetic statement regarding the potential of this disease to spread far wider than we were experiencing at the time: "Because we do not know the cause of this syndrome, any assumption that the syndrome will remain restricted to a particular segment of our society is truly an assumption without scientific basis." I felt that I needed to publicly explain my career change, and my seven years of Latin courses and the Jesuit in me prompted me to refer to this article as my apologia pro vita sua, or my apology or explanation for the direction of my life, referring to the article of the same title written in 1864 by John Henry Newman in defense of his religious opinions to Charles Kingsley of the Church of England.

It gave me no satisfaction to watch my prediction tragically come true. In November 1981, Dr. Gerald Friedland of Albert Einstein College of Medicine in the Bronx noted and in 1983 fully reported similar cases among heterosexual male and female injection drug users. This suggested that similar to hepatitis B this disease could be transmitted by blood-contaminated needles and syringes as well as by sexual contact. Over the next year and a half, the full scope of the domestic epidemic began to rear its ugly head. In rapid succession, the CDC reported in the *MMWR* the following: July 1982—cases in Haitians in the United States and people with hemophilia; December 1982—transfusion-associated cases and cases among infants; January 1983—infections among female sexual partners of males with AIDS as reported by Dr. Friedland. Similar cases were being reported from Europe, particularly France and Belgium. Of importance was the fact that many patients were being referred from Zaire (now the Democratic Republic of the Congo) to hospitals in Belgium with a syndrome almost identical to what was being observed in AIDS patients in the United States and Europe. Joseph McCormick of the CDC and Peter Piot of the University of Antwerp were reporting that many such patients were being seen in Zaire and interestingly there were equal numbers of men and women and the spread seemed due to heterosexual exposure. This was not just a U.S. and developed-world problem.

And no, this was not just a curiosity, and it certainly was not going to go away.

By 2023, there would be more than eighty-six million HIV infections throughout the world with forty million deaths.

The disease finally received a permanent name by mid-1982. We needed to get rid of the designation "gay-related immunodeficiency disease" because it was clear by then that the disease was not confined to gay men. On September 24, 1982, the CDC used the term "acquired immunodeficiency syndrome" for the first time in describing the case definition of the illness in *MMWR*. This was based on a series of meetings in which I participated that were led by HHS and the CDC. AIDS became the name universally now used for this dreadful disease.

Up Close and Painful

s our interest in studying AIDS patients became widely known through the medical grapevine, Cliff, Henry, and I did not have to wait long for patients to enter our new program. It was mid-February 1982 and the Washington, D.C., area was experiencing a blinding snowstorm that forced the closing of the federal government for the day. I had braved the drive up Wisconsin Avenue to the NIH Bethesda campus and was sitting in the office of my laboratory, the Laboratory of Immunoregulation, in the NIH Clinical Center. The phone rang and it was Dr. Jack Whitescarver, special assistant to Dr. Richard Krause, the then director of NIAID, who administratively was my boss. Jack had been called by a private physician who wanted to refer a patient with this disease to the NIH. I took the patient's contact information and arranged to have Henry see him. In taking a medical history, Henry found out that the patient, Ronald Rinaldi (the patient's name is changed for the purpose of confidentiality), had a healthy identical twin, so the potential of bone marrow transplantation from the healthy to the ill brother was immediately apparent, although retrospectively this was naive given what we were soon to learn about the cause of this disease, and we became inundated with AIDS patients.

In my previous decade, I had become used to treating—and usually curing—very sick patients with inflammatory diseases; only rarely did any of my patients die. Those were heady years, and I had been feeling pretty good about myself as a physician.

Not anymore.

I think of the years from 1982 until the late 1980s as the "dark years" of my medical career. The growing monster of this epidemic did not allow me ever to fully separate from my work. This also affected my personal life. In the spring of 1981, I married a young woman with whom I had had a yearslong relationship. But long-standing tensions in our relationship, compounded by the hours I was putting into my work on the raging AIDS outbreak, which surfaced just a few months after our wedding, unfortunately made the survival of our marriage impossible. We separated around the time of our second anniversary and got divorced amicably one year later.

There was little time for anything but taking care of very sick patients. Their pain, suffering, and fear were unimaginable. It is difficult to describe the intense emotional stress and frustration that a physician or health-care provider feels in caring for large numbers of desperately ill and usually terrified patients. Working alongside Cliff, Henry, and me were a group of talented and committed nurses, fellows, residents, and other health professionals who shared our burden and without whom we never would have been able to provide the patients with the extraordinary level of care they needed.

We did not know the cause of the disease, and we certainly did not have a cure. It felt as if we were putting Band-Aids on a hemorrhage. We had drugs that treated the opportunistic infections, but no sooner was one infection treated than others appeared that were ultimately killing the patients. The disease progressed relentlessly despite our best efforts. The median survival of our patients was nine to ten months, which means that half of them would be dead within that time. On any given day, our ward on the eleventh floor of the Clinical Center had a dozen or so such patients. I was trained for many years to be a healer, and during this period I was healing no one. The only saving grace in that experience was the inspiration we felt witnessing the courage and dignity of our uniformly young patients throughout the unthinkable ordeal to which they were subjected. Our patients usually remained in the hospital for extended periods before they either died or left for facilities such as hospice, and we physicians and nurses got to know them well. Watching them suffer and ultimately losing them weighed heavily on us, as it similarly did on my physician-colleagues and friends who were caring for the growing numbers of AIDS patients in hospitals in New York City, Los Angeles, San Francisco, and other large cities. We often compared notes by telephone and in visits to each other's medical centers, and our experiences were identical. Even today, I get flashbacks of scenes in the rooms of patients that gripped me then and evoke strong emotions in me more than forty years later. One scene in particular among many, many others comes back to me often.

After we had tried almost all available and ultimately inadequate interventions, including bone marrow transplantation and multiple lymphocyte infusions, on our first ward patient, Ron Rinaldi, his condition slowly deteriorated. Nonetheless, he remained cheerful under the circumstances. His immune system was practically destroyed, and he was prey to a number of opportunistic infections. One particularly difficult infection was cytomegalovirus, which can attack a number of organ systems such as the gut and the retina of the eye, leading to compromised vision.

We had been attempting to treat Ron for cytomegalovirus infection with available drugs such as acyclovir; however, the only way to stop the progression of the disease is to reconstitute the immune system at the same time as directly treating the cytomegalovirus infection. But we had no way of reconstituting his immune system. The lymphocyte infusions and bone marrow transplant that he had received from his twin brother had failed.

Ron was such a likable fellow that Cliff and I looked forward to speaking to him on the twice-daily formal rounds we made on our patients. I would walk in and stand by his bedside. He would say, "How's it going, Dr. Fauci? Nice to see you." Only one day on evening rounds, Cliff and I walked in; I approached Ron's bed and smiled at him. He looked straight at me and said, "Who's there?"

It was as if someone had stuck a spike in my chest. Ron had gone completely blind. The cytomegalovirus, despite treatment that was obviously inadequate, had literally chewed up the critical sight elements of his retina from the time we had made morning rounds to the time we walked into the room that evening. I constrained my emotions as Cliff and I comforted him about this devastating outcome, although he said to us he expected that this would happen because he had been gradually losing vision over the previous weeks. We left and finished our rounds. I went back to my office around the corner and down the hall from the patient ward, just out of sight of my team, and burst into tears. I was not just deeply shaken and saddened; I was profoundly frustrated and angry. Ron would soon die. This is just one such story.

I could not fully appreciate it at the time, but for us there were to be hundreds and hundreds of similar stories right here on our ward.

I had experienced grief before. I lost my mother to cancer when I was twenty-four, and I knew how it felt to lose someone whom I loved deeply. But the loss we were experiencing now was different by several magnitudes. It was chronic, pervasive. I had gone into medicine because I wanted to serve people, and as a clinician it was my job to heal patients, to find solutions, to pull them back from impending disaster. It was something I was very good at. I am also an optimist by temperament. Now, as wave upon wave of men, often in their twenties and thirties, were handed a death sentence, none of my training or temperament provided a bulwark against that horrible, inevitable outcome. Helpless was the only way to describe it, as if we were battling an unseen enemy in a war zone—an enemy that was steadily overtaking us. But the physicians, nurses, and health-care providers on our team could not give up. Burnout was not an option. The patients needed us, and even though we could not cure them, we could offer them what we had—clinical skill, empathy, and excellent care. We had to stick with it and we did. And except for the occasional moment of uncontrolled grief such as when I learned that Ron Rinaldi had lost his sight, all of us who worked on the ward with these patients had to stuff away our feelings of loss, day after day, just to be able to carry on.

I think those feelings can be stuffed down for only so long. Today, when I flash back to that time, tears spontaneously well up. I have read about post-traumatic stress disorder, and I am sure that in this very specific area, I have it. And I am not alone. I know from speaking to many of my colleagues who were in the trenches of AIDS during those years that they have had similar feelings. But what we went through was nothing compared with the suffering of our patients and their families.

The Human
Immunodeficiency Virus

If you are a medical researcher, when you know the cause of a disease, you direct your research toward interventions to alleviate or cure the disease. If the disease is a cancer, you approach it with surgery in certain circumstances and test various forms of chemotherapy. If you are dealing with a known infection, you treat it with drugs specifically directed against that infection. But when you do not know the cause of an infectious disease, as was the case with AIDS, you have to look for clues to try to understand mechanisms of the disease process and hopefully to discover the cause. The way to do this is by observing patients and studying the nature of their organ system dysfunction. This is referred to as delineating the pathogenesis of the disease. These patients had severe immune defects. My lab's expertise was in the area of immunology, so that was the direction our studies went. The virologists, whose expertise is identifying new viral agents, were working full time searching for the virus in the blood and tissues of the patients.

Ever since I returned to the NIH in 1972, I had been studying the regulation of the human immune system, which is that part of the body that protects one against a wide variety of infections and even from the development of certain types of cancers. It is the "defense department" of the body. It is made up of a variety of different cell types, the most important of which are called lymphocytes. The two major ones are T lymphocytes and B lymphocytes, generally referred to as T cells and B cells. T cells are given the designation *T* because they are originally derived from the thymus gland, which is a relatively small cell-rich tissue located below the throat immediately beneath the upper part of the chest. There are many different varieties of T cells, one of the most important of which is the helper T cell with the designation "CD4+." These cells are the "conductors of the orchestra" of the multifaceted immune system and turned out to be the primary target of the virus that causes AIDS.

B cells are given the designation *B* because they are derived from bone marrow in humans. B cells produce proteins—strings of connected amino acids—called antibodies that protect us from a variety of infections. I was particularly interested in abnormalities of the regulation of B cell function. When I approached the investigation of the immune defects in AIDS, the natural path for me to take was to carefully examine B cell function in our patients. Our findings were striking as well as confusing. When we examined the B cells under a microscope and used a technique to measure their activity, we saw that despite the immune deficiency seen in patients with AIDS, the B cell component of the immune system was aberrantly "turned on" or hyperactivated. Cliff and I published this observation in the August 25, 1983, issue of *The New England Journal of Medicine*. Little did we know that years later it would be appreciated that the exuberant activation of the body's immune system was in response to a virus, which was soon to be discovered by others and which would ultimately be called the human immunodeficiency virus, or HIV.

Understanding this aberrant hyperactivation of the entire immune system, affecting both B cells and T cells, was critical to understanding the mechanism by which the disease AIDS evolves. The underlying disease mechanism was a diabolical, self-propagating process of HIV replication causing the activation of the immune system. This activation in turn drove the virus to replicate even more efficiently. It was a vicious cycle.

From the very first reports of this strange new disease in 1981, it was noted that patients showed a profound decrease in the number of CD4+ T cells in their blood. This observation strongly suggested that whatever was responsible for AIDS was targeting and destroying CD4+ T cells. This was a critical clue that galvanized groups of investigators who had long been studying a class of viruses that targeted CD4+ T cells. These viruses were called retroviruses, and in 1979, Robert Gallo and his team at the National Cancer Institute at the NIH had described a retrovirus responsible for an unusual form of leukemia, which he named human T cell leukemia virus, or HTLV-I. Soon after, a similar group of viruses was discovered in injection drug users and referred to as HTLV-II. The search was on by a number of scientists throughout the world for a brand-new retrovirus that was likely causing AIDS. In 1983, the French scientists Luc Montagnier and Françoise Barré-Sinoussi and their colleagues at the Institut Pasteur in Paris discovered the virus HIV, and in 1984, Gallo definitively showed that it was indeed the cause of the disease AIDS. Montagnier and Barré-Sinoussi were awarded the Nobel Prize in Physiology or Medicine in 2008 for their discovery.

This discovery transformed the direction of my own research and the focus and activities of my institute, and had a huge impact on my entire professional circle. Finally, we knew what the enemy was, and we could target it with diagnostics and preventive efforts, and begin to develop treatments. In addition, the discovery opened the gateway for increasing numbers of scientists including virologists, epidemiologists, immunologists, drug developers, and vaccine specialists, among others, to enter the field of HIV/AIDS research. The beginning of the end of the dark years was in sight. We were no longer helpless.

SOON AFTER HIV was discovered, a blood test was developed that the FDA licensed in March 1985. In addition to serving the important function of screening the blood supply and essentially eliminating transfusion and blood-product-associated transmission of HIV, the blood test allowed the screening of at-risk populations. Known as a seroprevalence study, it indicated what percentage of a given population was infected even before they became clinically ill.

The CDC and other domestic and international organizations began to perform these seroprevalence studies, sampling various populations who might be at high risk, such as sexually active gay men, commercial sex workers, college students, pregnant women, hemophiliacs, and injection drug users.

This led to the shocking revelation that the number of people with full-blown AIDS who had been identified clinically represented only the tip of the iceberg of the number of people who were actually infected. One seroprevalence study of sexually active homosexual men in the Castro District of San Francisco estimated that about 50 percent were infected with HIV. A seroprevalence study conducted in western Pennsylvania of patients with hemophilia whose disease required transfusions of components from plasma to prevent bleeding demonstrated that 45 percent were living with HIV. It is an understatement to say that we were horrified. Thousands and thousands of people had been getting infected before we knew that the disease existed, and they were passing the infections on to others long before they showed symptoms of the disease itself. It was not yet clear what was the "incubation period" of the infection—the time from initial infection until the onset of a clinical diagnosis of AIDS. It became important to distinguish between infection with HIV and the disease AIDS. The CDC later put out certain criteria that constituted a diagnosis of AIDS. One of these criteria is a drop in the number of the critical CD4+ T lymphocytes to below a certain empiric level of two hundred cells per microliter of blood. When the cells fall below that level, there is a high risk of contracting one or more of the infections or cancers associated with HIV infection. Apart from the CD4+ T cell count, there is a list of infections, which when contracted automatically characterize the person as having AIDS.

By the end of 1985 the number of reported AIDS cases in the United States according to the CDC was 15,948 including 229 children. Seventy-five percent of the children were infected from an infected mother during pregnancy or at the time of passage through the birth canal, 5 percent were hemophiliacs and were infected by contaminated blood products, while 15 percent received contaminated blood products for other reasons. Among the adults, 73 percent were homosexual or bisexual men, 17 percent were injection drug users, and only 1 percent were infected through heterosexual sex. The relative proportion of infections through heterosexual sex gradually increased over the years; however, in the United States the predominant risk category of transmission remained men who have sex with men.

TYPICALLY, attending physicians in a research hospital such as at the NIH make morning rounds on their patients around 7:00 or 8:00 and then leave them in the care of residents, fellows, and other health-care providers until they return for evening rounds at around 5:00 or 6:00. Then, if the patients are stable, their day is a wrap, and they can usually go home for dinner. Only occasionally is an attending physician on such a ward called in for an emergency during the night.

But during the very early years of HIV, there was little that was typical when it came to treating AIDS patients on the eleventh floor of the NIH Clinical Center. On morning rounds Cliff and I saw each one of our dozen or so patients. On a regular uncomplicated research ward, this could take about one to one and a half hours. Not so with AIDS patients. Each room we entered greeted us with some form of medical complication such that rounds often took several hours. After that, we walked the fifty yards to our lab, where we, along with our ten or so research fellows and lab technicians, were conducting immunology research studies trying to uncover the complex mechanisms involved in the deterioration of our patients' immune systems. More often than not, we got called back again and again throughout the day to tend to an emergency or near emergency. A patient's condition could change from stable to critical in a matter of hours and sometimes within minutes. A patient might start bleeding from the Kaposi's sarcoma in their gut with the potential of bleeding out. Another patient's *Pneumocystis* pneumonia might be getting worse even on therapy. Yet another patient might be in such distress that we would have to transfer him to get intubated for assisted breathing at the Medical Intensive Care Unit, where Henry Masur, now firmly established as an attending there, would take over. In the face of these near-constant interruptions, our lab work plodded along, and our "days" usually lasted until around 10:00 p.m., after which I went home and heated up a Lean Cuisine in the microwave for dinner. Getting called back in the middle of the night was not a rare occurrence.

The AIDS world was permeated by suffering and death, and it was getting worse, not better, as more and more people were getting infected and the global nature of the pandemic was becoming increasingly apparent. Amid all of this, I felt compelled to break out and force more attention and, importantly, more resources toward this disease. But how was I going to do that? I was just the chief of a relatively small laboratory in a huge research agency.

MY PERSONAL LIFE took an unanticipated turn soon after I returned in September 1983 from a trip to China, where I had delivered a series of lectures on our experiences with AIDS patients. The French group had just published their discovery of HIV four months earlier. The nursing department at the NIH hospital was actively recruiting for clinical nurse specialists—nurses with an additional level of skills and competence in dealing with difficult clinical problems. These specialists were also expected to train other nurses in the next-higher level of clinical care. We needed their help. While I was away in China, one such clinical nurse specialist, Christine Grady, was hired and assigned to the eleventh floor. Ms. Grady had just completed a two-year stint with Project HOPE, where she ran a medical clinic in Maceió, Brazil, and she spoke fluent Portuguese. She was caring for a Brazilian patient suffering from a serious vasculitis syndrome who had been hospitalized for months and wanted to return home. She had gotten to know the patient well, even cooking Brazilian food at home and bringing it to him in the hospital. He pleaded with her to help him persuade the doctors to discharge him. Within days of my return from my trip, Ms. Grady requested a meeting with the patient and me. Because I was the attending physician, I would be the one to decide if he was well enough to leave.

I wanted to tell the patient that he was to restrict his activities upon return to Rio de Janeiro because he was recovering and was still weak. The wound on his leg from the vasculitis was gradually healing, but he needed to keep changing the dressing, elevate his leg, and take it easy. Because he did not speak English, I asked Ms.

Grady to convey this message. She did, and he responded animatedly. When I asked her what he had said, she hesitated just for a moment and then told me that the patient promised to follow my instructions. The patient actually said to her that he was going to go home and drink several double-shot cachaça caipirinhas (the national drink of Brazil) and dance the night away in a club near Copacabana Beach. I, in complete ignorance, told her, "I am happy to hear that. Please tell him that he can go back to Brazil." As it turned out, after I left the room, she stayed behind and told the patient that the only reason she did not translate his real response was that she realized how painful it would be for him to stay any longer. She felt on balance it would be to his benefit to go home. He could have some fun, she told him, but in moderation.

A couple of days later, I ran into Ms. Grady on rounds and asked if she could come to my office at the end of her shift. Christine was mortified, thinking that I had discovered she had duped me when she translated the patient's response. She walked into my office visibly tense, although it would be months before I found out how the conversation with the patient had played out. What she did not know was that I could not get this woman with bright blue eyes, auburn hair, and a radiant smile out of my thoughts. "Would you like to have dinner with me?" I asked after she had taken a seat. I was not crossing any lines of authority here. Christine did not work for me; she worked for the nursing department. I just happened to be the attending physician on the floor where she was assigned.

She stared dumbfounded at me for what seemed like a full minute and then said, "I would love to." It was October 1983. Our first date was at a fashionable Vietnamese restaurant named Germaine's on the edge of Georgetown. Our second date and many thereafter found us dancing at the Marquee Lounge in the storied Omni Shoreham Hotel, where they had a live band every Saturday night. We were attracted to each other, but we also understood each other's work and shared the pain of caring for young men with HIV whose lives were cut tragically short as well as the helplessness that accompanied it.

After we had dated for seven months, Christine and her aging dog, Willie, moved from her Capitol Hill apartment into the house I had bought in 1977 in Northwest Washington, D.C. It is the house we still live in today. We were married on May 18, 1985. She became the mother of our three daughters and my closest confidante in the years that lay ahead.

She was and is my best friend. We worked impossible hours, but when we played, we inevitably played together. Christine is an excellent athlete, and we decided to train for the 1984 Marine Corps Marathon, running in our neighborhood in the evenings and along the C&O Canal or in beautiful Rock Creek Park on the weekends to build up our miles from six per day to eighteen a week before the race. The race was a challenging but exhilarating experience. We stuck together for 26.1 miles, and I had visions of the two of us going over the finish line in the shadow of the Iwo Jima Memorial hand in hand. But the lovely Christine, eleven years younger than I, had another idea. With 0.1 miles left, she turned to me with a big smile and said, "I love you dearly, but see you later." Then she took off, sprinting the last few hundred feet and finishing seconds before me. She did the same thing a year later when we ran the New York City Marathon together. This extra bit of gas in the tank applied to more than running, as I came to fully realize over the years.

IN THE SUMMER of 1984, another event dramatically shaped my future. Dr. Richard Krause, the director of NIAID, accepted the position as dean of the Emory School of Medicine in Atlanta. A search committee to replace Dr. Krause was formed, and word was out that I was considered a top candidate for the job. I was aware of the rumors but was ambivalent about that possibility. I loved what I was doing in the lab and with our AIDS patients and had no interest in changing. Yet I was intrigued by the idea of using the elevated position to call attention to the global problems of infectious diseases in general and HIV/AIDS in particular. I would be able to directly advocate for a major increase in funding for AIDS research supported by NIAID because in my mind the resources allocated to AIDS were meager compared with the potential enormity of the public health problem. The idea of heading a major agency responsible for the conduct and support of basic and clinical research on *all* infectious diseases including established global killers such as tuberculosis, malaria, and neglected tropical diseases also held some appeal. In addition, as a person trained in both infectious diseases and immunology, I was interested in the fact that NIAID was responsible for allergy and immunology research including organ transplantation.

Until that time, it was unofficial policy that directors of NIH institutes not conduct their own research or care for patients. If I were to submit my name to the search committee and in the event that I might be chosen for the job, the idea that I could no longer have one-on-one relationships with patients, or try to solve the terrible puzzle of their disease, bothered me and was in fact a deal-breaker. When I called Shelly Wolff to ask his opinion, he strongly encouraged me to submit my name for consideration and to worry about the conditions of the job later. I also had numerous discussions about my dilemma with Christine, who was my fiancé at the time. Like Shelly, Christine, who now knew me better than anyone, said, "Examine your options and go with your gut." But sensing that I was beginning to feel less challenged in my current position, she favored my putting my hat in the ring. "You can negotiate the details if and when you're offered the job," she said. Cliff was of similar mind urging me to apply, particularly since he knew that I would insist on continuing to lead the lab and seeing patients with him.

My interview before the search committee took place in late September 1984 and was uneventful. They never asked if I wanted to continue to see patients and work in the laboratory, and I never brought it up. I walked out feeling that the interview went well, but I did not have a clue what their impression was or what they would recommend.

Weeks went by without a word. Finally, I received a call scheduling a meeting with Dr. James B. Wyngaarden, director of the NIH. I met with Dr. Wyngaarden a few days later in his office in Building 1 in the center of the NIH campus. He got right to the point and offered me the position of director of NIAID. He mentioned that he was choosing me ahead of several highly qualified candidates who had considerably more administrative experience than I had and asked whether I was confident I could do the job. He also mentioned as an aside that at age forty-three I was probably the youngest person ever appointed to head an NIH institute.

I told Jim that I was confident about my abilities to handle the job. "I would be honored to accept the position," I said, "but I have two nonnegotiable conditions. First, I need your blessing to continue to do AIDS research as the chief of the Laboratory of Immunoregulation at NIAID. Second, I want to continue to see and care for my patients at the NIH Clinical Center." I told him that I realized that looking forward this would have to be in a supervisory role only and that the day-to-day care of patients would have to now be delegated to someone else. That someone would be Cliff Lane. Jim remained silent for about ten seconds, which seemed to me to be ten minutes, and then said, "I have no problem with this arrangement. I believe from what I have heard about you and have observed from a distance that you can pull this off."

"I promise that you will not regret this decision," I said. We shook hands, and I bounded out of his office, realizing with much excitement and an undeniable touch of anxiety what I had just gotten myself into.

Taking the Reins

As long as I can remember, I have had a muted disdain for new administrative leaders who take over an institution and, before they really understand the place, feel compelled to make changes just to show that they are in charge. I decided right from the beginning that before I made any changes at NIAID, I would learn everything possible about the institute. I had been a basic scientist and clinical investigator within NIAID for fifteen years including my fellowship from 1968 to 1971, and I knew the science and clinical medicine as well as or better than anyone. But until this time, I had only supervised a small lab of about twenty people doing research very familiar to me with a total budget of a couple million dollars, and I had almost no classic administrative experience. Now I was leading a scientifically diverse organization of several divisions representing a wide range of research conducted by government scientists mostly on the Bethesda campus and by a much larger group of grantees and contractors at universities and medical centers throughout the country and to some extent the world. We had about eight hundred full-time employees and contractors with a budget of $370 million.

What I needed was to become the best possible administrator

without losing touch with the science and the bedside, and I
needed to do this quickly. Only when I knew the workings of the
institute inside out could I feel comfortable in pursuing my vision
for its direction. It took me about six months of sixteen-hour days
before I felt qualified and confident enough to start articulating and
implementing my vision. I visited all of the labs on the Bethesda
campus and our satellite campus in Hamilton, Montana. I traveled
throughout the country meeting the scientists and clinical investigators in the medical centers that NIAID was funding. I learned about
budgetary planning and managing the balance between support of
basic (in the labs) versus clinical (on the wards) research. I wanted
to know more about the institute than any individual on earth.

Even though there were many fine people who were directors
of various divisions within NIAID and who reported directly to
me, I realized that to some extent I had taken over a sleepy organization. What was lacking among several of them was a palpable
sense of urgency. Few were pushing the envelope to aggressively
attack the problems of infectious diseases or even to realize the
growing importance of and opportunities in the discipline of immunology and its relevance across all fields of medicine. In addition, there was little enthusiasm for expanding AIDS research
among the aging senior staff. Conscious or subconscious homo-
phobia in society might have contributed to this feeling; also, the
existing pot of money was only so big. Others in the infectious
disease community were concerned about putting too much emphasis on AIDS for fear that this would divert resources away from
the diseases that they were studying. At that time roughly 25 percent of all deaths worldwide were due to infectious diseases, making them the second leading cause of death worldwide and the
leading cause of death among young people from birth to forty-
nine years old. In the developing world, particularly in sub-Saharan

Africa, with malaria, tuberculosis, respiratory diseases, diarrheal diseases, and the gathering storm of HIV/AIDS, infectious diseases were the leading cause of disability-adjusted life years—the number of years lost to disability or premature death. In addition, there was the ever-present threat of a pandemic influenza outbreak. Given all of this, I asked myself, why was NIAID only the sixth-largest institute among what were then the eleven institutes at the NIH, and why was the NIH not crying out for more money for NIAID?

The time for me to act had come.

I learned quickly that it was not good form and in fact could get you in trouble if you asked for more money than was in the president's proposed budget for a given fiscal year, or if you even suggested publicly that the proposed budget, which was handed down to directors with little of our input, was not sufficient for the job at hand. This was referred to as budget busting. I began to appreciate that there was a fine line between busting the budget and articulating in an appropriate setting, such as in scientific lectures that would be picked up by the press or by direct discussions with congressional staff, the legitimate need for more resources. It was a fine line, but I walked it—budget-busting lite. As long as I defended the president's budget publicly, I saw nothing wrong with my articulating the importance of more resources to meet public health needs. If I did not ask for it, for sure we would not get it.

A fiscal year (FY) in the government runs from October 1 of the previous year to September 30 of the designated year. When I arrived as director of NIAID in November 1984 (FY 1985), the NIH budget was $5.149 billion, and the budget of NIAID was $370 million, with the total AIDS budget at $66 million. By comparison, the budget of the National Cancer Institute was $1.18 billion. AIDS in the United States was at that moment predominantly restricted to gay men and injection drug users. In other words, unlike cancer, AIDS was not a "generalized" epidemic in the United States, and most of the general population was not particularly concerned at the time. Even so, it was crystal clear to me that this amount of money was woefully inadequate considering the seriousness of this explosively emerging threat.

I then did something that to my knowledge had not been done before by individual institute directors. I pushed hard for a doubling of the AIDS budget among selected members of Congress, the Reagan administration, and constituency groups, and to my surprise I got it. The NIH received $147 million for AIDS research in FY 1986, an increase of $81 million over FY 1985. This was the largest single increase in any particular discipline for that year, and it was all additional and not redistributed funds, thanks to the support of both Dr. Wyngaarden and the HHS secretary, Margaret Heckler, and of course the U.S. Congress. I was thrilled. We were at last showing a degree of financial commitment to HIV/AIDS research, even though our needs for additional resources would continue to grow dramatically.

That experience taught me crucial lessons. Just because no one had ever done something like this before did not mean it could not be done. I also realized how important it was to cultivate relationships with people who are in a position to make things happen. Importantly, to win over the skeptics, I learned that the cause for which you are advocating must be legitimate, worthy, and not motivated by self-interest; your arguments must be evidence based; and you must be truthful and consistent in your reasons for asking for resources. People quickly see through anything less than that.

We used the additional resources we had just obtained for AIDS research and also began a massive drug-development program as well as started the task of trying to develop an HIV vaccine.

Now that my job had grown from lab chief and clinical investigator to director of NIAID, besides pushing for more resources, I wanted to see for myself what AIDS in the "real world" outside the NIH looked like. I decided to visit the epicenters of the epidemic. First, I went to Greenwich Village in lower Manhattan.

Greenwich Village occupies a special place of affection in my psyche. Both my parents were born in Little Italy within walking distance of the Village. I remember that when I was a young boy, my father brought my sister, Denise, and me to see the small apartment building on Elizabeth Street between Hester and Grand Streets where he was delivered by a midwife in 1910. My mother was born about a mile away on Bleecker Street and Sixth Avenue. I recalled my impression as a child of the vibrancy of the Village as my father took us through Washington Square Park. As a student at Regis High School in upper Manhattan, I occasionally took the subway to the Village with friends to experience the excitement of the streets. The young lady that I took to my high school prom lived in Greenwich Village on Waverly Place and Sixth Avenue. As a medical student, medical intern, and medical resident in the late 1960s and early 1970s, I liked to go to the Village to listen to folk music and jazz at places such as Gerde's Folk City, the Village Gate, and the Village Vanguard. To me, these blocks were part of my DNA, part of my heritage. Every association and memory that I had of the Village was of joy, vibrancy, and entertainment.

But now I was shocked. By 1985, I had already taken care of hundreds of AIDS patients at the NIH. I was intimately acquainted with the devastating nature of their illness. However, that was in a clinic and hospital setting where I was wearing a starched white physician's coat with a stethoscope hanging from my neck. Here I was a pedestrian observing very sick people walking the streets. I could not believe what I was seeing as I meandered through Washington Square

Park along Waverly Place, across MacDougal Street, and up through Christopher Street. I could easily spot several young men with AIDS as I passed by them. The telltale dark spots on their faces due to Kaposi's sarcoma, what people used to refer to as gay cancer, easily identified them. The drawn faces and appearance of physical wasting were now all too typical. The positive electricity of the neighborhood had been replaced by an atmosphere of pain, suffering, and imminent death. A dark and ominous cloud had settled over Greenwich Village. I went on to visit the clinics of my medical colleagues at Bellevue Hospital and Memorial Sloan Kettering in Manhattan and Downstate Medical Center in Brooklyn. In those hospitals, 20 to 40 percent of the beds were occupied with AIDS patients.

The same was true when I visited San Francisco. A walk through the Castro District or just standing on the corner of Castro and Eighteenth Streets was strikingly similar to the Greenwich Village scene. My friends and colleagues at San Francisco General Hospital were being deluged with AIDS patients similar to the experience in New York City and our experience at the NIH. It was clear to me that we needed to establish a highly focused research effort on AIDS.

THERE HAD NEVER BEEN a research program in NIAID that was devoted to a single disease, and there was considerable pushback to my creating one. Nonetheless, I went ahead and did so, establishing a separate Division of AIDS within NIAID, and not surprisingly this stirred resentment among the older generation of infectious disease scientists. This was my first real introduction to the sometimes painful process of leadership. I rejected the concept held by many that I was paying too much attention to a disease that had afflicted only a few thousand people in the United States and that many still thought would probably disappear in a year or two. I learned in this instance and in several situations over the coming years that a leader, particularly in an area of controversy, cannot make everyone happy all the time. If you do, you are probably not a good leader and you soon will not be respected. Having doubled the AIDS budget and created the Division of AIDS, I now faced the challenge of having to persuade the White House, HHS, and Congress to put even more resources into AIDS research so that we could further entice the best among the scientific and public health communities to join the struggle.

Besides scientists and clinicians, others would soon join the mounting response directed against HIV/AIDS. Some stood out much more than others. One was a pediatric surgeon who initially had little interest in AIDS.

Two Brooklyn Boys

I had first heard about the pioneering surgeon operating out
of the Children's Hospital of Philadelphia (CHOP) during
my years as a medical resident at The New York Hospital. Im-
pressionable young physicians such as I was at the time frequently
took particular notice of the careers of famous physicians who
might serve as role models, even from a distance. And Dr. C. Everett Koop was truly a legend in his own time. He had been the surgeon in chief of CHOP from 1948 through 1981. When I was in
training during the late 1960s and early 1970s, Dr. Koop was at the
peak of his career. He invented surgical procedures for the correction of congenital abnormalities that were previously considered
hopeless. Among these was the correction of esophageal atresia,
which is a lack of connection of the esophagus to the stomach, a
fatal condition. In addition, he developed new procedures for the
treatment of hydrocephalus, a condition where normal fluid (called
cerebrospinal fluid) accumulates around the brain because of an
obstruction to the free flow of the fluid. He also revolutionized
the surgical repair of pediatric inguinal hernias and the correction
of undescended testicles. In essence, he more than anyone created
the discipline of pediatric surgery. He gained true international

fame in 1974 by surgically separating twin girls who were born joined together at the trunk and pelvis, saving the lives of both of them. He felt strongly that society had an obligation to respect the sanctity of life, and in his profession this extended to doing whatever is possible and reasonable to save the life of a child with certain abnormalities for which he had developed these revolutionary surgical procedures. It would have been a great honor for me as a medical student or physician in training to just meet Dr. Koop and perhaps shake his hand. I never imagined that this would happen.

DR. KOOP'S REPUTATION as a defender of the right to life including his concerns about abortion had caught the attention of President-elect Ronald Reagan in late 1980. Reagan nominated Koop for surgeon general in 1981, and this triggered a series of hostile congressional hearings, public debates, and media commentaries that put Dr. Koop under a degree of stress that even his most difficult surgical procedures did not elicit.

Ever since I had returned to the NIH from my final year of clinical training, I was considered the "house physician" for many NIH staff and their families and assorted Washington VIPs. One day I received a call from the NIH director, Dr. Donald Fredrickson, telling me that Dr. Koop was "not feeling well" and that HHS would like one of the NIH physicians to see him.

At 8:30 one morning, I went to the nurses' station on the 11 East ward of the NIH Clinical Center, where I had been working for the past nine years, and waited for Dr. Koop to arrive. Out of the elevator and down the hall came this imposing man—tall (six feet, two inches) and ramrod straight, sporting his trademark Captain Ahab beard, and with a concerned expression on his face. We shook hands, and I led him into the treatment room to take a history and perform a complete physical examination.

Dr. Koop explained his symptoms to me: insomnia, a feeling of jumpiness, irritability, intermittent flushed sensation, occasional headaches, and lightheadedness. His physical examination was completely normal. I drew blood for a number of tests and arranged to see him again after the results of the blood work came back. Before I let him go, I asked, even though I already knew the answer, if anything was bothering him or causing him stress. He brushed off the possibility. I strongly suspected that his symptoms were all being caused by the fact that due to his pro-life stance he was getting trashed on a regular basis by the liberal media and that Senator Ted Kennedy, one of the most respected members of the Senate, was dead set against his nomination as surgeon general. Still, I had to rule out any physical cause. When the blood work, electrocardiogram, chest X-ray, and other laboratory tests came back as unremarkable, I was convinced that we were dealing with a reversible constellation of signs and symptoms. But reversibility is easier said than done. I first had to convince him that he was physically fine and that we could work this out. Because he was an accomplished surgeon, I told him that the bad news was that this was not a surgically correctable problem. However, the good news was that it was fixable. "I have a name for your condition, Dr. Koop. The welcome-to-Washington traumatic stress syndrome." He thought this was hilarious, and we shared the first of what would be a series of hearty laughs together over the next thirty years. I told him I planned to gradually diminish and ultimately discontinue some of the medications that various physicians had put him on over the past year because I did not think that he needed them. He agreed only under the condition that I not attempt to discontinue his beloved daily predinner dry martini. He also insisted that I stop calling him Dr. Koop. "My friends call me Chick," he said. I agreed and my friendship with the medical icon began.

OVER THE NEXT four years as the number of cases of AIDS increased at a sharp rate, Chick Koop was not actively engaged with AIDS and spent the bulk of his time on other issues such as the crusade against tobacco use. But starting in early 1986, I saw a distinct evolution in his growing appreciation of the devastating effect HIV/AIDS was having and of the potential role he, as surgeon general, could play in the nation's response to the epidemic. A peculiarity of the HHS allocation of housing for high-ranking employees played some role in this evolution. Although the office of the surgeon general is located in the main headquarters of HHS in the Hubert H. Humphrey Building at 200 Independence Avenue, S.W., in Washington, D.C., the living quarters of the surgeon general were at that time on the NIH campus in Bethesda, Maryland. The house in which Koop and his wife, Betty, lived was about a hundred yards from my office in the Claude Denson Pepper Building (Building 31). Upon entering the NIH campus, Chick had to walk directly past my building to get to his house. Starting in 1986 he began regularly stopping off for visits in the evening, usually around 7:30 after all my staff had already left for the day. He would arrive resplendent in his Public Health Service uniform, which is almost indistinguishable from the uniform of a U.S. Navy officer. The sleeves of his jacket displayed the thick bands of a vice admiral. He knocked softly and led off with the same introduction each time: "You work too hard; take a few minutes and relax with me." I put aside the manuscript I was working on in preparation for submission to a medical journal, and the few minutes inevitably turned into an hour as he probed me about every aspect of the scientific, medical, epidemiological, and policy issues of HIV/AIDS. It was clear that he wanted to learn everything he could about the disease. He referred to those sessions as his "nighttime tutorials." But it was not long until he became a true expert in his own right. During his evening visits, he described with passion and enthusiasm the visits he had begun making to AIDS clinics throughout the country and his interactions with patients, their families, and various constituency groups. He was about to enter the arena of AIDS in a big way.

In 1986, the Reagan administration asked Dr. Koop to prepare a report on AIDS. The *Surgeon General's Report on Acquired Immune Deficiency Syndrome*, released at a press conference on October 22, 1986, was a masterpiece of clarity, candor, evidence-based statements, and critically useful information. Chick dispensed with the niceties and talked about the epidemic in real-world terms. His descriptions of the risks of transmission by anal intercourse among gay men and his advocacy for the use of condoms to prevent transmission of HIV caused quite a stir among certain religious leaders and social conservatives. Chick was not deterred. To the contrary, he was concerned that such a daunting, technical report might not be widely read, particularly by the general public, who would most benefit from the information. Chick wanted to mail a pamphlet containing frank information about HIV infection and AIDS to every household in the United States. But because the Office of the Surgeon General was mostly thought of as a bully pulpit position and had a relative paucity of financial resources, his budget was too small to pull the project off.

Here is where we hatched what he jokingly called "the Brooklyn Scheme." Like me, Chick Koop was born and raised in Brooklyn. He grew up in Flatbush, originally populated by children and grandchildren of Dutch and German immigrants. It was just a few neighborhoods away from Bensonhurst. Chick's scheme was one Brooklyn boy helping another to enable the pamphlet to be produced and mailed in a timely fashion. It was early 1988, and NIAID now had a substantial budget of $740 million. It was not unusual for one component of a government agency to transfer a small amount of money to another component for services rendered through what is referred to as an interagency transfer. Because my institute was the leading government agency performing and supporting AIDS research, the pamphlet, which might help prevent HIV infection, was in the interest of NIAID. When the first mailing went out, Chick called me up and with a mischievous laugh said, "I guess we Brooklyn boys pulled it off!"

The pamphlet had a profound effect on the country's awareness of the seriousness of the AIDS epidemic and the risks of infection. It remains one of the most influential public health publications ever distributed by the U.S. government. It was both highly effective and controversial. This latter fact was illustrated by a syndicated cartoon that appeared in a number of newspapers showing a working mother leaving her home and telling her children as she walks out the door, "If anything comes in the mail from the Surgeon General, don't open it!"

CHICK KOOP REMAINED a force on issues related to public health for many years following his tenure as surgeon general. Our friendship endured, and Chick and I both were invited back to our medical school alma mater, Cornell University Medical College, in May 1992. I was to receive the Alumni Award of Distinction, and Chick was to deliver the commencement address. He decided that we should rent a limousine and take a tour of our childhood landmarks in Brooklyn. We visited his elementary school, the Flatbush School, and mine, Our Lady of Guadalupe; the sports fields where he played football and I played baseball; and other neighborhood hangouts. We finished the day by driving to Coney

Island to reprise one of the great treats of our childhood, a hot dog at Nathan's Famous. As we stood on line waiting to be served, a small crowd gathered around us and began staring at Chick. Soon you could hear people saying, "Hey, isn't that the surgeon general guy? That must be him, look at that crazy beard. What is he doing here?"

He heard the remark, started to laugh, and said, "What do you *think* I am doing here? I'm a Brooklyn guy, and this is Nathan's."

Building an AIDS
Research Program

Most progress in medical research on a disease is usually slow and incremental, and there are few eureka moments. The discovery of HIV as the cause of AIDS was one of those moments. It opened up the gates for all the subsequent studies on the disease. In contrast, much of the understanding of how the virus destroys the immune system of the body was incremental. This was true of the work that Cliff, my team, and I were doing in my lab and a growing number of scientists were doing in laboratories in the United States and throughout the world. It was during those early years that we only gradually began to understand the resiliency and destructive capability of HIV. But despite our growing knowledge of the disease, our patients were still suffering and dying at an alarming rate.

It was the mid-1980s, and we still had no effective therapy. Because of the desperate nature of the situation, people with HIV were willing to self-administer almost any substance or compound that showed even the slightest hint or rumor of being able to suppress the virus in a test tube. Searching for an effective treatment, patients were traveling to foreign countries to obtain drugs that were unavailable in their own country. One of the most celebrated examples was when Rock Hudson, who had advanced-stage AIDS, went to France in July 1985 to receive the experimental drug HPA-23, developed by scientists at the Institut Pasteur in Paris. In a later multicenter study that included our team at the NIH Clinical Center, HPA-23 proved to be ineffective in treating HIV infection. Rock Hudson died of AIDS on October 2, 1985, at age fifty-nine.

It became clear to me almost from the start that we needed to accelerate our drug discovery efforts. Soon after I established the Division of AIDS within NIAID, we initiated the National Cooperative Drug Discovery Groups (NCDDGs) modeled after an approach initiated in 1983 by the National Cancer Institute for the development of anticancer drugs. The NCDDGs were partnerships between academic institutions and pharmaceutical companies to develop drugs for HIV infection.

We also needed a mechanism to test these drugs on people with HIV. I expected that there would be multiple drugs that would be coming through the newly stimulated pipeline over the next couple of years. It was unlikely that any single clinical unit would be able to enroll enough patients to gather sufficient data to prove the safety and efficacy of the drugs. I felt we would need a network of clinical trial units to pool all the data and get solid answers to clinical questions. By mid-1986, we awarded contracts for more than a dozen AIDS Treatment Evaluation Units (ATEUs) nationwide that formed the core of the network. Not everyone at the NIH or in research institutions throughout the country was excited about spending the money to create such a network, especially when we did not have any drugs yet to test in these units. Some scientists were even saying that we were "throwing money away." But I knew that soon we would have more drugs than we were able to test, and so, despite the skepticism and criticism, I felt it was prudent to get the units set up quickly and ready to go. That turned out to be the correct decision as many new candidate drugs began to roll in.

The ATEUs were the forerunners of a much larger network of clinical trial sites called the AIDS Clinical Trials Group (ACTG) that over the coming years would be the vehicle where antiretroviral drugs would be tested individually and in combination for their ability to suppress the replication of HIV. The future impact of this network of clinical trial units would ultimately prove to be profound and transformative in the development of highly effective treatments for individuals with HIV.

At about the same time we were setting up the ATEUs, drug companies such as Burroughs Wellcome were examining compounds that had been developed for other diseases, particularly cancers, to determine if they might also be effective against HIV. Drs. Samuel Broder, Robert Yarchoan, and Hiroaki Mitsuya at the National Cancer Institute had developed a test to determine the ability of any compound to suppress the replication of HIV. In collaboration with scientists from Burroughs Wellcome, Broder and colleagues demonstrated that the drug azidothymidine, or AZT, had potent suppressive activity against HIV in the test tube.

Another eureka moment!

The results constituted the first real breakthrough in the treatment of people with HIV. I was excited about the test tube results, but I remained guarded because the proof of the pudding would be whether the drug worked in people.

Over a twenty-four-week period in 1986, 145 individuals with HIV received AZT, and 137 received the placebo. At the end of the study, 19 patients who received the placebo had died compared with only 1 death in the group that received AZT. Opportunistic infections such as *Pneumocystis* pneumonia developed in 45 subjects receiving the placebo compared with 24 subjects receiving AZT. These stunning results were published in *The New England*

Journal of Medicine on July 23, 1987. Now I felt as if shades in a dark room had been raised and flashes of sunlight were coming through.

As word spread in the gay community, despair switched overnight to optimism. It was a period of exuberance with demand for immediate access to the drug. The problem was that the application for approval by the Food and Drug Administration was just in its beginning stages, and the drug was not yet available on the market. The question was, How could we get this potentially lifesaving drug to the desperate people who needed it immediately? At that time, the end of 1986, the number of reported cases of AIDS in the United States was approximately twenty-nine thousand. There was no precedent to get a lifesaving drug to so many people prior to official approval by the FDA.

However, in the treatment of cancer, there was a precedent to assist a limited number of patients to obtain drugs, some of which were still experimental and not yet approved by the FDA. For several years the National Cancer Institute had operated a hotline for this purpose, contracted through a company called Biospherics in Rockville, Maryland, just up the road from the main NIH campus in Bethesda. It was not too much of a stretch to apply this concept to AZT distribution. We decided that NIAID would pay Biospherics to set up a twenty-four-hours-a-day, seven-days-a-week hotline for the distribution of AZT under the FDA's "Investigational New Drug" mechanism.

Because the supply was limited at that time, we had to determine who would get the drug first. We decided that patients had to currently have or have had at one time *Pneumocystis* pneumonia as an entry criterion to the program. We estimated that this made as many as six thousand people eligible to receive AZT in the United States.

The key to implementing this program was Deborah Katz, a

nurse employee of the National Cancer Institute who was assigned to the Biospherics contract. Debbie marshaled her friends and neighbors to staff the hotline, accepting applications around the clock. The applications had to be made by a physician on behalf of a specific patient. Every night, one of our young NIAID physicians reviewed the applications that had come in that day. Then the approved applications were sent to Burroughs Wellcome, which shipped out the drug to a pharmacy. Approximately five thousand patients received AZT through this program from September 1986 to March 1987, at which point AZT was approved by the FDA under the name zidovudine. The hotline was discontinued. From the time Burroughs Wellcome submitted the zidovudine application to the FDA to the time of approval was three and a half months—then the quickest approval of a drug by the FDA in its history.

But the promise of AZT was short-lived.

ONE OF THE characteristics of RNA viruses, particularly those such as HIV that replicate very rapidly, is that they make mistakes in copying themselves during the replicative process. These mistakes, known as mutations, may impart various characteristics to the virus. One characteristic can be resistance to an agent meant to kill the virus, such as an antiviral drug. During the course of therapy, AZT was killing those HIV viruses that were sensitive to its killing effects, but not those viruses that had mutated to become resistant to the drug. The lesson we learned was not that AZT was ineffective. The problem was that when it was administered alone, the virus almost inevitably outsmarted the drug as a result of its uncanny ability to mutate and evade killing. The solution would have to be to use a combination of drugs. This had been done successfully in the treatment of tuberculosis and certain cancers that were resistant to single drugs alone.

When a person is treated with two or more drugs that individually are effective, the virus finds itself "boxed in" and ultimately suppressed, so long as the patient continuously takes the combination of drugs. Despite best efforts, it took four years to develop the next effective anti-HIV drug—didanosine, manufactured by Bristol Myers Squibb. The FDA approved it in October 1991. These four years were extremely frustrating to me and my colleagues. Our patients were still suffering and dying, and by that time there were more than 200,000 cases of AIDS reported in the United States.

Drug discovery was steady but slow. The following year, 1992, the third anti-HIV drug, dideoxycytidine, manufactured by Hoffmann–La Roche, was approved by the FDA; then, in 1994, stavudine, manufactured by Bristol Myers Squibb, and in 1995 lamivudine, manufactured by GlaxoSmithKline, were approved.

Unfortunately, the virus was not slow. By the end of 1995 there had been more than 513,000 cases of AIDS reported in the United States. We were making considerable progress, but we were still losing the war. We were struggling with the balance between efficacy and drug toxicity. In other words, the drugs were prolonging life in many patients but not suppressing the virus completely, which was continuing to contribute to the deterioration of the patients' condition. Meanwhile drug side effects often took their toll. In some respects, this was similar to the toxicity that cancer patients experience with chemotherapy aimed at destroying their cancer.

We needed better drugs.

In the meantime, we got much better at the art of taking care of patients with HIV apart from treating HIV itself. The practice of HIV medicine was becoming a discrete subspecialty of internal medicine and a sub-subspecialty of infectious diseases. One area of infectious disease practice that was significantly altered because of the AIDS experience was the concept of prophylaxis, or treatment of patients with a variety of antimicrobial drugs to prevent the onset of infections that frequently occurred in individuals with HIV whose immune function was severely compromised. Instead of waiting for patients to get these opportunistic infections, we preemptively treated them to prevent disease. It was the wide implementation of this practice for diseases such as *Pneumocystis* pneumonia, cytomegalovirus disease, toxoplasmosis, and cryptococcosis that saved or prolonged countless lives before the availability of highly effective antiretroviral drugs that completely and durably suppressed HIV.

AIDS Strikes Close
to Home

I first met Dr. James Carroll Hill in 1974 when he was a program officer in the infectious disease grants program at NIAID ten years before I became director. A research microbiologist at Berkeley, he had been transferred from San Francisco in 1969 as a navy officer to head a division in the Department of Microbiology at the National Naval Medical Center in Bethesda. When he retired from the U.S. Navy in 1974, he joined NIAID. As much as he liked the East Coast, he still loved San Francisco and often visited friends in the Castro District in the late 1970s and early 1980s.

I remember quite clearly the first time I spoke with Jim, in the summer of 1975, long before we worked on AIDS together. We were both in the weekly meeting of the Executive Committee of NIAID in our seventh-floor conference room, where the director and program officers gathered to discuss administrative and policy issues of the institute. Jim was there to present and discuss a vaccine trial for meningococcal infection, a common cause of meningitis in college students, for which he was the program officer in charge. I was there to present a research project in my lab related to treatment of vasculitis. Jim was tall and immaculate in his appearance with perfectly trimmed hair, a tan suit, light blue shirt, and bright yellow tie. He caught my eye and introduced himself with a warm smile.

In 1983, after several years as a program officer, he left his scientific position and became an administrator in the NIAID intramural research program, where I had recently been made a laboratory chief. This was when our friendship began. Jim emanated kindness, dignity, and a refreshing lack of cynicism. I hoped that someday I would get the opportunity to work even more closely with him. The opportunity soon arrived when I became NIAID director in 1984.

I immediately asked Jim to become my special assistant. Special assistant in the federal government is a catchall phrase that can mean nothing—or everything. With Jim, it meant everything. He cared deeply about NIAID, the AIDS crisis, and me.

Before accepting the position, he asked to see me alone in my office. He closed the door, and with an anxious look on his face said, "Tony, I am gay, and I don't want this to cause you any embarrassment." At the time, being gay in a public government position was not widely accepted. Jim went on: "If you think that it will be a problem, just tell me and I will stay where I am. No hard feelings."

I put my arm around his shoulder and said with a smile, "Jim, you are totally clueless. I have known you were gay from the moment I met you ten years ago in the NIAID conference room." Jim was visibly relieved. But that encounter brought into sharp focus for me what I had witnessed with so many of my AIDS patients. Although many parents of AIDS patients embraced their children's sexual orientation and were with them constantly on our clinical wards, others did not know that their child was ill or even that he was gay. Often the patient was reluctant to tell his parents that he had a lethal disease for fear of rejection. Once Jim and I got that out of the way, we were off on our mission together.

Jim often made me laugh even when it seemed that everything was going wrong. He was born in Manila, Arkansas, a town that I along with probably a couple hundred million other Americans had never heard of. When visiting dignitaries, often from foreign countries, arrived at the NIH and I briefed them on our activities with HIV/AIDS, Jim always joined me. If they asked where we were from, I said Brooklyn, New York, and for better or worse, everyone had heard of Brooklyn. Jim said with a twinkle in his eye, "I am from Manila, Arkansas," a statement that was almost always met with a puzzled look. Jim would then say, "Just think of Manila this way: we sell Velveeta cheese in the gourmet section of our supermarkets." He had another Arkansas favorite that he would use when I looked particularly stressed. He just smiled and said in his Southern drawl, "Tony, back in Arkansas we would say that you look like hammered shit!" Jim was the only person I ever knew who could walk into a room during a crisis when I was seething about something and within a minute have me hysterical with laughter, merely by saying something disarming like "Well, aren't you a hoot today." Or his favorite was "Lighten up, Tony, things could be worse; we both could be picking cotton in Arkansas; trust me, I've done it." You just could not help but love him. When the deputy director of NIAID, whom I inherited from the previous director, stepped down, I immediately promoted Jim to that important position.

Jim had a deep understanding of the challenges faced by the at-risk gay community, and he continually taught me the nuances of these challenges. In addition, the gay community trusted him as one of their own, and this made it much easier for me to integrate myself into the community. Jim's Capitol Hill town house on Sixth and C Streets in Northeast D.C. served as the meeting place and gourmet restaurant where countless discussions took place between me and the activist communities. It was not an unusual sight to see AIDS activists sitting with me around the fireplace in Jim's living room debating the communities' most pressing questions. All the while Jim went back and forth serving wine and tending to the meal that he was preparing in the kitchen.

JIM WAS ALSO the world's greatest traveling companion, for me at least. He often accompanied me on international trips to AIDS scientific conferences where I usually gave a keynote lecture and participated in meetings with foreign health officials. Jim felt personally responsible for seeing to it that we were never late and never missed our flight. I was compulsive enough without Jim in the picture, but he brought the process to new heights. As we headed out to Dulles International Airport for a trip to Paris or Bangkok or Cape Town, Jim calculated the maximal time for each phase of the trip starting from leaving his town house on Capitol Hill to my house across town. Normally this was a fifteen-to-twenty-minute trip. Jim built in the possibility that there would be major traffic problems between those two destinations, and he allowed one hour for the trip. Never mind that it might be 6:00 a.m. on a Sunday with not a car in sight. He also factored in double the amount of time each step took to drive from my house to Dulles, check in at the airport, get to the gate, and board the plane. We often arrived several hours before flight time, long before this was the common protocol. In fact, we did this so many times that we became friendly with a waitress at one of the airport restaurants where we spent hours eating hot dogs and drinking beer as we waited and waited for our plane to board. After a few such encounters with her, when she saw us sit down one day for our usual hot dogs and beer, she came over and said with a straight face, "Hi, guys, flying to Europe? When does your plane leave . . . tomorrow?"

In 1978, four years after he joined NIAID and six years before I hired him as my deputy, Jim entered a clinical trial for a hepatitis B vaccine. As part of the trial's screening protocol Jim was discovered to already be infected with hepatitis B virus. Although he had no symptoms, he had mild chronic persistent hepatitis. This condition was common among sexually active gay men. This diagnosis put Jim under the care of one of the world's leading experts on hepatitis B, Dr. Jay Hoofnagle, who happened to be our colleague right there on the NIH campus at the National Institute of Diabetes and Digestive and Kidney Diseases.

One day in July 1985, I was sitting at my desk working on a lecture when Jim walked in looking worried and closed the door behind him. I instinctively knew that something was very wrong. His eyes were moist as he said that he was going to tell me something, and he would understand if I had to let him go as my deputy. I was struck with a terribly ominous feeling and blurted out, "Jim, for goodness' sake, what the hell are you talking about?" Tears ran down his face as he told me. "Dr. Hoofnagle just did the newly available test for HIV infection on my serum sample, and it came back positive." I lost my breath and could barely speak. I had taken care of endless AIDS patients over the past four years, but this was the first time a person so close to me, indeed someone whom I loved, was found to be infected. He repeated: "I would absolutely understand if you let me go. How bad and inappropriate would it appear and how would people react to the knowledge that the deputy to one of the leading AIDS researchers in the world, who was also the director of the National Institute of Allergy and Infectious Diseases, was stupid enough to get infected?"

I threw my arms around him and said, "Jim, you crazy son of a bitch, there is no way in the world that I would ever let you go. And so drop that idea right now." It was so typical of Jim to worry more about an imagined negative effect on my public image or that of the institute than about the fact that he now had a deadly disease with no known treatment. That was Jim Hill. But this situation was also representative of what was occurring every day out in the community. There was still so much stigma and shame associated with being infected, and it would take several years before that changed; even today in some parts of the world it has not completely disappeared.

Fortunately, his CD4+ T cell count was reasonably good, within the low-to-normal range, and the level of virus in his blood as measured by the crude techniques available in 1985 was not very high. We composed ourselves and mapped out a plan for his care. We would follow and watch him until a treatment became available and hope that his condition did not deteriorate rapidly.

THE YEARS WENT by and life went on for Jim and me, working intensively together on the business of the institute. We traveled together nationally and internationally, visiting medical centers that NIAID was funding. I often gave lectures, with Jim always making sure that everything went smoothly and the logistics were executed perfectly.

Jim became closer and closer to me and my family. He loved children and occasionally pinch-hit as a babysitter for our eldest daughter, Jennifer, who was born in 1986, and dropped in for dinner at our home. Then, on March 16, 1989, our second daughter,

Megan, was born. Christine and I were considering who would be a good choice to be her godfather, an important position of honor among Italian American and Irish American Catholic families. It took us less than a minute to decide that Jim was the man, and he became Uncle Jim not only to Jennifer and Megan but also to Alison, who was born three years later.

I began to see definite signs of Jim slipping in mid-1993 as he appeared physically weaker and began losing weight. He occasionally spoke of retirement, but never seriously pursued it. He was integral to our efforts against this devastating plague, and he wanted to remain in the fight. In the summer of 1994, Jim experienced episodes of gastrointestinal bleeding that required blood transfusions. That August, he underwent a procedure that successfully controlled the bleeding, after which he returned to work, albeit considerably weaker than before.

Soon thereafter Jim told me what I had been dreading to hear for some time. He felt that he had to retire since he could no longer give me the 110 percent he wanted to give me. I tried to convince him that as far as I was concerned Jim Hill even at half speed was better than most anyone else at full speed, but he would have none of it. I was crushed because I knew that now I would not be seeing him every day as I had for the past ten years and also because it was clear to me that he was physically slipping with regard to both his HIV disease and his chronic hepatitis. Jim was well aware of the seriousness of his illness, but in typical fashion he did not focus on himself, and retired at the end of 1994.

Jim volunteered in the clinic over the next two and a half years and quickly gained the respect and admiration of the clerks, nurses, physicians, and patients. He had always been a deeply religious man who often participated in the activities of St. James Episcopal Church near his home. His retirement now gave him more time to devote to church activities. He also allowed himself one indulgence. He had always wanted to own a pickup truck, and now he bought one so he could, as he said, "finally play out my identity as a true Southern boy." It was quite a sight to see Jim enter the NIH parking lot filled with gray or black Toyotas and Hondas driving his red Ford pickup.

I dropped in often to see Jim in the clinic when I made my in-patient rounds, and he looked weaker and weaker as the months went by. By the spring of 1997, he had terrible complications from his failing liver and the abnormal pressures in the veins connected to his liver. His kidneys also were beginning to fail. We admitted him to the NIH Clinical Center on June 20, 1997, for evaluation. It was clear that he needed surgery to address his problems, but the NIH did not have a person on staff who could perform the diffi-cult procedure required. We decided to transfer him to another hospital.

On June 24, Cliff Lane, Christine, Jim's close friend Dr. Jack Whitescarver, and I gathered around Jim's bed to wish him luck and send him off to the referral hospital. As I hugged Jim and kissed him on the cheek to say goodbye, he looked frightened, an expression that I had never seen on him before. He said that it was tough to explain, but he just had a "bad feeling." We all told him that everything would be fine and that he would be back working in the clinic in no time. Jack Whitescarver volunteered to accom-pany Jim to the other hospital and bring him home after the pro-cedure.

The surgery was scheduled to take place on June 27, and we anxiously awaited Jack's call telling us that all was well and that they would soon return to Bethesda. Around 8:30 that evening I heard from Jack. He told me that the unthinkable had happened. During the procedure the catheter had punctured a hole in Jim's he-patic vein, leading to a fatal hemorrhage. It is impossible to describe the shock, the pain, the anger I felt when I got the news. There was nothing that anyone could do now. Jim, not yet fifty-six years old, was gone, and the sense of grief was almost unbearable.

To this day, I still miss Jim and feel the loss. But he is with me in many ways. Whenever I am stressed out, I think of Jim smiling at me and saying, "Lighten up, Tony, things could be worse; we both could be picking cotton in Arkansas; trust me, I've done it."

A Global Catastrophe

In the summer of 1981, when the first cases of AIDS were reported from New York City, Los Angeles, and San Francisco, many assumed that this was a disease confined to gay men in the United States. However, soon thereafter, cases were reported from other developed countries, particularly European countries, and especially Belgium and France. But what gradually became apparent was that AIDS was really predominantly a disease of the developing world. The evidence of this was hidden in plain sight; we just did not appreciate it at the time.

Among the Europeans who were seeing AIDS patients was Peter Piot, a Belgian national who had studied infectious diseases at the University of Washington in Seattle and was now back at his home base at the University of Antwerp. Peter was also seeing Zairian nationals who had come to Belgium for medical care or were European nationals who had traveled to or lived in sub-Saharan countries including Zaire, now the Democratic Republic of the Congo. What was fascinating to Peter and those of us closely following the evolution of the AIDS epidemic was that many of these patients with an African connection were heterosexual. They had a disease identical to what we were seeing among gay men.

Few people believed that this was AIDS since AIDS was not supposed to happen via heterosexual sex.

At about the same time Piot was noticing these cases in Belgium, the CDC reported in 1982 that a disproportionate number of Haitians in the United States, many of whom were heterosexual, were being diagnosed with AIDS. As a result of this information, Dr. Richard Krause, my predecessor as director of NIAID, visited Port-au-Prince, Haiti, with a team of NIAID physician-scientists including two members of my lab, Cliff Lane and Dr. Tom Quinn, who had come from an infectious diseases fellowship at the University of Washington in Seattle. They wanted to determine if the disease was present in Haiti and how it was being transmitted. It soon became clear to them that many Haitians were afflicted with AIDS and that it affected both men and women, suggesting that heterosexual transmission might be common. They also became aware that from a historical perspective many Haitians had lived in Zaire over the prior ten years as a result of a bilateral arrangement between the governments of Haiti and Zaire. Many of these Haitians returned home in the early 1970s; some became ill with AIDS-like illnesses several years later.

We needed to know what was going on in southern Africa. Piot wanted to investigate the possibility that AIDS was present in a major way in Zaire. In 1984 with support from NIAID, a multi-institutional collaboration among the University of Antwerp, NIAID, and the CDC was established. The project was called Projet SIDA (syndrome d'immunodéficience acquise), and it launched a substantial epidemiological, clinical, and laboratory investigation. Within weeks it became clear to the group that heterosexual transmission of AIDS was occurring widely in Zaire and the epidemic likely had started in the early 1970s. Unlike the patterns in the United States, the male-to-female ratio of AIDS was one to one.

The investigations continued until 1992, when unrest in Zaire jeopardized the safety of our investigators. This forced me to evacuate my team by air out of Kinshasa. However, an extraordinary amount of important epidemiological data were collected from the project that, together with studies from other sub-Saharan countries, established definitively that HIV/AIDS was predominantly a disease of heterosexual transmission concentrated in the developing world, particularly in sub-Saharan Africa. Today more than 90 percent of cases are in low- and middle-income countries, and more than 65 percent are in sub-Saharan Africa.

In Zaire, percentages of infection among pregnant women and female sex workers were so high as to be almost unbelievable. For example, in some prenatal clinics, at least 20 to 40 percent of the pregnant women were infected. In certain locations, more than 80 percent of female sex workers were infected. In one study, from 1 to 18 percent of otherwise healthy blood donors were infected. In certain countries, the percentage of individuals fifteen to forty-nine years old who were infected was in double figures.

Beyond Zaire, by the time accurate surveillance was available in many sub-Saharan countries, the numbers of individuals who were infected were staggering. In Zimbabwe, Botswana, Swaziland (now Eswatini), and Lesotho, the percentage of people in the general population who were infected was about 20 percent. In South Africa that number was 11 percent in 1998, and it rose to 15.8 percent by 2005. Tom Quinn, who was the chief of the International HIV/Sexually Transmitted Diseases Section of my lab and who spent considerable time in Africa, reported back to me regularly with these astounding numbers months before he and his colleagues published them in the medical literature. This was horrible beyond our imagination. To make matters worse, even the modestly effective single-drug and two-drug anti-HIV treatments that were available in the developed world in the late 1980s and early 1990s were completely out of reach to most people with AIDS in southern Africa. Even simple treatments such as antibiotics and antivirals for the secondary opportunistic infections were mostly unavailable for many of these patients.

Relief was nowhere in sight.

AIDS Activism

Starting in the early 1980s, there was deep frustration among the gay community that the United States government was not doing enough to call attention to and act on the emerging AIDS epidemic. What was particularly galling was the fact that President Ronald Reagan had not mentioned AIDS in any public discussions until he used the word in a press conference on September 17, 1985, already well into his second term. At that time, there had been more than fifteen thousand cases of AIDS reported in the United States with more than eight thousand deaths. There was the perception, and in some respects the reality, that along with the federal government many local and state governments did not grasp the seriousness of the emerging plague. Few were moving quickly or forcefully enough to address this escalating problem by increasing awareness of the outbreak and putting money into prevention. In addition, the gay community justifiably felt that investments in basic and clinical research including in drug development were inadequate. Soon their frustration burst into protest and confrontation.

At about this time, I assumed the NIAID directorship. I felt that it was my responsibility not only to conduct and support biomedical research on AIDS but also to speak out in whatever venue possible about the seriousness of this pandemic, its devastating potential, and the need to do more. I began to realize that as an increasingly recognized public figure, I could focus more attention on gaining support for additional funding. On the downside, because I was one of the few government people in Washington talking about and being identified with AIDS, it was inevitable that I became the government's public face of AIDS and, with that, the target of the activists.

I started reading some of the literature put out by the activists as well as listening to their public statements. What came through and resonated deeply with me was not their confrontational style but the obvious fear and emotional pain they were feeling as they watched their friends and lovers die horrible deaths and as they feared a similar fate for themselves. I tried to put myself in their shoes, and it became clear to me that I would have been as vehement as they were in demanding a more concentrated and effective effort against this emerging plague. I knew I needed to make a connection with them, but they beat me to the punch. This did not happen in the way I had hoped.

Enter Larry Kramer.

BEFORE WE MET, I had heard a number of stories about how outrageous this man could be. Larry Kramer was the undisputed father of the activist movement, and his reputation preceded him. He had the unique capability of simultaneously offending a large number of people of diverse persuasions with his confrontational style and his iconoclastic approach to authority. He certainly was anathema to public health and government officials. I was warned by my friends and scientific colleagues in New York City that Larry Kramer was someone to be avoided. I ignored this advice. I was fascinated with his history and was particularly impressed by the passion that was evident in his March 1983 article in the *New York Native* titled "1,112 and Counting," in which he blasted President Reagan, the NIH, the CDC, New York City's mayor, Ed Koch, the city's health commissioner, the hospitals of New York City, New York City newspapers, and the entire gay community for what he considered an inadequate response to the AIDS epidemic.

Larry was a well-known screenwriter, author, and playwright before the epidemic, and was an early and outspoken critic of promiscuous gay relationships that he felt were destructive to the health of the gay community that he loved so deeply. His first big breakthrough was the screenplay for the movie *Women in Love* in 1969, which earned him an Academy Award nomination. His propensity toward controversy became evident with his 1978 novel, *Faggots*. It was in this book that he predicted dire physical and psychological health consequences for the gay community because of what he considered their sexually reckless lifestyle. This was not a message that much of the gay community wanted to hear, celebrating as they were their newfound freedom of sexual expression after the Stonewall Inn riots of June 1969. Larry was raining on their parade.

In essence, Larry had predicted a catastrophe like the AIDS pandemic years before AIDS emerged. He became involved with AIDS issues just a few months after the first cases were recognized in the United States in 1981. That year, Larry got together with his friends Nathan Fain, Lawrence Mass, Paul Popham, Paul Rapoport, and Edmund White in his Greenwich Village apartment, where they began an informal group to raise awareness around AIDS. The following year, they officially established an organization called Gay Men's Health Crisis. This story was vividly described in his Tony Award–winning play and acclaimed

HBO movie *The Normal Heart*. Larry soon became frustrated with what he referred to as the apathy of the gay community to the AIDS crisis. He dissociated himself from Gay Men's Health Crisis and in 1987 formed the activist group AIDS Coalition to Unleash Power, better known as ACT UP, which soon became the hub for highly talented, energetic, and passionate advocates for the cause. Over the ensuing years, members of ACT UP would have an extraordinary impact on AIDS awareness, public health policy, and, particularly relevant to me, the AIDS scientific agenda, the conduct of clinical trials for AIDS drugs, and the pace of FDA approval of potentially lifesaving drugs. This iconic organization would serve as the future prototype of advocacy for diseases beyond AIDS.

I got my first taste of Larry's confrontational style in the early 1980s when I saw him at a public meeting held in New York City where community constituents could discuss their AIDS-related concerns with federal and local public health officials. In the middle of a speech by an HHS official, Larry began to shout out obscenities, disrupting the proceedings. As I observed him from the back of the room, it was clear to me that sooner or later I would have to deal with Larry Kramer.

In late 1986, I arranged to meet him and some of his activist colleagues in a New York City hotel. It was a cordial meeting, but a turning point for me. We had a calm discussion about our plans to ratchet up the AIDS research effort. Soon thereafter, in early 1987 in a show of good faith I invited Larry down to visit me at the NIH to see how we at NIAID were building up our operation with the additional funds we had received. My staff was concerned about opening our doors to Kramer and strongly advised me not to, but I insisted. It was critical to interact with the activists, and the best way to do this was to get to know their leader.

I had recently established the Division of AIDS, and expanding our AIDS efforts would require hiring many new people and finding space for them in the usually cramped laboratories and administrative offices of NIAID. I spent a considerable amount of time explaining to Larry how difficult it is to get a major research and administrative operation up and running. I mentioned casually that as mundane as it might seem, office space was in short supply. It was just an offhand comment in a more substantive conversation concerning our beefed-up scientific agenda. I thought that his visit went well and that he now better understood the challenges and goals of our operation.

I was mistaken. A couple of weeks after his visit, an article ran in the *New York Native* sharply criticizing me as well as our AIDS efforts, with Larry writing, "People are dying, and the government's AIDS efforts are paralyzed because of lack of office space." My staff was furious and there were plenty of "I told you sos." Nonetheless, I still thought that embracing Larry was the right thing to do. I did not think he was intending to embarrass or attack me personally. He was frustrated with the federal government, and in his eyes I was the government.

In June 1988, I was sitting in my office when someone from our communications team came in with a "please do not shoot the messenger" look on her face. She handed me an article that had run the previous day in the *San Francisco Examiner* written by Larry titled "I Call You Murderers, an Open Letter to an Incompetent Idiot, Dr. Anthony Fauci." Larry accused me of being responsible for the deaths of hundreds if not thousands of persons with HIV. His rationale for the attack was that I had not demanded enough money for AIDS. He ignored the fact that I had requested from Congress and the president the largest increase in resources given to an NIH institute since the famous "war on cancer" in the 1970s. It hurt me as a physician devoted to alleviating suffering and saving lives to be called a "murderer." Yet, in a strange way, I still did not blame Larry. If I had been in his position, I would have been just as angry.

ONE OF THE MOST compelling issues for the activists was that very few people had access to the experimental drugs in clinical trials. Because the drugs were unproven (experimental), the number of people allowed in the trials by the FDA was limited, because the FDA needed clear-cut and definitive data uncomplicated by other factors to grant approval. The criteria for entry into and exclusion from the trials were rigid, leaving out many who wanted access to any possible treatment. For example, a person might be excluded from a trial because of the level of their CD4+ T cells, other infections they might have, or other drugs they might be on. This made sense from a pristine medical standpoint but not from the standpoint of a desperate person with AIDS. As Larry Kramer stated in the article, "The arithmetic is terrifyingly simple. An average study takes seven to ten years. The average life after diagnosis with AIDS is two years. Of course, activists are screaming for faster access to treatments. Otherwise, most of us won't be here when the answers come."

I was getting the picture. In February 1989, a group of activists descended on the NIH to demand a greater effort to develop better drugs than AZT, which was the only AIDS drug available at the time. I made what I consider now one of the most important decisions that I ever made regarding my involvement in AIDS policy. Instead of ignoring them, I asked if seven or eight of the protesters wanted to come upstairs to meet with me.

They were shocked. This was the first time in anyone's memory that a government official had invited them to sit down and talk on equal terms and on government turf. We met for two hours in my conference room. After a candid and sometimes heated discussion, I came away from that meeting with a positive feeling and convinced that we needed to have a sea change in the way we dealt with the activist community.

Word spread quickly that I was someone who cared about them and that I was willing to be an advocate for them in dealing with the faceless bureaucracy of the federal government. I was no longer the enemy, no longer the "murderer." I realized that I now embraced two roles, which I enthusiastically welcomed. One was my official job: to conduct my own research and lead NIAID. The other unofficial role was to use my visibility and scientific credibility to influence policy that would address the issues critical to people living with HIV in the United States and, as I would soon appreciate, throughout the world.

At first, my relationships with the activists consisted primarily in listening and responding to their concerns that there were not enough resources devoted to HIV/AIDS research, something I was working hard behind the scenes to remedy. However, as they became more sophisticated in their understanding of the process of clinical trial design and the regulation of drug approval, they and their ideas played an increasingly important role in shaping my thinking and policy in these areas. I soon found myself regularly on the phone and meeting with the younger of them, people whom Larry Kramer, then in his fifties, referred to as his "children." They came from diverse backgrounds and were universally intelligent, tough, passionate, determined, and thirsty for knowledge about AIDS. You can watch them all in action in the Academy Award–nominated documentary film *How to Survive a Plague*, directed by David France. Prominent in the film were Peter Staley, Mark Harrington, Jim Eigo, David Barr, Gregg Gonsalves, Spencer Cox, Bob Rafsky, Garance Franke-Ruta, Iris Long, Ann Northrop, Gregg Bordowitz, and Bill Bahlman with his ever-present movie camera filming every conversation I had with the group. I occasionally saw them in New York City, and they came to Washington, D.C., regularly (usually to demonstrate) and often visited me in my office or later at working dinners in the home of Jim Hill. Over the years I got to know a few of them well, and I grew to respect and like these brave young people very much even though we sometimes disagreed, and they did not hesitate to publicly criticize me over these disagreements. But we learned from each other, and as time went by, I valued more and more their unique insight into issues that affected them and their community.

I FIRST HEARD about Marty Delaney from my staff who were concerned that he would disrupt the clinical trials process because he was strongly advocating to make unproven drugs available to ill and despairing people with HIV. Martin "Marty" Delaney was a charismatic and articulate former Jesuit scholastic, business genius, and gay man who founded Project Inform in San Francisco in 1984. Marty was the reflective, intellectual, analytical counterpoint to the unbridled and iconoclastically passionate Larry Kramer. Project Inform was an education and public policy group that lobbied aggressively for increased support for HIV/AIDS research. It also pushed for greater flexibility of regulatory agencies in their dealings with clinical trials and approval of drugs for AIDS. Marty balanced time in the conference room with smuggling drugs from Mexico for distribution to individuals with HIV at a time, prior to the approval of AZT, when there were no approved drugs at all for the treatment of AIDS. For that specific activity, he was in some respects the gay ex-Jesuit version of Ron Woodroof, played in an Academy Award–winning performance by Matthew McConaughey in the movie *Dallas Buyers Club*. McConaughey's character was a heterosexual man who was HIV infected via injection drug use and who smuggled drugs across the Mexican border for AIDS patients in need of hope. In real life, Marty was much, much more than that. Even after the approval of AZT in 1987, Marty, impatient with the drug development process for AIDS, ran his own trial of a drug called Compound Q, which was made from extracts of a cucumber-like plant grown in Southeast Asia. This understandably rattled my staff, dedicated and hard-working scientists and health officials whose job was to design and support classical clinical trials to test candidate drugs for HIV in an orderly and traditional fashion.

Marty and his inner circle at Project Inform, particularly an engaging and committed young woman named Brenda Lein, wrote prolifically to educate the community of infected and at-risk individuals. They provided the latest information on HIV research and drug development, and pushed the envelope in what they considered an unduly slow process. I began reading some of their pamphlets and literature, and here again they were spot on. Given my eight years of Jesuit training, I was eager to meet Marty.

MARTY AND I did not always agree on strategy, but we both respected our differences of opinion. I can honestly say that I learned more from Marty about what was really going on in the trenches of the pandemic, in the Castro District of San Francisco and throughout the country, than Marty learned from me about the science and medicine related to HIV/AIDS. I visited Marty in his crowded Project Inform offices on more than one occasion. My most important visit came at Marty's invitation in June 1989. The issue of access to unlicensed experimental drugs for individuals with HIV was heating up on both the East and the West Coasts. A bone of contention among activists was the restriction on the availability of ganciclovir for cytomegalovirus disease in the eye.

In an ongoing clinical trial determining the safety and efficacy of ganciclovir, there were restrictions in the protocol: if patients wanted to receive ganciclovir, they could not simultaneously be taking AZT. The reason was based on the classic and time-honored FDA approach to clinical trials whereby there could not be any confounding elements when testing a specific drug. If a person were also taking AZT, it would be unclear which drug was responsible for any observed clinical effects or toxicities. On one level this made sense. But the patients did not care which drug did what. They just wanted to get better. This hit me hard during that June 1989 visit when Marty Delaney brought me to the Castro District apartment of a young teacher with HIV who was receiving AZT but was losing his vision due to progressive cytomegalovirus infection of his retina. He desperately needed and wanted ganciclovir. He was lying on a pullout couch in his living room, appearing chronically ill. As I approached him, he looked straight at me, but he was moving his head from side to side as if he were trying to get me in focus. He grabbed my arm and said, "Dr. Fauci, I appreciate all that you are doing for us with the research, but please get me some ganciclovir. Why do I have to make a choice of stopping my AZT and dying sooner versus staying on AZT, living a little longer, but going blind without ganciclovir?" I immediately thought back in horror and sadness to seven years earlier in 1982 and the scene at the NIH when my patient Ron Rinaldi went blind right in front of Cliff Lane and me on our evening clinical rounds when his cytomegalovirus chewed away the final critical areas of his retina. I was embarrassed, but all I could do was to say to myself, "What the hell are we doing? This is complete insanity."

I HAD TO DO something about this situation even though I had no official authority to overcome the regulatory hurdle. Jim Eigo of

ACT UP New York had been advocating for some time for a "parallel track" approach, as had Marty. Parallel track was a concept whereby a drug that was being tested in a controlled and restricted clinical trial could simultaneously be made available outside the structure of the clinical trial to patients who could potentially benefit from the drug, had no other available alternative intervention, and were not able to be in the clinical trial for any number of reasons. These could include a lack of geographic accessibility to the medical centers conducting the trial or a preexisting condition, medication, or abnormal laboratory test. Safety data would need to be collected on the patients participating in the parallel track approach, but the efficacy results would not affect the data collected in the official clinical trial. This all seemed logical, but the FDA was reluctant to consider it even though I knew that the FDA commissioner, Frank Young, was privately sympathetic to the concept.

The day after I visited the young man in his Castro District apartment, Marty arranged for me to be the keynote speaker at a town hall meeting held at a theater in downtown San Francisco on Friday, June 23, 1989. The night before at dinner in a small Italian restaurant in the Pacific Heights section of the city, Marty argued forcibly for me to just come out and publicly propose a parallel track approach to AIDS clinical trials. I knew what I had to do regardless of the enormous amount of flack that I was bound to catch for speaking out against established government regulatory policy. All I needed was a slight push. As Marty and I stood offstage before he walked out to introduce me, he said, "Tony, do it. Please do it." I took a deep breath, walked out onstage, and did it. Standing before a thousand people, I threw away my prepared remarks and gave an impassioned speech saying that I was now totally convinced we should embrace a parallel track approach to testing certain drugs for HIV/AIDS and its complications. The room erupted in a standing ovation. After my speech, Marty shook my hand, hugged me, and said very quietly, "Thank you, Tony. You cannot imagine the importance of what you have just done."

The next day Randy Shilts, award-winning author of the book *And the Band Played On*, describing the excruciating plight of the AIDS community, reported in the *San Francisco Chronicle*, "The federal government's top AIDS researcher yesterday called for opening up a 'parallel track' of drug testing that would greatly expand the availability of new treatments for AIDS sufferers." The following Monday, June 26, Gina Kolata reported in *The New York Times*, "In a major shift long sought by those involved in the fight against AIDS, the chief of Federal AIDS research has called for a new system that would allow patients far greater access to experimental drugs." In the same *New York Times* article, Mathilde Krim, the highly respected scientist-activist and founder of the American Foundation for AIDS Research, praised what I had done, saying, "It's a great step forward." Mark Harrington of ACT UP New York weighed in with support, and of course Marty Delaney himself, speaking on behalf of Project Inform, lent "total support" to the concept. The real question was, How would this break with the U.S. government establishment be received back in Washington?

As soon as I stepped off the plane from San Francisco, I phoned my office and found out. Officials at the FDA were furious that I had publicly declared my opinion, which contradicted their official position. I assumed that I would be in some sort of trouble, but I was not sure just how much trouble. I was counting on the adage that it was easier to ask for forgiveness than for permission. But I did wonder, Could I be fired for doing this? I was counting on support from the powers that be because I had already developed a warm personal relationship with President George H. W. Bush, whom I had met when he was vice president.

No sooner did I reach my office than I was told that the White House chief of staff, John Sununu, had called. John wanted to

know "what the hell was going on." I gulped and told him that this
was absolutely the right thing to do and that we should have done
it a long time ago. He seemed satisfied and said he would relay this
to the president. John called me back later that day to say that the
president was okay with what I had done and told me "not to
worry; all is well." Even the FDA commissioner, Frank Young, was
quoted as saying, "I've been pushing it as much as Tony has." Well,
certainly the bureaucracy of the FDA was not pushing it, but no
matter. At the end of the day, the strategy worked, and AIDS activists, particularly Jim Eigo and Marty, were justifiably credited
with moving the needle on this critical issue. In a twist of irony, at
an open government hearing on the subject of parallel track soon
after my San Francisco speech, Larry Kramer shouted out from
the back of the room with the same passion with which he usually
disrupted such public hearings, saying, "Tony, I have called you a
murderer in the past, but you are now my hero." Almost four years
later, in January 1993, I received a Certificate of Appreciation from
the HHS secretary, Louis Sullivan, stating, "With deep appreciation for your outstanding contribution in the implementation of
the Parallel Track initiative for the U.S. Department of Health
and Human Services." Go figure.

WITH THE VICTORY of parallel track behind us, Marty was not
finished with me. Many was the night that he called me at my
home at 8:00 San Francisco time and 11:00 East Coast time with
his usual comment: "I figured that you would be awake, and so can
we talk?" In a twenty-minute phone call, I would learn more about
what was going on in the trenches, and what he thought I should
be doing differently and/or better, than if I had five official briefings in my office. To his enduring credit, he never let our friendship stop him from being blunt: "Tony, this clinical trial is not

asking the right question." Likewise, I did not hesitate to disagree with him on issues, knowing that it would not negatively affect our friendship. "Marty, you know I love you, but you are wrong on this one." In fact, his advice was so valuable that I appointed him to the NIAID AIDS Research Advisory Committee, and he served on NIAID's National Advisory Allergy and Infectious Diseases Council.

Marty became keenly interested in the question of whether we could restore the damaged immune system in people with advanced-stage AIDS. This issue came up over a dinner we had during one of his visits to Washington, D.C., in 1990. We found a quiet booth at one of my favorite French bistros on M Street. "Tony, you really need to put a big effort into this," he said animatedly. I knew that Marty had a real talent in galvanizing people around a cause. "Okay, Marty. If you are so hot about this, then come up with some ideas to light a fire under it." Which he did shortly thereafter by talking up the subject among the scientific and advocacy communities, resulting in a number of workshops and conferences that led years later to a major effort supported by NIAID to cure AIDS.

FOR ALMOST THE NEXT TWENTY YEARS, my relationship and friendship with Marty Delaney flourished. Marty was not living with HIV, but he had a chronic hepatitis B infection, similar to Jim Hill. Despite adequate control of his disease over many years, his condition deteriorated, and chronic liver failure led to the development of hepatic cancer, a uniformly fatal condition. In his last years, Marty pushed hard for an accelerated effort to find a cure for HIV infection, because after 1996 anti-HIV drugs were highly successful in suppressing the virus but patients needed to take medicine every day for the rest of their lives. Marty wanted us to cure HIV infection so that patients would no longer require antiretroviral drugs. In recognition of his leadership in this area, I established a new initiative called the Martin Delaney Collaboratories for the development of a cure for HIV infection.

Marty had a calm, philosophical attitude toward his imminent death as we discussed what had been accomplished, his role in these accomplishments, and what still needed to be done.

Marty died on January 23, 2009, and Brenda Lein asked me to give one of the eulogies at his memorial ceremony in San Francisco that March. The ceremony was to be held at 4:30 p.m. at the Eureka Valley Recreation Center in the middle of the Castro District. I did not want to be late, so I arrived in San Francisco around midday. With plenty of time to kill, I took a taxi into town and spent the next hour or so just roaming around the Castro District, re-creating the walk that I took in 1985 right after I became director of NIAID and flew to San Francisco to see firsthand the devastation of the AIDS pandemic. But this time highly effective AIDS drugs were available and had transformed the lives of people with HIV. I did not see anyone with the telltale Kaposi's sarcoma lesions on their faces or the hollow looks that stared back at me as in 1985. We had come a very long way since then, and part of the success was due to the passion and commitment of activists like Marty Delaney.

ALTHOUGH I HAD BECOME popular with some of the AIDS activists after coming out in favor of the parallel track, there were still disagreements over other issues where certain activists felt that we were not moving quickly enough and there was not enough input on the part of activists regarding the research agenda. My relationship with the activists became complicated as we got to know, respect, and like each other at the same time that we sometimes disagreed. I tried to address these disagreements by making myself available for meetings and discussions. In my attempts to engage them, I often met them on their own turf. On one occasion, in October 1989, I took a chance and, together with my assistant at the time, Dr. Margaret "Peggy" Hamburg, attended a meeting with the ACT UP New York group in the Lesbian and Gay Community Services Center on West Thirteenth Street in Greenwich Village. The two of us sat in the center's packed ground-floor auditorium with exposed pipes overhead, surrounded by dozens and dozens of activists loaded with questions for me. One poignant exchange that evening took place with the ACT UP member Bob Rafsky, who excoriated me for not doing more to see that an antibiotic called Bactrim be officially recommended as prevention for *Pneumocystis* pneumonia. I tried to explain that I had no authority to declare recommendations or guidelines for treatment. It was my responsibility to provide scientific evidence for whether an intervention was safe and effective so that guidelines could be made based on this scientific evidence. It was a wrenching moment for me because I knew how difficult it was for the activists to hear this. I recall the pain, anger, and frustration in Bob's voice as he confronted me about the inadequacy of our system to address his needs and those of his suffering friends and colleagues. Bob was a fearless warrior and someone who was sharply critical of me, but for whom I felt deep empathy and respect. Bob, who died of AIDS in 1993, never forgave me for what he felt was a failing on my part.

In the documentary *How to Survive a Plague*, Bob is shown playing with his toddler daughter, Sara, shortly before his death. More than twenty-three years after Bob died, Peter Staley, who by 2016 had become a legend in the field of activism, had been awarded a fellowship at the Institute of Politics at the Harvard Kennedy School to teach a course on the history of AIDS activism. Peter and I had become close friends over the previous three decades, and he asked me to come to Cambridge, Massachusetts, in the fall of 2016 to participate in a class with him where he would interview me regarding our shared experiences during the heyday of AIDS activism. At the time, my daughter Jennifer was living in Cambridge while pursuing a Ph.D. in clinical psychology at Boston College. In an extraordinary coincidence, Jenny's apartment was a few blocks from Sara Rafsky's apartment. Sara was now thirty-one years old, a year older than Jenny. Peter invited both Jenny and Sara to the class, which included showing a clip from *How to Survive a Plague* of the interchange between Bob and me at the Gay and Lesbian Community Services Center. At the end of the class, which led to a standing ovation, Jenny and Sara looked at each other and hugged. It was a moving experience for all of us.

Besides access to certain drugs, a burning issue was the question of representation of activists at meetings and discussions that affected them. In late 1989, I had been discussing with Mark Harrington, a young Harvard graduate and brilliant strategist of ACT UP New York, my idea of allowing activists to be present at what had always been closed meetings of the NIAID AIDS Clinical Trials Group (ACTG). Against my staff's strong objections, I invited him and three of his colleagues to attend the next meeting on November 6–8, 1989, at a hotel near the NIH campus. I was not at the meeting that day but was informed that one of my senior staff opened the meeting by saying, "The issue of constituency representation at the ACTG meeting has been precipitated by ACT UP New York against our will; they have sent four representatives who are here today. We did not invite them, and we wish they were not here. Nonetheless, we did not wish to provoke a physical confrontation by attempting to secure their exit. They will not be permitted to talk in any of the meetings."

I was furious. I could not fire the senior NIAID official, because he was a civil servant who had not committed an offense that was serious enough for removal; nonetheless, I called him into my office and told him that given our fundamental differences in how to interact with the AIDS activist community, I wanted him to start looking for another job. This was difficult for me to do because he was a talented, energetic, and committed scientist and administrator. But he was completely wed to the classical paradigm that scientists and scientists alone should participate in the development of a scientific agenda and above all that activists had no place in the process.

As it turned out, my decision to open the doors to the activist community was one of the best administrative decisions I ever made. Over the years their input proved to be invaluable to our developing the optimal design of clinical trials that were user-friendly to the participants and still yielded the most valuable scientific and clinical information. The recalcitrant members of the scientific community realized that I was serious about involving the activists in our discussions and decisions and soon got over their objections.

IN EARLY SPRING 1990, I invited Peter Staley, Mark Harrington, and other members of ACT UP New York down to Washington, D.C., to discuss some of the most pressing issues in the AIDS struggle. That night, over glasses of Pinot Grigio and Jim Hill's famous Cuban pork, Peter told me that although he considered me a friend and that he was grateful to me for opening a dialogue between the scientific establishment and him and his activist colleagues, they felt that they needed to push us harder. They were going to complain in a public and confrontational way about the paucity of AIDS drugs, particularly drugs for opportunistic infections. He told me that they planned to "storm the NIH." I tried to convince them that this was not the way to go since it would hurt my efforts to get government officials, including President Bush, to resonate more with the plight of the activists and the entire HIV community. Peter, an Oberlin graduate and former Wall Street trader then in his late twenties, looked me straight in the eye and said, "Tony, I feel badly if this causes you problems, but when all is said and done, we still need to do this. The NIH is highly visible, and we need to do this in a visible setting. It's high time a bunch of us got arrested on the NIH campus." We agreed to disagree and had another glass of wine and some of Jim Hill's delicious cheesecake.

Two months later, on May 21, 1990, busloads of activists, some dressed in costumes, descended on the Bethesda campus and blocked access to buildings. They swarmed over the lawns and pathways chanting, "Storm the NIH," and set off colorful smoke bombs. A few carried fake caskets bearing the words "Fuck you, Fauci." As I watched the demonstrations from a window on the seventh floor of Building 31, I saw that Peter Staley had jumped on top of the concrete overhang at the entrance to the building as police tried to get him down. I ran down the stairs to make sure that he was all right and would not get hurt. When I reached the ground floor, I ran into Peter being taken away in handcuffs. With his hands shackled behind his back, Peter looked up with a big grin and said, "Tony, I did it! I was the first one arrested." The police officer looked at us in disbelief as he led Peter away.

In January 1992 members of the Treatment and Data Committee of ACT UP New York including Peter, Mark Harrington, Gregg Gonsalves, Spencer Cox, and David Barr left the parent ACT UP group to form the Treatment Action Group, or TAG. Their major goal was to influence the acceleration of treatment research for HIV and its complications. They were serious and scholarly and produced a number of policy reports that we in the federal government often referred to. We were entering a new era of AIDS activism in which street-like confrontation gave way to participation in advisory boards, workshops, and the planning of scientific meetings—a true partnership between scientists and involved constituencies.

EVEN AS WE had established a growing rapport with the younger activists, Larry Kramer did not refrain from lashing out at me publicly, criticizing me for what he considered the inadequate efforts of the federal government concerning the AIDS crisis. He also did this in private. He never failed to point out something that he thought I should be doing or not doing. Larry and I met by chance at the Fifth International AIDS Conference held on June 4 through 9, 1989, in Montreal. I was walking back to my hotel after dinner late at night with Jim Hill as Larry was just starting out on a walk with his dog, Molly. He asked Jim and me if we would walk a bit with him and chat. Larry, Jim, Molly, and I walked the streets of Montreal on this pleasant spring night. Larry was in a talkative mood and was acting friendly and warm. He seemed to want to put aside his usual hostility, and he admitted begrudgingly that he realized we were fighting for the same things. But he had a request. "Tony, you need to do something outrageous to bring more attention to the AIDS problem," he said. "Chain yourself to the White House fence or give a quote to *The New York Times* that the administration of George H. W. Bush are a bunch of murderers."

"Larry, I hear you, but that is a terrible idea," I replied. "Besides the fact that I disagree with you, if I did something like that, I would get one shot at attention and then my access to the administration would cease forever." Larry remained unconvinced.

Over the next year or two, as we got to know each other better and understand each other more, our relationship made Larry nervous. He worried that our growing friendship would compromise his ability to attack me as I went from an abstract public figure to a confidant. Larry would later describe our relationship to the press as "extremely complex." I would agree.

In 1991, Larry and I both appeared on *Nightline* with Ted Koppel. Larry was being piped in from the ABC studio in New York City and I was with Koppel in the ABC studio in D.C. As usual, Larry was relentlessly attacking the government's track record on AIDS. In the process, he became angry and began shouting at me for defending the NIH's accomplishments. Ted did a great job refereeing, but Larry was Larry. To viewers, it must have seemed that I was Larry's mortal enemy. Soon after I got home after the show, Larry telephoned me and said he thought that the program went "real well" and hoped that I agreed. After wondering what program he was referring to, I told him that everything was okay and that I looked forward to seeing him again soon.

Around this time, Larry began working on a new play titled *The Destiny of Me*. It is a magnificent story of his growing up as a young boy realizing that he was gay. He describes the painful relationship with various members of his family and how he dealt with the fact that he is HIV infected. The story is told in retrospect from his hospital room, which he chose to be at the NIH. The physician in his play was called Dr. Anthony Della Vida. Similar to my wife, Christine, Anthony Della Vida's wife in the play is an AIDS nurse who works closely with Dr. Della Vida.

As with all his work, Larry took the details of his playwriting seriously. I agreed to have the actor Bruce McCarty, who would play Della Vida, visit the NIH and follow me around for the day, including accompanying me on clinical rounds, to portray me as authentically as possible.

Christine and I were Larry's guests at the play's New York opening on October 11, 1992, at the Lucille Lortel Theatre on

Christopher Street in Greenwich Village. As I expected, Larry trashed Dr. Anthony Della Vida; however, by the end of the play, Della Vida emerges as a complicated character who is seen in a subtly sympathetic light. It was an outstanding play that received a standing ovation. As we regrouped in the lobby, I sensed that Larry was a bit uncomfortable over and above the jitters that naturally occur on opening night. He came up to me and asked sheepishly, "Tony, are you terribly pissed off at me?" I gave him a big hug and told him that the play was a masterpiece and that I was not the least bit offended. His relief was palpable. It was a terrific night for Larry, and it opened up my eyes a bit more to the painful experiences that he and so many of his friends and colleagues had growing up gay in a homophobic society, only to be confronted later with a deadly disease. The play would go on to receive rave reviews, win the 1993 Obie Award among other accolades, and be a finalist for the Pulitzer Prize.

LARRY GUESSED THAT he had been infected with HIV in the mid- to late 1970s. He was cared for by excellent physicians in New York City, but he kept me closely involved in his care, albeit from a distance. He had been receiving appropriate antiretroviral therapy for his HIV infection for many years and had done rather well. However, in 2001 he began to experience deterioration in his liver function due to his chronic hepatitis B infection. Larry's physical condition progressively worsened. After several phone discussions, it became clear to me that he needed a few days in a hospital to have his liver ailment fully evaluated. I brought him down to the NIH and admitted him to our Clinical Center. It was an eerie example of life imitating art. He now was in a hospital room at the NIH under the care of a team headed by the real Tony Fauci and not the fictitious Anthony Della Vida. We gave Larry a thorough workup and concluded that he desperately needed a liver transplant, which he received in December 2001.

The adaptation of *The Normal Heart* in 2014 as an HBO movie starring Mark Ruffalo received high critical acclaim. Unfortunately, Larry was too ill to attend the screening, and he did not have the pleasure of basking in the well-deserved glory and adulation associated with the film. I called him at his Greenwich Village apartment the evening before the first showing to congratulate him. His voice was barely audible.

Surprisingly, Larry's physical condition improved dramatically, but this did not last as his condition relentlessly deteriorated over the next couple of years. I occasionally visited Larry when I came to New York City. During a private dinner for just the two of us in his apartment, we reminisced like two aging warriors who recalled the battles we had fought together, how despite our initial adversarial relationship we ultimately became partners in an important struggle, and how differences of opinion, and even a history of antagonism, are entirely compatible with friendship. When I was leaving his apartment, we gave each other a prolonged hug, and as we parted, he said with a mischievous smile, "I still think that you should have chained yourself to the White House fence." Shortly before he died in May 2020, we had one last phone conversation that ended with Larry's saying, "I love you, Tony"; I tearfully responded, "I love you too, Larry." A complex relationship, indeed.

A President, a Gentleman,
and a Friend

Wednesday, April 8, 1987, was a typical mild spring day in D.C. But it had been far from typical for me because Vice President George H. W. Bush and his wife, Barbara, were coming to the NIH campus. Because we were given only forty-eight-hours' notice, everyone was scrambling to accommodate roughly fifty reporters and eight television crews. It was already widely understood that Bush was planning to run for president in 1988. As was well recognized, President Reagan had been less than proactive in dealing with the HIV/AIDS pandemic. It seemed that the vice president wanted to change that perception and reality for himself.

As we gathered on the eleventh floor of the NIH Clinical Center, the vice president extended his hand and gave me a warm smile. I briefed him on the work we were doing in my lab on HIV and AIDS and what NIAID was doing as an institute. The vice president was attentive and asked probing questions not just about the disease but about my background and training. He wanted to know how it felt to take care of such dreadfully ill and often dying patients on a day-to-day basis and how the patients themselves coped with their disease. By the time he left, I felt he had a good grasp on the complexities of HIV/AIDS.

To my great surprise he invited Christine and me to several social functions at the vice president's mansion on the grounds of the Naval Observatory in Northwest Washington, D.C., over the subsequent year and a half. He also called me from time to time to ask questions related to science or medicine. This embarrassed me on one occasion. I was in our weekly meeting of institute directors when an assistant administrator came in and announced in front of everyone including my boss, NIH director Jim Wyngaarden, that the vice president was on the phone and wanted to speak with me. He had a question about a friend's illness. The mouths of my fellow institute directors dropped as I got sheepishly out of my chair and took the call in Dr. Wyngaarden's office.

It was shortly after this that a dear and wise friend, Dr. James F. Dickson III, stopped by my office one afternoon and gave me sage advice that I have never forgotten. Jim was a thoracic surgeon who, after graduating from Harvard Medical School, trained in general and thoracic surgery at Boston City Hospital. In 1950, he was drafted into the U.S. Army and was deployed to South Korea as chief of surgery at the 8055th Mobile Army Surgical Hospital (MASH) during the Korean War. He was the real-life prototype for Trapper John from the hit television show *M*A*S*H*. Years later, he worked in the Nixon and Reagan administrations, where I first met him. We had a common academic heritage; he studied Latin and Greek under the Jesuits at Boston Latin School twenty years before I did the same at Regis High School. We became fast friends, and Jim assumed the role as my elder statesman adviser after I became director of NIAID.

I mentioned to him one day that I was on my way to the White House at the vice president's request. "Tony," he said, "it's a good rule when you are walking into the West Wing of the White

House to advise the president, vice president, or the White House staff to remind yourself that this might be the last time you will walk through that door. If you base your advice on the truth and on scientific evidence and do not sugarcoat anything, it is likely that sooner or later you will be telling the president or the vice president something they really don't want to hear, something that may point out a problem with how their administration is handling an issue. Sometimes when advisers do that, their opinion is no longer sought. It's a version of shooting the messenger. Some people might fall into the trap of never wanting to disappoint a powerful figure, and so they slant their advice toward pleasing rather than informing. Don't fall into that trap."

I hope I would have arrived at the wisdom Jim imparted on my own, but he was explicit about it, and continued, "If you're consistent and totally honest, you might risk being dropped as an adviser, but this approach with the right kind of president or vice president can also engender respect and a durable relationship."

It was well-known by this time that I was apolitical in my professional and public life, but I had developed friendships with government officials on both sides of the aisle. My personal relationship with a Republican vice president who was hoping to become president one day led to some awkward moments in my interactions with my Democratic friends in Congress. Such was the case when I testified at a contentious hearing on July 13, 1988, before the Senate Committee on Labor and Human Resources chaired by Senator Edward M. Kennedy. Senator Kennedy was concerned that the Reagan administration was not putting enough resources into drug development and testing for HIV. He knew that I consistently pushed for more support, financial and otherwise, for HIV/AIDS research, but he rarely lost the opportunity at a hearing to take a shot at the Reagan administration. I had been advising the vice president on certain health policy issues and advocated for more resources any chance I got, be it at a reception, a visit to the White House, or an occasional dinner at the vice president's mansion. At one such dinner, at a time when I was trying to hire more scientists, I brought up the fact that the development of clinical protocols and the testing of HIV drugs were being hampered more by a lack of staff than by a lack of money. In an article that ran in *The Washington Post* two weeks before the hearing, the columnist David S. Broder reported that the vice president said that "he did not favor an immediate increase in federal research funds because Dr. Anthony S. Fauci of the National Institutes of Health told him at a dinner at his home two nights ago that the funding allocated to NIH for that purpose was about right."

Obviously, that was not the point I was trying to make. At the hearing, Senator Kennedy looked down from his chairman's seat at me in the witness chair, pulled out the article, and read that paragraph aloud to the crowded hearing room with more than a slight bit of sarcasm in his voice. The clear implication was that having dinner at the vice president's house was equivalent to my going over to the dark side. Collateral damage, Washington style. However, at the end of the hearing Senator Kennedy called me over, put his arm around my shoulder, and said warmly, "Sorry I had to do that, Tony, it was nothing personal, but I just have to keep the pressure on. Anyway, keep up your great work."

I WAS AGAIN unwittingly brought into the political arena during a presidential debate between Vice President Bush and the Democratic candidate, Michael Dukakis, on October 13, 1988, in Los Angeles. The debate was moderated by Bernard Shaw of CNN together with Ann Compton of ABC News, Margaret Warner of *Newsweek*, and Andrea Mitchell of NBC News. Compton asked Governor Dukakis, "Governor . . . who are the heroes who are there in American life today? Who are the ones who you would point out to young Americans as figures who should inspire this country?" Dukakis rambled on, never really answering the question. Shaw then turned to Vice President Bush for his response. The vice president crisply answered that his heroes included Jaime Escalante, who was teaching calculus to underserved high school students (his story was told in the movie *Stand and Deliver*). He also named Armando Valladares, who had written an inspiring memoir titled *Against All Hope* about his decades in a Cuban prison. Then he went on to say, "I think of Dr. Fauci. Probably never heard of him." Ann Compton nodded her head in the affirmative. The vice president looked at her and said, "You did. Ann heard of him. He's a very fine researcher, top doctor, at the National Institutes of Health, working hard doing something about research on this disease of AIDS."

I had been out of town giving a lecture and had not watched the debate. The next day when I got on the elevator at work, several people started to applaud. I had no idea what was going on until one told me what had happened the night before in the debate. Although I did not fully appreciate it at the time, it was at that point that I transitioned from the classical role of an NIH institute director, responsible for the planning, conduct, and administrative oversight of research in a specific specialty, to someone who had the explicit respect of and thus access to the highest leaders of government. This would turn out to be true for me across party lines in both the White House and Congress. This public role was not in the job description of the director of NIAID or of any of the other NIH institute directors, but I believe my relationship with leaders in Washington served the NIH and science well. I am sure that it was due to the intense attention placed on the emerging epidemic of AIDS, for which I had a major responsibility. And perhaps I had a knack, possibly related to my years of schooling under the Jesuits, for "precision of thought and economy of expression," for explaining complicated scientific and policy issues in a way that makes sense to nonscientists. I addressed public policy only when it related to my scientific expertise, and I left politics to others, a practice I tried hard to adhere to for the rest of my career.

After Bush won the election, and throughout his tenure, I had the opportunity, sometimes for a moment at a reception and sometimes at prearranged briefings, to discuss AIDS-related issues with him or his immediate staff. One of the critical people in allowing me direct access to the president was Timothy J. McBride, an affable former business management consultant who had been personal aide to Vice President Bush for the previous four years and from 1989 through 1990 was special assistant to the president. Tim and I hit it off from the first time we met during the Bush vice presidency, and he was highly sympathetic to the urgency I felt about HIV/AIDS. He also understood the importance of getting information to the president directly from people on the front line in addition to the formal briefings from cabinet-level political appointees. It was through this dynamic that I began to understand how important personal relationships are in getting things done within a big government setting.

I was a scientist and clinician with no political affiliation and with extraordinary access to the president of the United States, and I came to fully appreciate Jim's very good advice. He was correct. It was exhilarating to talk to the president in the Oval Office, and natural to want to be asked back. It was easy to understand that it could be tempting to tell the president or his staff what you thought they wanted to hear so as not to disappoint them. That is exactly why it was crucial to be truthful and consistent in providing information based purely on scientific evidence and best judgment, and nothing else.

That was my rule, and George H. W. Bush was definitely

receptive to this approach and continually sought my opinion and advice.

At the end of each administration, all presidential appointees are required to hand in their resignation even when the new president is of the same political party as the former president. In January 1989, Dr. Wyngaarden, appointed NIH director by Ronald Reagan, submitted his resignation. Word was out that if the president accepted Dr. Wyngaarden's resignation, he might want me to replace him. This thought filled me with anxiety. I loved my job and the hands-on exposure to the lab and to AIDS patients. To give it all up to assume as NIH director the administrative responsibility for the more than twenty NIH institutes with such diverse mandates as cancer, heart disease, diabetes, and neurological and mental disorders was something I did not want to do. Since I did not want to be put into the position of saying no to the president of the United States, I subtly let out the word that I was not interested in the job.

Nonetheless, I received the phone call I dreaded. It came from Dr. Louis Sullivan, the secretary of HHS, who knew where I stood on becoming NIH director. "Tony, the White House is all over me to get you to take the job," he said. "You are making my life very difficult. If someone is going to say no to the president, it is going to be you, not me."

I was mortified, but I knew what I had to do. Accompanying me to the White House in his government car on October 30, 1989, Secretary Sullivan used the ride to try to convince me one last time to change my mind. As we waited outside the Oval Office, I rehearsed what I was going to say to the president. A few moments later, the president's chief of staff, John Sununu, opened the door to the Oval Office and ushered Dr. Sullivan and me in. The president greeted me warmly, I sat down to the left of the Resolute Desk, and he got directly to the point. He offered me the job. I took a deep breath. "Mr. President," I said, "I believe that I can serve you and the country better if I remain where I am. This is what I want to do, what I love to do, and what I do very well, and I believe that in the long run this is really what you would want me to do, and so I will have to respectfully decline your offer."

I could not read his expression, and I was afraid he would not react well. "You know, Tony," he replied, "I respected you greatly before today, but now I respect you even more. The country needs you. So go back and do your thing, and I promise you we will stay in touch."

I cannot describe the relief I felt. We both stood up and shook hands. As I walked out of the Oval Office with Secretary Sullivan and John Sununu, John put his hand on my shoulder and with a resigned smile said, "You son of a bitch. Nobody says no to the president."

THE PUBLIC IMPRESSION among some people, particularly AIDS activists, was that President Bush was an insensitive and unsympathetic right-wing conservative when it came to HIV/AIDS. True, his politics were conservative. But what was most apparent to me was his kindness and empathy to the suffering of others. During his visit to the NIH on December 22, 1989, with his wife, Barbara, and son George, he attended one of our regularly scheduled support group meetings for the patients. I was struck by the fact he spoke to every single patient. Even when his staff hinted that it was time to move on, he stayed and continued to listen to their problems and concerns.

The president's flexibility and open-mindedness within the

conservative circles of his administration were also evident when he backed my statement in favor of the parallel track at the town hall meeting in San Francisco in June 1989. I am still convinced that had it not been for my relationship with the president, I would have been in a very difficult situation for speaking out against an established FDA and government position on the regulation of clinical trials.

In fiscal year 1988, the last year of his vice presidency, the AIDS budget for the NIH went from $500 million to $742 million. Over the four fiscal years (1989 to 1992) for which his administration forged the NIH budget, AIDS spending rose to $1.05 billion. Of course, a willing and generous Congress was very influential in achieving these increases, but the president also played an active role, much more so than the AIDS activists gave him credit for. Yet, despite these increases, the activists were quite correct in continuing to push for more resources, because more were clearly needed.

THE PRESIDENT'S EMPATHY and his and Congress's role in increasing funding for AIDS research did not erase the fact that the years 1989 to 1992 were bleak for HIV/AIDS.

At the end of 1988, a month before he assumed the presidency, there had been 82,764 cumulative cases of AIDS in the United States. The numbers of cases globally were less well recorded, but it was estimated that there were more than 6 million cases worldwide. At the end of 1992, shortly before George H. W. Bush left the presidency, there were 253,448 cumulative cases of AIDS in the United States, and the global numbers had reached an estimated 12.6 million. That same year, AIDS had become the leading cause of death in the United States for men between the ages of twenty-five and forty-four.

Given these stunning numbers of cases and deaths, it was not surprising that the HIV/AIDS pandemic loomed large in the public consciousness. In 1985 the first major AIDS film made for TV, *An Early Frost*, starred Aidan Quinn as a young gay lawyer who reveals his homosexuality and the fact that he has AIDS to his parents, played by Ben Gazzara and Gena Rowlands. The first major Hollywood movie on AIDS, *Philadelphia*, starring Tom Hanks in his Academy Award–winning role as Andrew Beckett, a young lawyer who suffers terrible discrimination in his law firm when it is discovered that he has AIDS, came out in 1993. Tony Kushner's play *Angels in America* about AIDS won both the Pulitzer Prize and a Tony Award. I had been taking care of AIDS patients for twelve years by then and had been director of NIAID for the prior nine years. Still, I was deeply moved when I watched these outstanding dramas. My colleagues and I had taken care of dozens and dozens of Andrew Becketts as patients on our wards. To see them portrayed on the stage and big screen was emotionally draining. Now the general public also was beginning to appreciate the depth and breadth of suffering in our society both from dramatic portrayals such as in these films and plays and from the fact that more and more people came to know someone who was living with HIV.

In real life, famous and often admired figures were also dying of AIDS, calling even more public attention to the severity of the ongoing catastrophe. In 1989, the world-renowned photographer Robert Mapplethorpe died. In 1990, Ryan White, a hemophiliac who became infected as a child after receiving HIV-contaminated blood products, died at age eighteen, and in 1991 Freddie Mercury, the iconic lead singer and songwriter of the rock band Queen, died at age forty-five. Mercury's heart-wrenching rendition of the song "Bohemian Rhapsody" remains in my opinion one of the greatest performances by a rock singer in a generation. That same year the

NBA superstar Earvin "Magic" Johnson announced that he was HIV positive and retired from the Los Angeles Lakers. And in 1992, the much-admired tennis star Arthur Ashe announced that he too had AIDS, which he contracted from a contaminated blood transfusion received during heart surgery. I had the privilege of providing consultations to both Magic and Arthur. Unfortunately, like so many others, Arthur died of AIDS on February 6, 1993, a few months after our visit.

AFTER THE PRESIDENT left office in January 1993, in addition to his Christmas cards, I received over the years an occasional hand-written note from him mentioning that he had seen me on TV or had read a newspaper article about me in association with some public health issue. On my sixtieth birthday, almost eight years after he had left office, he sent me a letter starting off with "Dear Tony, You 60? No way!!" His letter helped to make that birthday very special, ending with "Warm regards from your friend."

My lasting impression of George H. W. Bush is that he brought decency, dignity, and integrity to the office of the presidency. An appreciation of this fact was evidenced by the warmth and affection for him on full display at his funeral service at the National Cathedral, which I had the privilege to attend on December 5, 2018, at the invitation of the Bush family.

La Famiglia

From the moment in 1984 that Christine and I decided to get married, the idea of having children was foremost on our minds. I anticipated that children would enrich our lives together, but I could not have appreciated the depth of joy that our three daughters would bring to us. I was forty-five when our first child was born, and my life changed forever. With our children, I came to fully understand what unconditional love is. Watching them develop from infancy to childhood to adolescence to young ladies to professionally accomplished women has been an awe-inspiring experience.

In the broad sense, I am the father of three daughters, but in reality I have three distinct and separate relationships. Jennifer is the oldest, feisty and opinionated since the day we brought her home from the hospital in 1986. Jenny does not hesitate to question and challenge me, but always with an undertone of respect and affection. She cares deeply about the plight of the underserved. Megan followed three years later. She is our gentle, sensitive middle child. Shy and reserved on the outside, but with a will and determination of steel. Megan is beloved by every child she has ever met, especially the ones she teaches in elementary school. Alison completed our family in 1992. Ali is the scholar-athlete of the family. She is intellectually brilliant, fun loving, but known for her generous nature and perpetual willingness to help others, a quality that was obvious since middle school. The common denominator among us all is a deep feeling of love.

I was making my way as a parent during a transitional time in society. Like most fathers in America in the 1940s and 1950s, my father left the cooking, housework, and childcare strictly up to my mother, who also put in long hours at the Fauci Pharmacy. I knew my dad deeply loved my sister, Denise, and me, but his almost impossible hours at work in the pharmacy did not allow him much time to toss a baseball or shoot hoops with me.

Societal expectations about the division of labor had changed somewhat by the time I became a father. But the culture had not yet reached the point we are at now, where fathers and mothers are expected to share the parenting and the housework. I thought my primary job was to be the family provider as I focused on my mission in science and public health.

And it was a challenge—sometimes a big challenge—to effectively carry out the responsibilities of my job and at the same time to be the kind of parent that I hoped to be. I got to my office before 7:00 a.m., and I rarely got home before 8:00 p.m. I also did a lot of traveling to give lectures and attend medical conferences. Because I witnessed so much suffering on the part of my patients at the NIH, particularly during the early years of HIV when my daughters were young, it was often difficult for me to let go of my work at the end of the day as I drove the five miles from Bethesda back to our house in Washington, D.C. Even when I got home, I was often preoccupied, ruminating about work.

But one routine was firm. When the girls were very young, as soon as I put down my briefcase and kissed Christine hello, I climbed the steep stairs to the second floor. As I rounded the corner to the bedroom where my children were getting ready to go to bed, I transformed from Dr. Fauci, NIAID director, to Chewbacca, Han Solo's furry sidekick in *Star Wars*. My guttural animal growls and wild gestures sent the girls into peals of laughter and mock terror. On many a night, I acted out a new story about Chewbacca's adventures saving the Fauci sisters from pythons in the woods threatening to swallow them, rampaging elephants, and other perils. Besides Chewbacca, I used to pretend to be different animals—a giraffe, a lion, a wildebeest. I was not sure who enjoyed this playacting more, me or the girls.

CHRISTINE ALSO NAVIGATED the balance between her profession and family, a task much more demanding of her than of me. As a nurse at the NIH Clinical Center, Christine experienced a deep satisfaction taking care of patients, mostly those with HIV, but she decided to expand her career options. She had developed an interest in the relatively new field of bioethics, which explores ethical dilemmas in medicine and clinical research. Starting in 1985, she worked full time as a nurse while pursuing a Ph.D. in philosophy at Georgetown University, where she had gone as an undergraduate. After Megan was born in 1989, Christine worked and went to school part time, which she continued even after Ali was born in 1992.

During this seemingly impossible stretch of time, Christine climbed out of bed at 4:00 a.m. to catch up on her schoolwork, woke the girls at 7:00, got them ready, and drove them to school. At the end of the day, she made dinner and gave baths, and on the nights that I was out of town or arrived home very late, she performed bedtime rituals by herself, often falling asleep midsentence while reading a children's book aloud. She was the one who took the girls to birthday parties, supervised the Brownie troop, and attended school and athletic events. Most of all, she was always available to them. From the time Jenny was a baby until Ali was in elementary school, we were lucky to have a live-in nanny, Jo, who loved the girls, and they loved her. She supported the children in their daily activities and, by helping us take care of them, was indispensable in allowing Christine and me to continue to flourish professionally. In 1993, once again, my brilliant wife burst through the tape at the finish line of her marathon—this time by receiving her Ph.D. and becoming Dr. Grady.

Amid all our busyness, we continually tried to figure out ways to spend more time together as a family. And so, when Jenny was three years old and Megan had just been born, Christine and I sat down at the kitchen table and came up with a solution. I continued to work on Saturdays, but Sundays belonged to our family. We adhered to this schedule religiously, even after Ali was born. Sometimes we went down to the National Mall, riding the carousel, visiting the dinosaurs at the Museum of Natural History, watching the baby ducks in the reflecting pool, or walking up the steps to the Lincoln Memorial. Other times, we ate lunch on the waterfront in Georgetown, went to the National Zoo, hiked the Billy Goat Trail along the Potomac River, or fished for catfish along the C&O Canal.

Alongside child rearing, certain enjoyable activities fell by the wayside. Although Christine was still an avid runner, she stopped training for marathons as soon as she got pregnant with Jenny. Marathon training for me was not as much fun without her, but I persisted anyway. When our daughters were ages seven, four, and one, I ran my second Marine Corps Marathon, and my family came out to cheer me on, with Christine carrying Ali in a backpack and pushing Megan in a stroller.

I ran to let off steam. Many nights, when training for a marathon or 10K race, I walked in the door and immediately announced to Christine, "I'll be right back. I need to go for a run." I did not realize how inconsiderate this was until Christine pointed it out to me. It was a revelation. After that, I tried hard to be aware of the fact that when I got home, my priority was my family.

Although I did not spend as much time with my daughters as I would have liked during their childhood years, when they went on to college and beyond, we developed a different kind of relationship, founded in love but functioning as a wonderful "friendship" where each of them understands and respects my commitment to my job and cuts me a lot of slack to do my thing at work. Part of our evolved relationship is their acceptance of and amusement with some of my antics. My daughters delight in teasing me, and I admit I gave them a lot of material. I put on the Bee Gees and danced around the kitchen to "Stayin' Alive" as if I were Tony Manero, the fictional Italian American character living in Brooklyn played by John Travolta, in the 1977 movie *Saturday Night Fever*. When they are at home, I also sing Italian songs to them as I make my morning espresso. I really enjoy being with them.

There is no doubt that my near-total devotion to my work was a strain on both Christine and me, but we worked hard at and succeeded in staying close. Almost everything I do and enjoy outside work is with Christine. She has a successful career as a bioethicist and now is internationally recognized as she directs the Department of Bioethics at the NIH Clinical Center.

I am incredibly grateful. I could never have had the career or the life I have had without Christine Grady.

The Changing of
the Guard

HIV and AIDS were fully on the radar screen of national politics for the 1992 presidential election. Both parties had people with HIV give major addresses at their respective conventions: Mary Fisher, a heterosexual white woman, at the Republican National Convention in Houston, Texas, and Bob Hattoy, an openly gay man, at the Democratic National Convention in New York City. On January 20, 1993, Bill Clinton was sworn in as the forty-second president of the United States, and the Democrats now controlled both the House and the Senate. Hattoy was quickly appointed as a deputy in President Clinton's Office of Presidential Personnel. With that came the hope of many activists that this would be an administration much more friendly and sympathetic to the needs of the at-risk community, as well as people living with HIV. Indeed, this expectation was in many respects met, particularly with regard to the access of gay activists to the White House. I was not sure yet what if any role I might have to play in the new administration. Shortly after being appointed secretary of HHS in early 1993, Donna Shalala telephoned me. Donna does not mince words, as I would quickly learn. "Tony, I just want you to know that you are my person for HIV/AIDS, and I am going to rely very heavily on you for advice and guidance. We have a lot of work to do."

She was not kidding.

It had been clear since 1987 that a single drug alone (AZT) was not sufficient for the durable suppression of the replication of HIV. Combinations of two or even three drugs were significantly better. Even so, although the progression of disease was slowed, most patients continued to gradually deteriorate. We found out why when Michael Piatak, Jeffrey Lifson, and other researchers in 1993 developed a highly sensitive test for the level of HIV in the blood. Finally, we could measure to the lowest level the amount of virus that was produced in a person with HIV and precisely determine how effective the anti-HIV drugs were in suppressing the virus. The test told us that we were suppressing the virus substantially but not completely. This information was critical because as long as the virus was replicating, it was insidiously destroying the body's immune system, making patients ever more susceptible to the host of complicating or opportunistic infections and cancers that were killing them.

As RESEARCHERS DEVELOPED additional drugs in the 1990s, we were also learning a considerable amount about how HIV affects the body and how the clinical disease of AIDS develops in a person. In my own lab I had promoted Cliff Lane to clinical director of NIAID, where he, in addition to his own research on the pathogenesis of HIV, would have the major responsibility for the clinical study and care of patients throughout the institute. I also recruited and trained a considerable number of talented young people who worked closely with me at the lab bench where we designed the experiments, collected and analyzed data, discussed future directions, and wrote up our results for publication in the scientific literature. One such project studied the accumulation and persistence of HIV in the lymphoid tissues of the body. This would turn out to be a major stumbling block in future attempts to eradicate HIV completely from the body and thus cure the patient.

The residual virus in the body is referred to as the reservoir. One of the big unknowns was whether this reservoir of virus was actively replicating and damaging the immune system early in the course of infection when patients were feeling relatively well. This was referred to as the clinically inactive stage of HIV disease. In fact, HIV disease was not inactive. In what is considered by many a groundbreaking study in how the disease of AIDS evolves undetected, Giuseppe "Gepi" Pantaleo and I demonstrated that HIV was actively replicating in lymphoid tissues such as lymph nodes even when patients showed no symptoms. In other words, the virus was stealthily eroding the body's immune system unbeknownst to the patient and the physician. Gepi, who was from Bari, Italy, came to my lab in 1989 following a fellowship in Genoa under my close friend and long-term colleague Dr. Lorenzo Moretta, one of the top immunologists in Europe. Simultaneously, my colleague and old friend Ashley Haase from the University of Minnesota demonstrated similar findings in his group of patients. Ashley and I had been trainees together at NIAID under Shelly Wolff. We both published our findings in the same issue of the prestigious scientific journal *Nature* in 1993, which generated a considerable amount of attention in the scientific community. In 1995, two other groups, led by David Ho in New York and George Shaw in Birmingham, Alabama, working independently, demonstrated the extraordinary degree of replication and turnover of virus and its destructive effects on the body's immune cells. This finding showed us that HIV was unique in its ability to persistently replicate over years from the earliest stages of disease to the point of advanced destruction of the immune system. This knowledge would prove to be even more important later when highly effective drugs that could completely suppress the virus became available. These and other studies served as evidence that it was essential to initiate therapy as early as possible.

THE RESERVOIR OF HIV was one of the major stumbling blocks to the cure of HIV. In 1997, I recruited Dr. Tae-Wook Chun fresh out of his doctoral studies at Johns Hopkins Medical Center in Baltimore. During his many years in my lab, Tae-Wook studied the HIV reservoir and attempted to eliminate or suppress it. Our studies on HIV pathogenesis were done in parallel with our other studies on how the body's immune system responds to HIV. I performed most of these latter studies with Dr. Susan Moir, whom I had recruited as a postdoctoral fellow immediately following the receipt of her Ph.D. degree in Canada. Susan and I probed the complexities of how HIV evades the body's immune response, particularly the antibody response to the virus. These studies were relevant because the development of an effective vaccine depended on the production by the body of a protective antibody response against the virus.

The gratification I felt from contributing to these incremental but critical studies that fit another piece of knowledge into the puzzle of HIV/AIDS and brought us closer to meaningful solutions is exactly what I had hoped for when I decided to pursue a career as a physician-scientist instead of a physician in private practice. My lab's contributions went well beyond the individual patient for whom we were caring. It is a very different but equally powerful feeling when a patient leaves a hospital free from disease as a result of our clinical skills.

I had three roles to play in the fight against HIV. First, I was director of a large government institution responsible for the over-all conduct of research on all infectious diseases including HIV/AIDS. Second, I was a physician responsible for clinical research on and care of people with HIV. Third, I was chief of a research laboratory doing basic and clinical research on HIV. The combi-nation was intense, exhausting, and exhilarating.

The Search for
an HIV Vaccine

While we were making steady progress in developing effective drugs to treat HIV infection, this was not the case with vaccines to prevent the infection. One reason why we had been so successful in developing vaccines against other important infections such as smallpox, polio, measles, and a wide variety of childhood diseases was that the human body had provided an example to us regarding its ability to control and clear these infections. While a significant number of unvaccinated people get seriously ill and die from these infections, most people recover spontaneously and become resistant to future infections with the same pathogen. So how does that help us develop vaccines? The answer is that scientists try to mimic natural infection with their vaccines by inducing in the body the same response that natural infection induces but without causing the disease associated with natural infection. Thus, the immune response to natural infection is a blueprint for the development of a vaccine.

We have no such blueprint with regard to HIV because the body, for reasons that we still do not fully understand, does not mount an effective immune response to HIV infection. This explains why virtually no one who has established HIV infection has ever cleared the virus spontaneously from their body through their immune response. While a subset of patients referred to as elite controllers are capable of long-term suppression of the virus, they do not eradicate it. Therefore, without this blueprint we had to figure out how to direct the body's immune system to make a potent and protective response against HIV through vaccination.

The problem was that soon after HIV was discovered in 1983, we, as a scientific discipline, naively assumed that because we had the virus in hand, we would successfully proceed with the tried-and-true steps of classical vaccine development. Unfortunately, this was not the case, because we did not realize how much we did not know. Scientists were concerned about testing a live attenuated HIV vaccine or even a killed or inactivated HIV vaccine, approaches that had successfully worked in the development of other vaccines including those for smallpox, polio, and measles. Vaccines, if not properly and completely inactivated, could lead to a public health disaster such as the infamous "Cutter incident" of 1955 when improperly inactivated polio vaccines manufactured by Cutter Laboratories were distributed, leading to a tragic vaccine-induced outbreak of polio. We could not risk this happening with an HIV vaccine, because we were dealing with a virus that was virtually 100 percent fatal.

The first phase 1 HIV vaccine clinical trial to be conducted in the United States was initiated in August 1987 using a specific component of the outer covering of the virus called the HIV envelope. We cleared the first hurdle; the vaccine was shown to be safe. But it did not produce the right kind of antibodies. It induced an immune response in the form of antibodies incapable of blocking the virus, but not antibodies that can kill the virus, which are called neutralizing antibodies. Over the subsequent years, we and other groups of vaccine scientists throughout the United States and the world studied antibodies naturally produced by individuals with HIV as well as antibodies induced by vaccines tested in uninfected individuals. We soon found that these antibodies were able to neutralize viruses grown in test tubes, but mysteriously they often could not neutralize isolates of virus taken directly from people with HIV.

This was chilling news to all of us. If natural infection could not readily induce neutralizing antibodies and vaccine candidates could only induce antibodies that neutralize HIV viruses that have been adapted to cell culture, then we could be in serious trouble in our quest for an HIV vaccine. We soon learned that HIV was very different from any other viruses with which we had dealt. For example, HIV disease almost invariably progresses despite an ongoing detectable immune response against the virus, underscoring that the immune response the body is generating is inadequate to suppress and eradicate the virus.

Another confounding fact we learned only years later is that persons with HIV can also be infected a second and even a third time with HIV, a phenomenon referred to as superinfection. The reason this is important is that the ongoing immune response in a person with HIV is not powerful enough to protect the person against reinfection with the same virus. In contrast, when you are infected with measles or smallpox, you will not be infected by another exposure to measles or smallpox during your ongoing infection, and you certainly will not be infected again by measles or smallpox after you recover. The immune response your body generated against these infections will protect you for decades and in some situations even for your lifetime. Thus, developing successful vaccines against measles and smallpox was straightforward. In contrast, in the case of an HIV vaccine, we would have to do *better* than natural infection in inducing a protective immune response against HIV. Along the way, certain highly respected vaccine experts gave an ominous prediction of how difficult this might be.

Every once in a while you have the privilege and excitement of meeting as an adult someone who was a legend when you were a child. As a young boy, I always wanted to meet the New York Yankees superstar Mickey Mantle and shake his hand. I never got the opportunity. But I did get a chance to meet a different kind of legend. The man was Albert Sabin, the developer of the oral polio vaccine. Albert had been admitted for a minor infection to the NIH Clinical Center in the early 1970s soon after I returned from New York. Shelly Wolff assigned me as the primary care physician for Dr. Sabin, who had a reputation of being a sometimes grumpy person and someone who did not suffer fools lightly. I was excited and a little intimidated that I would get to meet the man responsible for the sugar cubes saturated with polio vaccine that had protected millions and millions of people from contracting polio throughout the world.

What transpired in that hospital room after I introduced myself was a scene that I will never forget. Albert was courteous, but he immediately began questioning, or shall I say grilling, me about everything from the type and dosage of antibiotics that I would give him to the amount and makeup of the fluids in his intravenous bag, the need or lack thereof for blood tests that I ordered, and on and on. He demanded a valid scientific reason for everything I did or planned to do.

If there was one thing I was confident of at that time, it was my ability as a clinician. That mattered nothing to Albert. He was challenging me, the way that all his life he had challenged everyone who spoke science. After completing that first visit, I said good night and began to walk out of the room. Albert called out to me and, with a twinkle in his eye and a broad smile that I would get to know well over the years, said in his booming voice, "Dr. Fauci, you did quite well tonight; I will allow you to come back and see me again." Only Albert Sabin could have said that. He was a patient being taken care of at the prestigious NIH, but he made it perfectly clear even lying there in his hospital gown he was in charge.

Over the years, we developed a warm friendship, and Albert took a great interest in my research as well as in my role as NIAID director in leading the effort toward the development of an HIV vaccine. Albert was a scientist in the purest sense. His world was one of theories, hypotheses, probabilities, and facts. When Albert took me aside at a black-tie function in Washington, D.C., almost two decades after I had taken care of him at the NIH, and said that he doubted very seriously given the unique nature of this virus that we would ever have a vaccine for HIV, I became even more convinced of the formidable challenge in front of us.

As it turned out, Albert's prediction thus far has proven to be correct. Two major phase 3 trials involving thousands of volunteers failed outright in showing any indication of efficacy. Other trials failed in the early stages. Another trial involved sixteen thousand volunteers in Thailand and was cosponsored by NIAID and the U.S. Army's Military HIV Research Program, or MHRP. Along with Colonels Jerome Kim and Nelson Michael, both physicians, one of the leaders of the MHRP group was Colonel Deborah Birx, also a physician. Deb was an old friend whom I had known from the time that she was a trainee in the 1980s when she rotated through our clinical service at NIAID. I had the pleasure of mentoring her during that early phase of her career. The Thai trial proved initially modestly successful with a 31 percent efficacy and brought new hope to the field. However, three subsequent large phase 3 trials—one performed in South Africa, one in several countries in sub-Saharan Africa, and one in Europe and the Americas—all used a concept similar to the Thai trial but did not corroborate the Thai trial results. A later vaccine trial in Africa was discontinued early when it was determined in 2023 that it was highly unlikely to show efficacy.

ON DECEMBER 3, 1996, President Clinton invited the HHS secretary, Donna Shalala, the NIH director, Harold Varmus, me, and other NIH and HHS officials to the Oval Office to discuss the status of the HIV/AIDS pandemic. After we were finished with that discussion and as we were walking from the Oval Office to participate in a press briefing in the Rose Garden, President Clinton turned to me and asked, "Since as you told me HIV was first recognized in 1983 and it is now 1996, why do we not yet have an HIV vaccine?" I explained to the president the inherent difficulty in developing such a vaccine, and stressed that any chance of achieving this goal would require the close interaction and collaboration of basic scientists such as immunologists, virologists, structural biologists, vaccine experts, and other scientists, together with clinicians. No one segment of the scientific community alone could develop a vaccine for HIV. "It would be extremely helpful, Mr. President," I said, "if we had a single entity in which all of these components were physically in the same location working together, exchanging ideas, and collaborating with each other. No such institution or entity exists. What we need is a Vaccine Research Center, preferably at the NIH."

To my amazement, President Clinton turned to his White House chief of staff, Leon Panetta, who was walking with us into the Rose Garden, and said, "Leon, is this something that we can do? Please look into how we can make this happen." Panetta nodded in assent, smiled, and as we walked out into the Rose Garden said, "Of course we can make this happen." I thought that the conversation between the president and Panetta might just be a show of courtesy.

Not so.

Within days, I got a call from White House staff asking us to think in more detail about what a Vaccine Research Center for HIV would look like. Five months later during a commencement address on May 18, 1997, at Morgan State University in Baltimore, President Clinton called for "a new national goal for science," namely to develop a vaccine for AIDS within a decade. He announced that the NIH would establish an AIDS vaccine research center that would centralize vaccine research and would involve as many as fifty scientists.

What President Clinton did was truly remarkable. Given our past experience with new construction on campus, we at the NIH were skeptical about how long this process would take. Here again, I learned a lesson about what happens when a president wants to get something done. Clinton clearly wanted this center built while he was still president. The Vaccine Research Center (VRC) was dedicated on June 9, 1999, just two years following President Clinton's commencement address at Morgan State. Standing with the NIH director, Harold Varmus, and President Clinton as the ceremony was about to get under way, I turned to Clinton and said, "I guess you were not kidding that day in the Oval Office." He laughed and remarked, "You know, being president can be a lot of fun."

We tapped as our first director Dr. Gary Nabel, a highly productive and brilliant molecular biologist from the Howard Hughes Medical Institute at the University of Michigan. Together with Gary, we recruited an extraordinary group of young scientists from all over the country, from basic researchers to clinical scientists to bioengineers with experience in developing a vaccine product.

Unfortunately, despite the enormous talents and efforts of the center's vaccine scientists as well as the hundreds of vaccine scientists throughout the country and the world, an effective vaccine for HIV is still nowhere in sight. I hope that one day we will prove my dear friend Albert Sabin to have been incorrect in his judgment about an HIV vaccine.

Nonetheless, the enormous scientific productivity of the VRC soon became apparent. Not only has it been a leader in the arduous quest for an HIV vaccine but its extraordinary team of scientists confronted other public health threats such as West Nile virus; severe acute respiratory syndrome, or SARS; bird flu; respiratory syncytial virus; chikungunya, a mosquito-transmitted virus that reached the Western Hemisphere in the Caribbean in 2013 and 2014; Ebola during the historic 2014–16 outbreak in West Africa and the 2018–20 outbreak in the Democratic Republic of the Congo; and Zika during the 2015–16 outbreak in South America. Perhaps of greatest importance, scientists at the Vaccine Research Center played a monumental role in the development of a highly effective vaccine for COVID some twenty years later.

The Lazarus Effect

In the later 1980s and early 1990s, with no immediate hope of a vaccine, highly effective antiretroviral drugs were the holy grail of our work on HIV infection. This was a long, tortuous, and incremental quest. Since 1987 with the FDA's approval of AZT, additional drugs used alone and in combination had had only modest and temporary effects in slowing the progression of disease, and none completely stopped disease progression.

Several pharmaceutical companies including Hoffmann–La Roche, Merck, and Abbott Laboratories, among others, were simultaneously and independently developing a unique class of anti-HIV drugs called protease inhibitors. These drugs were directed against an enzyme that the virus uses to cleave off certain proteins as its progeny emerges from an infected cell so that the virus particle can go on to infect another cell. Roche's saquinavir was the first protease inhibitor approved by the FDA in December 1995, followed soon thereafter by the approval of Abbott's ritonavir and Merck's indinavir in March 1996.

At first the impact of these novel drugs was not fully appreciated; they were initially tested as single drugs rather than as a part of combination therapy because companies such as Merck were aiming for a breakthrough with a single drug. However, as was the case with other anti-HIV drugs when used alone, resistance to the drug often developed rapidly. As a result, Merck was seriously considering abandoning the protease drug development program. My colleague and friend Dr. Ed Scolnick, whom I knew from his former position in the National Cancer Institute at the NIH, called me at home late one evening with considerable frustration in his voice. He and his colleague at Merck Dr. Emilio Emini wanted to continue studies on indinavir by using it in combination with other antiretroviral drugs. Ed wanted to know my thoughts, and he wanted to go back to the officials in his company with my support for pursing the combination path. I totally agreed with Ed and Emilio and strongly recommended that they go with their instincts. They did so, and when indinavir was combined with the drugs AZT and 3TC, which targeted a different viral enzyme (reverse transcriptase), the results were truly stunning. The level of virus in the blood dropped dramatically to below the level of detection and remained down. This was accompanied by an equally dramatic improvement in the clinical condition of the patients.

The results of the triple combination indinavir trial were presented publicly as a last-minute add-on (Late Breaker) session to the International AIDS Society meeting that took place in July 1996 in Vancouver, British Columbia, and later were published in *The New England Journal of Medicine*. Other publications reported equally dramatic results with combination therapies using protease inhibitors produced by other pharmaceutical companies. I can remember sitting in Hall C, room B1 of the Vancouver Convention Centre filled with thousands of people on July 11, 1996, when the data were presented. The room was buzzing. I knew what was coming because I'd already seen the data, and yet I still felt like screaming out "Yes!" The audience clearly felt the same way. They erupted in sustained applause as soon as the data were presented. It was a truly historic moment. A game changer if there ever was one. No sooner did the session end than I was grabbed by Christy Feig, the CNN producer assigned to the Vancouver meeting, who hurried me out of the convention center for an interview. We ran out to the pier jutting into beautiful Vancouver Harbor where Christy had CNN holding for a live shot. She interviewed me about the breakthrough, and the news instantly exploded on to the American and global public.

The era of highly effective and lifesaving anti-HIV treatment had begun. AIDS was no longer an inevitable death sentence.

IT WAS ASTOUNDING how quickly the triple combination antiretroviral drugs began to be used throughout the developed world and even in certain regions in the developing world. We immediately adopted that approach with our patients at the NIH, and the results took my and my colleagues' breaths away. Patients who had been close to death walked out of the hospital sometimes within weeks of initiating the combination therapy, having gained back much of the weight that they had lost. When we saw them in follow-up clinic after several more months of therapy, many looked healthy again. We at the NIH certainly were not alone in this experience. Our colleagues in San Francisco, Los Angeles, New York, and other hot spots of HIV/AIDS throughout the country were seeing identical results, as were our colleagues in Europe, Australia, and Canada. Even in certain isolated segments of the developing world these findings were being replicated. My dear friends and fellow physicians Paul Farmer and Jean "Bill" Pape began treating their patients in Haiti with the triple combination, and the results were equally striking. Paul sent me a picture of one of his patients before and a few months following the initiation of the triple combination drugs using one of the protease inhibitors, and it was clear that he was seeing exactly what we were seeing here in the United States.

This phenomenon became known as the Lazarus effect, drawing on the biblical story of Jesus performing a miracle and bringing back Lazarus from the dead. It did feel like a miracle after our fifteen-year struggle with this deadly disease. Patients who had been preparing for death soon found that they now needed to plan their futures. Many were going back to work and resuming normal relationships. It was an extraordinary time.

Within a couple of years, hospices that cared for hundreds of dying people with AIDS closed their doors because of a paucity of patients. HIV/AIDS had been almost exclusively a disease of hospitalized patients, where desperately ill people with HIV at one time occupied up to 40 percent of the beds in certain hospitals in cities such as San Francisco and New York. Now it became a disease that was managed in outpatient clinics. In addition, as testing for HIV infection became more widespread and as we developed more knowledge of the pathogenesis of HIV infection and became more confident in the use of these drugs, we began treating people earlier in the course of their infection. We were now finally acting as healers as opposed to ministers to the dying. In addition, and importantly, over time we went from requiring more than twenty pills per day given over multiple doses to the first triple-drug combination, Atripla, a single pill administered once per day, which was approved by the FDA in 2006.

The development of these highly effective drugs was a striking example of the positive synergy between the basic and the clinical science funded by the NIH and the ingenuity of pharmaceutical companies that developed and manufactured these drugs. There was another component of this success story. Many of the studies to establish the optimal use of the drugs in clinical practice were conducted through the NIAID AIDS Clinical Trials Group. The ACTG was an expanded network of medical centers performing clinical trials. This network had grown extensively from the original evaluation units that we at NIAID had established in 1986 in anticipation of testing drugs that did not yet exist. Now we had the drugs, and through this network we were learning an enormous amount about the best way to treat individuals with HIV, and we were getting better and better at it.

When Cliff Lane, Henry Masur, and I were taking care of patients with HIV in the early 1980s prior to the availability of AZT, the median survival of our patients was roughly nine to ten months from the time they were diagnosed. This meant that 50 percent of our patients would be dead within that time frame. By 2007, more than ten years after effective combination anti-HIV therapy became available, a modeling study in the United States and Canada found that if a twenty-year-old individual with HIV was put on combination antiretroviral therapy, that person could be expected to live into their early seventies, providing a life expectancy approaching that of the general population. Without a doubt, this represents one of the greatest achievements in medical research and implementation in the history of medicine.

THE ONLY DOWNSIDE of this extraordinary achievement was the fact that these drugs had a range, depending on the drugs in question, of long-term, cumulative toxicities that could have devastating effects on bone marrow, the kidneys, and the liver. In addition, some drugs had cosmetic effects such as facial fat tissue atrophy, which gave patients a characteristic gaunt appearance, and redistribution of fat tissue on various parts of the body, particularly the abdomen, resulting in a potbelly. Other drugs had psychological effects such as depression, anxiety, and sleep disturbances. Despite these side effects, a series of studies clearly demonstrated that the risk of toxicities of the drugs was far less than the risk of the damaging effects of uncontrolled virus replication in the body, and that starting therapy immediately was much better than delaying it. Newer drugs resulted in markedly diminished toxic effects. Ultimately, based on studies reported in 2015, the HHS Guidelines Panel as well as other international HIV treatment guidelines panels recommended that all persons with HIV be treated with combination antiretroviral drugs as soon as they became aware that they had HIV. This would have the dual effect of preventing them from getting ill while also suppressing the level of virus in their body to levels undetectable by standard tests. This high-level suppression of the virus was ultimately shown to totally eliminate the possibility that a person with HIV would pass the infection on to an uninfected sexual partner.

HIV Denialism

An insidious phenomenon that reared its destructive head early in the AIDS saga was what came to be known as HIV denialism: the belief, contradicted by overwhelming and conclusive medical evidence, that HIV does not cause AIDS.

I first became aware of this terrible issue in 1987 when Dr. Peter Duesberg began openly questioning whether HIV was the cause of the disease AIDS. Conspiracy theories regarding HIV had abounded ever since French investigators discovered HIV in 1983 and Bob Gallo proved that it was the cause of AIDS in 1984. Among the far-fetched and inflammatory theories put forth was that the CIA had created the virus to eliminate the gay population of the country and the world. But the fact that Peter Duesberg was a staunch denialist was most problematic. A German American molecular biologist, he was at the time a professor of molecular and cell biology at the University of California at Berkeley and a member of the prestigious National Academy of Sciences. This high honor, bestowed upon a scientist by one's peers, by definition means that he was considered a highly respected and accomplished scientist.

Peter Duesberg shocked the scientific community with his new claims. Denying that HIV caused AIDS became his passion, and he soon devoted much of his time to promoting the idea. At the time, members of the academy could publish their papers in the academy's journal, the *Proceedings of the National Academy of Sciences*, without going through peer review, and it was much to the chagrin of the editors of the journal and despite the outrage of most of the scientific community that Duesberg used this privilege as an academy member to publish his "theory." In this 1991 paper the abstract states, "It is concluded that American AIDS is not infectious, and suggested that unidentified, mostly noninfectious pathogens cause AIDS."

Soon others with scientific credentials joined the denialism bandwagon, and even Dr. Kary Mullis, who won the Nobel Prize in Chemistry in 1993 for development of the polymerase chain reaction, a transforming tool in molecular biology, showed solidarity with the denialists. It was inconceivable to me and all of my colleagues who worked daily in the arena of HIV and AIDS that people such as these, many with substantial scientific backgrounds, could deny the overwhelming evidence proving that HIV was the cause of AIDS. At first, I just ignored them since their ideas were so preposterous and fell apart on close scrutiny; however, denialism started to gain the attention of the media, and soon I and some of my scientific colleagues were left with no choice but to debate this topic with these deniers, usually Peter Duesberg. My comment in one such debate quoted in a *Washington Post* article on April 10, 1988, summarized the baselessness of the denialist argument that lifestyle alone and not HIV leads to AIDS. "'What kind of risk behavior does the infant born of an infected mother have?' asked Anthony S. Fauci, the coordinator of AIDS research for the National Institutes of Health. 'And what about the 50-year-old woman who received a blood transfusion from an infected donor? The data overwhelmingly suggest that HIV is the cause of AIDS.'"

But no matter how many times we refuted it, the denialism movement would not go away. On several occasions, most concentrated in 1993 through 1995, I was drawn into discussions and debates with denialists, some on national television and often to the confusion of TV viewers. On the one hand, Peter Duesberg, who was a member of the prestigious National Academy of Sciences, was saying that HIV did not cause AIDS and was a harmless virus. On the other hand, Dr. Tony Fauci, also a member of the National Academy of Sciences, was saying that HIV was the unequivocal cause of AIDS. Inadvertently, the press, by attempting to report on this in an unbiased manner, was giving these senseless claims false equivalency with the established scientific facts. But the claims of each side were not equivalent. One side was overwhelmingly incorrect and the argument never should have taken place. And every time we debated the denialists, we gave them public exposure, which only compounded the problem.

Finally, I became fed up and asked a member of my staff, Greg Folkers, who was well versed in the medical literature related to HIV and AIDS, to put together a scientifically based point-by-point proof of HIV causality of AIDS and thus provide a formal refutation of the denialists' spurious claims. We published the resulting "Relationship Between the Human Immunodeficiency Virus and the Acquired Immunodeficiency Syndrome" in hard copy and online in 1995. After that, whenever I was asked to engage in this debate, I referred the party in question to our publication. I thought that we were finally finished with this nonsense; sadly, I was wrong.

ALTHOUGH THE FUROR over HIV denialism died down in the United States, a more insidious situation soon arose across the Atlantic Ocean. For reasons that are difficult to explain, Thabo

Mbeki, the president of South Africa, became enamored of Dues-berg's denialist claims. In addition, his minister of health, Dr. Manto Tshabalala-Msimang, was even more of a denialist. She re-jected the idea of treating people with AIDS with antiretroviral drugs, believing instead that AIDS should be treated with natural products such as garlic, beetroot, lemon juice, and olive oil. She even went on to say that the antiretroviral drugs exacerbated the disease. This led to a public health disaster. Mbeki and Tshabalala-Msimang refused to provide universal access to AIDS drugs for the people of South Africa, a country that had more people with HIV than any other country in the world. There were more than four million people with HIV in South Africa in the year 2000.

At the Thirteenth International AIDS Conference held in Durban, South Africa, that year, President Mbeki addressed the conference and expressed his view to the thousands of scientists and activists in the audience that HIV was not the cause of AIDS. Hundreds of delegates walked out during his speech. It was clear to virtually everyone outside the small denialist group that Mbe-ki's behavior was aberrant, prompting a group of scientists and ac-tivists to develop the Durban Declaration, signed by more than five thousand individuals, declaring that HIV was unquestionably the cause of AIDS. Nonetheless, Mbeki and Tshabalala-Msimang were unrelenting.

The activist community of South Africa was enraged at the South African government's dereliction of responsibility and mounted massive demonstrations under the leadership of the South African film director and activist Abdurrazack "Zackie" Achmat and the Treatment Action Campaign that he cofounded. They demanded universal access to antiretroviral drugs. In fact, Zackie, who publicly announced his HIV status in 1998, became world famous because of his refusal to take antiretroviral drugs until they were made available to everyone who needed them in South

Africa. It was the drug equivalent of a hunger strike for a noble cause. He kept his pledge for five years until 2003, when the South African cabinet overruled Mbeki's objections to provide such access. Zackie came to visit me in my office at the NIH on November 7, 2003, shortly after he began taking antiretroviral drugs, to thank me for leading NIAID's efforts in the development and testing of the drugs that were now saving his life and the lives of so many of his countrymen.

The tragedy is that a number of studies have estimated that between the years 2000 and 2005 more than 330,000 deaths and an estimated 35,000 infant HIV infections occurred in South Africa due to the government's failure to make the drugs available. And so what started out in 1987 as a completely unfounded movement instigated by a small group of misguided scientists turned out to be responsible for the avoidable deaths of hundreds of thousands of people.

An Unequal World

B y the time we reached the year 2000, AIDS was no longer a death sentence—that is, if you lived in a country where AIDS drugs were available. My satisfaction and joy for my patients who just a few short years previously would have died, as did my beloved friend Jim Hill, were tempered by the fact that millions of people in the developing world, especially in sub-Saharan Africa, were dying purely because they did not have access to these lifesaving drugs.

During the last two years of the Clinton administration, interest within various sectors of society, particularly the faith-based community, turned toward making these drugs available in the developing world. The first and most direct approach was to lower the prices of the drugs. The cost of the triple combination of anti-retroviral drugs without cost reductions ranged from $15,000 to $18,000 per year per patient, well beyond the reach of most people in the developing world. Yet the pharmaceutical companies were initially reluctant to institute a two-tiered pricing arrangement: a markedly reduced price for the developing world simultaneously with a full price for the developed world. They felt that this would be the beginning of a slippery slope to drive down the prices for everyone. Their argument was that the prices of the drugs were essential to fund the research and development of successful drugs and to defray the cost of the many failures in product development of experimental drugs that never reached the market. In an attempt to help counter the prohibitive pricing of these drugs, on May 10, 2000, President Clinton issued an executive order to assist developing countries in importing and producing generic forms of the HIV drugs without fear of trade retaliation.

IN THE YEAR 2000, the issue of AIDS in the developing world also attracted considerable attention in the international diplomatic world. The U.S. government and the UN Security Council declared the HIV/AIDS pandemic a global security threat. The potential impact on political and economic stability was real. Of note was the fact that the militaries in certain African countries often had the highest percentages of infected individuals, adding to the concern of weakening global security.

The theme of the Thirteenth International AIDS Conference held in Durban, South Africa, that year was "Breaking the Silence," which set out, among other goals, "the urgent need to break the silence on equal access to treatment and care."

Time ran out on the Clinton administration before any concrete program to address these disparities could be put together. My opportunity to address this global suffering would come, but it would have to wait just a bit longer.

THROUGHOUT THIS PERIOD, my lab and the institute were making steady gains. We had published several notable papers dissecting out the pathogenic mechanisms of how HIV destroys the body's immune system. NIAID grantees and contractors were making inroads in perfecting the treatment and prevention of HIV infection. Much had been accomplished, but much yet had to be done.

In the meantime, the Fauci family was going strong. Jenny was now fourteen years old, Megan was eleven, and Ali was eight. The two older girls were enrolled in the National Cathedral School, and Ali joined them there in fourth grade. I was gratified that they excelled academically and equally pleased that they all were exceptional athletes. They were passionate about gymnastics, putting in long hours on the bars, vault, beam, and floor. I still stayed late at work, but now I had a firm evening schedule. Five nights a week I picked up at least two of the three girls at 8:00 p.m. from their gymnastics club not far from the NIH campus and then drove us all home to D.C. We spent our time in the car playing those "name that whatever" games: state capitals, capitals of countries, products from states—apples from Washington State, oranges from Florida, cheese from Wisconsin, and so on. Sometimes as I was parking in front of our house, I marveled at how the empty house that I had bought as a bachelor in 1977 was such a lively, happy home inhabited by the woman I loved and the family we had created and were raising together.

This schedule meant that we sat down to dinner at 9:00 p.m. This was a meaningful time for our family and always included our gentle dog, Bubba, lying on top of our feet under the table. We caught up on each person's day, but sometimes the meal was quick because the girls had homework to finish. Other times, we lingered, talking about all sorts of things, from movies to pop music, school, and sports to deeper conversations including our values, many of which Christine and I had learned at our dinner tables growing up: the importance of caring for and about others, of acknowledging the privilege and debts of education, and of always doing your best.

Part Three

THE WARS ON TERROR
AND DISEASE

Widening the Battle

On January 20, 2001, as I watched the inauguration of George W. Bush on TV, I thought about when I had first met the forty-third president. It was less than twelve years earlier when he came with his father to visit the NIH in 1989. As I introduced the Bushes to several of our patients during the tour I gave them through our laboratories and wards, George W. seemed to have a genuine interest in the topic of AIDS.

Each time a new president was sworn in, I wondered the same things: How would this new president view the global HIV/AIDS pandemic, and what would my role, and NIAID's, if any, be in this process? As with the Clinton administration, I did not have to wait long to find out.

The new HHS secretary, Tommy Thompson, the longest-serving governor of Wisconsin from 1987 to 2001, came to this job with no background in global health. Yet he became very curious about HIV and its impact in the developing world. On April 3, 2001, I was invited to brief Thompson and his staff, after which he called me into his office to speak with him further. Thompson told me that he had heard a lot about me from a number of people in the new administration and Congress and that he wanted me to be his go-to person on AIDS. He mentioned that he and Secretary of State Colin Powell would be leading an administration task force on international AIDS.

I was delighted and surprised at how quickly things were moving when, two days later, on April 5, 2001, I was invited to my first meeting in the Situation Room, a secure (leave your cell phones at the door) conference room on the ground floor of the West Wing of the White House across from the Navy Mess. The meeting was chaired by Gary Edson, one of National Security Advisor Condoleezza Rice's deputies at the National Security Council. Bill Steiger, Tommy Thompson's point person on international affairs, had been charged with developing a white paper to use as a framework for international AIDS initiatives, and they wanted my input. Gary and I, along with other people from HHS and the White House, went back and forth on several drafts, and the finished product then went to Thompson and Powell to use in an upcoming presidential briefing.

There had been discussions as early as 2000 about the possibility of creating a process for the developed nations of the world to jointly support southern African countries suffering most from HIV/AIDS. This idea of what would ultimately be called the Global Fund originated with and was advocated for by many influential people around the world, including the UN secretary-general, Kofi Annan, and leading macroeconomist Jeffrey Sachs. The topic was raised again in late March 2001 at an international gathering in Taormina, Italy—a precursor to the July 2001 G8 meeting in Genoa—and had prompted the white paper.

During the discussions surrounding the white paper, I expressed my long-standing strong feeling that the United States has a moral obligation to provide leadership in mobilizing resources for international health. Slowing down and stopping the spread of infectious diseases to the extent possible in the developing world was also in our own self-interest. The threats of HIV/AIDS and other infectious diseases such as malaria and tuberculosis were destabilizing influences in Africa and other regions of the world. What's more, the majority of tuberculosis cases in the United States are among people born outside the United States. In addition, it was important to support the development of sustainable health infrastructure in the most affected countries so that they could adequately meet future public health challenges on their own.

The discussion among staff at the White House during the spring of 2001 was that there would inevitably be some form of multilateral global fund. Given that we would likely be the major donor, the president felt that the United States should have a strong say in how the fund was organized and managed. He articulated this publicly in a Rose Garden speech on May 11, 2001, following discussions that he had just had with the Nigerian president, Olusegun Obasanjo, and Kofi Annan. He summarized the devastating impact that HIV/AIDS had had across the African continent and the entire world and told the audience how important it was to show leadership and share responsibility, praising the international efforts thus far. The president then commited $200 million to support a new worldwide fund.

The following month, Tommy Thompson asked me to be part of the U.S. delegation that he and Secretary Powell were leading at the United Nations General Assembly Special Session on HIV/AIDS, held on June 25–27, 2001, in New York City. I was sitting a few seats down from Secretaries Powell and Thompson and among heads of state, ambassadors, and ministers of health from countries across the world in the gallery of the UN General Assembly. I could not help but recall that exactly twenty years earlier when Cliff, Henry, and I admitted our first AIDS patients to the NIH Clinical Center before the disease even had a name, there was very little interest in it. Now I was witnessing a whole new attitude and commitment to the catastrophic global AIDS pandemic as the United Nations Global Fund to Fight AIDS, Tuberculosis, and Malaria was agreed upon in concept based on the financial pledges of the United States and other countries. The rest of the world was finally taking notice of HIV/AIDS at the highest levels of governments.

Kofi Annan gave a magnificent speech on the compelling reasons why such a fund was necessary. Secretary Powell was equally eloquent, with much of his speech drawn from material in our white paper. He brought up the issue that he emphasized often over the next few years: in addition to a substantial health problem, AIDS in certain southern African countries as well as in other poor countries of the world was a national and global security problem.

The Global Fund was officially established six months later on January 28, 2002. In the meantime, unanticipated events dramatically upended the focus on global AIDS.

The Day the World Changed

My US Airways shuttle landed at LaGuardia Airport at approximately 8:00 a.m. I jumped into a cab and headed to midtown Manhattan for a board meeting of a charitable foundation of which I was a trustee. As I approached the city from the airport in Queens, I was impressed by the beauty of the New York City skyline against the backdrop of a clear blue sky. When we emerged from the Midtown Tunnel on East Thirty-fourth Street, I saw a concentrated bit of smoke in the distance toward the downtown area.

The date was September 11, 2001.

As I got off the elevator on the nineteenth floor of a building on West Fifty-second Street, instead of the usual crowding around the coffee and pastries, my trustee colleagues were planted in front of the wide-screen television in the conference room. They told me that apparently a small plane had gone off course and slammed into the North Tower of the World Trade Center at about the ninety-fifth floor. As I looked at the TV image of the smoke rising from the tower, I suspected this was the smoke that I had just seen from my taxi. Just as we were discussing how odd it was that a small commercial plane could be so far off course as to hit a sky-scraper in lower Manhattan, the unthinkable happened. At 9:03 a.m., a plane that was unquestionably a full-size commercial jet airliner smashed into the south face of the South Tower. The TV cameras had caught the image of an enormous fireball as it splashed out over the New York City skyline. We all rushed to the windows to see if we could get a view downtown, but we could not due to the way the windows were angled and the location of our building. Like tens of millions of other people we stared dumbfounded at the TV, watching the fiery smoke pouring out of both towers. It was clear that the United States was under attack, and like every-one else watching this unfold, we were in total shock. We had no idea who was attacking us or why. One thing was certain. Our world would not be the same.

AFTER A QUICK CALL to Christine to let her know I was safe, I called my office in Bethesda. My staff told me that Tommy Thompson wanted to speak with me. I had gotten to know and become close with Thompson over the prior several months, and we had dis-cussed the role of HHS in biodefense preparation and response. He was calling me to ask my advice on what HHS could do to help in that moment. "Tommy, I am actually here in New York City about fifty city blocks from the Twin Towers," I said.

He replied, "Do you think you can get down to the site and re-port back to me?"

"I'll do my very best."

Things kept getting worse. At 9:37 a.m., American Airlines Flight 77 crashed into the west side of the Pentagon just outside Washington, D.C., and TV coverage shifted back and forth from the World Trade Center to the Pentagon. Shortly after 10:00 a.m., we learned that another plane, United Airlines Flight 93, rumored to be headed for the U.S. Capitol or the White House, crashed in an open field in Somerset County, Pennsylvania. The hijackers were overtaken by a group of courageous passengers, who in the course of a struggle with the hijackers caused the plane to crash.

My anxiety shot up even further because I realized that my three daughters, whom just a few hours earlier I had kissed good-bye as they lay sleeping in their beds, were now sitting in class at school. The National Cathedral School is located on the grounds of the National Cathedral, which sits atop an elevated landscape overlooking Washington, D.C.—the highest elevation in the city. I had no idea how many planes were involved in this onslaught, and I worried that the National Cathedral would be a perfect target for another plane attack. I tried desperately to call Christine again at her NIH office. By this time, though, the telephone lines were completely clogged. This meant I also could not reach my father, who now lived on East Sixty-eighth Street in Manhattan, but because he rarely, if ever, went downtown, I was all but certain he was okay.

I later learned that Christine and the girls were terrified for me because they knew that I was in Manhattan, and the attacks were all the more real to my daughters as they saw from the windows of their classrooms smoke emanating from the Pentagon.

The horror of the day continued when it was shown on TV that people were jumping out of the windows of the upper floors of the towers to escape the swirling flames at their backs. Of all the tragedies associated with 9/11, the sight of those innocent people jumping to their deaths struck at me in a way that I will never, ever forget. It was at that point that my horror turned to deep anger and rage at those who propagated this atrocity.

The next unfathomable blows came at 9:59 and 10:28 a.m. when the South and North Towers collapsed in full view of billions of people watching TV throughout the world. A feeling of helplessness and deep depression descended on all of us in the room.

I felt that I needed to at least attempt to keep my promise to Thompson to get downtown to the site. As soon as I walked out onto Fifth Avenue and Fifty-second Street, it became apparent to me that I was going nowhere by taxi, bus, or any other vehicle. There was a complete shutdown of all traffic, and I decided to walk. By chance, I ran into a New York City police lieutenant huddling with a group of officers on the corner of Fifth Avenue and Fiftieth Street. I explained to him that Secretary Thompson had asked me to go down to the site and report back to him. He looked at me quizzically at best and as if I were insane at worst, and said, "Who's Secretary Thompson? Buddy, the only people we are letting in down there are the police, ambulances, and firefighters."

I had no choice but to return to the foundation headquarters. I tried repeatedly over the next couple of hours to call my office to no avail. Miraculously, I finally did get through, and my assistant told me that Secretary Thompson wanted me back in Washington immediately. There would be high-level meetings to plan how we might respond to a potential bioterror attack that might follow the airplane attacks, and he wanted me there.

ALL PLANE TRAFFIC HAD STOPPED, but I had to get back to Washington that evening. My only chance, though slim, was Amtrak. I took off with my fellow board member Nan Keohane, then president of Duke University, and headed for Penn Station on Seventh Avenue and West Thirty-second Street. Because the only way to get there was on foot, we set out walking south through a surrealistic midtown Manhattan. I had never seen anything like it. There were hardly any vehicles on the streets at all. We literally walked through Times Square in the middle of Broadway. It was an eerie feeling, reminding me of some of the movies I have seen over the years where the streets of New York City are totally empty after a deadly disaster. When we arrived at Penn Station after our thirty-five-minute walk, I got lucky. I was able to get on a train heading south to Washington, D.C., that evening.

As we emerged out of the tunnel on the way to the first stop at Newark, where the smoke and the glow from Ground Zero were fully visible from the train, I saw an abrupt explosion of smoke, dust, and glow from the site. I thought that another plane might have struck yet another building. I just could not believe what was happening. I sat numb in my seat for the trip to Washington not knowing what awaited me back home. I found out as soon as I arrived that the burst of smoke and dust was the collapse of the forty-seven-story building at 7 World Trade Center, referred to as Tower 7. It had not been hit by a plane, but had caught fire as collateral damage from the explosions, fire, and collapse of the North and South Towers.

ON THE TAXI RIDE from Union Station to our house, I saw military police stationed at almost every major intersection. Reagan National Airport and Dulles International Airport were closed indefinitely. There were reports on the taxi's radio that the FBI was claiming several terrorist sleeper cells were still in the United States with plans to carry out further attacks with Washington, D.C., as the prime target. I could not stop hugging my daughters as I walked in the door. Christine and I lay in bed that night to the sound of F-16 jets flying in combat formation over the city, ready to intercept any further attacks.

The following day, Tommy Thompson told me that HHS would

be one of the lead government agencies in preparing our defense against possible future bioterror attacks and asked me to be his point man in this effort. In a flash, at least for the time being, HIV and AIDS fell off the radar screen of just about everyone in the U.S. government, and in the entire country for that matter. Over the next few days, I participated in a number of meetings at the White House chaired by Richard Falkenrath, director for proliferation strategy at the National Security Council. The meetings were aimed at putting together short- and long-term plans for how to handle a bioterror attack.

The general feeling of the group was that such an attack was inevitable, and of all the possible bioterror agents that could be used against us, aerosolized smallpox virus was believed to be the primary threat. Smallpox was a historically deadly disease that spread from person to person. It was well-known from defected Soviet officials that the Soviet Union had stockpiled massive amounts of smallpox virus, among other deadly infectious agents, during the Cold War as potential bioweapons to be used in the event open hostilities broke out between the Soviet Union and the Western allies. In the chaos that followed the dissolution of the Soviet Union, it was unclear whether any of the bioweapons stocks had fallen into the hands of al-Qaeda or other radical Islamic groups. The White House was taking seriously the possibility, however remote, that such weapons had become available to terrorists.

THE MEETINGS STARTED to pile up at HHS Washington headquarters in the Hubert H. Humphrey Building. The underlying theme of the discussions was that with this new bioterror threat we needed to develop countermeasures in the form of diagnostics, treatments, and vaccines. The agency tapped to take the lead in this effort: NIAID. It would be our job to design and coordinate the direction of the research, carried out by our grantees and contractors, who would develop the required countermeasures. The task took on even greater urgency when another shock wave hit our nation.

Anthrax

On September 30, 2001, Robert Stevens, a sixty-three-year-old photo editor at the supermarket tabloid the *Sun*, published in Boca Raton, Florida, began feeling ill on the last day of a five-day vacation at his daughter's home in North Carolina. He was admitted to the John F. Kennedy Medical Center emergency room in Palm Beach County, Florida, on the early morning of October 2. He was disoriented and vomiting, had a high fever, and was unable to speak. Multiple tests conducted over the next two days at the hospital labs, the State of Florida, and the CDC confirmed that he had anthrax, a disease caused by a bacteria called *Bacillus anthracis* that predominantly infects animals but can cause serious and even fatal disease in humans. Although rare, cases of inhalational anthrax (spores of the bacteria being inhaled and entering the lung) occur sporadically without much public notice. Given the proximity of this event to the 9/11 attacks and the growing concern within the administration and among the general public about the possibility of bioterror attacks on our country by al-Qaeda sleeper cells, bioterror as a possible cause of Mr. Stevens's illness was on almost everyone's mind.

WHAT UNFOLDED OVER the next several months thrust me front and center into an escalating national state of anxiety and crisis. In addition, it brought Secretary Thompson and me closer together as colleagues and friends, an unusual relationship between a cabinet secretary and a director of one of the many institutes within a department of which he was in charge. It was typical of Thompson to pick out a small group of people whom he trusted and make them his go-to team. I, together with a young attorney named Stewart Simonson, one of the inner circle that he brought with him from his Wisconsin governor's office, became his closest confidants. During this extraordinary period of national crisis, Stewart and I also grew closer, a relationship that has lasted to this day. Stewart, Christine, and I, along with John Gallin, then director of the NIH Clinical Center, and his wife, Elaine, still spend every New Year's Eve together celebrating with a late-night dinner at my home.

ALMOST EVERY DAY for weeks, and even months, a new surprise heightened public anxiety and confusion. The media, with strong encouragement from the White House, turned to me for answers to questions concerning anthrax. This soon became almost all-consuming because, unfortunately, the anthrax issue did not end with Robert Stevens, who died on October 5.

The assumption was that this was an attack by al-Qaeda and there would be more, possibly with other bioterror agents such as smallpox and botulism toxin. This concern was intensified after October 7, 2001, when the United States together with the British invaded Afghanistan in Operation Enduring Freedom to hunt down the 9/11 mastermind, Osama bin Laden, and expel al-Qaeda from the country. The conventional wisdom at HHS and the White

House was that al-Qaeda would likely intensify its efforts to attack the United States with biological weapons as payback.

Even though the evolving anthrax situation was causing great uncertainty, the White House began to fear that the next bioterror attack would be with smallpox. The reason for this concern was that smallpox had been declared by the World Health Organization (WHO) to be eradicated in 1980 and most of the world had stopped vaccinating for smallpox years earlier. For example, routine vaccinations for smallpox were halted in the United States in 1972 since the risk of adverse events from the vaccine was judged to be far greater than the risk of contracting smallpox in an era of essentially no naturally occurring smallpox cases. Thus, the majority of people younger than thirty living in the United States and most other countries were now vulnerable to smallpox because they had not been vaccinated. In addition, the supply of smallpox vaccinations in our Strategic National Stockpile contained only fifteen million doses, certainly not enough to address a massive outbreak of this deadly disease. HHS focused on setting up contracts to manufacture the next generation of smallpox vaccines. The question we had to face was whether the United States should preemptively vaccinate the general public in anticipation of a smallpox bioterror attack if and when enough doses became available rather than wait for an attack. To answer that, Tommy Thompson asked me to work with several smallpox experts to develop a plan on how we might best protect ourselves against a potential smallpox attack. Paramount among them was Dr. Donald Ainslie (D.A.) Henderson, a legendary public health figure who had led the WHO's successful effort to eradicate smallpox from the planet. Our challenge now, besides expanding our smallpox vaccine supplies, was to begin developing an antiviral drug for smallpox. No small task.

The situation with anthrax was quite different. We had been

routinely administering our anthrax vaccine to personnel in the U.S. armed forces. In addition, there were several highly effective antibiotics against anthrax, most prominently ciprofloxacin, referred to as Cipro. The effort against anthrax was concentrated on increasing our supplies of vaccine and stockpiling large amounts of Cipro.

These discussions were not merely academic. Virtually every day new cases of anthrax were popping up in New York City, Washington, D.C., and Connecticut, the pattern of which became clear only in retrospect. Utter confusion and even panic prevailed. By the third week of October, there had been nine cases of anthrax with one death from inhalation, two additional serious inhalation anthrax cases, six cutaneous cases, and about forty cases of documented exposures who had not yet shown signs of infection. The exposures were predominantly related to people who might have handled mail because by this time it was becoming evident that the method of attack was sending highly infectious anthrax spores through the postal system. The machines that sorted the mail were demonstrated to push out an invisible puff of spores into the mail rooms, putting postal workers in these facilities at risk. The Senate majority leader, Tom Daschle of South Dakota, and Senator Pat Leahy of Vermont had received anthrax-spiked letters addressed to them, exposing several of their staffers to the spores.

It is amazing what your adrenaline can allow you to do. For a period of several weeks, on a good night I got only four hours of sleep purely because of the demands on my time that inevitably pushed late into the night. When I did get to bed, my mind was running like an engine in overdrive. I often found myself staring at the ceiling playing out what happened during that day and anticipating the events of the next day. It is difficult to describe to young people now who were not yet born or who were too young at the time what it felt like to not know when there would randomly be another attack that could harm or kill. Superimposed on this was the responsibility that Tommy Thompson and White House officials had put on me to oversee the development of countermeasures for anthrax and other potential agents of bioterror. Time was not on our side, to say the least, as more and more cases of anthrax appeared.

My nature has always been to remain calm under very difficult circumstances. I can get animated and annoyed over trivial things like getting caught in a traffic jam, yet, when important issues are at stake, I am totally focused and unemotional. I imagine that this characteristic was fine-tuned during my internship and residency training, where I was always extremely busy taking care of some of the sickest patients in New York City. The on-call schedule imposed on interns and residents at that time was nothing like it is today. For better or worse, we were formally on call every other day, every other night, and every other weekend, and on your on-call day or days (if it was a weekend) you rarely got any sleep. In addition, if your patient was critically ill, you did not leave their bedside until you stabilized them as best as you could. Every once in a while, the intern or resident in your rotation got sick with the flu or some other infection that put them out of action. The solution was that you just continued to be on call without relief. This happened to me a few times during my residency training, and I found myself simultaneously taking care of several critically ill patients with little or no sleep for days in a row. As surprising as that may seem to an outside observer, and I am certain that this does not apply to everyone, I was at my best under those circumstances. The sicker the patients and the more stressful and demanding the challenges, the better I functioned. The stakes were high; failing to rise to the occasion was definitely not an option.

I felt just like that many times during those weeks in October and November 2001. I can remember one day in late October when my basic physiology and emotions slipped temporarily out from under the umbrella of the adrenaline surge. After spending the entire day at HHS and the White House in intense meetings, I returned to my office at the NIH since I also needed to discharge at least some of the duties of my day job as NIAID director. At about 2:30 a.m., I finally left my office to drive home. As I got off the elevator in the lobby of Building 31 and walked the short distance toward my car, suddenly and without warning I broke into tears. It is a good thing that it was the middle of the night because I would have been terribly embarrassed if any of my colleagues had seen that. However, after about a minute and a half, I felt fine, and the brief outburst reminded me that indeed I still could express genuine human emotions despite a job that required that I remain as cold as ice.

ON SUNDAY, October 21, 2001, I appeared on NBC's *Meet the Press*, moderated by Tim Russert, to talk about the broad issues of bioterrorism and the U.S. government's biodefense efforts. After an extended discussion about our preparedness against potential attacks, and as the segment came to a close, Tim had one final question: "Take thirty seconds and tell the country how they should deal with their anxiety about bioterrorism." My response centered on a message that I would repeat again and again on countless future media appearances in slightly different ways. The gist of my message was that there was reason to be concerned and there would be some understandable anxiety. But we should not push ourselves over the edge to panic. We should productively channel that anxiety and concern into heightened alertness and preparedness. The purpose of the bioterrorist is to instill terror, and we should not aid them in their goal.

———

As INTENSE FEAR of the possibility of other imminent bioterror attacks unfolded and the FBI began a yearslong investigation to determine who was perpetrating the attacks, unexplained anthrax cases trickled in. The latest was an employee working in the Brentwood Postal Service Facility in Northeast Washington, D.C. Investigators concluded that the anthrax-afflicted postal worker never directly touched a contaminated letter, but was exposed to aerosolized anthrax spores likely released in that facility when letters to Senators Daschle and Leahy passed through. Along with verified anthrax cases, suspicious powder was identified in various locations that ultimately turned out to be false alarms, contributing to the public anxiety that was swirling around.

SIMULTANEOUSLY with the anthrax scare, we were having high-level discussions at HHS with Secretary Thompson and at the White House with Vice President Dick Cheney and his chief of staff, Lewis "Scooter" Libby, about our lack of preparedness for a massive smallpox bioterror assault on the country. Cheney and Thompson felt that we needed to mount an intense effort to provide in our stockpile a dose of smallpox vaccine for every person in the United States. Even if we were successful in demonstrating that we could effectively dilute the 15 million doses in our stockpile to 75 million doses, we still would fall short of the projected goal. But there was considerable debate as to whether we actually needed as many as 300 million doses or whether a far smaller amount would suffice for an adequate response to a smallpox bioterror attack. I agreed with Dr. Henderson, who felt that something along the lines of 100 million doses would suffice. Nonetheless, Cheney and his team together with Thompson felt strongly that we should expand the stockpile to the maximal amount as quickly as possible.

The state of high anxiety was compounded by constant rumors of impending bioterror attacks. On October 24, I was called to an emergency meeting in Secretary Thompson's office. Thompson walked into his conference room looking concerned. With the CDC director, Jeffrey Koplan, connected to us by teleconference, Thompson told us that he was hearing that the United States would be hit with a major bioterror attack (agent unknown) within the next seven days. Thompson felt that because smallpox was high on the list for a possible bioterror attack, we should definitely accelerate the replenishment of our smallpox vaccine stockpile. Jeff did not seem particularly engaged or responsive to Thompson's urgency, bringing into clearer focus a growing and obvious tension between the CDC and the HHS leadership.

This was not solely a peculiarity of Jeff's. The CDC, established in 1946 to eradicate malaria in the United States, had evolved to address public health and safety more broadly. Employing thousands of talented, hardworking people, it looked upon itself as an elite academic institution whose job was to collect and analyze data for publication in the scientific literature and to take the lead in responding to crises by advising state and local public health officials. In addition, located in Atlanta, it operated somewhat more independently from HHS leadership compared with the close relationship between HHS and the NIH and FDA, all located in the Washington, D.C., area. Thompson wanted much more direct contact with and influence over the activities of the CDC particularly regarding our response to bioterror attacks. I had known Jeff for several years and found him to be a superb public health official with an outstanding track record. This growing undercurrent between CDC and HHS leadership antedated Jeff, having existed beneath the surface for many years. The conflict got worse over the next couple of months, which ultimately led to Koplan's resignation in February 2002. Thompson was just too strong a personality with a governor's style of running a program to let the CDC function as it traditionally had. During the closing months of 2001, the CDC official Julie Gerberding, an old friend and physician whom I had known from her years of work on HIV/AIDS when she was at San Francisco General Hospital, assumed a greater role as the voice and face of the CDC in response to real and potential bioterror attacks. Thompson ultimately appointed Julie to succeed Koplan as director of the CDC.

BETWEEN OCTOBER 25 and 28, more cases of inhalational anthrax were recognized, including five more cases in Washington, D.C., among postal workers. People were more and more afraid to open their mail, and some were even stockpiling Cipro. The first anthrax infection in New Jersey was reported in a woman who developed cutaneous anthrax even though she had no direct connection with the postal service. The theory was later proposed that a contaminated letter from the Hamilton Township Post Office in New Jersey went to her home or place of employment. At the time, her case remained a mystery. In addition, the first case in New York City was reported in a sixty-one-year-old woman named Kathy Nguyen who had unexplained inhalational anthrax, also with no connection to the postal system.

There was a growing feeling among the general public and expressed in the press that the government's response to bioterrorism should be officially led by someone with a scientific background instead of Tommy Thompson and Tom Ridge, the new assistant to the president for homeland security and former governor of Pennsylvania. Both were experienced and talented politicians but had little knowledge and experience in public health. An editorial in *The Washington Post* by Charles Krauthammer on October 26 underscored this point and strongly suggested that I be made the official spokesperson on the bioweapons war front: "Have him brief the press and the nation. Every day. Same time. The way Gens. Colin Powell and Norman Schwartzkopf [*sic*] did during the Gulf War." In fact, a day did not go by where someone in the media was not asking me for an interview, a quote, or a comment.

On October 31, Kathy Nguyen died of inhalational anthrax, putting the country further on edge. The public's need to understand where we were headed dominated every conversation. I felt it was critically important to tell the public exactly what we knew and what we did not know. The day Kathy Nguyen died, I led a previously scheduled conference on anthrax and bioterrorism at the NIH. This was supposed to be attended almost exclusively by NIH staff including physicians, scientists, and trainees. Historically, it was virtually unheard of for media to attend such conferences. But as I looked out from the podium in the NIH auditorium, I saw that the back of the room was crowded with cameras representing all major networks, cable, and *PBS NewsHour.*

I gladly assumed the growing responsibility in terms of both becoming a major spokesperson for the federal government and putting together a substantial long-term biodefense research effort. But there were days when these tasks completely consumed me, leaving too little time for my other responsibilities as director of NIAID including leading the NIH HIV/AIDS efforts. To make matters worse, or better, depending on your perspective, the U.S. Congress became increasingly interested and involved in our activities in response to the anthrax attacks. I was asked to brief the Senate Democratic Caucus including Senators Lieberman, Daschle, and Biden on bioterrorism at a lunch meeting at the U.S. Capitol on November 1. In all, there were about thirty Democratic senators present. I told them everything that we knew from a public health and medical standpoint concerning the anthrax situation. Several of them expressed a strong desire that I lead the nation's biodefense efforts as my full-time job. I said no on the spot.

EVEN CATASTROPHE PROVIDED some light moments. For example, my debut (of sorts) on *Saturday Night Live* on November 3 had Darrell Hammond playing Attorney General John Ashcroft and Chris Kattan playing me. It spoofed the fact that the Environmental Protection Agency was having a tough time decontaminating the buildings the anthrax letters had passed through. Just when they thought that a building was clean, another, more sensitive test showed that there were still spores present, and it was not clear what the minimal accepted number of spores was for people to safely reoccupy the buildings. Activities in several government buildings had been severely disrupted even though, apart from the Brentwood Post Office, no one had gotten infected inside a government building. There was great frustration among staff and senators who wanted to return to their Senate offices. This was perfect fodder for satire. "Good evening," Hammond as John Ashcroft said. "These are, indeed, complicated times for a great nation. But tonight, the United States Justice Department simply wishes to say: Get on with your lives. Do whatever you would normally do. Also, in the next three days, there's probably gonna be a terrorist attack on our country." Then Hammond said, "Well, there ya go! Look, everyone, please go back to normalcy, live your lives, just relax. And now, here with an update on the vicious, seemingly unstoppable anthrax scourge, from the National Institute of Health, is Dr. Anthony Fauci." At that point I (Chris Kattan) said, "Thank you. I'd like to reassure the American public by saying this: we have cleaned the State Department, the White

House, the Supreme Court, and the Capitol building with state-of-the-art decontamination instruments, and have installed dozens of $20 million irradiation lasers to keep all dangerous substances away from the U.S. government." In contrast to what we were doing about the federal buildings, when asked what we were doing about decontaminating the post offices, Kattan had me say, "We've given each post office some baby wipes and a dust buster." A reporter then asks, "But what about the contaminated buildings in New York? Are they safe?" Kattan responds, "I don't know, lady! I haven't been to New York in weeks! Do you think I'm crazy?"

No sooner did we believe that things were quieting down than another fatal case of anthrax was recognized in late November 2001. Ottilie Lundgren was a ninety-four-year-old woman from Oxford, Connecticut, a rural community thirty miles from Hartford, who developed inhalational anthrax and died on November 21. Careful detective work on the part of the CDC and the FBI suggested that her exposure might have been through a tertiary mail contamination. A letter that might have passed through the Trenton, New Jersey, postal facility along with the letter to Senator Leahy likely got contaminated and subsequently went on to a post office in Connecticut. Lundgren received a letter that at some time was probably physically next to the secondary contaminated letter. The mystery was never solved. Lundgren turned out to be the final anthrax case in this extraordinary saga, which in the end killed five people and sickened an additional seventeen.

It would not be an overstatement to say that the country was close to outright panic. People continued to be afraid to open their mail, and the postal service took to irradiating the mail before delivery to homes and offices. Most people thought al-Qaeda perpetrated these attacks and that additional attacks were sure to come. But I and several of my colleagues in the security and public health sectors had doubts as to whether this attack really was carried out by al-Qaeda. It seemed that if al-Qaeda wanted to perpetrate mass damage and terror, they would have picked a more effective approach than sending out a few letters with a couple of grams of anthrax spores. As I stated in a *New York Times* interview, the attacks were "high on terror, but low on biomedical impact."

Furthermore, al-Qaeda had already proven themselves to our dismay to be highly competent in executing terror attacks. There was a certain amateurishness to these letters that contained the anthrax spores. The notes in one set of letters dated "09-11-01" read,

> *This is next*
> *Take Penacilin now*
> *Death to America*
> *Death to Israel*
> *Allah is great*

This did not sound to me like a ruthless al-Qaeda operative. Nor did the note in the second group of letters to Senators Daschle and Leahy also dated "09-11-01," which read,

> *You cannot stop us.*
> *We have this anthrax.*
> *You die now.*
> *Are you afraid?*
> *Death to America.*
> *Death to Israel.*
> *Allah is great.*

Al-Qaeda's lack of involvement only became clear after several years of tortuous investigation by the FBI. In April 2007, an intensive investigation focused on Bruce E. Ivins, a civilian employee of the Department of Defense who worked as a microbiologist biodefense researcher and an expert on anthrax at the U.S. Army facility at Fort Detrick, Maryland. In July 2008 the FBI informed Ivins that it was about to press charges against him as the perpetrator of the 2001 anthrax attacks. Soon after, Ivins died by suicide on July 29, 2008, taking an overdose of Tylenol with codeine. Although the FBI was convinced that he was the guilty party, it was never definitively proven that Ivins sent the anthrax letters.

It had been almost seven years since the anthrax attacks in the fall of 2001, bringing to relative closure a frightening chapter in U.S. history.

Going Global with
AIDS Relief

E ven as we were intensively focused on anthrax and the bioterror threat, AIDS continued to rage, particularly in southern Africa. My concern for the dire situation there crystallized during a trip I took to Uganda in the spring of 2001, months before 9/11 and the anthrax attacks.

I had been invited to give a lecture at a meeting titled "AIDS Care in Africa" that was held in the Ugandan capital of Kampala. I welcomed this as an opportunity to visit some of the facilities that NIAID was supporting in the country. As I traveled throughout Uganda, certain riveting scenes became embedded in my consciousness and remain with me to this day.

The percentage of HIV positivity among pregnant women in Uganda had previously been as high as 40 to 50 percent; but due to intensive counseling on risk reduction over the past couple of years the percentage had dropped to 20 percent, still an astoundingly high number. When I visited the antenatal clinic at Mulago Hospital, it was totally packed, with little room to squeeze by. While many women appeared to be healthy, several clearly had AIDS, which I could easily recognize by their emaciated appearance. If they had a small amount of money, they could possibly pay for some treatment for their opportunistic infections such as candida, a common fungal infection among AIDS patients. Others might afford Bactrim, a sulfa-based drug used to prevent and treat *Pneumocystis* pneumonia and other infectious complications of HIV. But virtually no one was receiving the lifesaving antiretroviral drugs widely available in the developed world. As I mingled in the clinic, my frustration and anger rose at the lack of fairness to these struggling and courageous people. These were people who would be saved if they had been born in a richer country.

Next, I went to the Joint Clinical Research Centre, known as the JCRC. I was shown around by Dr. Peter Mugyenyi, the head of the clinic, and his deputy, Dr. Cissy Kityo Mutuluza. Peter Mugyenyi was an important physician in Uganda because of his leadership role in addressing the HIV/AIDS pandemic. The talent, organization, and performance of the medical staff he had assembled was impressive. Most of his colleagues had spent some time in the United States learning medical techniques as well as getting clinical experience. Peter, Cissy, and their team were making the most of the scarce amount of money that they received from philanthropic sources to purchase and successfully administer antiretroviral drugs to a small number of patients. I remember thinking that if we could give these health-care providers more resources, their operation could serve as an excellent model for HIV prevention, treatment, and care in southern Africa.

Later that day when I made ward rounds back at Mulago Hospital, I saw that the wards were completely packed. There were no private or semiprivate rooms; the wards were wide open with beds lined up next to each other. This reminded me so much of the old Bellevue Hospital on First Avenue in New York City, the overcrowded public hospital, where as second-year medical students at Cornell we rotated through to learn the art of physical diagnosis.

The difference here was that the beds were jammed next to each other, and some people were lying in the hallways on makeshift futons and cots. Patients also overflowed onto the open-air verandas. The sheer volume of patients was overwhelming. I had made ward rounds on thousands of patients over the years, and I had never experienced anything like this even during the worst years in the early 1980s when Cliff Lane and I were taking care of ten to fifteen AIDS patients at a time at the NIH. To make matters worse, most of these patients were extremely ill. Even though this was 2001, a full five years since combination antiretroviral therapy had proven to dramatically turn around the course of HIV infection in those people who had access to the drugs, there was little to no access to the drugs for most of these patients. Similar to the situation in the antenatal clinic, not only did these patients not get antiretroviral treatment, but the overwhelming majority of these people were not being treated for some of their opportunistic infections, including tuberculosis. As was the case earlier, if the patient could not pay even a small amount such as a dollar or two, then they would get no specific treatment at all. If they were poor but could pay something, certain common medications were made available to them. Only a very small group of relatively wealthy patients were put in a different ward where they had access to chest X-rays and other imaging studies as well as blood tests, treatment for their opportunistic infections, and even occasionally antiretroviral therapy for their HIV infection.

As we walked through the ward, I saw patient after patient with advanced HIV disease. I remember clearly a seventeen-year-old girl, a mere two years older than my daughter Jenny, with a frightened expression on her face. She had been diagnosed with HIV disease by observation alone. She showed the typical wasting as well as an oral candida infection. She also very likely had a form of fungal meningitis called cryptococcal meningitis commonly seen in people with HIV. The diagnosis can be made by examining the cerebrospinal fluid with a special stain called an India ink stain. But the physicians decided not to perform the test because they could not do anything for her anyway. She could not afford the very expensive medications commonly being used in the United States for these infections. The plan was to hydrate her, give her some analgesics, and discharge her home to her mother. I was embarrassed that I just could not conceal the moistness in my eyes as I left the bed of this suffering and frightened young girl. Two beds down was a similar case of a man in his early thirties with obvious HIV disease and likely tuberculosis that had spread throughout his body. Again, no specific therapy for this man. It hit me like a Mack truck. I was witnessing an unspeakable tragedy.

Together with Dr. Nelson Sewankambo, dean of the Makerere School of Medicine, and his colleague Dr. David Serwadda, I visited the Rakai district of Uganda in the southern part of the country near the borders of Tanzania and Rwanda. I had thought that I had seen everything up to that point, but apparently not. The health facilities in Rakai made Mulago Hospital in Kampala look modern. There was a hospital along with antenatal and general medical clinics in the town of Kalisizo, but just getting there was a huge battle for patients and their families. The roads were unpaved, and the best of them were almost impassable with large ruts and gigantic potholes. Even with a four-wheel-drive van, we barely made it to our destination because it was the rainy season and segments of the road were washed away. Once patients got there, their problems continued—benches full of people waiting to be registered and hallways crowded with people waiting to be seen. Some patients, being attended to by their families, were lying without beds on the walkways. The pediatric ward had two children per bed. I was told that, in addition to HIV and tuberculosis, the majority of the people in the wards, especially the children, had malaria. Now that it was 2001, the blood supply was being screened for HIV. I could only imagine how many children had been infected with HIV just a few years earlier, before the transfusions that were given for malaria were screened. I am still haunted by the faces of the patients on the ward. Blank stares and silence. No one made a sound, not even the sickest of them.

The Kalisizo Hospital was staffed by three physicians whose training consisted of medical school and one to two years at the most of residency training. These dedicated young physicians did everything that did not absolutely require advanced technical procedures typical of major hospitals. They performed deliveries, even Cesarean sections; abdominal surgery including bowel resection; tended to bone fractures and other trauma; and performed some types of chest surgery. There was no senior attending physician supervising them. As frightening as this may seem to those of us used to teams of highly trained physicians with years of specialty training, experienced nurses, and well-equipped facilities, I was impressed with these dedicated physicians who were learning on the job and saving lives on the way.

Upon my return from Rakai to Kampala, I gave the opening address at the "AIDS Care in Africa" meeting on April 19, 2001. I had prepared my remarks before I left the United States, but I needed to modify them after what I had just seen. It was clear to me, and I expressed this during my remarks, that there needed to be a greater focus on treating Africans with HIV while also accelerating prevention measures such as condoms. However, it would be extremely difficult to provide a comprehensive HIV treatment and prevention program without addressing at least in part the existing health-care infrastructure problem. I stressed in my talk that we had to enlarge our ambitions. We had to bring in and train researchers who could tackle the health problems of the region as well as address other basic health-care issues such as clean water,

treatment, and prophylaxis for malaria and tuberculosis; vaccination against childhood diseases; and treatment of diarrheal and
acute respiratory diseases. I knew that this was aspirational and
likely not easily attainable, but I felt this was the time and place to
lay out expectations. I needed to state it clearly and forcefully so
that we could set it as a goal for the future.

After the meeting we drove to the Uganda Virus Research Institute in Entebbe on the way to the airport. The institute was an
excellent facility, and the view from the main building was magnificent because the structure was perched overlooking the shores
of Lake Victoria. As I gazed out on the reflection of the setting
sun on the waters of this historic lake, I could not help feel an even
greater conviction that it was our moral responsibility to help the
wonderful people of this region who were suffering so greatly.

NINE MONTHS AFTER my return from Uganda, the Global Fund
was formally established in January 2002. The United States was
contributing roughly one-third of the funding, but President Bush
was looking for more direct and bilateral ways to positively affect
the global HIV/AIDS pandemic, particularly in southern Africa.
To this end, the president sent Tommy Thompson and me together
with a small delegation to southern Africa on March 31, 2002, to
gather facts on the ground. We visited Mozambique, South Africa,
Botswana, and Côte d'Ivoire, and the AIDS situation in these
countries was similar in many respects to what I had seen the previous year in Uganda. I became even more convinced of my con-
clusions that the United States could and should provide resources
to southern Africa to address their dire situation with HIV/AIDS.
I realized one of the most compelling needs was the prevention
of mother-to-child transmission of HIV. A study published in
1999 indicated that a single dose of a drug called nevirapine

administered during labor and delivery together with a single dose of the drug to the baby within seventy-two hours of birth substantially reduced the risk of HIV transmission from mother to infant. This relatively inexpensive regimen seemed perfectly suited to the developing world and seemed to be low-hanging fruit. As we left Africa, I was determined to put together such a proposal to the president and his staff. As soon as I got back to Washington, with the indispensable help of Dr. Mark Dybul, we got to work on the proposal.

Mark was at the time a young physician who had joined my lab in 1995 as a trainee in infectious diseases. He had attended Georgetown University both as an undergraduate and as a medical student followed by a medical residency at the University of Chicago Medical Center. In 1998, as he was approaching the end of his NIAID fellowship, he was faced with an important career decision. He was a superb clinical physician, and he felt somewhat unfulfilled doing only basic research. He came to me for advice. Because he was quite interested in the policy side of biomedical research and public health, I suggested that he leave the lab and come over to my office to serve as my assistant. It was in this capacity that I called upon Mark to help me formulate the mother-to-child transmission program in May 2002.

Our proposed five-year plan aimed to save 146,000 babies per year from being infected from their mothers during pregnancy or at the time of birth (referred to as perinatal transmission) for a cost of about $100 million annually. Gary Edson and Jay Lefkowitz, deputy assistant to the president for domestic policy, liked the plan and said they wanted to present it to the president within a couple of days. They told me that the president wanted to announce a major global health initiative at the G8 summit during the upcoming summer meeting in Ottawa and they felt that this plan would perfectly suit that need.

On May 29, 2002, in the Cabinet Room of the West Wing packed with White House and cabinet officials, I presented the Prevention of Mother to Child Transmission initiative to President Bush. After asking several insightful questions, the president seemed very pleased with the proposal and said that he would likely go ahead with it but said he wanted to hear comments from others in the room.

At that moment, a surprising dynamic unfolded. Andrew Natsios, the administrator of the U.S. Agency for International Development (USAID), became visibly upset that this initiative was an HHS proposal and got into a heated argument with Tommy Thompson right in front of the president. He pointed out that he had a memorandum of understanding with the CDC, part of HHS, indicating that USAID had the lead with regard to AIDS in Africa. I was stunned that a turf argument could occur in this setting. I knew nothing about the memorandum, nor apparently did Tommy Thompson. Natsios was clearly upset, but Thompson did not back down, and they went at it. The president did not seem at all amused. Sounding annoyed, he said that despite this interagency argument the only thing he knew was that "I like Tony's plan, and so let's implement it." He then abruptly said that HHS and USAID should "work it out." From my standpoint, despite the awkward exchanges between Natsios and Thompson, the meeting was an overwhelming success because the president accepted the plan and a lot of babies were now going to be saved in Africa.

About two weeks later on June 10, Secretary of the Treasury Paul O'Neill, who had heard of my recent presentation to the president, invited me to breakfast in his office in the Treasury Building. He had just returned from a ten-day tour of Africa with Bono, leader of the rock band U2. Bono had been a major advocate for

HIV/AIDS assistance to developing nations. O'Neill mentioned that both he and Bono were deeply moved during their tour by the suffering due to HIV/AIDS that they witnessed in southern Africa. They were particularly struck by the desperate situation for children with HIV who had essentially no hope of surviving to adulthood. O'Neill wanted to compare notes on our respective trips, and he was extremely enthusiastic about our going forward with the proposed Prevention of Mother to Child Transmission initiative.

June 19, 2002, turned out to be one of the most exciting days in my involvement in the global fight against HIV/AIDS as I joined President Bush and other dignitaries in a Rose Garden ceremony to announce the $500 million Prevention of Mother to Child Transmission program. The president spoke to me with Josh Bolten, deputy chief of staff for policy, before we walked out to the Rose Garden. I had provided talking points for the president's speech, and he was gracious and thanked me for the work that I had done on this project.

But he had more to say. He asked me to work together with Josh on a proposal for a much bigger and broader global HIV/AIDS program, something that went well beyond what he was about to announce. "As a rich country," he said, "we have a moral responsibility to not allow people to die from a preventable and treatable disease because of where they happened to have been born. For those to whom much is given, much is required."

I could not fathom at the time what extraordinary and transformative implications that simple statement by the president to Josh and me would have for global HIV/AIDS.

Immediately after the ceremony Josh called a meeting of our small group that included Gary Edson; Jay Lefkowitz; Kristen

Silverberg, deputy assistant to the president and adviser to the chief of staff; Margaret Spellings, domestic policy adviser to the president; along with Robin Cleveland from the Office of Management and Budget (OMB). Josh was explicit; the president did not want word of this expanded plan to leave the room. Gary and Jay underscored to me that I could not discuss this subject with people outside the group and this included even my immediate boss, the newly appointed NIH director, Dr. Elias Zerhouni. The White House was concerned that leaks to the press and others might derail the process. I promised Gary and Jay that I would go along with their request, but that this was going to be awkward for me. I was known as a team player, and my team had always been the NIH. Nonetheless, if this is what the president of the United States wanted, then this was the way it was going to be.

JOSH WAS OPEN to all possibilities about what the plan would look like and said that we should put impact ahead of cost. One option was to do a massive, high-tech, scientific project to develop an HIV vaccine, similar to the massive effort of the Manhattan Project that developed the atomic bomb. Another was to invest in providing HIV prevention and treatment on a wide scale in the developing world, particularly southern Africa. Although a major accelerated investment in vaccine research would have meant considerably more resources for my own institute, I told Josh that I did not think that this was the best approach. It would take several years at best to develop a vaccine, and as far as Africa and the developing world were concerned, we were dealing with a true global health emergency. As we started our work, Josh clearly favored a treatment and prevention plan with immediate impact and indicated that the president likely would also.

I could barely contain my excitement. As I left the White House and walked to the Metro station to return to the NIH, I called Mark Dybul and told him that I believed we might be given the opportunity to do something huge. I considered Mark an integral part of the team and so I was not breaking confidence. "Mark, we should act now, preemptively, and start putting together a plan. I am almost positive that Josh will come back sometime soon and ask us to do just that." Mark was in total agreement and seemed as pumped up as I was.

Over the next couple of weeks Mark and I struggled with the concept of what such a program for southern Africa would look like. When I was in Africa, I had observed the successful implementation of treatment and prevention programs, albeit on a very small scale where scarce resources were made available. This was particularly true for the program run by Dr. Peter Mugyenyi at the JCRC in Kampala. Peter and his colleagues had been treating considerable numbers of Ugandans in a community-based program with antiretroviral therapy paid for predominantly by philanthropic organizations.

I headed off to the Fourteenth International AIDS Conference in Barcelona on July 7–12, 2002, to give a keynote speech. At that conference Mark and I arranged a meeting in my room at the Fira Palace Hotel with Peter and Cissy Kityo Mutuluza. Peter showed Mark and me the outline of his program. It included a main center with highly trained physicians as well as regional satellites and subgroups of the satellites with progressively less technical capabilities but with the capacity to see patients and administer antiretroviral drugs. Each low-tech clinic cost only $30,000 a year. Mark and I were impressed with Peter's program and decided to use this as a potential model to present to Josh Bolten, Gary Edson, and the folks at the White House.

The 2002 Barcelona meeting also was Tommy Thompson's first encounter with AIDS activists. On July 9, Thompson, as the ranking U.S. government official at the meeting, gave a major speech. It was almost a foregone conclusion that there would be a demonstration against any U.S. administration official at an international AIDS meeting. Activists were determined to keep the pressure on the U.S. government to provide additional resources for the AIDS effort, especially for the Global Fund. I had heard from my friend and ACT UP member Gregg Gonsalves that ACT UP was planning to demonstrate against Thompson. The idea was that they would protest for a while and then allow him to speak provided that he meet with them afterward. I explained this to Thompson, and he agreed to meet with them; even so, they shouted him down throughout his entire speech. I advised Tommy beforehand that this might happen and that he should just calmly continue with his speech and then leave the stage when he was finished. This is what he did, but he was terribly upset and hurt that they had attacked him. He just could not believe that people would attack him when he was doing everything he could to help them. I liked Tommy a lot by now, so it was up to me to explain to him in words that I knew he would understand that for the activists this was like the iconic line from the movie *The Godfather*—"It's not personal, it's strictly business"—and he should just let it go. He seemed to understand, but later he told me he was puzzled as to why he was not appreciated even though he was doing his best. I understood how Tommy felt because I had been there. He just needed to come to grips with the reality of activists who were fighting for their lives.

In mid-July, I met at the White House with Gary Edson and Jay Lefkowitz, who gave us a short turnaround to put together a proposal based on the "Mugyenyi Model." They wanted something on paper before the president left for his August break. Gary and

Jay were considering that the president might bring a proposal for such an initiative with him on his planned trip to Africa in January. Clearly, Mark and I had a lot of work to do over the next several days. My NIAID budget officer, Ralph Tate, who was fluent in computer modeling of large budgets, was helpful over the coming months with the part of our proposed initiative that required mathematical modeling. For example, we needed to determine how many individuals with HIV were living in the countries that we were considering to include in the program, what percentage of them we could likely reach in a treatment and prevention program, and how much all of this would cost.

On July 26, Gary sent me an email asking whether we had completed the plan so that he could determine if it was ready to present to the president. That was code for hurry up! We finished the draft within the next two days and set up a meeting with Gary for August 1.

That same day I got another taste of hard-core Washington politics and interagency competition. I, together with the HHS deputy secretary, Claude Allen, was called to an unusual meeting at the Rayburn House Office Building with Chairman Jim Kolbe of the House Appropriations Committee, Subcommittee on Foreign Operations, and the staff director of the committee, Charles Flickner. Here was a powerful congressional committee, and Kolbe, a Republican from Arizona, and Flickner were clearly upset with Gary that the president made the announcement of the Prevention of Mother to Child Transmission initiative without consulting them. They vented their intense displeasure on Claude and me, although we were not the immediate object of their concern. They disparagingly referred to Gary as "Emperor Edson." I was taken aback by the degree of their hostility. This was obviously a turf issue, and I was uncomfortable being in the middle of it. But as I was quickly learning, keeping important issues close to the vest was the way this president operated, and although he was a collegial and considerate person, he acted decisively when he made up his mind. When I mentioned the encounter with Kolbe and Flickner to Gary, he just shrugged his shoulders and said, "Who cares? I work for the president, not for them."

AFTER THREE WEEKS of back-and-forth with the White House, Margaret Spellings and Gary responded to our latest revised proposal questioning what the impact of such a large international program would be on domestic AIDS programs. Specifically, would we be criticized for putting so many resources into global problems when access to care was still difficult among some individuals with HIV here in the United States? I proposed that we strengthen the Ryan White HIV/AIDS Program, which provided federal funds for community-based treatment for people living with HIV in this country. Also, the effect this new program would have on our support for the Global Fund was obviously a sticky point. The UN secretary-general, Kofi Annan, was already concerned that not enough resources were being put into the Global Fund.

I felt that we could do both. A huge independent, bilateral effort led by the United States in the form of a presidential initiative could complement the multilateral Global Fund so long as the United States stood by our agreement of providing up to 30 percent of total resources given to the Global Fund.

Another issue was whether we should include Russia, India, and China among the countries that would receive aid from our program. I was strongly against doing so because I felt that although AIDS was an important issue in all three countries, they had the resources to address their own problems. This was in sharp contrast to the poor countries in sub-Saharan Africa that were in desperate need of assistance. What we were proposing would cost billions of dollars per year, and I felt that this would be diluted if Russia, India, and China were included. Also, in discussion with Josh Bolten several weeks earlier I had mentioned that we would provide the president with multiple alternatives, which I referred to as the "Chevrolet plan" for the inexpensive version, the "Oldsmobile plan" for a more expensive version, and the "Mercedes plan" for the truly expensive version. After several revisions, we seemed to be heading toward a new Mercedes.

NOTHING GETS DONE in Washington without a lot of meetings, and over the next few months we had a full dose. A memorable one came in late August in the White House Situation Room. Several minutes into my presentation Robin Cleveland and another OMB official walked into the meeting. Without even having heard the first part of my presentation, Robin interrupted me and expressed skepticism about the entire concept in general and my proposal in particular. She questioned whether Peter Mugyenyi's model would work, even though she had never heard the details of what the model actually was. Her attitude was really starting to irritate me. Gary immediately sensed this and intervened, defending my presentation and indicating that we would get back to her with more details about the Uganda model. I got it that Robin was doing her job employing due diligence as an OMB official. But it raised a red flag for me about the internal resistance that we might consistently meet as we moved forward with the proposal. After all, we would be proposing a multibillion-dollar project, an amount that would cause OMB to instinctively flinch.

Over the next month we worked to address the concerns, and Robin seemed less antagonistic, if not entirely satisfied. By mid-September, I was as ready as I would ever be and made my last pitch to Josh. It was clear by the time I finished that he was thoroughly convinced this was something we should do. However, he pointed out that a major problem would be the question of where we were going to get the money this late in the normal budget process; the 2003 budget had already been submitted to Congress.

THE NEXT DAY, something entirely unexpected happened. Around midday, I received a telephone call from Jamie Drummond, who worked closely with Bono. Apparently, word had leaked out to Bono that I was "up to something" with regard to trying to get AIDS treatment, prevention, and care to sub-Saharan Africa. AIDS in Africa was a subject of great interest to Bono as I knew from my breakfast with Paul O'Neill. Because Bono had been actively advocating for rich nations to make major investments in the AIDS effort in that region of the world, he wanted to hear more about what I was doing. Jamie told me that Bono and his staff were currently in Chicago and that Bono was hoping to speak with me in person that evening. He could fly to Washington that afternoon and meet me in a place where we could talk privately. I suggested that the easiest thing to do would be for them to come to my home in Washington, where Christine and I would be happy to cook up a quick Italian meal for them. Jamie thought that this was a great idea.

I was thrilled. Not only was Bono a world-famous performer but he was emerging as a true hero in the fight against global HIV/AIDS. I immediately called Christine in her NIH office and filled her in on our new evening plans. I asked her not to clue in our daughters. At that time, Jenny was sixteen, Megan was thirteen, and Ali was ten. Jenny and Megan, like many teenagers (and adults), were enthusiastic fans of Bono and U2, and I thought that I would give them a little surprise. When Bono and his group landed, Jamie called and said they would be here in about twenty-five minutes. I told the girls that a group of people from my office were coming for dinner and that they would be arriving soon. As you might expect of children their age, they did not care much one way or another. When I saw Bono's SUV pull up in front of our house, I deliberately went into the kitchen, and when the doorbell rang, I asked Jennifer to let in our guests. About ten seconds later she let out a clearly audible gasp at the front door. She called out, "Daddy, Bono is here!" I calmly said, "Well, let him in." Bono was genuinely gracious, warm, and friendly. He spent a considerable amount of time talking with the girls and posing for pictures with them. Accompanying Bono was a staff of four. They had stopped off at a local wine store and brought with them three bottles of exquisite Italian wine. Christine cooked rigatoni with marinara sauce, and we settled in with warm Italian bread, a Caesar salad, and the terrific wine. We sat out on my back deck talking for hours well into the night.

Bono is an admired public persona. Face-to-face, he is even better. He came across as intelligent and inquisitive, passionate about helping to alleviate the suffering and death associated with AIDS, particularly in the developing world. He admitted that he had heard "through the grapevine" that I was working on some sort of AIDS proposal for sub-Saharan Africa to present to the president. So much for total secrecy in the White House inner circle. I apologized but said I could not give him the details of what I was doing because of my promise of confidentiality to Josh, Gary, and Jay. "When the time is right," I said, "I will explain everything." He asked how he could be helpful and promised that he would do all he could to support me and President Bush. I congratulated him for his wonderful work and assured him that we would stay in close touch.

———————

MORE THAN THREE WEEKS went by before I heard anything from the White House. I learned that this was a pattern—several intense meetings followed by long silent gaps.

The suspense was broken on October 10, 2002, when I was called to a meeting at the White House with Gary, Jay, and OMB's ever-skeptical Robin Cleveland. Jay wanted a breakdown of how much would be spent for condom distribution versus sex worker education versus needle exchange versus family counseling. He said the more conservative factions in the White House would not support some of these preventive interventions, especially those dealing with commercial sex workers and injection drug users, and that we had to be prepared for these questions. I insisted to Jay and Gary that the prevention component of the plan could not be viable without large-scale distribution of condoms and engagement with commercial sex workers who were important drivers of the epidemic in certain southern African countries.

Also, I began to realize that some in the White House were vacillating between making this initiative part of the Global Fund and creating a purely bilateral program led by the president between the United States and the recipient host countries. Bernhard Schwartländer, the WHO point person on AIDS, and other WHO officials wanted to treat three million people over three years, which would cost about $10 to $15 billion, and they hoped that the United States would contribute $4 to $5 billion, thus sticking to the formula of the United States contributing one-third to the Global Fund. They wanted to make this announcement on World AIDS Day, which was December 1. In my mind, there were pros and cons to this approach. On the upside, we could give the money under the condition that they coordinate their activities with our own plan. The president could get credit for providing leadership as well as contributing to a multilateral global fund. Also, it would avoid the inevitable impression that we Americans were going off on our own, something that Kofi Annan frowned upon. On the downside, it would take away from our ability to get things done quickly and efficiently, and I was still very much in favor of the president's initiative driven by the United States alone. I still felt we could support both the Global Fund and the president's initiative at the same time, and I was not shy about letting my opinion be known in the White House.

While all this was happening, Bono, still unaware of the details of what we were up to, continued to push for more resources for the global AIDS effort. We had breakfast in October, and he mentioned that he would be meeting with Condoleezza Rice that afternoon and would push for the United States to make major commitments of new money as well as to provide leadership in the global AIDS effort. Condi Rice was in a situation similar to me, since she had been working quietly, but effectively, behind the scenes strongly supporting the president's initiative as it evolved. That breakfast underscored for me what an extraordinarily compassionate humanitarian Bono was. My only disappointment was that I could not yet tell him about the program we were developing at the White House.

By the first week of November the White House seemed on the verge of making a decision, but OMB still wanted more due diligence. In particular Robin Cleveland wanted outside opinions as to whether the plan was feasible or advisable. Gary asked me to bring together a small group of people who worked firsthand in developing countries to a White House meeting with OMB to discuss our plan. And they wanted to do so without my being present.

I GAVE GARY a short list of people who I felt would be favorably disposed: Peter Mugyenyi and Jean "Bill" Pape, my Haitian friend who trained at my alma mater Cornell University Medical College and who was the director of the highly esteemed GHESKIO AIDS program in Port-au-Prince, Haiti. Also on the list were Eric Goosby, my good friend with whom I had worked closely during his years directing AIDS programs at HHS and the White House during the Clinton administration and who was now the CEO of the Pangaea Global AIDS Foundation working in Rwanda on HIV/AIDS programs; and my longtime friend and colleague Paul Farmer, cofounder of Partners in Health who was working in his clinics in Haiti.

To my amazement and luck, and as a testimony to our friendship and their commitment to HIV/AIDS, I was able to get all four of them to Washington within forty-eight hours. Even though I had promised Gary that I would not pre-brief our group of advisers, I was certain that he knew this is exactly what I would do. In fact, knowing Gary, I was convinced that he actually was counting on it. In my best clandestine manner, I arranged for us to meet on the evening of Tuesday, November 12, at the Trattoria Sorrento, a family restaurant on Cordell Avenue in downtown Bethesda. It was one of my favorite restaurants because in addition to serving good Italian food, it was quiet, especially during the week.

As I walked into the restaurant, my colleagues were already sitting at the table. After greeting each one warmly, I joked that this secretive meeting in a quiet Italian restaurant reminded me of that iconic scene in *The Godfather* where Michael Corleone, played by Al Pacino, meets with and ultimately shoots and kills the corrupt New York City police captain Mark McCluskey, played by Sterling Hayden, and the drug trafficker Virgil "the Turk" Sollozzo, played by Al Lettieri. This meeting turned out to have a happier ending, because my four colleagues enthusiastically supported the program we had put together—both the concept of a separate president's initiative and the amount of money that I felt was essential for the success of the program. I briefed them on the types of questions that Robin and the OMB director, Mitch Daniels, would likely ask and the potential traps that might be set for them. Above all, they needed to stick firmly to the concept that this program was essential and that it potentially could save millions of lives. After some calamari appetizers, delicious pastas, and a couple of bottles of Italian wine, I left the dinner confident we would triumph.

The meeting with OMB took place the following day, November 13. Soon afterward, Gary called me to say that all had gone extremely well. Robin brought her own chosen consultant to the meeting in the person of Nils Daulaire, a knowledgeable former public servant now in the private sector who agreed with the necessity and importance of our plan.

ALMOST TWO WEEKS went by without hearing another word. My already ever-present anxiety intensified on Wednesday, December 4. Gary was getting ready to meet with Mitch Daniels about the AIDS plan, but he had heard that Mitch was balking and trying to steamroll Gary by bringing up a *Washington Post* article published two days earlier about the failure of an AIDS treatment and prevention program in Botswana. It had been initiated by the Harvard AIDS Institute, the Bill & Melinda Gates Foundation, and the Merck pharmaceutical company. OMB was now raising the question that if the Botswana program failed, why should we believe that our program would succeed? Gary needed to forcefully counter that argument and asked me to contact our colleagues who were working on HIV/AIDS in Africa to get their opinion. He gave me thirty minutes. I frantically got on the phone and was able to contact Peter Mugyenyi; Sam Kibende, deputy director of the national AIDS research center in Uganda; and Eric Goosby, who was back in Rwanda. All helped explain why what we were proposing for the president's initiative was quite different from the Botswana program. Peter mentioned the big mistake made in Botswana was that it was a top-down plan. The Botswana government employed the Harvard AIDS Institute, which developed a high-tech Harvard-like approach using CD-ROMs for developing voluntary counseling and testing. Peter said that such a plan was doomed to failure from the beginning. I relayed this to Gary, who was satisfied that he could now push back on Mitch Daniels's argument comparing our program with the Botswana program. Thus, we hurdled over another potential OMB roadblock.

CHRISTMAS AND NEW Year's Eve came and went and still no word from the White House. My anxiety skyrocketed. Then, in the third week of January, Gary and Jay called me to give me a heads-up that things were starting to move. To my great surprise, I received a call on January 24, 2003, from Gary and Jay telling me that they wanted me to again bring back Peter Mugyenyi from Uganda to meet with Mitch Daniels. Two days later Peter joined us for a late lunch / early dinner at Mark Dybul's house. It was Super Bowl Sunday and the Tampa Bay Buccaneers would defeat the Oakland Raiders by a score of 48 to 21. But we paid very little attention to football as Mark and I intensively rehearsed Peter on what he might expect the next day on his visit with the good folks from OMB.

It worked. The next day, Peter and I met with Mitch Daniels, who seemed genuinely moved by Peter's description of the desperate situation of AIDS in Africa and was now fully on board with our plan.

Tuesday, January 28, the day of the State of the Union address, turned out to be one of the most exciting days of my life. I'd been asked to plan to spend the entire day at the White House, and when I arrived in the West Wing, Gary and Jay were all smiles as they delivered the news that the president had decided to adopt our AIDS plan—$15 billion over five years starting out with $2 billion in fiscal year 2004. The program would be separate from but complementary to the Global Fund to Fight AIDS, Tuberculosis, and Malaria. I spent the day working with Mike Gerson, the president's principal speechwriter, drafting the wording of the paragraph in the State of the Union address that would announce the president's plan. Mike had been a strong advocate inside the White House for the initiative throughout the entire process. After much discussion, we decided to call it the President's Emergency Plan for AIDS Relief, or PEPFAR.

I worked with Jay, Gary, and Kristen Silverberg on questions and answers that the White House would use in the expected public reaction to the president's announcement. I also was tasked by Josh to help call up leading members of Congress to inform them of what the president would be announcing that evening so they would not be taken by surprise. The mood was festive in the White House, and I was especially delighted when I heard that the president had asked Peter Mugyenyi to sit next to First Lady Laura Bush in her box at the Capitol during the State of the Union address.

On that night of January 28, 2003, tears of joy and exhaustion welled up in my eyes as Christine and I sat in front of the television watching the president announce the PEPFAR program to the millions of viewers who had tuned in to the State of the Union address. His words reflected the results of what we had been doing for the past eight months: "Ladies and gentlemen, seldom has history offered a greater opportunity to do so much for so many. We have confronted and will continue to confront HIV/AIDS in our own country. And to meet a severe and urgent crisis abroad, tonight I propose the Emergency Plan for AIDS Relief, a work of mercy beyond all current international efforts to help the people of Africa. This comprehensive plan will prevent 7 million new AIDS infections, treat at least 2 million people with life-extending drugs, and provide humane care for millions of people suffering from AIDS and for children orphaned by AIDS. I ask the Congress to commit $15 billion over the next five years, including nearly $10 billion in new money, to turn the tide against AIDS in the most afflicted nations of Africa and the Caribbean."

Here was a U.S. president, to his enduring credit, using the full weight of his position to help those who have few resources to help themselves.

PEPFAR WAS THE largest global health initiative for a single disease by any country in history. The announcement of the program was met with considerable enthusiasm throughout the world. Because the White House began referring all questions and requests for information about PEPFAR to me, I began receiving hundreds of enthusiastic phone calls and emails from friends, colleagues, and strangers around the globe praising the initiative and asking questions.

On February 13, I received a wonderful fax from Bono, who congratulated me on our efforts in developing PEPFAR and referred to himself and me as "partners in crime." He hosted a private dinner at Galileo, an Italian restaurant in downtown Washington, D.C., on March 16, in part to celebrate the creation of PEPFAR. Along with Josh, he invited several U.S. senators and other Washington notables. Josh was exceptionally kind to me by toasting me as the "principal architect of PEPFAR." As I sipped my prosecco, I realized that without President Bush's unflinching will to create such a program and the extraordinary commitment and skill of Josh and White House staff, particularly Gary, Jay,

Condi Rice, and Mike Gerson, among several others, as well as the invaluable partnership of Mark Dybul, PEPFAR would not have happened.

PEPFAR officially became a reality a few months later when it received its congressional authorization in legislation as a $15 billion, five-year initiative for fifteen countries. The fifteen countries were those that Mark and I had originally proposed. Twelve were in southern Africa: Botswana, Ethiopia, Mozambique, Nigeria, South Africa, Uganda, Zambia, Côte d'Ivoire, Kenya, Namibia, Rwanda, and Tanzania. One, Haiti, was in the Caribbean; another, Guyana, was in South America. The fifteenth country was Vietnam.

On May 28, 2003, President Bush signed the authorizing legislation for PEPFAR in front of a full house in the Dean Acheson Auditorium of the State Department headquarters a block from the Lincoln Memorial.

For a change, I slept very well that night.

Today, as I write, after more than twenty years, over $100 billion has been spent on the PEPFAR program in more than fifty countries, resulting in the saving of twenty-five million lives and counting.

Smallpox and Stockpiles

PEPFAR was on its way, but the problem of bioterrorism and smallpox vaccines and the question of what we needed to protect the country had not gone away. One thing we did know was that our stockpile of smallpox vaccines was inadequate.

One of the first projects that we pursued to correct that problem after 9/11 was to demonstrate in a clinical study that we could dilute the existing stock of smallpox vaccine by one to five or one to ten and still maintain the desired potency. This meant that the 15 million doses of undiluted vaccine in our stockpile could now be extended to anywhere between 75 and 150 million doses. There would likely be even more doses available because we had contracted months before to produce a second-generation smallpox vaccine that would raise our supply to more than 280 million doses by the end of 2002.

There was considerable disagreement over what to do with this expanded supply. Some U.S. public health officials and politicians argued that we should now vaccinate all first responders and emergency personnel in anticipation of a smallpox bioterror attack. A recently updated plan and guidelines put out by the CDC recommended a "ring vaccination" approach; if cases of smallpox were identified, patients with suspected or confirmed smallpox would be isolated, and their contacts would be traced, vaccinated, and kept under close surveillance, as would the household members of those contacts. The plan called for identifying other high-risk people who might have had direct or indirect contact with the patients and who therefore also should be vaccinated. In essence, one would vaccinate in "rings" around the index or original case. Local quarantining and travel restrictions also could be enforced if deemed appropriate. This approach had been successfully used in the global smallpox eradication program. While the CDC did not recommend mass vaccination campaigns either in response to documented cases of smallpox or in anticipation of a potential outbreak, some argued for just the opposite—preemptive mass vaccination of the general population because this would essentially take off the table the threat of smallpox as an agent of bioterrorism. A supporting argument for this approach was that this would eliminate any confusion and panic that would most likely accompany simultaneous attacks at different locations. Weighing against preemptive mass vaccination was the concern about vaccine-related adverse events. Historically, there was an incidence of one to two deaths per million recipients of the vaccine in addition to hundreds of cases of serious complications such as generalized vaccinia, which is characterized by spread of the virus throughout the skin and other parts of the body, as well as post-vaccine encephalitis, or inflammation of the brain.

I was leaning heavily against universal vaccination from the start. I wanted to clarify the issue of incidence of adverse events. I reviewed the medical literature on the subject. It was clear that the rate of complications in previously unvaccinated people, predominantly the younger people in the population, was considerably higher than the complications in the previously vaccinated group, namely those who were old enough to have been vaccinated during childhood many years ago, before smallpox vaccinations were discontinued in 1972. There was a considerable amount of residual immunity in the population among those who had been vaccinated even decades ago. In other words, they would likely already be protected in the event of a smallpox attack. This argued against the need of vaccinating the entire population of the United States even if there were a massive smallpox attack. My reluctance to go along with universal vaccination was strengthened by this information.

Vice President Cheney, however, was leaning toward a broader vaccination program. It soon became clear why. It was all about Iraq. There were continual rumors that we would soon preemptively attack Iraq to neutralize it before it used or obtained the capacity to employ weapons of mass destruction, including a deliberate release of smallpox in the United States or in an allied nation such as Israel.

Over the following weeks, the palpable tension regarding possible war with Iraq intensified. Carol Kuntz, special assistant to Vice President Cheney, told me that the president would soon announce that the Pentagon was ordering that 250,000 to 500,000 frontline military personnel in high-risk areas be vaccinated. Once the vaccinations of the military began, a policy regarding vaccination of civilians would have to be put in place. I was in favor of the voluntary, not mandatory, vaccination of up to 500,000 members of smallpox response teams and emergency personnel. However, my default recommendation was not to take the vaccine if you were just a member of the general public. I believed that the risk of a massive smallpox bioterror attack was just too small compared with the risk of the rare but serious incidence of adverse events with the vaccine.

I found myself in one meeting after another at HHS headquarters to nail down what would be the most appropriate vaccination program in case of a smallpox terror attack. Saddam Hussein was reportedly refusing to allow international inspections to rule out the possibility that he had weapons of mass destruction. An invasion of Iraq seemed inevitable. The press was reporting that the president planned to start bombing Iraq sometime during the second week of January 2003. President Bush wanted to start vaccinating the half a million people who would constitute the country's smallpox response teams by December 1, 2002. The atmosphere was heavy and tense.

Project BioShield

The smallpox vaccination program was part of a much broader biodefense strategy at NIAID. We had been working for months on a comprehensive research agenda for the development of countermeasures for biodefense. It was a new paradigm for government-sponsored research. I had no idea how it would be received when I presented it to Scooter Libby, Carol Kuntz, and my good friend Stewart Simonson in the fall of 2002. "There will need to be greater regulatory flexibility by the FDA so that we can move the approval process more quickly without compromising safety or proof of efficacy," I told the group gathered in the West Wing. I explained that we would need the authority to implement sole-source contracts in situations in which it was essential that we move quickly for the safety of the nation. I also brought up that we would likely need a special fund to purchase vaccines and drugs so that the pharmaceutical industry would have an incentive to partner with us in the development of countermeasures for biodefense, just as the automobile industry made planes and tanks during World War II. I did not anticipate at the time how this would evolve into a whole new approach for development of countermeasures to combat infectious diseases or how deeply I would be involved in the development of vaccines against newly emerging infections a couple of decades later.

It was clear to me that my job was changing, and quickly. Stewart Simonson, Carol Kuntz, and I met to discuss what new administrative authorities would be needed for me to adequately do that new job. This included sole-source contracting authority and the ability to rapidly award research grants as opposed to the eight to ten months usually required from submission of a grant application to awarding of the grant. Some of these authorities were similar to those already given to the Defense Advanced Research Projects Agency (DARPA). DARPA is an agency of the Department of Defense tasked with making transformational as opposed to incremental advances in technologies. Its projects are high risk, but high impact. I was skeptical that these same powers would be granted to a classical biomedical research organization such as NIAID; however, Stewart felt that it was worth a try.

New authorities are fine but meaningless without the money to support them. For months the vice president's team, Stewart, and I had been discussing the need for a vaccine trust fund to enable the advanced development and purchase of vaccines as well as other countermeasures to prepare for a bioterror attack. This included plans not only for anthrax and smallpox but also for botulism, plague, Ebola, tularemia, Rift Valley fever, a variety of mosquito-borne encephalitides, staphylococcal enterotoxin, pandemic influenza, and West Nile virus. I suggested to Scooter Libby that we give the entire program including the proposed new flexible implementation authorities, the FDA issues, and now the vaccine trust fund the name Project BioShield. It was reminiscent of Operation Desert Shield, the name of the preparatory military operation in 1990 under President George H. W. Bush in response to Iraq's invasion of Kuwait. Scooter liked the name and was fast becoming a staunch ally for the project.

The big day for the president's smallpox vaccination program announcement came on Friday, December 13, 2002. I was called to the White House for the 2:15 p.m. event. President Bush had decided to get vaccinated because he felt that as commander in chief of the armed forces and in recognition of the fact that certain risks and adverse events were possible, he did not want to order the troops to do something that he himself would not do. He did, however, say that Laura and his daughters, Barbara and Jenna, would not be vaccinated, because they were part of the general public. He felt that the risk of a bioterror attack was minimal, and there likely would be time for them to get vaccinated if there was a massive terrorist-driven smallpox outbreak in the United States. Apparently, the president had heard what I had been saying for the past few months. I would have made the same decision for my own family.

The smallpox announcement was only the beginning of a long and complicated process of getting the country ready for bioterror attacks. The next hurdle was to gain full White House and ultimately congressional support for Project BioShield.

WHETHER AND HOW a program gets funded can make all the difference. There was considerable discussion and often disagreement even within the White House about how we should secure funding. It was clear to Scooter Libby, Vice President Cheney, and me that for the program to be successful, the money would have to be guaranteed. This meant that the fund would have to fall under the category of mandatory spending. The money would come directly out of the Treasury year after year just like Social Security and would not have to go through the normal annual appropriations process. Staff from OMB and the White House economic team, on the other hand, vastly preferred year-by-year appropriations.

Before a meeting at the White House to weigh the pros and cons of each approach began, OMB official Nancy Dorn pulled me aside and whispered to me in exasperation out of earshot of the others, "Every time you come into the White House, it costs us billions of dollars." Nancy was only doing her job making sure that money was well spent, but, between the vaccine trust and PEP-FAR, I was not making friends among the OMB team.

When the meeting got started, the vice president called upon me to present the proposal. Nancy began to push back immediately. She argued that we could not include in the purchasing authority anything that was not already licensed. I had proposed that we include countermeasures that were "licensable"—namely diagnostics, vaccines, and treatments on the way to licensure by the FDA, but perhaps months away from actual approval. Nancy seemed completely frustrated by what was rolling out in front of her. But the vice president made no attempts to hide whose side he was on. "Nancy," he said, "do you expect me to go to the president and to the American people and say that we cannot provide countermeasures against threats that we either know or strongly suspect that Iraq has in its possession because we do not want to broaden authorities due to bureaucratic processes that will not allow it?"

The result was swift. Nancy said she would work with us to get this done. By the end of the meeting I knew that some reasonable form of Project BioShield would emerge.

The Christmas holidays in December 2002 turned out not to be holidays at all, because we worked right through the Christmas week and into the New Year hammering out the details of Project BioShield. All this was happening while I sweated out whether PEPFAR would be a go. On December 24, I had a pleasant surprise that momentarily broke the tension. At 1:00 p.m. the phone rang in my office at the NIH. I answered it myself because my staff had left for Christmas Eve. On the other end of the phone a familiar voice broke out in the full verse of "Happy Birthday." It was Tommy Thompson calling on his cell phone from a shopping center in Wisconsin.

THE MEETING WITH Nancy Dorn turned out to be only the first skirmish in what became an open battle between OMB and the vice president's team. I was continually asked for more supporting material to justify the program, which would ultimately require legislation both for authorization and appropriations.

Mentioning Project BioShield in the upcoming State of the Union address on January 28, 2003, would be a major step. Over the next several days I was consumed with fashioning the precise language that might be used if the president decided to include the program in his speech. The vice president's team, Stewart Simonson, and I spent hours in meetings to push Project BioShield forward.

It was worth it. Along with the PEPFAR announcement, Project BioShield did make it into the State of the Union address. "I ask you tonight to add to our future security with a major research and production effort to guard our people against bioterrorism, called Project BioShield," the president announced. "The budget I send you will propose almost $6 billion. . . . We must assume that our enemies would use these diseases as weapons, and we must act before the dangers are upon us."

I was thrilled about getting both of these initiatives this far, but it was exhausting me. While I had spent a part of almost every day up to that point either on the phone with the White House or physically in the West Wing working on both Project Bio-Shield and PEPFAR, I had also been dutifully performing my day job as director of NIAID, usually late into the night. I had been functioning on a maximum of four hours of sleep a night, and I had barely interacted with my children in a meaningful way in weeks. Christine was holding things together at home and was a true source of steadiness during this frenetic period. I knew things were getting out of hand when I ran into Karl Rove, senior adviser and deputy chief of staff to the president, in the hallway of the West Wing during one of my many visits to the White House. He had seen me multiple times during the previous few days and jokingly asked me where my West Wing office was.

Josh Bolten, who was becoming a good colleague and friend, must have noticed my fatigued look and felt sorry for me. He thought he would cheer me up. As I passed his office during a visit to the West Wing a few days before the State of the Union address, he said he wanted me to meet a friend of his. Sitting in Josh's office was Clark T. Randt Jr., the U.S. ambassador to China. Josh asked me to chat briefly with Ambassador Randt about our collaboration with China on AIDS research. But Josh had something else in mind. As I walked into his office, also standing there was Bo Derek looking as stunning as she did in that iconic scene in the movie *10* when she and Dudley Moore were running toward each other on the beach during one of Moore's daydreams. Derek was charming in our brief conversation. The White House is always full of surprises!

THE IRAQ WAR started on March 20, 2003, and by the week of April 11, 2003, U.S. troops occupied essentially all of Iraq. The effort now began in earnest to find the elusive weapons of mass destruction. The inability to find any weapons had a dampening effect on the intensity surrounding the biodefense effort, particularly the smallpox vaccination program. At the same time, as we had feared, we were receiving reports of adverse events associated with smallpox vaccination including myocarditis, or inflammation of the heart muscle. As knowledge of these complications spread, people became more and more reluctant to come forward to be vaccinated. In the end, relatively few people outside the military, where smallpox vaccination was mandatory, opted to get vaccinated. Thankfully, we never had a smallpox bioterror attack.

MEANWHILE, we were being attacked by another source: Mother Nature. In November 2002, health officials in mainland China had started seeing several cases of an unusual severe acute respiratory syndrome. The Chinese first reported that these cases represented severe, atypical influenza. But when a cluster of cases occurred in Hong Kong and then spread to several countries throughout the world, it became clear that we were dealing with a new infectious disease caused by a novel coronavirus, ultimately given the name SARS, indicating just what it was—namely, a severe acute respiratory syndrome. As the months went by, more and more cases would be described. SARS was evolving into a global health emergency. By March 2003, four hundred people were recognized to have been infected and several had died.

Travel to and from Hong Kong and other cities in China all but came to a standstill. By April 11, 2003, there were thirty-four hundred cases reported worldwide, but there were relatively few cases in the United States, with little indication that it was spreading to any great extent. Nonetheless, the U.S. press became energized about this possibility. During the month of April, I was interviewed on dozens of TV shows about SARS, and I tried to provide the general public with some perspective about the actual risk and alleviate some of their concerns.

By the time the outbreak burned itself out in July 2003, there had been more than 8,000 reported cases and over 750 deaths in 37 countries, with the majority of cases in Hong Kong, where the economic effects were devastating. As far as pandemics go, although the SARS outbreak was successfully contained by low-tech public health measures such as identification of infected individuals, isolation, contact tracing, and quarantines, nonetheless it validated the exact point that I had been making in countless discussions regarding our biodefense efforts including Project BioShield. Months before the SARS outbreak during a trip with the president on Air Force One on February 5, 2002, on our way back from a speech that he gave in Pittsburgh about early warning systems for bioterror attacks, he asked me, "Tony, what keeps you awake at night?"

"It's not so much the possibility of another deliberate bioterror attack, Mr. President," I said, "but more the possibility of a naturally occurring disaster such as a brand-new emerging respiratory virus that has pandemic potential."

History had taught us and it had always been in the front of my mind that nature was a more likely and more formidable bioterrorist than a human terrorist group.

You Have to Love Yogi

mid the fear of bioterror and the SARS outbreak, the stress and tension I felt were almost stifling. A bit of relief came in an unexpected way. On April 10, 2003, I flew to New York City and took the ferry to Ellis Island to receive the Ellis Island Family Heritage Award given to individuals who had made notable contributions to society and who had immigrated themselves or had ancestors who had arrived at Ellis Island or other ports. I was accompanied by Christine; my sister, Denise, and her husband, Jack Scorce; and my ninety-three-year-old father, whose father and mother at separate times had left Sicily and stepped off an ocean liner at Ellis Island at the turn of the twentieth century. It was a real thrill for my father, who, although he was born in New York City, spoke fluent Italian and taught Italian language and history as a teaching assistant when he was a student at Columbia University in the late 1920s. My mother would have loved this event because her parents had arrived at Ellis Island from Naples, Italy, at the turn of the century.

The elegant ceremony included a skillfully crafted video highlighting my personal history and professional accomplishments. I was presented with a copy of the ship's manifest containing my

grandfather's name and a photograph of the ship that brought An-
tonino Fauci, for whom I am named, to New York City in 1902.
Other awardees that day were Bob Hope (represented by his son),
the actress Cicely Tyson, Abie Abraham (hero of the Bataan Death
March), and my childhood hero Yogi Berra.

I have been an avid baseball fan for as long as I can remember.
If you were a youngster growing up in Brooklyn in the 1940s and
into the mid- to late 1950s, you had the luxury of cheering for the
New York Yankees, the New York Giants, or the Brooklyn Dodg-
ers. For reasons I cannot divine, hardly anyone in Brooklyn was a
New York Giants fan even though the Polo Grounds, where the
Giants played in upper Manhattan, and Yankee Stadium, where
the Yankees played in the Bronx, were almost equidistant from
Brooklyn. The Giants just never connected with kids from Brooklyn except for the universal adoration of their iconic center fielder
Willie Mays. In Brooklyn, you were either a Dodger fan or a Yankee fan. I was a staunch Yankee fan. In Bensonhurst, my almost
exclusively Italian American neighborhood, the first-generation
Italian American Yankee star center fielder Joe DiMaggio and shortstop Phil Rizzuto were idolized.

Another Italian American, Lawrence Berra—universally known
as Yogi—came up from the minor leagues and played his first
game with the New York Yankees on September 22, 1946, when I
was just shy of my sixth birthday. It was near the end of the season,
and Yogi played only seven games. It was not a good year for the
Yankees, who finished in third place in the American League
standings, and no one much noticed Yogi. But the fall of 1946 was
only a year after the end of World War II, and the war was still
much on the minds of the grown-ups. Yogi was a bona fide war
hero, having served in the U.S. Navy on an attack ship, the USS
Bayfield, during the D-Day invasion of Normandy. As part of a

crew that engaged in active combat, he received commendations for bravery in battle. Thus even before he swung a bat at Yankee Stadium, he started off in the good graces of New Yorkers, including Brooklynites. The next year, 1947, Yogi exploded onto the scene and was a major contributor to the New York Yankees' long and glorious string of World Series championships. He won the most valuable player in the American League three times—in 1951, 1954, and 1955. I was twenty-two years old when he stepped down as a Yankee player in 1963.

Besides being an amazing Hall of Fame athlete, Yogi was a colorful character. From the time I was five years old I idolized him. Whenever I think about baseball, Yogi is not far from my mind. And here at Ellis Island, at age sixty-two, I was sitting next to my seventy-seven-year-old hero at lunch. We chatted at length about my playing baseball on the sandlot parks of Brooklyn and how as a young boy I knew his precise batting average every day as the numbers changed depending on how many base hits he did or did not get in a game. Yogi told me how much he loved to see the exasperated expression on the opposing pitcher's face every time he whacked a base hit off a pitch way outside the strike zone. I nodded, telling him, "Yogi, my friends and I used to go nuts with glee when you drilled a high outside ball off the left field wall from the right side of the plate, especially if it was against the Brooklyn Dodgers in the World Series."

The combination of spending time with the incomparable Yogi Berra and a deep nostalgia for how I had felt about him and baseball as a young boy made for one of the most memorable days of my life. As the day ended, off I went back to the reality of Washington, D.C., the Iraq War, the fear of a bioterror attack, and the SARS epidemic.

A Reluctant Congress

By mid-April 2003, despite an exhaustive search, no weapons of mass destruction had been found in Iraq. But there was still the concern that such weapons had gotten into the hands of al-Qaeda and that this posed a clear and present danger of a biological terror attack on our homeland. Now that it appeared we had "officially" defeated Iraq, Vice President Cheney and Scooter Libby felt even more strongly that we needed the resources to protect the nation against bioterror attacks that might be a reaction to the war. They were genuinely anxious, more so than many, about the danger of future bioterror attacks.

For the first two weeks of May 2003, I spent almost all my time working with the White House staff trying to help shape the Project BioShield legislation in both the Senate and the House. I was working fourteen-to-sixteen-hour days including weekends, with almost daily briefings on Capitol Hill to help whip up support with a number of senators and congressmen. This included a memorable encounter with Senator Robert Byrd, the iconic and long-serving Democrat from West Virginia. I walked into his imposing office and gave him my well-practiced speech on why it was important for him to support mandatory spending in the Project

BioShield bill. A dignified man of eighty-five, he was courteous and let me speak uninterrupted. When I finished, he calmly reached into the left vest pocket of his sport jacket, which covered his characteristic red vest. He pulled out a three-by-five-inch booklet and waved it in front of me. In a serious tone of voice he said, "Young man"—I was sixty-two years old at the time—"do you know what this is? It is the Constitution of the United States of America, and it grants to me and my colleagues in the legislative branch what we refer to as the power of the purse. And so you go back to Vice President Cheney and tell him that I have no intention of supporting a mandatory, permanent, and indefinite appropriation."

ULTIMATELY, Project BioShield was authorized to spend $6 billion over a ten-year period from fiscal year 2004 through fiscal year 2013. The funding was not permanent, indefinite, or mandatory, and the power of the purse remained with the appropriators in Congress (Senator Byrd was pleased). However, virtually all other aspects of Project BioShield that we had argued for remained intact. The program included three key elements. First was the funding for needed medical countermeasures such as vaccines, therapeutics, and diagnostics. This fund would become available to the secretary of HHS for procurements following interagency and White House approval.

Next was the facilitation of research and development. Here Project BioShield granted me as director of NIAID the special authorities, referred to as other transactions authorities, to expedite the solicitation and award of grants and contracts for the development of critical medical countermeasures.

Finally, Project BioShield established for the FDA an emergency use authorization to provide access to the best available medical countermeasures following a declaration of emergency by the secretary of HHS. The declaration could be based on the secretary's determination of either a public health emergency with a significant potential to affect national security or a high risk of a chemical, biological, radiological, or nuclear attack on the public or on U.S. military forces.

Before BioShield, our efforts to develop nuclear and radiological countermeasures were fragmented. After the fall of the Soviet Union and the end of the cold war, the Department of Defense understandably gave that program a low priority. Vice President Cheney was quite concerned about this potential gap in our preparedness and encouraged a ramping up of activity to develop a series of medical interventions that would counter the effects of radiological attacks such as a dirty bomb that might not cause immediate and massive destruction but that might have insidious long-term effects.

The concepts that we had established with Project BioShield were extended a few years later when, under the leadership of the North Carolina Republican senator Richard Burr, Congress passed and President Bush signed the Pandemic and All-Hazards Preparedness Act. The purpose of the act was to "improve the nation's public health and medical preparedness and response capabilities for emergencies, whether deliberate, accidental, or natural." The act established within HHS a new assistant secretary for preparedness and response. Tommy Thompson appointed Stewart Simonson, who had been my strong ally in developing Project BioShield, as the first assistant secretary of this new entity. The act also provided new authorities for a number of programs including the Biomedical Advanced Research and Development Authority (BARDA). BARDA would become the lead component within HHS for the development of medical countermeasures. The new legislation provided BARDA with both authorities and funding that would enable more flexible contracting to support advanced research and development of medical countermeasures. Importantly, these new authorities and funding could be directed as much to naturally occurring microbial outbreaks as to deliberate bioterror attacks. This is something for which I had been pushing ever since we began the biodefense program following the attacks of 9/11 and has been put to use for every naturally occurring emerging infectious disease outbreak since.

Iraq

I had never been anywhere near a war zone. I was born as World
War II was beginning to unfold. I was a young boy during the
Korean War, and I had the privilege of helping to take care of
navy and marine personnel who were wounded during the Vietnam War when I served from the late 1960s to the early 1970s as
an infectious disease consultant to the Bethesda Naval Hospital
across the street from the NIH. I served for twenty-seven years in
the U.S. Public Health Service, achieving the rank of rear admiral
before I retired from the service and continued on at the NIH as a
civil servant. But I had never served in the armed forces and
thus had never been anywhere near harm's way during hostile activities.

It had been just under a year since the United States had invaded Iraq, and I had long wanted to visit the country, to show my
respect for members of our armed forces and to bolster the morale
of the medical establishment there, which had been severely neglected by Saddam Hussein. Security concerns had delayed the
trip, and given the evolving insurgency situation, I was not sure
how great the risk would be. Recently there had been a substantial
escalation of insurgent activity and terrorism with many suicide

bombings and rocket-propelled grenade attacks on both military and civilian targets. It appeared that the insurgents were targeting Iraqis who were cooperating with U.S. officials who were trying to rebuild the country.

In February 2004, I was asked to be part of an official presidentially sponsored delegation led by Tommy Thompson to evaluate the health and medical situation in Iraq and to determine if the U.S. government, particularly HHS, could provide assistance there. The hope was that this might be the beginning of a program to bring more medical assistance to the Middle East to counterbalance our military presence there. Christine and particularly our daughters—now seventeen, fourteen, and eleven—were very worried about my going and tried to talk me out of it. Christine was close to adamant about my not going. Jenny, not unexpectedly, was the most vocal: "Dad, I really don't want you to go." But during an intense family meeting around our breakfast room table, I argued that my visit would be important symbolically, that this was something I really wanted to do, and that the risks were probably minimal because I would have heavy security as part of a presidential delegation. Finally, they said, "Okay, if you must go, then go, but please come back in one piece."

THE DELEGATION TOOK OFF for Amman, Jordan, on February 26, 2004, from Andrews Air Force Base (now named Joint Base Andrews) in Prince George's County, Maryland, a few miles outside Washington, D.C. The initial leg of the trip was in a U.S. Air Force Gulfstream jet. In addition to Tommy Thompson, the team included Bill Steiger, now head of the Office of Global Affairs at HHS, and Dr. Andrew von Eschenbach, director of the National Cancer Institute, as well as Admiral Craig Vanderwagen of the U.S. Public Health Service. We also were joined by several members of the press including my longtime friends CNN producer Christy Feig and CNN medical correspondent Dr. Sanjay Gupta.

We landed at Marka International Airport in Amman after an eleven-hour flight and almost immediately changed planes to a much less comfortable but much larger Air Force C-141 transport plane that took us on the brief flight to Baghdad. It was toward the end of this flight that I got my first taste of what it was like to be in a war zone. In the approach to Baghdad International Airport just outside central Baghdad, the air force pilot initiated what the air force personnel told me later was a sharp corkscrew landing that terrifyingly felt from inside the plane as if we had actually flipped over. They explained to us that this was the standard way to lessen the likelihood of being hit by a shoulder-fired surface-to-air missile as well as by sporadic fire from AK-47 assault rifles fired by insurgents. They also said that the airport was randomly attacked by mortars every day. Our air force hosts assured us that these were just pockets of insurgents who rarely hit their targets. I did not ask what "rarely" actually meant in military terms. The real targets were the convoys of troops that accompanied the armored SUVs in which I would soon be riding.

Almost immediately upon landing at Baghdad International Airport, we began the trip along a highway that was referred to as "ambush alley" because of the number of insurgent attacks on convoys traveling from the airport to the relatively safe Green Zone in downtown Baghdad, where we were headed. Our convoy consisted of several carloads of security personnel from the Department of Defense, all armed with M4 automatic rifles, as well as U.S. Army Military Police in four Humvees with a fixed .50-caliber machine gun on each vehicle. The trip into Baghdad was both exhilarating and frightening because we had no idea what to expect. Tommy had me sit with him in his car. The drill during the motorcade was that every time we passed a person walking along the highway or a parked car, someone in the security detail either on foot or in their vehicle would insert themselves between the "suspects" and our car. As we approached an overpass, the military police in the Humvees aimed their machine guns up and swung around the gun turret as we drove under the overpass and emerged on the other side. I later asked the reason for such a maneuver and was told that frequently insurgents dropped explosive devices from the overpasses and then ran away. I was beginning to appreciate and empathize with the extraordinary stress that our military in Iraq was under day after day.

Our first stop in the Baghdad Green Zone was at the headquarters of the Coalition Provisional Authority (CPA) located in the main imperial palace, which had been used by Saddam Hussein. Here we met with Ambassador Paul "Jerry" Bremer, the head of the CPA. We had an enlightening discussion with Ambassador Bremer regarding the difficulties in transitioning from control of the country by the CPA to control by the Iraqi Governing Council. Bremer made the interesting statement that democracy was a difficult concept for some Iraqis to grasp and that they were having a hard time agreeing what form their new government should take. In the United States democracy means that the majority rules, but the minority also has considerable influence, and the balance of power can and does change with elections. But, Bremer explained, the Iraqis in general were suspicious of majority rule because in their experience minorities often had been severely persecuted. Only later, as the years went by and the situation in Iraq became more complicated after the U.S. military phased out and the CPA gave way to the Iraqi Governing Council, did I fully realize the significance of this conversation. It became clear to me how difficult it is for certain countries and societies to live comfortably and peacefully under a democratic system. I was getting a first-hand glimpse of the problems that would beset Iraq in the ensuing years.

THE DEFINING EXPERIENCE of that first day in Iraq was our visit to the famous Ibn Sina Hospital in the Green Zone, which had been converted to the combat trauma support hospital for the U.S. military. I had seen wounded marines and naval personnel at the Bethesda Naval Hospital during the Vietnam War. I was not naive to the terrible effects of combat on the human body and mind. However, my experience at the Ibn Sina Hospital was more intense by orders of magnitude. In the States, wounded service men and women had been evacuated by air days, weeks, or even months before to the state-of-the-art Bethesda Naval Hospital. Here these men and women had been wounded minutes to hours earlier, and there was a continual stream of wounded being brought into the hospital. Another obvious difference was that here everyone carried a weapon including the military doctors who were performing procedures either in the operating room or in the trauma rooms. This was usually a Beretta M9 pistol either attached to a waist belt and strapped to their thigh or in a shoulder holster. No one went anywhere without a weapon. I tried but could not imagine myself making rounds on my patients at the NIH Clinical Center with a weapon on my hip.

I saw several young soldiers and marines who ranged in age from eighteen to early twenties with all forms of wounds including shattered legs and abdominal wounds mostly from improvised explosive devices. As I was walking through the ward, a soldier was wheeled in right in front of me. He had been shot in the face, and the bullet went cheek to cheek, entering one side of his face and coming out the other without hitting any vital structures apart from a few teeth. He was wincing in pain and seemed to be in a state of mental shock that I guessed would not go away anytime soon. A medic explained to me that the troops wore body armor up to their neck and a helmet down to their eyes, and so their faces were one of the few exposed parts of the upper body.

Soldiers and marines were not the only people who were cared for at the hospital. I saw several wounded Iraqi citizens who had been caught in cross fire as well as Iraqi insurgents. One wounded insurgent getting an X-ray was being guarded by someone who almost certainly was a U.S. Special Forces soldier because he was not wearing a typical military uniform; he had a well-trimmed beard and wore a brown T-shirt underneath a khaki vest, sunglasses, a bandanna wrapped around his neck, and a baseball cap. I also saw an Iraqi who I was told had been working as a translator with a Special Forces unit. Apparently, another Iraqi had come up to him when no one was around and shot him in the back of the head; the bullet miraculously missed his brain, passing through his left posterior jaw and exiting his face. When he was taken to the hospital, he told the Special Forces soldier who had helped bring him in who his attacker was and where he could likely be found. The Special Forces soldier turned around and without saying a word stormed out of the hospital. The medical team told me they could only imagine where he was going and what he was about to do.

I was barely able to shake these searing images as I left the trauma unit and went on to tour the rest of the hospital. I spent the next forty-five minutes shaking hands and chatting with the physicians and nurses. Some of them recognized me from my recent TV news appearances, but more often they had studied from the frequently updated medical textbook *Harrison's Principles of Internal Medicine*, of which I had been an editor since 1983, while they were in medical school and during their residency training. They seemed excited to meet me, which made me feel totally embarrassed because I felt so privileged to be in the same room with them and to have the opportunity to thank them personally for their service. That hospital experience dramatically demonstrated to me, the way no written account could, the horrors of war as well as the bravery and commitment of our young men and women in uniform.

FEBRUARY 29, 2004, my last day in Iraq, was as eventful as the others. We spent almost the entire day in the Red Zone, the designated unsafe area, and the security was intense. The traffic was heavy as our convoy worked its way from facility to facility including the office of the Iraqi Ministry of Health as well as several local medical clinics. The tension in the members of our security detail was palpable as we got stuck in traffic jams in narrow streets. Most of the time, our detail jumped out of their vehicles and walked or jogged alongside our SUVs, M4s cocked, hyperalert to the cars and people that we passed as well as to the rooftops of the buildings we passed. Although I never felt that I was in any real danger, I was still glad my daughters were not observing this!

We then left for Baghdad airport, where we met General Curtis "Mike" Scaparrotti, the highly decorated chief of combat maneuvers. He brought Tommy Thompson and me into the base command room to show us how they tracked hostilities in real time on a computerized map screen. He introduced us to his chief of intelligence and his combat coordinator, and they walked us through some of the activities on the screen. An ambush had just taken place in the Red Zone, and they described how a unit was immediately dispatched to help out. It was an eerie experience to watch events so near to us play out on a screen.

WE THEN LOADED into three Black Hawk helicopters to fly to Balad Air Base to catch a C-17 to Rhein-Main Air Base in Germany, where we would pick up the Gulfstream and fly back to Andrews Air Force Base. The trip in the Black Hawk was the last of the truly unnerving experiences on this incredible trip. We flew about a hundred to two hundred feet off the ground in pitch darkness with nothing but a few dim red lights in the cabin of the helicopter. I sat about two feet from the machine gunner, who was clutching the handles on a .50-caliber gun. He told me that his job was to focus on the ground and look for flashes from small arms fire and hopefully not a rocket-propelled grenade. If he saw the flash from the latter, he would notify the pilot to take evasive maneuvers. He said he was not really worried about small arms fire because it almost never hit the speeding helicopter. As I recall, I took some comfort in his confidence . . . I think.

Influenza Meets
the Supply Chain

Never a dull moment in Washington. We had just returned from Iraq. My family, who had been on pins and needles for the entire time I was away, was enormously relieved to have me home, but there was little time to absorb all that I had seen. Something was brewing in my area of infectious disease that had bubbled over into the public consciousness and was causing anxiety. It was related to an influenza virus that had emerged among chickens and was beginning to infect humans in China. The fact that humans became infected with a bird virus immediately generated concerns throughout the world, including in the United States, about the possibility of a pandemic influenza outbreak.

People have feared this kind of natural disaster since the historic global pandemic of influenza in 1918, often referred to erroneously as the Spanish flu. In reality, that global pandemic might have actually started in the United States toward the end of World War I, and it claimed the lives of between 50 and 100 million people worldwide. The population of the world then was 1.8 billion, making this equivalent to 200 to 400 million deaths today. There were more deaths due to influenza among military personnel on both sides of the conflict than deaths due to bullets and bombs. At that time there were no vaccines for influenza, no antibiotics for the secondary bacterial infections that killed many influenza-infected people, and no intensive care units that might have saved many lives and thus might have mitigated the impact of the pandemic.

Of note, in 1918 the influenza virus had not yet been identified. Today we know an enormous amount about influenza. There are two major types of influenza: influenza A and influenza B. The most common type is influenza A, which has been the cause of all known influenza pandemics. Different influenza A viruses are designated by an international classification according to the types of protein on the surface of the virus. Two of the most important influenza surface proteins are hemagglutinin and neuraminidase, represented by the letters *H* and *N*, respectively, together with a number next to each letter. There are eighteen separate H proteins and eleven separate N proteins among influenza A viruses. Each virus has an *H* with a given number and an *N* with a given number. The pandemic of 1918 was caused by an influenza virus with the designation of H1N1. Influenza viruses did not start off evolutionarily as human viruses, and only a small proportion of these have infected humans. The remainder are animal influenzas, primarily viruses of wild waterfowl such as ducks.

Over centuries, certain of the influenza viruses have adapted very well to humans such that now we generally consider them human viruses, although they remain prevalent in many species of birds including chickens, as well as in mammals such as pigs, hence the term "swine flu" for some viruses. The pandemic of 1918 is thought to have originated from a bird influenza that jumped species to humans.

Each year human outbreaks of influenza occur almost invariably during the winter season in a given region of the world. In the

United States and other Northern Hemisphere countries, this seasonal outbreak usually takes place from December through March. In the Southern Hemisphere in countries such as Australia, the winter flu season is June through September. The occurrence of seasonal influenza is predictable in that we are almost guaranteed to have an outbreak every winter. However, the precise influenza virus that will dominate during any given winter is much less predictable.

From one year to another there is usually a slight change in the circulating influenza virus caused mostly by mutations in the genetic makeup of the virus. This slight change is referred to as a drift. Because of exposures to influenza viruses over previous years as well as the protection afforded by vaccinations, most of the world has some degree of what is known as background immunity to influenza. This at least partially protects us from actual infection or from serious disease caused by the infection. This is the reason we do not have a global catastrophic outbreak of influenza every year.

In contrast, when an influenza virus emerges that is markedly different from previous years, the phenomenon is referred to as a shift in the virus. Because this very different virus is new to most people, there is little background protection against the novel strain. This can lead to a high rate of global infection and an increased level of suffering and death. Such outbreaks are referred to as pandemics.

After the pandemic of 1918, the next pandemic occurred in 1957 with a brand-new influenza virus referred to as H2N2. During that pandemic there were 1 to 2 million deaths globally. A subsequent pandemic occurred in 1968 with a new influenza virus referred to as H3N2. This pandemic resulted in roughly 700,000 deaths worldwide. Since then, H3N2 influenza viruses have transitioned and evolved over the years to become the typical seasonal

My parents, Eugenia (age nineteen) and Stephen (age eighteen), on their wedding day, 1929.
Credit: Fauci collection

In my stroller at age two in Bensonhurst, Brooklyn, 1943.
Credit: Fauci collection

My father's drugstore in Dyker Heights, Brooklyn, circa 1950.
We lived in the apartment above the store. *Credit: Fauci collection*

My parents working together in the Fauci Pharmacy in the midfifties.
Credit: Fauci collection

Playing point guard (#4) for Regis High School, 1958.
Credit: Fauci collection

Graduating medical school, 1966.
Credit: Fauci collection

The first year of my fellowship at NIH, 1969. Group portrait of the Laboratory of Clinical Investigation with insets of me and my mentor, Dr. Shelly Wolff. *Credit: Fauci collection*

Me (bottom row, far right) as chief medical resident at The New York Hospital–Cornell Medical Center with senior staff and fellow residents, 1971. *Credit: Fauci collection*

With my longtime colleague Dr. Cliff Lane, working together as usual during the AIDS years, circa 1986. *Credit: NIH*

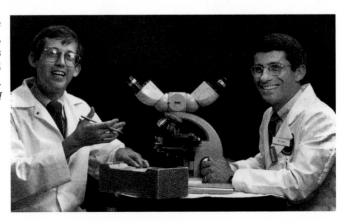

Christine and me
on our wedding day,
May 18, 1985.
*Credit: Fauci/Grady
collection*

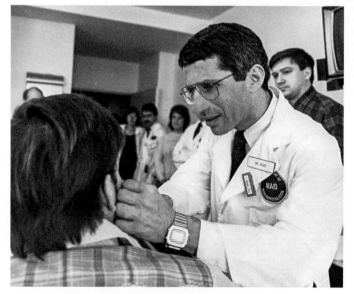

Making rounds
on a patient
with my team,
circa 1982.
Credit: NIH

Christine and me running the Marine Corps Marathon in Washington, D.C., November 1984. This was taken just before she sprinted ahead of me to cross the finish line.
Credit: Fauci/Grady collection

Dr. C. Everett Koop, surgeon general of the United States and my good friend, giving me the Surgeon General's Medal just prior to his retirement, 1989. I am wearing my rear admiral uniform of the U.S. Public Health Service.
Credit: NIH

"Uncle" Jim Hill, my beloved friend and NIAID deputy director, with two-year-old Jenny, 1988.
Credit: Fauci/Grady collection

In the Oval Office, turning down President George H. W. Bush's
offer to become director of NIH, 1989.
Credit: The White House

Meeting with members of ACT UP New York at the Gay and Lesbian
Community Center in Greenwich Village, New York, 1989. *Credit: T.L. Litt*

Christine and me
on vacation in
San Gimignano,
Italy, 2006.
*Credit: Fauci/Grady
collection*

From left to right, my daughters Jenny, Megan, and Alison on the beach
at Beach Haven, New Jersey, 1996. *Credit Fauci/Grady collection*

With children in a remote village in Uganda in 2001, one of my several trips to Africa that convinced me of the need for a PEPFAR-like program in southern Africa.

Credit: Fauci collection

My trip to Iraq, February 2004. Pictured here after landing at Baghdad International Airport with the U.S. Army Military Police unit that escorted us to the Green Zone. Civilians from left to right: Howard Zucker (HHS), me, HHS Secretary Tommy Thompson, National Cancer Institute Director Andrew von Eschenbach. *Credit: Fauci collection*

President George W. Bush presenting me with the Presidential Medal of Freedom for my role in the creation of PEPFAR, June 19, 2008. *Credit: Ron Edmonds/AP*

Making ward rounds with the senior staff, fellows, residents, nurses, and other providers on our patients at the NIH Clinical Center, circa 2018. Cliff Lane is on the far right. *Credit: Fauci collection*

Briefing President Obama in the White House Situation Room on pandemic preparedness, February 12, 2010. *Credit: The White House*

We cared for Nina Pham, an Ebola patient, at the NIH Clinical Center. On her release on October 24, 2014, I hugged her in front of dozens of TV cameras to help dispel the stigma associated with Ebola patients.
Credit: Pablo Martínez Monsiváis /AP

Getting dressed ("donned") with extensive personal protective equipment (PPE) in preparation for entering a room to care for an Ebola patient at NIH, March 2015.
Credit: NIH

With my youthful
seventy-nine-year-old
sister, Denise, 2017.
Credit: Fauci collection

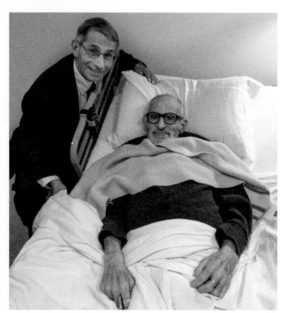

Visiting my dear friend Larry
Kramer in a convalescent
facility in Greenwich Village,
New York, in 2019. Larry
died on May 27, 2020.
Credit: Fauci collection

At the podium of the White House press briefing room during one of many COVID briefings, circa March 2020. President Trump and Vice President Pence are looking on. *Credit: The White House*

Throwing out the "aberrant" first pitch on opening day at Nationals Park, July 23, 2020. *Credit: Alex Brandon/AP*

In the White House press briefing room during the Biden Administration with Press Secretary Jen Psaki and COVID Response Coordinator Jeff Zients, April 13, 2021. *Credit: The White House*

The head of my HHS security team, Special Agent Brett Rowland, became a close friend to me and Christine, November 2020.
Credit: Fauci/Grady collection

My successful attempt at timpano, an Italian pasta delicacy inspired by actor Stanley Tucci in the movie *Big Night*, December 2022. Christine celebrated with me.
Credit: Fauci/Grady collection

The Fauci Family on a 2023 trip to Sicily. Left to right: me, Ali, Jenny, Megan, and Christine holding granddaughter Lina.
Credit: Fauci/Grady collection

Celebrating my retirement from NIH with my good friend Peter Staley, former ACT UP New York activist, in a Washington, D.C., restaurant, December 2022. *Credit: Fauci collection*

Christine and me saying goodbye to President Joe Biden in the Oval Office after I stepped down as his chief medical adviser, January 2023. *Credit: The White House*

Playing with and loving my eight-month-old granddaughter, Lina, during a Christmas visit, December 2023. *Credit: Fauci/Grady collection*

influenza virus that we experience with varying degrees of drifts each year. The most recent influenza pandemic, which occurred in 2009, originated somewhere near the border of California and Mexico. This was a relatively mild pandemic referred to as H1N1 swine flu because it jumped species from a pig to the human population. The global mortality estimates from that pandemic ranged from 151,000 to 575,000.

Influenza viruses have long been an intermittent and sometimes major problem for chickens—and chicken farmers. Entire flocks of chickens can get infected and either die or need to be culled to prevent further spread to other flocks. Note, not all chicken influenza viruses are especially harmful to the chickens and do not require dramatic measures such as massive culling. While chicken influenzas occur worldwide, they are most common in the Far East, particularly in China. Occasionally, one of these chicken influenza viruses jumps species to infect one or two people, but these occurrences are rare and do not attract much attention. This was not the case in the spring of 1997, when an influenza virus designated H5N1 infected and caused high mortality in three chicken farms in Hong Kong. Soon thereafter there were reports from Hong Kong of avian influenza H5N1 infections that had jumped from chickens to eighteen humans. The more troubling problem was that six of these people died, a case fatality rate of 33 percent. This was astronomical compared with the usual death rate of seasonal influenza, which is a fraction of 1 percent. Even in the catastrophic 1918 pandemic, the mortality rate was only 1 to 2 percent.

The fear that this virus might develop the capability of spreading easily from human to human, together with the economic considerations associated with a highly pathogenic chicken virus spreading to other chicken farms, led the health authorities in Hong Kong to take drastic measures. They did a mass culling, killing essentially all of the chickens in Hong Kong. This draconian course of action ended the 1997 H5N1 outbreak among chickens, and thus there were no additional human infections.

FOR THE NEXT six years H5N1 fell off the radar screen. That changed in 2003 when it reemerged in China and spread to countries in Asia and Southeast Asia. Of concern were the sporadic human cases that occurred. In one situation, health officials could not rule out the possibility of human-to-human transmission within a family unit. This is what we were facing at the end of February 2004, when I returned from Iraq.

Over the twenty years that I had been director of NIAID, threats of pandemics almost never turned into actual pandemics, and there was no solid evidence at that point of efficient or sustained human-to-human transmission of H5N1 influenza, which would be the first indication of a looming pandemic. Nonetheless, we began the public health and scientific process of preparing for the worst. In the broad sense, the CDC was responsible for the public health aspects of the preparedness and response to a potential outbreak. They carefully tracked the cases in collaboration with their Chinese and other Asian counterparts and were prepared to identify, isolate, and contact trace infected individuals if the virus ever entered our country. At NIAID my colleagues and I began the process of doing what we do best—developing and testing vaccines against this new influenza strain.

As part of this effort, in the early fall of 2004, we launched the NIAID Influenza Genome Sequencing Project in collaboration with other HHS agencies and other non-HHS organizations to determine the complete genetic sequences of H5N1 viruses from thousands of chickens and from the occasional human who was infected. We rapidly provided the sequences to the broader scientific community funded predominantly by NIAID. This was information they required both to do the nuts-and-bolts research on the testing of sensitivity to known anti-influenza drugs such as Tamiflu and to begin the important process of developing a pre-pandemic vaccine. All this was proceeding very well. But then we hit a trouble spot on another front that diverted our attention.

THE SUPPLY OF INFLUENZA vaccines administered in the United States each year for seasonal influenza generally becomes available in the early fall preceding the winter influenza season. The United States usually obtains its seasonal influenza vaccines from several pharmaceutical companies based throughout the world. For the 2004–5 influenza season we were expecting between forty-six and forty-eight million doses from the Chiron Corporation and about fifty-two million doses from other companies. During the summer of 2004 at the peak time of vaccine preparation and production, the FDA and the CDC were informed that there was a "minor problem" with about four million doses being produced in Chiron's Liverpool, U.K., plant due to bacterial contamination. The FDA and the CDC were led to believe that this problem was "being taken care of." But on October 5, 2004, the British regulatory agency abruptly suspended Chiron's license to ship the influenza vaccine to the United States because the Liverpool plant failed to pass inspection. This came as a big surprise to the FDA and was a huge issue for the United States because this would result in a severe shortage of seasonal influenza vaccine doses in the fall and winter of 2004–5. So the rising concern for a potential H5N1 bird flu pandemic was compounded by the reality of a vaccine shortage for seasonal flu. And what had started off as a purely public health issue quickly evolved into a political hot potato as we happened to be in the final months of the 2004 election campaign.

Almost immediately there was an explosion of press interest and an array of congressional hearings. On October 8, 2004, just three days after the British regulatory agency suspended the Chiron license, the CDC director, Julie Gerberding, the acting FDA commissioner, Lester Crawford, and I testified before the House Government Reform Committee regarding the broader issue of the fragility of the influenza vaccine supply. I totally believed that my FDA colleagues were telling the truth when they said they were not told about the seriousness of the situation in the Liverpool plant until the British announced the suspension of the Chiron license.

On October 12, I gave a White House briefing in which I reiterated my confidence that the FDA was correct because I was hearing from other sources that their story matched with the way others had seen the events unfold. But the damage had already been done from a public perception standpoint, and we had to deal with it. The president's aides were concerned that Senator John Kerry, the Democratic nominee for president, would try to embarrass President Bush in the presidential debate to be held the next night by claiming that the FDA knew about the problem and covered it up. The last thing that I wanted to do was to get involved in a fight between political parties, something I had successfully avoided for so many years as director of NIAID. But the political game was on. I offered my humble suggestion that they just come out with the plain truth, and that the president state outright that a contamination in the vaccine plant was the cause of our potential vaccine shortage.

During the debate, that is how it played out. President Bush admitted right up front in response to a question from one of the moderators, Bob Schieffer of CBS, that "we relied upon a company out of England to provide about half of the flu vaccines for the United States citizens, and it turned out that the vaccine they were producing was contaminated." The president then took the high ground: "And so we took the right action and didn't allow contaminated medicine into our country." When asked to comment on President Bush's answer, Senator Kerry changed the subject and talked about the weaknesses in our health-care system and how they had gotten worse over the past four years of the Bush administration. The debate went on to other issues.

George W. Bush was reelected on November 2, 2004. I doubt if the issue of the Chiron vaccine debacle had any effect one way or another on the voting. And the fact that the election was over seemed to defuse the tension around this issue. The 2004–5 influenza season came and went without incident. Relatively speaking, the public health impact of the vaccine shortage was insignificant. We were lucky.

No sooner had the second term of the Bush administration begun than the situation with H5N1 influenza started heating up again. In January 2005 we learned of the first documented human-to-human transmission of the H5N1 bird flu in Thailand. The bird flu issue again loomed large, and we accelerated the process of developing a pre-pandemic vaccine against the circulating H5N1 bird flu.

The development of a vaccine against an emerging influenza virus such as H5N1 is a complicated process that starts off with the isolation of the virus in question. Usually the CDC as well as the WHO obtains the virus specimens and creates what is referred to as seed viruses that are manipulated to grow readily in chicken eggs. Growing the virus in eggs is the standard method of obtaining enough virus to produce an influenza vaccine. A consensus is developed as to what the best seed virus is—that is, the one that grows most efficiently in eggs—and then this virus is distributed to various pharmaceutical companies so that they can manufacture test doses of vaccine. Some of these doses are then given to us at NIAID to test in various clinical trials.

When a new vaccine is being made, you need to know if it is safe and if it induces a response (immunogenicity) in the person being injected that would predict that when that person gets exposed to the actual virus, they will be protected. In other words, if I vaccinate you, I can measure antibodies in your blood that tell me even before you get exposed to or infected with the virus whether those antibodies will protect you against infection. That is called "predictive of being protective against exposure to the virus," and it is an important aspect in NIAID's early clinical trials.

At the same time the NIAID vaccine trials are being conducted, the various pharmaceutical companies begin accelerated production of vaccine that the government ultimately purchases for the stockpile. The clinical trials tell us what the optimal dosage and number of doses are for the various populations who might receive the vaccine, such as adults, the elderly, and children. This entire process takes several months at a minimum.

ON APRIL 27, 2005, Julie Gerberding and I briefed President Bush and his senior staff in the White House about the current situation with the H5N1 bird flu. The epicenter of bird-to-human transmissions had shifted to Vietnam, where several individual cases were reported.

The president was in good spirits as he entered the Roosevelt

Room from the Oval Office, joking with people in the room including the newly appointed HHS secretary, Mike Leavitt, former governor of Utah, before taking his seat at the center of the large wooden table. Julie gave a quick summary on the increasing number of bird-to-human cases and human-to-human cases being reported from Southeast Asia and Indonesia. The president turned to me: "Okay, Fauci, your turn." "Mr. President, thus far the safety and potency of the candidate H5N1 vaccine look good," I said. Discussion turned to the need to stockpile H5N1 influenza vaccine once it was adequately tested. This was of particular interest to Vice President Cheney and Scooter Libby because both of them had been major driving forces in establishing Project BioShield and supporting the Strategic National Stockpile.

By August, we had successfully demonstrated in normal volunteers that with the proper dose we could induce responses that we could predict would be protective against the H5N1 influenza were it to develop into an outbreak. The remaining challenge was to make enough vaccine in the immediate future to have a sufficient stockpile of tens of millions of doses and to be able to scale up to hundreds of millions of doses in the event of a pandemic.

The good news regarding the potential efficacy of the vaccine was tempered by the recent sobering news that migratory birds that likely were infected by the chickens in China and the Far East had brought the H5N1 infection to chicken flocks in Russia, Mongolia, and Kazakhstan, and birds using established flyways would likely bring the infection to India and Europe. Given the international implications of the virus's spread, I was asked to brief Condoleezza Rice, now secretary of state, on August 17. Although the tone of the briefing was serious, Condi joked that every time we met it was about some real or potential global health crisis. She said she was glad to see me, but we both knew the truth.

THE POSSIBILITY OF an influenza pandemic was completely overshadowed by a real catastrophe that took place on August 23, 2005, when Hurricane Katrina struck Louisiana and Mississippi. In the aftermath of this tragedy—one of the most horrific natural disasters in the history of the United States—the Bush administration, particularly the Federal Emergency Management Agency, and even the president himself were sharply criticized for their inadequate response to the hurricane. This criticism generated an increased sensitivity on the part of the administration to never again be unprepared for natural disasters. When I again briefed the president in the Roosevelt Room on our progress in developing a pre-pandemic vaccine about ten days after Katrina made landfall, he was emphatic: "Fauci, failure is not an option here."

ON OCTOBER 6, Mike Leavitt and I briefed President Bush and his senior staff in the Oval Office for a meeting the next day with the senior executives of major pharmaceutical companies. The president sat in his usual chair in front of the fireplace. "Mr. President," I said, "our capacity to manufacture influenza vaccines is rather fragile. Remember the disaster with the Liverpool contamination." I went on to tell him that our ability to scale up rapidly in response to a pandemic outbreak was weak, particularly when we had to rely on the rate of growth of viruses in eggs to produce vaccines. For this reason I said we needed to get more companies to invest in newer technologies and that it would be helpful if he emphasized this point.

The next day, the president walked into his meeting and got

right to the point. He emphasized the importance of revitalizing our vaccine production capacity not only for the immediate issue of H5N1 influenza but also for every seasonal influenza. He told the pharmaceutical executives that we needed to ramp up capacity and create a sustainable market for seasonal influenza vaccine that would provide a major head start in the event of a pandemic flu.

The pharmaceutical executives left that meeting with a clear message from the president. How they would respond was less clear.

I left with clarity on a different issue. We did not just need to increase our vaccine production capacity. That would be only an incremental improvement. What we needed was a game changer. We just had to do better than continually chasing after each new emerging influenza strain. We needed a "universal" influenza vaccine—one vaccine for all strains of influenza, be they seasonal or pandemic. In 2010, we began in earnest a concentrated research effort at NIAID to develop one.

FOR THE NEXT YEAR, the interest in H5N1 influenza among the media, Congress, and the general public waxed and waned depending on the occurrence or not of new infections in chickens in various parts of the Far East, eastern Europe, and North Africa. Despite this interest the number of actual cases in humans remained relatively low. By the end of May 2006 there had been 218 confirmed cases of bird flu in humans associated with 124 deaths.

By late 2008, from a countermeasures standpoint we were as prepared as we could be. We had successfully developed an H5N1 vaccine and had stockpiled forty million doses to be able to vaccinate twenty million people with the required two doses apiece. In addition, we had stockpiled a considerable amount of antiflu medications, particularly Tamiflu. While the virus continued to smolder among chickens, it never evolved the capacity to spread efficiently from human to human, there were no human infections of bird flu in the United States, and we never experienced a pandemic outbreak of H5N1.

But once again, we were lucky. I believed then that as long as there were viruses or other pathogens that infect animals and that could evolve molecularly to infect humans, there was a risk of spillover, similar to what we had seen with SARS in 2002–3. This was especially true in places such as Southeast Asia where animals live in proximity to humans—on farms or in the wild—known as the animal-human interface.

One might imagine that it would be terribly frustrating to put in enormous efforts of preparation for events that never happen. However, that is not how I feel. At NIAID, our job was to conduct and support the basic and clinical research that would allow us to develop the best possible vaccines, treatments, and diagnostics for any future pandemics. I knew that sooner or later the day could come when our efforts at preparedness might save millions of lives.

Legacies

T oward the end of any presidential administration regardless of the party in power, there is a growing sense of urgency to complete projects and initiate new projects that might serve as a presidential legacy before the hard deadline of stepping down.

It was already clear that PEPFAR would be a major part of the Bush legacy. Now Josh Bolten, Gary Edson, and Mike Gerson were talking about whether and how to apply a PEPFAR-like approach to other diseases of global health importance, particularly malaria, tuberculosis, and what are referred to as neglected tropical diseases. These latter diseases include the helminths, or roundworms, that so often infest the gastrointestinal tracts of people (especially children) in developing countries, leading to severe malnutrition and wasting. They also include leprosy and African sleeping sickness. The mortality of these diseases is not as high as tuberculosis, malaria, or untreated HIV infection, but they cause significant morbidity and chronic suffering, as well as impede the economic development of the countries involved.

NIAID was the leading funder in the world of research on the treatment and prevention of malaria and tuberculosis. The Bill &

Melinda Gates Foundation was a close second. Most malaria experts agreed that any program aimed at controlling and eliminating malaria would have to go well beyond just research support and would have to involve implementation of many of the tools that were already available to us. It was this latter step that was lagging. Mike Gerson made this his thing.

Mike had transitioned from being President Bush's primary speechwriter to now his senior adviser and assistant. On March 7, 2005, he came to my office at the NIH for a crash course in malaria. While he was there, he wanted me to show him around the mosquito insectarium, a room full of glass cases where millions of swarming *Anopheles* mosquitoes are bred for a variety of experiments on malaria. A visit to the insectarium was not usually a stop on the typical NIH tour, but this showed the deep dive Mike was taking into this subject.

With Malaria 101 under his belt, Mike went on to play a major role in putting together the President's Malaria Initiative, established in June 2005. The goal of this program was to reduce malaria-related mortality by 50 percent in fifteen highly affected countries in sub-Saharan Africa through a rapid scale-up of highly effective malaria prevention and treatment measures. These included insecticide-treated mosquito nets; indoor residual spraying with insecticides; accurate diagnosis and prompt treatment with artemisinin-based combination therapies (artemisinin is one of the most highly effective antimalarial drugs ever developed); and intermittent preventive treatment of pregnant women. Within ten years the program was associated with a dramatic decrease in annual global deaths due to malaria from more than 600,000 to about 400,000 deaths per year.

Although we had never formally met, Bill Gates was a potentially strong ally and partner in the fight against malaria. Bill, through the Bill & Melinda Gates Foundation, was agitating for the scientific and global health community to boldly consider the possibility of actually eradicating malaria from the planet, and he wanted to work with the U.S. government and NIAID in particular toward this goal.

When I finally met Bill, it was at a private dinner that he held for a group of international global health leaders. As Melinda gave the group a tour of their magnificent home, Xanadu 2.0, just outside Seattle, Bill pulled me aside for a one-on-one conversation in his elegantly appointed library. As we sat surrounded by floor-to-ceiling bookcases that reflected his reputation as a prodigious reader, he peppered me with questions about how I ran NIAID; what my management structure was for the institute; how I navigated the politics of Washington, D.C., while running a scientific enterprise; how I prioritized our research efforts; how much flexibility I had with the budget; what it was like to have put together the PEP-FAR program for President Bush; and on and on. His intellectual acumen, curiosity, and willingness to learn were on clear display. I was given a quick window into what makes Bill Gates tick. Over several subsequent years we became friends and collaborated in diverse areas—not just on malaria but also on developing an HIV vaccine, and tuberculosis research and control, among other public health issues.

ABOUT 1.3 MILLION people die from tuberculosis each year throughout the world. Although NIAID was the leading global funder of tuberculosis research, I still felt that tuberculosis research and control did not get the international attention that they deserved. I was vocal about my feelings, and I was pleased that Gary Edson and others in the Bush administration were of like minds and considered it a possible legacy item.

There was a considerable amount of scrambling at the White

House to position options for the president's consideration to include in his final State of the Union address on January 28, 2008, which increased greatly the likelihood that the initiative would be realized. As it turned out, malaria and PEPFAR were the two health issues brought up in the State of the Union address, with President Bush asking for $30 billion for PEPFAR and praising the President's Malaria Initiative, but without committing resources to it. As much as we tried, tuberculosis did not make it into the speech.

In Washington, you never get everything you want.

ON FRIDAY AFTERNOON, July 27, 2007, I headed to the White House as I had on countless occasions, but instead of meeting with administration officials or briefing the president, I was a guest. I was ushered into the East Room to join the seven other recipients of the National Medal of Science. This is the highest honor bestowed by the president of the United States to individuals for accomplishment in science and engineering. The White House was a couple of years behind in the actual awarding of the medals; we were receiving the 2005 medals in 2007. The conferring of the awards was a formal process with a U.S. Army officer in dress uniform announcing the name of each of us as we approached the platform, walked up to the president, and did an about-face so that the president could slip the medal over our heads from behind. When my turn came, the army officer announced into the microphone "Dr. Anthony S. Foosseee." I do not expect everyone to intuitively know the correct Italian pronunciation of my name, which is "Fowchee." I cut the fellow some slack and acted as if there were nothing wrong especially because the military staff in the White House are usually heroes who had almost always served one or more combat tours in Iraq or Afghanistan. But as I approached

President Bush, he put his arm around me and whispered in my ear, "Hey, Tony. No sweat. Maybe this young man does not know who you are, but I certainly do. Congratulations!" Classic George W. Bush!

Secretary of State Condi Rice did not miss a beat as she approached me at the reception following the awards ceremony. She gave me a hug and with a big smile on her face said, "Congratulations, Dr. Foosseee." I could not hold back my laughter.

I HAD THOUGHT that receiving the National Medal of Science from the president was the high-water mark for my professional career. Then the president one-upped me. On June 11, 2008, the White House announced that I would be receiving the Presidential Medal of Freedom for my work with HIV/AIDS and particularly my role in helping to develop the PEPFAR program. I was stunned and humbled, because this was the highest honor that could be given to a civilian by the president of the United States.

Eight days later I once again took an unusual route into the White House as I entered the East Room with my group of ten guests including Christine, Jenny, and Ali, who was still in high school. Megan was not present, because she was finishing a post-high-school gap year as a teacher's assistant in a charter school on the South Side of Chicago. Also with us were my proud sister and brother-in-law, Denise and Jack Scorce, and several of my senior staff from NIAID. The highlight of the day for me came after the ceremony as my guests and I stood together for a photo with the president. He gave me a hug and whispered in my ear, "We love you, Tony. Thanks for all you do for our country and the world. I will not miss Washington very much when I leave, but I will miss you and people like you."

For me, there was no doubt that President George W. Bush

ranks second to none in leading efforts toward the alleviation of suffering and prevention of deaths due to infectious diseases throughout the world.

I knew that this extraordinary phase in my life would soon be coming to an end, and I wondered whether I would ever again get such an opportunity to advise a U.S. president.

Part Four

EXPECTING THE UNEXPECTED

Enter Obama

Within days of the January 20, 2009, inauguration of President Barack Obama, there began the typical Washington-style stressful activity of positioning oneself for the jobs that would soon be filled and that would influence different areas of policy. I was lucky. This was not a concern for me, since I was not a political appointee. Nonetheless, I had been afforded opportunities not usually available to directors of NIH institutes. I had had the privilege over the past twenty-five years of going in and out of the White House, traveling as a part of presidential delegations, and having one-on-one meetings with presidents of the United States on substantive matters of domestic and global health involving the emergence of new infections. I had ridden in presidential motorcades and flown in Air Force One. In addition, I had testified before the Senate and the House of Representatives numerous times.

But my "day job" as NIAID director and chief of a basic and clinical research laboratory was still my core activity. I loved my job. It was exciting and fun, and the scientific challenges were plentiful. In my own lab, the Laboratory of Immunoregulation, which was established with me as chief of the lab in 1980, I provided broad direction and administrative support for several senior scientists whom I had trained over the years and who were now independently pursuing various questions related to HIV. I also directly supervised a much smaller group of three or four scientists together with a number of younger pre- and postdoctoral trainees. Our interest was how to contain and hopefully eliminate the reservoir of HIV that remains in the body even when active replication is suppressed by antiretroviral drugs. In other words, we were trying to "cure" HIV. As part of my role as a practicing clinical investigator, I never stopped seeing patients with HIV in the NIH Clinical Center on teaching rounds at least twice a week. Some were critically ill, and others were admitted for routine studies.

As director of NIAID, my main responsibility was more as science administrator than lab chief and clinical physician, providing direction and overall support for thousands of scientists involved in research conducted at universities throughout the country as well as some internationally on immunology, allergy, transplantation, and HIV and more than two hundred other infectious diseases including malaria, tuberculosis, influenza, and a wide variety of common infections. We still had not achieved the goal of ending the HIV pandemic, and although effective, lifesaving therapies were available, we were still diligently searching for the scientific holy grail of an AIDS vaccine. My director role also meant that the intramural NIAID Vaccine Research Center reported directly to me. Another part of my job was to travel around the country and the world delivering lectures on my own research as well as attending conferences where I would describe the broader research supported by NIAID and keep up to date on the activities in my field of research interest. At the beginning of the Obama Administration, I relished getting back to my traditional schedule of being physically at the NIH most of the time during the usual working hours instead of going back and forth to the White House and playing catch-up on weekends and nights as I had done during the previous public health crises. I thought I was back to business as usual. But as I have said so many times, "Expect the unexpected."

THE ANNUAL SEASONAL INFLUENZA outbreaks that occur every winter usually peak around January or February. This was the case in the 2008–9 winter. By March there are usually very few cases, and by April the flu season is almost always declared over. But on April 17, 2009, public health officials in California noticed a few cases of a novel influenza, which the CDC identified as a "swine flu" of the H1N1 type. At about the same time, a few similar cases were reported in Mexico.

In the past, there had been cases of "one-offs" where the virus had jumped from pigs or birds to humans but did not spread from human to human. Such was the case during the Bush administration with the H5N1 bird flu. These recent swine flu cases were worrisome, however, because they were being transmitted from person to person among people who had had no contact with pigs. This was a brand-new virus for which there was little or no background immunity in the population, which meant there was a clear danger that this could evolve into a true pandemic. Indeed, within days to weeks, additional cases were reported in several states and soon in other countries. Most public health officials expected the next novel influenza with pandemic potential to arise in the Far East, likely China, as was usually the case. Here we had a virus that very likely originated somewhere along the California-Mexico border. Soon we were in battle mode at HHS with almost continual conference calls involving the CDC, the FDA, and me representing NIAID and the NIH to put together a strategy to prepare for a pandemic that was all but certain in the coming winter.

So much for my return to "normalcy."

THE TIME FRAME for developing an influenza vaccine from the moment the virus is identified until the vaccine is produced and put into arms is roughly six to seven months. Because the swine flu virus was recognized in April, this meant vaccine development would begin in May and the first doses would be ready for distribution at the end of October with the bulk of the vaccines available by November and into December 2009. Because cases of influenza usually peak in January, we were counting on having sufficient doses already administered throughout the U.S. population before the outbreak peaked.

There is an old adage that the only thing predictable about influenza is that it is unpredictable. We would soon learn the truth of that saying.

By the end of May, the spring outbreak of the swine flu had abated in the United States but not elsewhere. Infections in other regions of the world continued with the outbreak especially severe in Mexico. Another ominous sign: winter was approaching in the Southern Hemisphere and countries such as Australia, New Zealand, and Argentina were already experiencing an outbreak of swine flu. It was becoming more and more clear that we in the United States would have a significant outbreak in our upcoming winter. As we proceeded into June and July, Congress and the press became focused on the question of whether the vaccine would be ready in time.

The U.S. government had made contractual arrangements with a few pharmaceutical companies, some of them foreign, to produce the H1N1 vaccine. The Biomedical Advanced Research and Development Authority, which we had established during the George W. Bush administration, was responsible for purchasing the vaccine doses from the companies, many of which were receiving U.S. government funding. The companies had promised BARDA, headed at the time by Dr. Robin Robinson, that they would have 160 million doses of vaccine by October 15, 2009. I was very skeptical about the fulfillment of this promise. Schedules almost never work out exactly as planned in vaccine production, usually through no one's fault but because of the uncertainties inherent in growing, purifying, inactivating, or attenuating virus for use as an influenza vaccine.

As was the case with other vaccines, our responsibility at NIAID was to test the pilot lots of vaccine as they became available in clinical trials in various groups of individuals to determine safety, to determine whether the vaccine induced an appropriate immune response predicted to protect against infections and to determine the correct dose. I had predicted that our clinical trials in adults and the elderly would begin by August 2009, and I was holding my breath that some technical or logistical glitch did not delay the start of the trials. The press was watching closely, and I was aware that any failure in meeting promised timetables would be closely scrutinized.

In late June 2009, I found myself presenting my identification at the entrance gate to the West Wing of the White House for the first time since the end of the George W. Bush administration. I had been invited to a meeting to discuss the impending pandemic and our preparedness. Nothing and everything had changed with the new administration. The building was the same, but all the people were different, as were the countless photographs on the walls, which had gone from capturing Bush and his team in action to team Obama.

The meeting in the Roosevelt Room was attended by a number of high-ranking administration officials including several cabinet secretaries. But it was the presence of nongovernment attendees, in particular Dr. David Sencer, that signaled there was a specific agenda. David had been director of the CDC during the infamous 1976 swine flu fiasco. Also sitting at the table were David Mathews, who in 1976 was secretary of the Department of Health, Education, and Welfare, now HHS, as well as Walter Dowdle, who was at the CDC in 1976, and Dr. Harvey Fineberg, president of the Institute of Medicine and coauthor of the 1978 book *The Swine Flu Affair*, which analyzed the events surrounding the public health fiasco.

In January 1976, several U.S. Army recruits at Fort Dix, New Jersey, became ill with a respiratory illness. One of the recruits had died. The cause of the respiratory illness was an H1N1 influenza believed to have originated from a pig and said to be similar to the H1N1 influenza that had caused the catastrophic pandemic of 1918. The potential for another 1918-like pandemic generated considerable anxiety among public health officials who urged President Gerald Ford to have every person in the United States vaccinated against this new influenza. The government initiated a crash program costing $135 million, and between October and December 1976 forty million Americans received the swine flu vaccine.

Then something terrible happened. There began to appear cases of Guillain-Barré syndrome, a paralyzing condition of the peripheral nervous system that was a known complication of certain infections and even certain vaccines. It was estimated that the risk of developing Guillain-Barré syndrome increased 8.8-fold in those vaccinated with this new vaccine. In an ironic twist, no outbreak of swine flu occurred. It was a premature and ill-fated decision to recommend mass vaccination before there was any evidence of an actual outbreak. Almost immediately the blame game was on. David Sencer was asked to resign and Assistant Secretary for Health Theodore Cooper also left his post.

We did not want to repeat the mistakes of the past, and we listened closely to the stories of the people involved in the 1976 fiasco. This was clearly a different situation from that in 1976. A global outbreak was already under way, and it was just a matter of time before it came to the United States. Our challenge was not to agonize over whether we should or should not vaccinate people but to have enough vaccine available in time to distribute to people in the United States before the inevitable influenza outbreak occurred.

Well into the meeting, President Obama walked in. Presidents do not just slip into a meeting. Everyone stopped our discussion and stood up. After he took his seat, we sat down again. I had met President Obama a few times when he was a senator during hearings where I testified on a variety of subjects, particularly the H5N1 pandemic influenza threat. Then as now he listened attentively, asking questions that were on point.

As WE PROCEEDED into the typically hot, muggy days of the Washington, D.C., summer, the White House's focus on the impending pandemic was intense, accompanied by equally intense interest and reporting by the press. Everyone wanted to know if we would have enough vaccine and if it would arrive on time. The answer, of course, depended on the pharmaceutical companies.

I had planned to start the clinical trials in August, and fortunately we met that projection. This meant that we would have the critical information from the trials by mid-October, when the first shipments of vaccine were supposed to be available to the public. Our part of the multifaceted plan was on time and good to go. We knew that we were going to get hit hard by the influenza virus because, as we began the vaccine trials in August, which was winter in the Southern Hemisphere, it was clear that part of the world was already in the middle of a major H1N1 influenza outbreak. No doubt, the world was experiencing the first global influenza pandemic of the twenty-first century. If we could get most of the people vaccinated by early October, we could probably blunt the outbreak here in the United States. I was spending most of my time explaining all of this to the public.

MY INITIAL SKEPTICISM that the pharmaceutical companies would have the promised number of doses to us in time would soon unfortunately prove to be justified. Around the time we got the vaccine trials under way, we began to receive some disturbing indications of production problems from the pharmaceutical companies. Robin Robinson told us that the virus was growing in eggs more slowly than they had anticipated. The slow growth was not the fault of the companies. Such are the vicissitudes of this type of vaccine development, which was beyond their control. It was the overpromising that was the problem. This is exactly why I had questioned the pharmaceutical companies' timetable. I knew that the process of vaccine development, particularly that which depends on growth of virus in eggs, is fraught with risks. I had been pushing for some time to get away from growing the virus in eggs and move toward the development of vaccines by molecular biological techniques, which would be considerably more predictable. But the influenza vaccine manufacturing field was so entrenched in the tried-and-true techniques of growing the virus in eggs that it was not likely to change for some time. Such a transition would take years to implement. Be that as it may, we had a problem now with the timetable of vaccine availability on the cusp of an approaching pandemic.

We had expected to have 140 to 160 million doses of the vaccine available for distribution by October 15, 2009. Besides the problem of the slow-growing virus, now we had another problem. One of the companies to which BARDA had contracted to produce vaccine virus for us was Australian. Because Australia was right then in the middle of a major pandemic outbreak, the Australian government decided that they would take all of the doses for themselves that the company had promised to the United States.

Now we really had a serious shortage.

There was one way that we might be able to catch up. That was if the outbreak did not start until late fall or early winter and peaked in January as did most seasonal influenza outbreaks. Unfortunately, no such luck for us.

THE PROBLEM BECAME EVIDENT as soon as children returned to elementary and high schools from their summer vacations in late August and early September. We started to notice a growing number of reported H1N1 infections. This was much earlier than usual. Typically, most people who would get vaccinated receive the vaccine in October or early November, several weeks or even months before the bulk of the flu cases appear. Now we were seeing infections in September and early October, and yet there was little if any vaccine to distribute.

By mid- to late October 2009, the problem had intensified. The cases of influenza began to accelerate, and the pharmaceutical companies had delivered only 11 million of the 160 million promised doses. We found ourselves in the middle of a major gap between supply and demand, leading to long lines for vaccine at a time when there was already widespread influenza activity in forty-six of the fifty states. The perfect storm had hit: the first pandemic of the twenty-first century; unmet promises of vaccine supply by the pharmaceutical companies; and the arrival of the outbreak months before it was predicted to occur.

As expected, critics were quick to pounce. Certain Republicans in Congress were calling this "Obama's Katrina." I had seen this movie before. It was a reverse playback from almost five years ago to the day when many Democrats blamed the Bush administration for the shortage of influenza vaccine associated with the bacterial contamination of Chiron's Liverpool, England, production plant right before the November 2004 presidential election.

Just the catchphrase "Obama's Katrina" triggered an explosion of press coverage, and soon the CDC director, Tom Frieden, and I found ourselves spending a substantial proportion of our time appearing in the media almost every day for several weeks in October and November 2009. I tried to explain to the American public how this unfortunate situation was not the fault of President Obama, the CDC, the FDA, or even the pharmaceutical companies. If there was one sin, it was that the companies had overpromised the time frame for delivery of the vaccines. Such is the fragile nature of the process of preparedness and response to emerging infectious disease outbreaks, and such was the nature of my complicated job. I was back in the role of chief explainer.

SOON CRITICISM BECAME focused directly and unfairly on the CDC even though there was virtually nothing that it could have done to change the situation. The optics and messaging issues for the CDC, which is responsible for distribution of vaccines during an emergency situation such as an influenza pandemic, really began to deteriorate when it was reported on November 5 that Goldman Sachs, Citibank, and other Wall Street firms had received vaccines from the CDC while pregnant women in clinics throughout the country were waiting in line for the scarce supplies. In fact, the CDC takes procurement orders from state and local governments and agencies and then distributes the vaccines through a contract with McKesson Corporation, which sends the vaccine to more than 150,000 distribution sites within the states according to how the cities and states themselves had decided to distribute the vaccine based on their best judgment. Because the Wall Street firms had large clinics, they could easily distribute vaccine to their pregnant employees and those with underlying conditions. They had publicly stated that this was their intention. It was actually an efficient way to distribute vaccine to the high-risk groups. But it did not look good, particularly because we were in the middle of the terrible economic crisis of 2008–9 and Wall Street was extremely unpopular.

By mid- to late November 2009, the vaccine finally started to become available in large quantities just at the time that the pandemic began to taper off. Here was a classic example of the unpredictability of influenza. As mentioned, seasonal outbreaks usually peak in January. Here we were in November and the pandemic had already peaked. Nonetheless, although the peak had occurred, there were still plenty of cases of influenza in November and December; people could still benefit from the vaccine. We encouraged people to get vaccinated in November, yet few wanted the vaccine at that point even though just weeks previously, when there had been a vaccine shortage, there were long lines for people to receive the scarce supply.

What happened next was an example of the inscrutability of human nature. Now that the vaccine was available, the long lines were replaced by many people saying that they did not trust the CDC, which was encouraging them to get vaccinated, nor did some trust the safety of the vaccine since it was a new vaccine and they were afraid of possible side effects. This, even though the vaccine had been shown to be safe. Go figure!

Because of the widespread global nature of the outbreak and its efficient transmissibility, this was by definition a true pandemic.

Fortunately, however, the mortality, at least in the United States, was not particularly high. In fact, there were fewer total deaths than in an average seasonal flu outbreak, likely because the elderly had some natural degree of protection due to exposure during their youth to a similar virus. But of course we did not know that this would be the case at the time that the pandemic was unfolding in the United States.

Moving Toward an
HIV-Free World

One of the most discouraging days in the realm of HIV vaccines was when I got the call from my dear friend Larry Corey, a professor in the Vaccine and Infectious Diseases Division of the Fred Hutch Cancer Center in Seattle, who directed our HIV Vaccine Trials Network. Larry and his South African colleagues were conducting a clinical trial in South Africa using a vaccine similar to the vaccine that was used in the modestly successful (31 percent efficacy) Thai trial from 2009. The South African trial was aimed at corroborating or disproving the Thai trial in a different population. Usually a sunshine type of guy, Larry's voice was choking and hesitant. He told me that the trial in South Africa had not produced the same results as the Thai trial. In fact, there was no effect at all. Larry had been working with this trial for nine years, and now we had nothing positive to show for it. It was not the design and implementation of the trial. They were impeccable. The vaccine just did not work. As Larry fought back tears, I tried to encourage him because there were other ongoing trials testing the same general type of vaccine.

The situation became darker a few months later when Carl

Dieffenbach, my trusted colleague who directs the NIAID Division of AIDS, told me in a sober tone that a second trial, this one in women, conducted in several southern African countries also was a bust. And then finally a third trial with a similar vaccine conducted in North and South America and a few European countries also showed negative results. I immediately recalled the sobering discussions that I had years earlier with my "wise uncle" friend Albert Sabin, who was skeptical about our ability to develop an effective HIV vaccine. Science can be hard and heartbreaking. We were back at square one and still had not even proven the concept that a vaccine would work.

Vaccine research using concepts different from that of the Thai and other trials is ongoing. The most promising is one that induces a type of antibody called broadly neutralizing antibodies, which could knock out all of the many versions of HIV. That approach is still aspirational, and as I write this, any success is still years away, if it is at all possible.

IN CONTRAST TO the disappointing results with vaccines, in 2010 and well into 2011 the number of advances in the field of HIV prevention and treatment were truly transforming. In November 2010, Carl Dieffenbach called to tell me the exciting results of an important NIAID-sponsored clinical trial for the prevention of HIV infection. Carl is usually a reserved and measured person, and this was the happiest and most animated I had ever heard him. In a major study in which men who have sex with men and who were at high risk for HIV infection were given either a single pill containing two antiretroviral drugs under the trade name Truvada or a placebo, Truvada significantly decreased the acquisition of HIV infection compared with the people in the placebo group. This phenomenon is called pre-exposure prophylaxis, or PrEP, and was a major advance in providing yet another tool for preventing HIV among high-risk populations. This approach was later shown to be more than 95 percent effective in preventing HIV infection if the trial participants took the pill every day. This advance was particularly important because the incidence of HIV infection in the United States was still unacceptably high with forty to fifty thousand new infections each year, mostly among men who have sex with men and disproportionately among African American men who have sex with men. Human nature being what it is, complete abstinence from sex was not feasible, and many people were still not using condoms consistently or at all. We needed another tool for our prevention tool kit and PrEP looked like it might be it.

Perhaps the most important breakthrough in HIV treatment and prevention following the transformational development of triple combination antiretroviral therapy in 1996 occurred in May 2011. The report of an NIAID-sponsored international clinical trial involving predominantly (97 percent) heterosexual couples published by Myron "Mike" Cohen and his colleagues from the University of North Carolina clearly demonstrated that in a sexual relationship in which one partner was infected and the other was not, if you suppressed the virus early with antiretroviral therapy in the person with HIV, you could decrease the likelihood that the individual with HIV would infect his or her sexual partner by more than 95 percent. *Science* magazine hailed this as the "Scientific Breakthrough of the Year" in 2011, an accolade that is a huge deal for a clinical study.

I had known Mike Cohen since he was an infectious disease fellow at Yale University Medical Center in the late 1970s. He is one of a tight-knit group of domestic and international clinical investigators who are out in the field directing large international clinical trials that sometimes fail, but when they succeed, the impact can be enormous. He had been working on this project for at least six years, and now he had blown it out of the water. A subsequent study published in 2016, also by Mike and colleagues, showed that the initially observed effect was even more impressive in that it was durable after five years. Because this effect was seen predominantly among heterosexual couples, an important question remained: Would the same outcome be seen in couples of men who have sex with men? A study involving both gay and heterosexual couples titled "PARTNER" partially answered that question, which was fully answered by the PARTNER2 study involving eight hundred only-gay men who had condomless sex more than seventy-seven thousand times without a single case of "linked" transmission. Linked transmission is when examination of the virus in both subjects shows that individual A clearly passed the virus to individual B. These results, which were presented at the 2018 International AIDS Conference in Amsterdam, firmly established that when the virus was suppressed by antiretroviral therapy to below detectable levels, it completely eliminated the possibility that the person with HIV would pass the infection on to a sexual partner without HIV. The activist community designated this phenomenon as "undetectable equals untransmittable," or $U = U$. These extraordinary drugs not only saved the life of the person with HIV but also prevented the further transmission of the virus. This was a lifesaving double bonus. Another huge benefit of $U = U$ was that it removed the stigma from a person with HIV who was properly treated because it made clear that such a person was not a danger to anyone else. Although all of this was fully realized in 2018 and beyond, it all started with the six-year study that Mike Cohen and his colleagues published in 2011. This is a classic example of the building blocks and iterative nature of science.

So, if we could identify everyone who was HIV infected and put them on antiretroviral drugs, we could interrupt the chain of transmission, theoretically slowing and even halting the momentum of the pandemic and ultimately ending it. In addition, if we implemented PrEP in those people who are at high risk of infection, we could even further accelerate the end of the pandemic.

Easier said than done. It was difficult in the United States and even more so throughout the resource-poor regions of the world to identify everyone with HIV, much less put them on and sustain them on antiretroviral therapy. However, as difficult as this task was, we finally had the evidence-based tools to accomplish it. We could end the global HIV/AIDS pandemic even in the absence of a vaccine.

OVER THE PREVIOUS FEW YEARS, the intensity of public interest in the domestic and global AIDS pandemic had leveled off. It was true that countless lives were being saved throughout the world by the treatment and prevention of HIV infection implemented through PEPFAR and the Global Fund to Fight AIDS, Tuberculosis, and Malaria, as well as through various host country programs. But there was not much public discussion about actually ending HIV/AIDS as a global pandemic. This mindset was fueled by the fact that budgets for the NIH, the CDC, PEPFAR, and the Global Fund were essentially flat due to fiscal constraints associated with the economic crash in 2008–9, from which we had not yet fully recovered. This meant there was very little wiggle room for new initiatives.

However, the year 2011 was the thirtieth anniversary of the recognition of AIDS as a new disease, and the attention paid to this landmark rekindled interest in and attention to the HIV pandemic. I saw this as an opportunity to galvanize support within the administration, particularly in HHS and at the White House and among AIDS constituency groups with the goal of turning around the trajectory of the pandemic, leading to its ultimate termination.

I became obsessed with this mission. I was excited by the prospect of what ending the AIDS epidemic would mean, but frustrated by the fact that we were not on a clear pathway toward making it happen. We needed to put into play a strategy backed by substantial resources to achieve this goal. I just could not get it out of my mind. I harped on it with Cliff Lane, and I ruminated on it during my daily six-mile run in Rock Creek Park. I spoke about it constantly at dinner with Christine, who encouraged me to push the idea, and I brought it up with colleagues at other institutions at every opportunity. Finally my ideas gelled enough for me to test out in a peer-reviewed article that I wrote for *Science* magazine on July 1, 2011, titled "AIDS: Let Science Inform Policy." I emphasized the transforming nature of the "treatment as prevention" findings from Mike Cohen's clinical trial and called for an expanded global commitment of resources. "For the first time in the history of HIV/AIDS," I wrote, "controlling and ending the pandemic are feasible; however, a truly global commitment, including investments by those rich and middle-income countries whose contributions have thus far been limited, is essential. Major investments in implementation now will save even greater expenditures in the future; and in the meantime, countless lives can be saved."

The activist community became energized around my article. The day it was published, Gregg Gonsalves, a former ACT UP member who had become a good friend over the years and who was now pursuing a Ph.D. in the epidemiology of microbial diseases at Yale (but who had not abandoned his activist instincts), wrote an email to his LISTSERV referring to my article: "This is one of the most important pieces to be written on HIV/AIDS in a very, very long time. Dr. Fauci is a cautious scientist and for him to step out so publicly, so unequivocally in this way, particularly when he works for an administration, which is unlikely to heed his words, is a tremendous statement of moral and political courage."

Although I appreciated Gregg's support and sentiments, I hoped that this broader attention would not offend members of the Obama administration who could make the ending of the AIDS pandemic in its current form a major legacy for them comparable to the indelible legacy of PEPFAR for the George W. Bush administration. I hoped to have the opportunity to make my case.

I soon got the chance.

THERE WAS, IN FACT, sincere interest on the part of several senior administration officials in achieving an end to the epidemic. Denis McDonough, deputy to National Security Advisor Thomas Donilon, emerged as a powerful advocate for our cause. He asked me to take the lead on what he called a blue-sky proposal that in addition to optimizing existing resources added significant additional resources of about $2.5 billion with the goal of putting eight million people globally on HIV treatment by 2013 and ten million by 2015.

Mathematical modeling done by Tom Frieden's team at the CDC indicated that this would tip the curve of HIV incidence of new infections sharply downward and would also have the benefits of saving the lives and avoiding hospitalizations of those who were already infected. When Denis gave me the task of putting together a plan to implement this approach, I was a little uneasy, because there was considerable skepticism that sufficient resources would be made available to achieve our goal.

In a series of meetings in the White House Situation Room in November 2011, Jack Lew, director of OMB, though sympathetic to what we were trying to do, frankly stated that he felt it would be impossible for the president to agree to a $2.5 billion budget increase given all the commitments that he had already made to other aid programs. This came down like a bucket of cold water on our discussions; however, I and my like-minded colleagues Eric

Goosby, the PEPFAR ambassador, and Tom Frieden did not give up. We plowed ahead with support from McDonough and Susan Rice, who was the ambassador to the United Nations. As a teenager, Susan had been a star point guard for the National Cathedral School, which all three of my daughters had attended. Being a former point guard, I immediately felt an affinity for her, and our friendship would deepen well beyond our similar basketball histories.

Another person in our corner was Secretary of State Hillary Clinton. Notwithstanding the pessimism around whether we would get any significant amount of new money, she remained enthusiastic about getting a substantial number of additional people on anti-HIV therapy, and she wanted to push for it by giving a major speech to that effect. Her staff, particularly her chief of staff, Cheryl Mills, and I worked on the speech together.

On November 8, 2011, the NIH campus was buzzing in anticipation of Secretary Clinton's visit. Hillary Clinton was extremely popular in the NIH community and was widely respected by the AIDS constituency groups. When the NIH director, Francis Collins, and I greeted the secretary, she was in good spirits. I showed her a picture of us shaking hands during her first visit to the NIH Clinical Center in 1994, seventeen years earlier, when she was First Lady. She burst into laughter and joked that we looked like "a couple of kids" back then. As Francis and I escorted her into the massive Masur Auditorium of the NIH Clinical Center, she was greeted with a standing ovation by the enthusiastic crowd of NIH physicians, scientists, nurses, and other staff. She passionately articulated many of the goals about ending the HIV/AIDS pandemic that we had been discussing over the prior several months. She coined the phrase "an AIDS-free generation" that became the catchphrase for our efforts over the coming years. The audience loved it.

And then something unusual happened. I had written and submitted an op-ed for *The New York Times* titled "Toward an AIDS-Free Generation" in which I discussed the possibility of ending the HIV/AIDS pandemic and focused on Secretary Clinton's speech. I got clearance to submit the op-ed from HHS (a routine requirement) and the State Department (because I referred to Secretary Clinton in the op-ed). It was timed to come out within days after her NIH visit.

In the op-ed, I mentioned the importance of scaling up the efforts in treatment as prevention, including "increased financial resources toward global AIDS efforts." I closed my editorial by stating, "An AIDS-free generation is possible; indeed, it is a moral and public health imperative that we strive, collectively, toward this goal. No single nation or organization can accomplish this. A truly global commitment and effort are required; however, United States leadership is essential. It is just this message that Secretary of State Hillary Rodham Clinton so cogently delivered in her November 8, 2011, speech at the National Institutes of Health calling for global action toward the goal of an AIDS-free generation. The world should listen carefully to that message. We have a unique opportunity to participate in a historic global health victory. We must act now. In the long run, expenditures will decrease and more lives will be saved. History itself will judge us harshly if we let this opportunity pass."

I thought it was a pretty good piece that reflected what we had been discussing with the administration.

After I submitted it for clearance, I went down to the White House to a meeting in the Situation Room to discuss the topic at hand. The meeting was chaired by Tom Donilon and attended by Secretary Clinton, Denis McDonough, and Jack Lew. Disagreement within the room continued regarding the feasibility and advisability of asking for more resources versus trying to accomplish more with already available money. It was still an open question as the meeting ended. And then, after I left the White House, things got more complicated.

When I returned to my NIH office, I was told by my director of communications, Courtney Billet, that the White House had contacted HHS and told them to have me recall the op-ed from *The New York Times* because, after reading it, they found it to be "off message." I was stunned and embarrassed. Of the many op-eds and opinion pieces that I had submitted for publication over the years, this was the first time that I had to withdraw anything. I have had several submissions rejected by newspapers, but never did I have to withdraw something myself. Someone in the White House, likely OMB officials, had obviously read my op-ed carefully and seen that I had mentioned the need for "increased financial resources." The issue almost certainly never made it all the way up to the level of the president. No matter. Despite our high-level support, we were not going to receive the additional resources that I had hoped for, at least not at this point. The frustrating realities of Washington, D.C.

SINCE 1988, December 1 had been designated World AIDS Day, a day when cities around the world held special events to bring people together and heighten attention in the battle against HIV/AIDS. This year, 2011, had special energy. President Obama himself gave remarks at the event in Washington, D.C. Afterward, a panel discussion was held moderated by CNN's Dr. Sanjay Gupta. The panel included my friend and "partner in crime" Bono; singer

Alicia Keys; California congresswoman Barbara Lee; Kay Warren, author and wife of the evangelical pastor Rick Warren; and Florida senator Marco Rubio. Sanjay, whom I had known for years since his first assignment as a medical correspondent for CNN, had alerted me a few days earlier that he would turn to me to make comments from the audience during the panel discussion. He asked me to talk about the science behind the medical advances that had been made in the field. I took the opportunity to underscore what I had been lecturing on and promoting heavily over the past year, namely that the science had provided us with the tools to end the pandemic and it was now a question of whether we had the will to implement those tools. When I was finished, Bono chimed in with some glee and told the audience the story of when he had visited my home nine years earlier. He said with a big smile that he was glad that after all these years I "was still at it."

Bono was correct. I was still at it. Despite the likelihood that we would not receive additional resources, I kept hammering away at my message in speeches I gave and buttonholed anyone I thought could help. As I said before, I was obsessed.

MY PUSH FOR a new initiative reached a peak at the Nineteenth International AIDS Conference, which took place in Washington, D.C., on July 22–27, 2012. In 1989, activists insisted on banning the United States as a venue for the meeting in response to the ill-advised 1987 U.S. immigration ban on entry of individuals with HIV into the country. After twenty-two years the immigration restrictions had finally been lifted, a process that began toward the end of the George W. Bush administration and was finalized under Obama.

The atmosphere at the meeting was supercharged, made all the more so because the data of Mike Cohen's treatment-as-prevention study were being publicly presented in detail. Sitting together with Mike in the front row of the Walter E. Washington Convention Center taking it all in, I threw my arms around Mike after the presentation. "We did it, we did it," I said, referring to the efforts led by Mike, Carl Dieffenbach, and his NIAID Division of AIDS, as well as the hundreds of clinical investigators on the ground and thousands of study participants who made the study happen. In response to the enormous implications of the data, the entire audience of ten thousand people jumped to their feet for a prolonged standing ovation.

Hillary Clinton and I both gave speeches that were enthusiastically received. Later, at a large and elegant gala sponsored by the organization ONE held at the Eisenhower Theater of the Kennedy Center, I gave a few remarks from the stage together with Kay Warren on what it would mean to actually have an AIDS-free generation. We also had a lot of help from Alicia Keys, Annie Lennox, and Herbie Hancock, who came onstage promoting this concept together with Congresswomen Barbara Lee and Nancy Pelosi. To put the crowd in a good frame of mind, Annie Lennox performed a smashing rendition of her hit song "Sweet Dreams." The legendary Sir Elton John amplified the excitement. He had recently written a book titled *Love Is the Cure* focused on how his friendship with Ryan White turned his own life around. At the time Elton was a cocaine addict as well as an alcoholic and bulimic. He had now been clean for twenty-two years. The Open Society Foundations held a reception at its Washington, D.C., headquarters that afternoon to celebrate the book's publication. To my great surprise, Sir Elton had requested that I introduce him before his remarks at the book party.

The movement was taking on a momentum of its own. At the subsequent World AIDS Day commemoration the following year held at the State Department, Secretary Clinton unveiled the "PEP-

FAR Blueprint: Creating an AIDS-Free Generation" to guide future PEPFAR efforts to end the AIDS pandemic. It was a document whose development was led by Eric Goosby. Eric had enlisted my help, which I gladly provided, in putting together various drafts. The final version did a good job of laying out a road map to reach this important goal.

With all of the mounting energy behind the concept of ending HIV, concrete headway was beginning to be made at the local, state, and country levels. In the United States, for example, the city of San Francisco had initiated an aggressive program called RAPID that seeks out people with HIV infection, initiates therapy on the spot, and closely follows them to assure adherence. In addition, it had energetically implemented a PrEP program for uninfected people practicing high-risk behavior. This program had resulted in a significant decrease in the incidence of new HIV infections in San Francisco, which is the first step toward ending the epidemic in that city.

THE NEW YORK *Times* in its Sunday, June 29, 2014, edition picked up on a speech I gave in Aspen, Colorado, on ending the AIDS epidemic. It was reporting on the then New York governor Andrew Cuomo's plans to implement in New York the program that I was pushing. "Thirty years ago, New York was the epicenter of the AIDS crisis," the article quoted Governor Cuomo as saying. The article went on to state, "The prospect of ending the AIDS epidemic is gaining momentum in epidemiological circles. It is based on studies showing that AIDS drugs have a double-barreled effect not just as treatment but as a means of blocking transmission. On Tuesday, Dr. Anthony S. Fauci, a leading AIDS researcher, argued at the Aspen Ideas Festival that 'we can end the AIDS pandemic in the next 10 years.'"

As I think back to our early painful experiences of caring for people with HIV infection before we had adequate interventions to save their lives, and I see how well equipped we now are to do so, I believe even more strongly that history will indeed judge us harshly as a global community if we do not seize the opportunity within our grasp to end one of the most devastating pandemics in the history of our civilization.

Epidemics of Disease
and Fear

When Francis Collins was director of the National Human Genome Research Institute prior to becoming the director of the NIH, I joked with him that he could go to bed at night and never have to worry about waking up to a genomic emergency or a genomic global health crisis. In contrast, I went to sleep knowing that upon waking and reading *The Washington Post* or *The New York Times* or more likely just glancing at my iPhone for CNN alerts, I could easily find out that something had happened in my world of infectious diseases during the night that would now consume me for the next few days, weeks, or even months.

This is exactly what happened with Ebola in 2014.

Ebola is a virus that causes severe disease characterized by the acute onset of fatigue, headache, muscle pain, severe vomiting, diarrhea, and skin rash, and often progresses to multisystem failure particularly of the kidney and liver, very often leading to death. The virus was first discovered in 1976 during two simultaneous outbreaks in the Democratic Republic of the Congo (DRC) and South Sudan. The virus got its name from the Ebola River, which is adjacent to a village in the DRC where the first outbreak occurred. It was formally referred to as Ebola hemorrhagic fever because of early reports of oozing of blood from the gastrointestinal tract and other mucosal surfaces such as the eyes, nose, and gums. The natural animal reservoir of Ebola is not entirely clear, although fruit bats are strongly suspected to harbor the virus and pass it on to humans who come into contact with bats or other infected animals such as monkeys and other forest animals. Once a human is infected, the spread from person to person sustains an outbreak. Spread among humans is by direct contact with bodily fluids such as vomit, blood, and feces during the time a person is acutely ill. Because of this pattern of transmissibility, family members, friends, and health-care workers are particularly vulnerable to infection. This is especially true when they take care of Ebola-infected people without adequate personal protective equipment designed to prevent direct exposure of any part of their body to infected material.

From 1976 until 2014 there had been at least eighteen separate outbreaks of Ebola virus disease, nearly all occurring in Central African countries. Outbreaks ranged in size from one to a few cases up to several hundred. The case fatality rate ranged between 25 percent and 90 percent depending upon the outbreak in question, the subtype of virus involved, and the location. These outbreaks had mostly been confined to remote areas, and all were ultimately contained by isolating the infected individuals and tracing and isolating their contacts until it became clear that they were not infected. Between outbreaks, the disease seems to disappear from the human population.

Although Ebola had never been a problem outside Africa, there was a lingering concern that somehow this frightening disease might one day strike us here in the United States, Europe, and other countries and regions in the developed world. This subliminal concern was heightened by such fictional accounts of potential outbreaks as depicted in the 1995 film *Outbreak* starring Dustin Hoffman, Rene Russo, and Morgan Freeman. The movie focuses on an outbreak in the United States of a fictional Ebola-like virus called Motaba that mutates and spreads through the respiratory route.

The last previous Ebola outbreak had been in 2012 in the DRC with thirty-eight cases and thirteen deaths. The DRC had had years of experience dealing with and successfully containing prior outbreaks of Ebola of various magnitudes.

In March 2014 disturbing reports were coming from the WHO about a cluster of Ebola cases occurring in the West African country of Guinea that began in December 2013. The cases were spreading and were not being controlled by standard measures. Unlike the DRC, Uganda, and other Central African countries, Guinea had no prior experience in dealing with Ebola outbreaks, nor did the neighboring countries of Liberia and Sierra Leone. This inexperience would contribute to an impending catastrophe for those countries.

The index case in Guinea, or the original person to whom the outbreak could be traced, was thought to be a one-year-old boy who died of Ebola virus disease in December 2013 in the village of Meliandou, Guéckédou Prefecture, Guinea. The boy's home was near a large colony of Angolan free-tailed bats. Soon after he died, his mother, sister, and grandmother became ill with Ebola and died, as did several people close to the family who had helped care for the boy or who had attended his funeral and burial rites. As quickly became clear, the sacred traditions and customs of the

West African people in expressing respect and affection for their deceased loved ones were a tragic source of spread of the infection. Relatives and friends washed the bodies that were often covered with infected materials in the form of blood, feces, urine, respiratory secretions, and other bodily fluids and embraced and kissed them as a way of saying goodbye. Traditional funerals became a major source of spread of the disease. As infected people left the young boy's funeral and went to their respective homes, the infection spread rapidly to other villages. In addition, health-care workers whose personal protective equipment was inadequate as they cared for seriously ill patients were also at high risk of becoming infected. At the time, little to no international attention was paid to this outbreak.

Three months later, on March 23, 2014, the WHO reported forty-nine suspected cases of Ebola, including twenty-nine deaths in Guinea, with more cases under investigation. Greg Folkers, my indispensable source of critical information, updated me daily on the increasing cases in West Africa reported from the WHO and the CDC. Until this point press interest in Ebola in the United States was muted, perhaps because in previous outbreaks, which occurred in remote areas of Central African countries, the spread of infection was normally controlled within a short period of time.

Another issue that probably clouded the potential importance of this outbreak in a faraway land was the fact that there was at the time the continued reporting of cases of a new disease in the Middle East, particularly in Saudi Arabia, called the Middle East respiratory syndrome coronavirus, or MERS-CoV. This disease was caused by a coronavirus spread by the respiratory route and was believed to be originally transmitted by contact with infected dromedary camels, although bats were believed to be the primary reservoir for the virus. The critical issue was that the case fatality rate of MERS-CoV was a frighteningly high 35 percent. Although the first cases were recognized in September 2012, there were still smoldering mini-outbreaks in Saudi Arabia and other Middle East countries in the spring of 2014, which overlapped with the beginning of the Ebola outbreak in West Africa. The concern about MERS-CoV was heightened by the fact that on May 1, 2014, the first imported case of MERS-CoV came to the United States from Riyadh, Saudi Arabia, to Indiana, and another case arrived on May 11 from Riyadh through London to Boston to Atlanta with final destination in Orlando, Florida. If there was one "foreign" disease that the American press and people were concerned would "come to the United States" and result in a lethal outbreak, it was MERS-CoV, not Ebola. Not yet anyway. As it turned out, these were the first and only two imported cases of MERS-CoV in the United States, and public anxiety about the disease soon dwindled.

Despite this public inattention, what was happening in West Africa was what I would soon continually be describing to the press as a "perfect storm" of circumstances that were contributing to a historic outbreak. Besides the inexperience of people in this region with Ebola, many tended to be deeply suspicious of authorities, particularly outside authorities because the region had suffered in recent years from destructive civil wars and oppressive government regimes. This played out when members of organizations such as Médecins Sans Frontières (Doctors Without Borders), Samaritan's Purse, and the CDC arrived to assist. They had difficulty in getting full cooperation in matters such as avoiding unprotected contact with sick and dead people, a problem compounded by the fact that the health-care infrastructure was negligible. Moreover, borders with the neighboring countries of Liberia and Sierra Leone were porous. Finally, unlike prior outbreaks, this one struck densely populated cities. The infection rapidly spread to Liberia, and by mid-April 2014 cases were reported in the Liberian capital of Monrovia. By late May the outbreak had spread to

Conakry, the capital of Guinea with a population of about 1.7 million people. By July cases were reported in Freetown, the capital of Sierra Leone. The WHO was severely criticized for its delay in realizing the seriousness and potential catastrophic nature of the outbreak and its sluggishness in addressing it. It was not until August 8, 2014, that the WHO declared the outbreak a "Public Health Emergency of International Concern."

WITH RELATIVELY LITTLE global attention being paid, the Ebola situation in West Africa became increasingly ominous. Over the ensuing weeks and months more than 1,000 cumulative cases were reported in Guinea, Liberia, and Sierra Leone and over 620 deaths by the end of July 2014, giving it an approximately 60 percent fatality rate and already making it the largest single Ebola outbreak on record.

By this time Médecins Sans Frontières and Samaritan's Purse, among others, were playing a major role in caring for the growing number of patients infected with Ebola. Several U.S. physicians and other health-care providers were volunteering to serve with these organizations including a member of the NIH Clinical Center staff, Dr. Dan Chertow. Dan volunteered in September 2014 to directly take care of Ebola patients in Liberia under the auspices of Médecins Sans Frontières. Many health-care workers, almost all Liberians, Guineans, and Sierra Leoneans, had been infected and many had died of the disease. Also, as would be expected, people native to one country were getting infected and then traveling to faraway countries where their illness became obvious.

Such was the case at the end of July 2014 when an American citizen named Patrick Sawyer became infected from his sister in Liberia and flew to Lagos, Nigeria, where he died of Ebola virus disease. He passed on the virus to several health-care providers in

Lagos who, unaware that he was infected, took care of him without proper personal protective equipment. The outbreak that Patrick Sawyer brought into Nigeria resulted in nineteen infections and eight deaths. This stirred up considerable fear that there would now be a major outbreak in Nigeria, the most populous country in Africa. Fortunately, this did not happen, due to Nigeria's effective public health infrastructure. Other individual travel-related cases were later detected in Mali and Senegal, where health officials who had more experience and resources than were present in Liberia, Sierra Leone, and Guinea were able to prevent the spread that was raging in West Africa. Nonetheless, these events began to kindle worry that sooner or later Ebola would come to the United States. The Peace Corps decided to bring home 340 of its volunteers from the three West African countries involved.

EBOLA FINALLY DID COME to the United States on August 2, 2014, not in a swarm of uncontrolled infection but calmly and with our knowledge. Two American health-care workers, Dr. Kent Brantly and the nurse Nancy Writebol, who had been working in Liberia with the organization Samaritan's Purse, became infected and were flown in a special containment air ambulance to Emory University's designated unit to care for patients with diseases that require high containment. At the time, there were three designated units in the United States that had the physical facilities and personnel trained in providing intensive care to patients while being dressed in full-containment space suits: Emory University in Atlanta; the University of Nebraska Medical Center in Omaha; and our Special Clinical Studies Unit (SCSU) at the NIH Clinical Center in Bethesda, Maryland.

Even though it was fairly well established that Ebola could only be spread from one person to another by direct contact with infected blood, vomit, feces, and other body fluids, there was fear among some in the public that now that we had Ebola patients in the United States, it was bound to spread. This anxiety was soon greatly compounded as additional infected individuals entered the United States intentionally to receive medical care or accidentally without realizing that they were infected.

Tom Frieden made his first visit to Liberia in August 2014 to personally assess the situation and came back with a dire report. He expressed great concern at our almost daily HHS conference calls and in his public remarks that the outbreak was exploding in West Africa and 100,000 or more people could ultimately be infected. This prediction proved to be problematic for Tom, particularly within HHS and the White House, because this turned out to be a considerable overestimate. In Tom's defense, it certainly was not outlandish that this could have been the case given that at that particular time hundreds of new cases were being reported each week.

I met Tom when he was commissioner of the New York City Department of Health and Mental Hygiene from 2002 to 2009 where he established a stellar reputation as a passionate advocate for public health. Like me he was born and raised in New York City, and we immediately clicked. We got to know each other well when we began working closely together after he was appointed director of the CDC by President Obama in 2009 as we struggled through the 2009 H1N1 pandemic. Tom was responsible for disease surveillance and infection control, and I was responsible for developing a vaccine for the pandemic influenza virus.

Tom is an impressive public health figure: pragmatic and impatient with red tape. During the Ebola crisis, he had little tolerance for certain aspects of the government bureaucracy, which sometimes put him at odds with HHS officials including the HHS secretary, Sylvia Burwell, and her immediate staff. Sylvia had replaced the HHS secretary Kathleen Sebelius for President Obama's second term. She had come from the Bill & Melinda Gates Foundation and had been deputy director of OMB during the Clinton administration and director of OMB under Obama. Tom and I soon became close friends as I would often find myself explaining "what he really meant" after he had put off or offended someone at HHS or even the White House. I looked upon Tom as sort of a very talented younger brother whom I had to defend every once in a while. I also developed a good working relationship with Secretary Burwell and as a result served as a buffer between Tom and Sylvia.

While Tom was focusing on the outbreak in West Africa, I was busy shaping a clinical research agenda. We were trying to balance gaining information that would help us in this and other emerging infectious disease outbreaks while simultaneously being sensitive to the needs of the afflicted people in West Africa, particularly Liberia, which had a historically strong relationship with the United States. I once again called upon my trusted colleague Cliff Lane, who by this time had worked with me for thirty-three years. Now in 2014 he was a deputy director of NIAID and a key member of my research laboratory. Over the years he had emerged as one of the top clinical infectious disease scientists in the world.

Our goal was to test candidate vaccines for Ebola as well as drugs to treat the disease, and Cliff was the ideal person to lead a collaborative research effort with our Liberian colleagues. Our prior experience in conducting international research prompted us to make sure that the host country, in this case Liberia, actually wanted us to conduct such research. Cliff got Walter Gwenigale, the Liberian minister of Health and Social Welfare, to write a letter on August 22, 2014, to Sylvia Burwell requesting the assistance of the U.S. government and HHS in conducting research in his country on therapeutics and vaccines for Ebola. After the letter of request cleared the usual bureaucratic and diplomatic hurdles, Sylvia wrote back to Minister Gwenigale on October 2, agreeing to initiate a research collaboration in his country, and at my recommendation she designated Cliff as the point person. Cliff enthusiastically accepted this responsibility and over the ensuing year and a half made about twenty separate trips to Liberia to set up an outstanding research program that he called PREVAIL, standing for Partnership for Research on Ebola Virus in Liberia. Unlike in southern Africa, where we put together the PEPFAR program based on an existing model that Peter Mugyenyi had initiated in Uganda, Cliff was essentially starting at square one in Liberia. Under his leadership, the program conducted clinical trials for Ebola vaccines, tested drugs for treatment of Ebola virus disease, and followed the survivors of Ebola to determine the long-term consequences of Ebola infection. He proved that one could conduct well-designed, ethically sound clinical trials even in the context of a raging outbreak of a deadly disease.

Although his efforts ultimately proved successful, they were not without controversy, and we received criticism from some who felt that because of the urgency of the situation we should distribute unproven drugs or vaccines immediately without necessarily testing them for safety and efficacy. We felt that, in the long run, if drugs and vaccines are not tested in well-controlled clinical trials, one can do harm by distributing potentially toxic interventions, and at the end of the day you may never know what really is or is not effective. Both Cliff and I had been through this during the early years of the AIDS pandemic when desperate people with HIV infection would take ineffective, potentially toxic drugs because no drugs proven to be effective were yet available. Our long, sometimes painful experience over the years in clinical research taught us that compassionate use of unproven interventions outside a clinical trial does have a place under certain circumstances such as with the "parallel track" program. We had established this with HIV whereby unproven drugs could be made available to people on a compassionate basis outside a clinical trial as long as the process does not interfere with the simultaneous (parallel) conduct of the clinical trial.

After the Ebola outbreak was brought under control, the U.S. National Academies of Sciences, Engineering, and Medicine issued a report in April 2017 reviewing the experience during the Ebola outbreak. It concluded that the core principles of science and ethics in conducting clinical research should not change during an epidemic and that randomized clinical trials are ethical and appropriate and are the most efficient and reliable way to determine the safety and efficacy of the intervention in question and get the most effective interventions to the greatest number of people in the shortest period of time.

IN THE MEANTIME, the Ebola saga continued to unfold as the global response to the outbreak intensified. The CDC had deployed hundreds of staff to the West African countries to assist in infection control. USAID also was actively participating in the on-the-ground response. Médecins Sans Frontières was bearing a considerable amount of the burden on the front lines caring for increasing numbers of patients. A number of other nongovernment organizations such as Samaritan's Purse had been in West Africa almost from the beginning of the outbreak. On September 15, 2014, Paul Farmer left Haiti for Liberia to set up Ebola treatment units under the auspices of Partners in Health, an organization that he created together with Ophelia Dahl and Jim Yong Kim, who was now the president of the World Bank. Other nations including China, Italy, the U.K., and Spain sent contingents to one or more of the three countries to assist in the response. Tom Frieden and I had been calling for the Department of Defense to provide logistical support in the form of transportation and building of facilities such as field hospitals to serve as Ebola treatment units; this eventually happened.

Since the first week in August 2014, I was on almost daily conference calls, sometimes over the weekends, usually with Secretary Burwell leading the call. Sylvia showed the right stuff as the crisis evolved, exhibiting hands-on leadership, in-depth understanding of the problems and their nuances, and insistence on being kept informed without micromanaging us. Besides me, the main players on the calls were Tom Frieden, Luciana Borio from the FDA, and Nicole "Nicki" Lurie, the HHS assistant secretary for preparedness and response, as well as a number of HHS officials who occasionally participated.

While these conference calls within HHS continued, given that now multiple U.S. government agencies were involved, the center of coordination shifted in the early fall from HHS to the White House with Homeland Security Advisor Lisa Monaco taking the lead. And take the lead she did. Lisa was a no-nonsense person who well understood the urgency of the situation.

Given the burden of now coordinating what had evolved into an all-of-government response, President Obama named Ron Klain as the Ebola response coordinator. Ron, who had been chief of staff to both Vice President Biden and former vice president Al Gore, would now report directly to Lisa Monaco and National Security Advisor Susan Rice. There was grumbling that he was a political operative (which he was), was not a medical doctor (which he was not), and therefore was not qualified to be the Ebola response coordinator. But Ron immediately dispelled the skeptics' reservations. He had a special talent for making sure that all the bases were covered and that there was no wrangling over turf, and at the same time he never micromanaged the subject matter experts.

Despite these intensive efforts, for the next few months, the infections mounted in West Africa, and with that so did multiple concerns: that the outbreak would essentially overwhelm the three countries involved; that the outbreak would spread to other populous countries in Africa; and that we would have an Africa-like outbreak here. This fear for the United States was fueled by reports and photographs appearing in major newspapers such as *The New York Times* and *The Washington Post* of dead bodies lying in hospitals or in the streets of major cities such as Monrovia, Liberia; Freetown, Sierra Leone; and Conakry, Guinea.

WE ALL SUSPECTED that eventually someone who became infected in West Africa would travel to the United States before symptoms appeared and develop full-blown Ebola virus disease once they were here. Such was the case with Thomas Eric Duncan. On September 15, 2014, Duncan was exposed to a woman with Ebola virus disease as he helped transport her by taxi to an Ebola treatment unit in Monrovia. On September 19, he flew from Monrovia to the United States, landing in Dallas, Texas, on September 20 to visit his son and his son's mother. Before flying, he had denied contact with Ebola on an airport questionnaire. After arrival in Texas he began experiencing symptoms of nasal congestion and abdominal pain and on September 24 went to the Texas Health Presbyterian Hospital emergency room. Unfortunately, there was miscommunication about his travel history, and Ebola was not considered in the diagnosis. He was given Tylenol and a prescription for an antibiotic and sent home. Four days later, on September 28, he re-turned to the emergency room severely ill with diarrhea, abdomi-nal pain, and fever. Duncan was admitted to the intensive care unit and diagnosed with Ebola virus disease on September 30 on the basis of a positive laboratory test. Duncan died of his disease on October 8, 2014. The fact that someone had slipped through the airport exit-screening protocol triggered a surge of public anxiety and a frenzy of media interest.

Then things went a bit over the edge. There were calls to close the borders and not allow anyone to enter or leave the three West African countries. I completely disagreed with this approach and was not shy about saying so. If we cut off these countries from the outside world, the outbreak would surely accelerate from within and likely spread throughout Africa as people inevitably slipped through the porous borders. Tom Frieden and I were continually appearing in public to explain the lack of rationale of completely cutting off these countries from outside assistance by "locking them in."

I now experienced something that I had not encountered since the early days of the HIV/AIDS pandemic—aggressive hate mail, by email and snail mail. With AIDS it was homophobically moti-vated, criticizing me for wasting time trying to save mostly gay men who "brought this all on themselves by their aberrant behav-ior." With Ebola, the hate mail began with the arrival of Thomas Duncan and my articulating publicly that we should not isolate the West African countries, and it continued for months as we debated quarantining American health-care workers who were returning to the United States after volunteering their services in the Ebola-stricken countries. The hate mail seemed to be related to the per-ception by white supremacist types that I favored Black Africans over the health of our country. Some of the milder comments in-cluded "Where did you get your degree from, North Korea? You love Africa and Ebola so much, you go there." "You are a liberal ass-hole, selling out to Obama. Go rot in hell." "I pray that if Ebola does break out in the USA that somehow it only attacks dumbass liberals like you and removes you from your misery."

OCTOBER 12, 2014, was going to be a hectic day because I was scheduled to appear on several of the Sunday morning TV shows including *This Week with George Stephanopoulos*, *Meet the Press* with Chuck Todd, and CNN's *State of the Union with Candy Crowley*. Thomas Duncan had died four days earlier, and the public's fear of Ebola coming to the United States leading to an outbreak was to be the topic of discussion. I went to my computer at 5:45 a.m. and saw an email alerting me that there would be an important conference call that morning with Secretary Burwell, Lisa Monaco, White House communications director Jennifer Palmieri, Tom Frieden, and me as well as other White House and HHS officials on a "breaking situation."

The call was a bombshell.

A twenty-six-year-old nurse, Nina Pham, who had taken care of Thomas Duncan in intensive care at the Dallas hospital developed symptoms and was now diagnosed with Ebola. This would become particularly problematic for the CDC and for Tom Frieden because Tom, in trying to calm the country, had been using words like "we have everything under control" and "we can stop Ebola in its tracks." Tom was correct, but his statements just did not come out quite right, and we were now faced with a credibility gap. I defended the CDC during my media appearances and tried to explain to the public that it was not surprising that an initially unrecognized Ebola-infected individual inadvertently got into the country and this by no means indicated that there would be an outbreak due to the way Ebola spreads. We had been confident that by tracing and isolating Thomas Duncan's contacts such as his partner and others, we would be able to prevent a major outbreak.

But Nina Pham had gotten infected, and as we would find out the next day, so had Amber Vinson, another intensive care nurse who took care of Thomas Duncan on a different shift from that of Nina. These nurses had bravely put themselves in harm's way by taking care of Duncan under the difficult circumstances of intensive care. This was totally different from the risk to the general population. No matter. Public angst was growing, as reflected by an editorial in *USA Today* on October 14, 2014, titled "Fear Spreads Faster Than Ebola: Our View."

PUBLIC CONFIDENCE IN the government, particularly in the CDC, was further strained because of events surrounding Amber Vinson. Vinson had flown from Dallas to her home in Cleveland before any symptoms or fever had appeared. While in Cleveland she developed a temperature of 99.3 degrees Fahrenheit, below the CDC cutoff of 101 degrees Fahrenheit for suspicion of Ebola infection, a parameter that was used to block someone from flying. When Vinson called the CDC to ask if she could fly back to Dallas, the CDC person cleared her to fly. By the time she returned to Dallas, it was clear that she did have a fever and that theoretically she had exposed the passengers on her flight from Cleveland to Dallas even though it was well-known that because she was not acutely ill and no one was exposed to her "body fluids," the risk of spread to her fellow passengers was extremely low and very likely nonexistent. Nonetheless, the CDC initiated a massive contact tracing of passengers on her flight, many of whom had already taken connecting flights. It turned out there were no secondary infections related to either Nina Pham or Amber Vinson. However, this all triggered a crisis of confidence in the CDC and unfortunately in Tom Frieden.

No doubt, it was poor judgment on the part of the CDC person to let Vinson fly, especially given the depth of public concern around the possibility, albeit remote, of an Ebola outbreak in the United States. Within a couple of days, Bill O'Reilly on his Fox TV show called for Tom to resign. Tom was not at all involved in the decision to let Vinson fly, but in Washington it seems that someone always needs to be blamed.

It was clear that we were dealing with an epidemic of fear rather than an epidemic of Ebola virus disease. The White House understood that the task at hand was to manage the growing sense of panic including the public perception that the U.S. government was mishandling the crisis. Lisa Monaco, White House chief of staff Denis McDonough, and others pushed and succeeded in getting me to appear on October 19, 2014, on all five of the major Sunday TV shows. The goal was for me to calm the nation and explain the scientific and medical facts in a way that the American public could understand. Andrea Purse, director of media broadcast for White House communications, was given a White House vehicle and driver and was assigned the task of making sure that I got to each of the five studios scattered around Washington in time for a taping or a live hit. Andrea was relentless in her mission as she whipped us through downtown Washington from TV studio to studio in the early Sunday morning hours.

NINA PHAM WAS ORIGINALLY cared for at Texas Health Presbyterian Hospital in Dallas, as was Amber Vinson. However, because of the concern that the hospital would be overwhelmed with other infections that might soon be appearing in Dallas related to Duncan, health officials decided that Amber would be transferred to

Emory University Hospital and Nina would be transferred to us in the Special Clinical Studies Unit at the NIH Clinical Center.

At the NIH, we had already admitted under the strict containment protocols two health-care workers who had a high-risk exposure to Ebola while taking care of patients in one of the West African countries. Neither of them turned out to have contracted Ebola virus, which meant that Nina was the Clinical Center's first patient who actually had documented Ebola virus disease. Since I had asked my staff to put themselves at risk taking care of patients with documented Ebola virus disease, I did not want to ask them to do something that I myself would not also do. Although I had been previously certified to work in the Special Clinical Studies Unit, I quickly had myself recertified to care for Ebola patients by taking the training refresher course given by one of our unit nurses and passing the test.

At 11:54 p.m. on Thursday, October 16, 2014, Nina Pham arrived at the NIH by police escort in an ambulance specially fitted for high containment coming from the Frederick, Maryland, airport. She had flown from Dallas in a specially equipped plane. Anthony Suffredini, one of our senior intensive care physicians, dressed in full space suit PPE and accompanied Nina in the ambulance. I waited to greet them at the back entrance to the NIH Clinical Center with Rick Davey, the head of the Special Clinical Studies Unit, Cliff Lane, and John Gallin, director of the NIH Clinical Center. Tara Palmore, hospital epidemiologist and senior infectious disease physician, was dressed in personal protective equipment ready to help get Nina admitted to our unit. Nina was obviously very ill, but not in dire straits. Three hours later we got her officially plugged into the unit and comfortably settled.

Because Nina's arrival at the NIH was widely broadcast over the media, many of the eighteen thousand NIH staff were understandably concerned about what was going on. On only three hours of sleep, the following morning John Gallin, Cliff Lane, and I, dressed in our fresh white coats, held a standing-room-only (much to the dismay of the fire marshal) town hall meeting for NIH staff in the expansive Masur Auditorium of the NIH Clinical Center. The crowd overflowed to a backup auditorium and several other rooms, and still more people watched via webcast. John Gallin confirmed to the gathered crowd that indeed we had admitted an acutely ill Ebola patient to our hospital the previous night. I then explained why we felt that this was an important duty of ours as public servants working in a government hospital. I did not want to appear melodramatic, but I told the audience, "We are a part of the government medical SWAT team, and this is what we do. Whatever risks there may be, this is still what we do."

Most people were entirely supportive, but during the question-and-answer period, a few objected to what we were doing, concerned that one or more of our staff would get infected and would then infect others in the hospital. Even to this medically sophisticated audience, I had to explain once again that one only gets infected by direct contact with bodily fluids from an acutely ill patient and that all of the staff taking care of Nina would be monitored twice a day for fever, which is usually the first sign of infection. I also said that in the unlikely possibility that one of us got infected, we would be isolated well before we became infective to others.

Over the next several days, because there were no approved drugs to treat Ebola, all we could do was provide Nina with supportive care: mostly intravenous fluids, analgesics, and fever control. Her signs and symptoms, mostly liver toxicity, were related in part to the experimental drugs that she had been given while at Texas Health Presbyterian Hospital. Each day she continued to improve. When the virus in her blood dropped to a very low level, we could enter Nina's room in modified contact protective clothing and mask, making it much easier and more comfortable to communicate with her, allowing me to spend a considerable amount of time with her over the duration of her stay. My staff and I immediately developed a rapport with her; her mother, Diana; and her sister Cathy, who remained in Bethesda for the entire time of her admission.

As Nina became more comfortable confiding in me, I wanted to find out if possible how she might have gotten infected while taking care of Thomas Duncan. When it had become public that she had gotten infected while taking care of an Ebola patient, it was reported that she must have "broken protocol" or had some procedural lapse. I was getting to know her pretty well, and I could not believe that this was the case because I asked her if she had done anything to break protocol. She insisted that she had not. Then I asked her to describe step by step how she got dressed in personal protective equipment. This was critical because if we were going to take care of acutely ill Ebola patients in our unit and we were wearing equipment that did not fully protect us, we needed to know about it.

I was shocked by what she told me. She did indeed follow to the letter the protocol that she was given. But when I asked her if any part of her skin or hair was exposed while she was in the intensive care unit, she told me that the first day she took care of Thomas Duncan much of her neck, her ears, and a considerable amount of the hair on the back of her head were exposed. What's more, after she removed her protective equipment, she did not "shower out."

We discovered that the protocol Nina followed was the protocol used in the field where patients were taken care of in tents and field hospitals. That setting is entirely different from a truly intensive care situation where multiple intravenous lines are inserted and tended to, patients are intubated with endotracheal tubes, and rectal tubes and urinary catheters are placed, as was the case with Duncan. In the protocol that we, Emory, and Nebraska were using, no part of the body was exposed, and one's personal protective equipment had to be removed in a precisely specified manner to avoid personal contamination. The person must then immediately shower and dress in a fresh set of scrubs. Therefore, Nina did not break protocol; she was initially given a protocol that was not appropriate for intensive care of an Ebola patient.

Thank goodness she was steadily improving.

I had been speaking with Secretary Burwell on a daily basis, briefing her on Nina's progress. Late in the evening of October 20, 2014, as I pulled up in front of my house, I received a now common nighttime phone call from the secretary. When I explained to Sylvia what Nina had told me about her personal protective equipment and how she got infected through no fault of her own, I could hear Sylvia struggling to hold back tears. No question, this was an intense and stressful time for all of us.

As NINA CONTINUED to improve, she would soon be ready to return home to Texas. One day as we were chatting in her room, she told me that she was worried she might be stigmatized after we discharged her. We were already aware of this issue from prior experience in West Africa. People who had fully recovered from Ebola were often not just stigmatized but ostracized as if they posed a continual danger to others. This problem was compounded by the growing concern, without any scientific basis, that healthcare workers including our team who took care of Ebola patients, even though they appeared to be healthy, could actually be infected and transmit the infection to others.

The media had followed Nina's case day by day during her stay at the NIH, and we decided to discharge her publicly at the north entrance to the NIH Clinical Center. That day, October 24, 2014, NIH communications director John Burklow; NIH director Francis Collins; Rick Davey; Cliff Lane; the nurses, technicians, and physicians who had cared for Nina; and I gathered in the main lobby of the Clinical Center at around noon. Seeing a wall of more than a dozen television cameras and essentially every Washington, D.C.–based reporter who had ever interviewed me, I decided right then and there that this was my chance to address the stigma issue. As we all walked out to the applause of the waiting crowd, I put my arm around Nina. After I gave a few introductory remarks to emphasize that Nina was now truly free from Ebola, I called her up to the lectern. As she approached, I gave her a long and warm hug. The photograph of that hug ran on the front page of *The Washington Post* the next day, went viral on social media, and was shown on virtually every TV broadcast throughout the world that evening. Nina gave a beautiful, heartfelt speech thanking the NIH staff for taking such good care of her. Following her discharge, she and her family, Cliff Lane, Rick Davey, and I went to the White House to meet with President Obama in the Oval Office. Without hesitation the president hugged Nina in front of a collection of photographers snapping away. When we parted ways, it was a bittersweet goodbye because I had become so fond of Nina and her family. I gave her my cell phone number, and for some time thereafter we communicated on FaceTime as she continued to regain her strength.

SIMULTANEOUSLY INTERWOVEN WITH the positive outcome of Nina's recovery were a series of events that compounded the frenzy around Ebola in the United States and thrust me into the middle of a politically sensitive debate that I would have preferred to avoid.

On October 23, 2014, the day before I discharged Nina from
the NIH, it was reported that Craig Spencer, a thirty-three-year-
old physician from the New York–Presbyterian/Columbia University Medical Center who had volunteered to take care of Ebola
patients with Doctors Without Borders in Guinea, had returned
to New York City a few days earlier and was now infected and admitted to Bellevue Hospital. Bellevue had recently begun to train
and prepare itself for such an emergency. The problem was that
Dr. Spencer had traveled around the city before it became apparent that he was infected. He had no fever at the time of his return.
On Tuesday, October 21, he felt a little "worn down," but still had
no fever. He had been in contact with a few friends as well as with
his fiancé. On Wednesday, October 22, he took two subway trains
from his apartment in Harlem to a bowling alley in Brooklyn. He
then took an Uber home. On Thursday, October 23, he developed
a fever of 103 degrees Fahrenheit. He followed protocol and notified authorities that he was febrile, was evacuated by hazmat-
dressed emergency responders, and was admitted to the Bellevue
intensive care unit. A few hours later a confirmatory test came
back positive for Ebola. Dr. Spencer, who soon became seriously
ill, recovered completely after an extended hospital stay. But this
episode stirred up a public debate on how to handle returning
health-care workers who cared for Ebola patients.

The plot then thickened.

A day after Dr. Spencer was noted to be infected, Kaci Hickox,
a nurse who had been taking care of Ebola patients in Sierra Leone, returned to Newark International Airport. On that same day,
related to the circumstances surrounding Dr. Spencer's return
from Guinea, New Jersey's governor, Chris Christie, and New
York's governor, Andrew Cuomo, ordered that all returning travelers to New Jersey and New York who had had contact with
Ebola patients in West Africa be quarantined for twenty-one days.

Ms. Hickox was the first returning Ebola caregiver to get caught up in this new policy. Officials at the Newark airport thought that she had a fever after taking a skin temperature. As it turned out, she was just flushed from the long trip, her correct temperature actually was normal, and she was not infected. Nonetheless, she was detained at the airport under conditions to which she strenuously objected, which triggered a battle between her and Governor Christie. Ultimately, she was released to drive to Maine to see her boyfriend.

Here was a situation where we had multiple federal departments (HHS, State, Homeland Security, Transportation) in the mix as well as the governors of two states.

It was just this type of complicated situation that justified having Ron Klain on board with a cool head, competence, and good judgment to help sort things out.

Right smack in the middle of all of this, I was doing the five Sunday TV shows and multiple other media appearances. As might have been expected, I was asked what my opinion was of the quarantine order by the two governors. This was dicey because I did not want to get into a public skirmish with the governors who were just trying to do their jobs. Governor Christie was particularly vocal about his insistence on quarantine, while Governor Cuomo was a bit more reserved. I had a lot of respect for Governor Christie, and I really did not want to start sparring with him publicly. Yet I could not back down, because a blanket quarantine was beyond the CDC recommendations. On each of the shows, I articulated two fundamental principles: First, that the safety of the American people came first and it was part of my responsibility to safeguard the public. I wanted to make sure that everyone understood that. However, second, all of our policies relating to the monitoring and movement of and restrictions on returning health-care workers should be based on sound scientific principles and scientific evidence. A person who was without symptoms did not transmit Ebola, and one must come into direct contact with the body fluids of an acutely ill person to become infected.

Returning health-care workers were well instructed to report symptoms and self-isolate the way Craig Spencer correctly did. Importantly, if a twenty-one-day quarantine was implemented across the board for all health-care workers who volunteered to care for Ebola patients, then I was certain, as were Tom Frieden and several of my colleagues who had volunteered or who were considering volunteering, that we would soon run out of people willing to care for these patients. A quarantine would mean that those of us, including myself, who were caring for Ebola patients in the United States would automatically be putting ourselves out of action for twenty-one days after taking care of even a single person. I was especially careful not to directly criticize the governors, and I said in the TV interviews that I could understand how they may sincerely feel that they were doing what was best for their constituencies. I did feel that they had a point in that we should consider stricter attention to the movements of potentially exposed health-care workers. But a blanket quarantine, in my mind, was going too far. President Obama would soon get involved in helping us reach an acceptable compromise.

THE POLICY ON monitoring and controlling movement of returning health-care workers was what was referred to as passive monitoring. This meant that the person in question took their own temperature and evaluated themselves for symptoms, only reporting them if there was a fever or other symptoms. This is exactly what Craig Spencer had done. This approach leaves the entire responsibility on the individual involved. Spencer had acted appropriately and everything worked out well. Active monitoring is the same as passive, except that you tell someone else each day whether you do or do not have a fever or symptoms. In this way, there is another person involved on a daily basis, but you are still the primary person to monitor yourself and you relay the correct information to the second party. Direct active monitoring is when another qualified person directly monitors you, taking your temperature and asking about symptoms at least once per day. That person and not the health-care worker then decides the degree of restriction or not of movement.

On Sunday, October 26, 2014, I went to the White House for a 12:30 p.m. meeting with the Homeland Security Council and the president. The meeting was scheduled for an hour, and it lasted two and a half hours. In Situation Room meetings, particularly those involving the president, the participants always get there about ten minutes early and make small talk as they wait for the arrival of the president. This day was no exception. Usually President Obama started the meeting in a light manner, casually chatting with one or more of the principals. That day he seemed more detached than usual and even a bit tired. No wonder, I thought. He had a lot of other important things on his mind, and it was Sunday after what had been a tough week. But in typical Obama fashion he immediately became totally engaged in the conversation.

The president asked my opinion on the best approach to the monitoring and movement of returning health-care workers. "Mr. President, speaking for myself and Tom Frieden," I said, "we believe that the direct active monitoring approach is the best way to abide by sound scientific principles that are applicable to the risk of Ebola. This alleviates as best as possible the concerns of the public, and does not resort to a broad policy of quarantine." I suggested that we match the level of the risk experienced by each returning health-care worker to the level of the restriction of movement that we would impose on the worker. For example, if a health-care provider had been working in an Ebola Treatment Unit, but had not been directly exposed to contaminated body fluids, their risk would be considered less than that of a person who was directly exposed, and so their movements would be less restricted. In this way, we could achieve the protective effect of a broad quarantine without actually imposing a broad quarantine.

The president liked this approach. As we closed the meeting, he told us that we had better get this right and that we needed to be crystal clear in what the policy was and why we had arrived at it. He reflected that over the past three weeks he had spent most of his time on Ebola and, tragic as the disease was, Ebola had killed only one person in the United States, at the same time that he was dealing with ISIS, Iran, the Affordable Care Act, border children, and just two days previously (Friday) a deranged high school student in Washington State who had killed two fellow students, wounded several others, and then shot himself. The president's marching orders were clear. The next day (October 27, 2014), Tom Frieden came out with revised CDC guidelines based on direct active monitoring.

Some Republicans criticized the president for his decision not to quarantine, and I continued to get hate mail including such intellectually constructive messages as "Fuck you and Fuck your opinions." The next day I was informed by the NIH Office of the General Counsel that I had been named in a civil action lawsuit along with President Obama, Secretary Burwell, Homeland Security Secretary Jeh Johnson, and Tom Frieden for promoting terrorism and discrimination. We were being accused of colluding with President Obama, whom they claimed was a Muslim citizen of Kenya, and of trying to destroy our country by introducing Ebola into American society. You just cannot make this stuff up.

Because the president came out strongly against blanket quarantine and had recently asked Congress for $6.18 billion for the multiagency Ebola response, congressional hearings inevitably followed, and anyone who knows anything about Washington, D.C., knew that the hearings would reflect which party controlled which chamber.

On November 12, 2014, Tom Frieden and I accompanied Secretaries Burwell and Johnson along with representatives of the Departments of Defense and State to testify before the full Senate Appropriations Committee. The Democrats had lost control of the Senate for 2015 as a result of the November 4 elections, but it was November 12, and the Democrats still held the chair of the committee with Senator Barbara Mikulski of Maryland; the Republican senator Richard Shelby of Alabama was ranking member. Shelby was a gentleman and relatively neutral in his comments, while Senators Mikulski and Tom Harkin of Iowa praised the administration's response to the Ebola outbreak. They were especially complimentary to Tom Frieden and me and were sympathetic to the budget request.

In contrast, on November 19, I testified before the House Energy and Commerce Committee controlled by the Republicans and chaired by Congressman Joseph Pitts, Republican of Pennsylvania, with Mike Burgess, Republican of Texas, as vice-chair. The hearing was primarily about product development for Ebola, but the discussion also included the quarantine issue. It was a lively hearing, but not a friendly one. Republican congressman Tim Murphy of Pennsylvania jumped all over me both for the quarantine issue and for the fact that we were doing controlled clinical trials in Ebola instead of just giving out the vaccine and experimental drugs. After his statement, without giving me a chance to respond, he got up and left. Clearly, Murphy was not happy with me, and this bothered me because, as tough as he was, I respected his intelligence and his fund of knowledge even though I disagreed with him. Next, Republican congresswoman Marsha Blackburn of Tennessee made a statement that we were moving too slowly in developing products and that industry could do much better. She too got up and left without giving me a chance to explain that the NIH does not make products; we do the basic and clinical research allowing industry to make products. It is a synergistic relationship between the NIH and industry. After thirty years of testifying before Congress and seeing this duel play out between the party in the White House and the parties that control the House and/or the Senate, none of this surprised me in the least. Finally, Congressman Mike Burgess, who had always been fair with me, gave me the opportunity to respond to Murphy's and Blackburn's comments.

MY TEAM AT NIAID along with other collaborators had just published in *The New England Journal of Medicine* the preliminary report of results of a phase 1 study that showed the safety (not yet the efficacy) of an Ebola vaccine candidate. I suggested to Denis McDonough that if the president could possibly fit it into his schedule, it would be great if he could visit the NIH. Denis said that the president had actually mentioned this to him and wanted to do this to thank our staff for their work on the vaccine trial. The president visited the NIH on December 2, 2014, and I showed him around the Vaccine Research Center just as I had done with President Clinton at the VRC groundbreaking back in 1999 and as I had done with Vice President Cheney and President George W. Bush during our biodefense efforts. I introduced President Obama to Dr. Nancy Sullivan, a veteran virologist who had been working on an Ebola vaccine for more than a decade. Not content to merely meet and greet, the president asked to go over Nancy's data book with her. She explained her first experiments from ten years earlier that led to the vaccine that had just been tested for safety.

After the VRC tour, I rode in the presidential limousine with Obama on the short trip across the NIH campus to the packed Masur Auditorium, where he addressed the NIH community. Impressed with what Nancy had shown him, he spoke eloquently about the importance of basic biomedical research in preventing, diagnosing, and treating diseases in the United States and worldwide. The audience, made up predominantly of people involved directly or indirectly in basic biomedical research, erupted in applause that seemed to go on for minutes. The president's sense of humor brought down the house when he pointed to me in the first row and said, "Tony and I were fondly reminiscing about the days of SARS and H1N1 pandemic flu."

Then, flashing a big smile, he asked the audience, "That's what you guys do for fun?"

WITH EBOLA NOW beginning to wane, Ron Klain decided that February 11, 2015, would be his last day as the White House Ebola response coordinator and that he would return to his position in the private sector. Ron had promised President Obama that he would stay until the Ebola situation was under control, and he had done his job exceptionally well. There was virtually no one involved in the White House Ebola response who was not sad that Ron was leaving. He had proved those who had been skeptical about his appointment to be wrong. Ron demonstrated the importance of surrounding oneself with the best possible people, pointing them in the right direction, being totally available for consultation, and staying out of their way. He had coordinated a vast multiagency effort in a crisis. I decided that I could not just let him leave without some recognition, and so I had a certificate made and framed thanking him on behalf of the NIH for his extraordinary efforts.

I wanted to deliver it to him personally, and so I took the Washington, D.C., Metro from the NIH to his office in downtown Washington to present it to him. Unfortunately, he was out having lunch when I arrived, and so I just left the certificate with his assistant and headed back. When he returned to his office, he immediately wrote me an email: "Tony: I so rarely go out to lunch—so I was completely crushed that I missed the extraordinary moment when one of the world's leading doctors paid me a house call. Thank you so much for the wonderful letter and incredible gift. I can tell people now that while I infamously do NOT have a medical degree I DO have a certificate from the NIH!!!!"

Ron might have been through with Ebola. But I soon found out that Ebola was not through with me.

Patient X

It was 1:45 a.m. on Friday, March 13, 2015, when my alarm clock blasted and I forced myself out of bed, to begin the first day of one of the most all-consuming four weeks of my life as a practicing physician. We had been notified the day before that a young health professional had become infected while caring for Ebola patients with Paul Farmer's Partners in Health group in Sierra Leone. Paul had emailed me several times and wanted very much for me and our group at the NIH to take care of his colleague. It turned out the NIH happened to be next in line to receive an Ebola patient according to the rotation among the three designated hospitals—University of Nebraska, Emory, and the NIH. We gladly accepted. The patient was being flown by chartered flight from Sierra Leone to Dulles International Airport in Virginia and would then come to the NIH by a police-escorted ambulance specially equipped for high containment. Although Nina Pham was public about her illness, this patient preferred to remain anonymous. For the sake of confidentiality I will refer to him as Robert, which was not his name.

I arrived at the NIH about 3:00 a.m. Robert landed at Dulles airport at 3:16 a.m. The same Special Clinical Studies Unit staff of nurses, physicians, and other health-care providers who had cared for Nina waited for the ambulance, which arrived at the back entrance of the NIH Clinical Center at 4:45 a.m. The team was led by the SCSU director, Dr. Rick Davey, together with Drs. Tara Palmore, Anthony Suffredini, and Dan Chertow, among others. Robert was immediately taken up to the SCSU on the fifth floor. Everyone knew what their responsibility was, and the transfer was flawless. Unlike Nina, who came to us from Texas Health Presbyterian Hospital critically ill but in the recovery phase, Robert was acutely ill and getting worse before our eyes. As the team got him into the bed of his specially equipped room, he was vomiting, had profuse diarrhea, profound weakness with liver function, and metabolic abnormalities. This was going to be intense because, although we would all be dressed in the state-of-the-art personal protective equipment with every millimeter of our bodies protected, there was no doubt that contaminated body fluids would get on our PPE. At the time that Robert was admitted to the NIH, more than eight hundred health-care workers had contracted the disease from taking care of patients in West Africa, and approximately five hundred had died.

As was the situation with Nina Pham, I did not want my team to take a risk that I was not willing to take myself, so I insisted on being part of Robert's care team. Rick Davey and the NIH physicians trained in intensive care got Robert settled in for the first shift. The protocol was clear. Those not directly involved at that point, including me, just needed to watch and stay out of the way. Our turn would come. Now I needed to get over to my office for the day's work, albeit a bit early.

I remember with great clarity taking the elevator down from the fifth floor, where the SCSU was located, to the Clinical Center lobby and walking through the spacious but completely empty atrium at 5:05 a.m. I had this extraordinary déjà vu of walking the hospital halls late at night more than forty years earlier as an in-tern and resident, when I very often stayed up through the night taking care of extremely ill patients. It might sound strange, but this is when I felt most at home. I was doing something that I have always loved to do and still love to do—taking care of very sick patients in the middle of the night when there were only skilled people around doing their thing. Very quiet, very intense. It is amazing how wide awake an adrenaline surge makes you feel at five in the morning.

THE NEXT DAY at 8:00 a.m., Saturday, it was my turn. I joined the Ebola team who had gathered for morning report, where the team that had just been taking care of Robert through the night was handing over the reins to the next shift.

There were always two or three nurses who staffed the nurses' station and audio and video links from the nurses' station to Robert's high-containment room. The nurses' lounge where we took morning report and gathered before and after our shifts was adjacent to the nurses' station. The hallway was where our PPE was stacked and where we donned, or put on, our PPE. Off the hallway was the anteroom where we doffed, or took off, our potentially contaminated protective clothing. The anteroom led directly into Robert's private room.

We followed a strict protocol. Always present on-site and rotating in and out of Robert's room were an infectious disease specialist (the category that Rick Davey and I were in), an intensive care specialist (the category that Anthony Suffredini and Dan Chertow were in), and several highly trained and skilled nurses. One of the most important members of the team was the WatSan. The term "WatSan" derives from old-time public health officials who were "water and sanitation specialists." With Ebola, the term applied mostly to nurses but also to physicians and laboratory workers, who were specially trained and whose responsibility was to ensure that each step in the donning and doffing of those who entered and exited Robert's room was followed to the letter. The multistep donning was strictly prescribed: underlying scrubs, impermeable gown, multiple layers of gloves with extended cuffs, shoe covers, disposable aprons, full face shield, and PAPR (powered air-purifying respirator). Before we entered the anteroom, the WatSan in the hallway would carefully inspect our PPE to verify that every area of the body was covered. When we left Robert's room by way of the anteroom, the WatSan carefully checked off every step in the doffing process. Doffing was the trickiest and potentially most dangerous step because you were removing contaminated protective clothing. Very intense moments. There was no small talk or joking around while donning and certainly not when doffing. No room for mistakes. Also, no matter who you were, and whatever your rank or seniority, when you donned and doffed, the WatSan was the boss and you strictly followed that person's instructions. When you were in the room with Robert, there was always a properly donned nurse watching your every move to make sure that there were no breaches in protocol. Shifts in the room were timed and with few exceptions did not exceed two hours. Moving around in the space suit PPE was uncomfortable, and despite the temperature control, which made it temperate compared with the extreme heat that our colleagues in West Africa were experiencing with PPE, one still became exhausted at about two hours, and that is when most mistakes and accidents occur. And so, the rules were two hours and out; doff, take a shower, put on a fresh set of scrubs, and report back to the lounge to brief the next shift.

My first shift in Robert's room was with Anthony Suffredini and Rick Davey. Over my many years at the NIH, I had been involved directly or indirectly in the training of all of the infectious disease physicians on the team; I was their mentor and technically speaking I was their administrative boss. However, in that room rank did not matter. It was teamwork at its best with two goals: to save Robert's life, and to not get ourselves infected in the process.

It was clear from the moment I entered the room that Robert was seriously ill. He had a high fever; a rash covering his body; was extremely weak, though able to communicate; and was putting out copious diarrhea (typical of Ebola infection) through and around a rectal tube. His platelets (cells that prevent you from bleeding) were rapidly dropping, and most of his blood chemistries were abnormal to a greater or lesser degree. In adjusting his rectal tube, positioning his urinary catheter, attending to the various intravenous lines plugged into him, and listening to his frequent coughing as we moved him about in bed to examine him, it was clear that we were being exposed to a fair amount of Ebola virus because the level of Ebola in his blood was still very high according to our lab tests. The team in the room was thinking the same thing: thank goodness for our PPE.

Around 10:00 a.m., after Rick, Anthony, and I doffed and showered out, we waited for Robert's parents to arrive. Bible in hand, they came into the lounge where Rick, Cliff Lane, and I spent more than an hour with them explaining the seriousness of the situation and what our plans were in caring for Robert. We then brought them into the nurses' station, where they could speak to their son through the video link. His parents were obviously deeply concerned as they watched the intense activity of the physicians and nurses centered on their critically ill son. After a tender conversation between parents and child, Robert's father read a passage to Robert from the Old Testament. He then turned to those of us in the nurses' station and said, "What a wonderful country we live in that would put so much effort into saving the life of one person—our dear son."

As battle-tested physicians and nurses as we were, there was not a dry eye in the room.

THE EFFORT TO SAVE Robert's life intensified as the days went by. I spent the entire next day, Sunday, March 15, in the SCSU rotating in and out of his room. We learned a sobering fact about Ebola. We had assumed that if we could monitor and maintain Robert's fluid and electrolyte (essential elements in the plasma) balance and his blood pressure, provide oxygen to alleviate his breathing difficulty, and treat any secondary infections, his immune system would suppress the Ebola virus and he would spontaneously improve without further organ system dysfunction. Unfortunately, the Ebola virus was not cooperative. As strictly as we maintained his body functions, his organ systems began to fail, one by one. First, his lungs failed. Despite the administration of nasal oxygen at a high flow, the saturation of oxygen in his blood fell to dangerously low levels, and to compensate, his respirations increased to forty per minute, which was untenable for any sustained period of time because this rate of breathing would ultimately exhaust him and he would die a respiratory death. On Sunday evening during my shift with Rick Davey, Bob Danner, one of our intensive care physicians, performed an elective intubation, placing a breathing tube through Robert's mouth into his trachea and attaching the tube to a ventilator. The machine would mechanically breathe for Robert, providing him with sufficient oxygen without his having to put in any effort. Robert's tracheal intubation exposed all of us to aerosolized Ebola virus. His respiratory secretions sprayed all over us as Bob inserted the tube. Each of us was thinking to take extra special care in doffing our PPE later. Robert's respiratory distress immediately improved, his blood oxygen level returned to normal, and we were over that hump for now. However, there were more challenges ahead.

Over the next few days, the failures of his organ systems continued. His kidneys gradually lost function, and we came close to having to dialyze him. Fortunately, his kidney function stabilized and began to improve over a few days. Next, he developed abnormalities of liver function, and more important, he developed a condition known as meningoencephalitis, which means that the Ebola virus had invaded his brain and the tissue covering (meninges) around his brain. He was deeply sedated so that the ventilator could breathe for him; so we could not carry out a thorough neurological exam. But it was clear that he had classic signs of neurological dysfunction. Soon thereafter, his heart began to fail due likely to direct involvement of Ebola virus with his heart muscle (cardiomyopathy). His condition was critical, and all we could do was to maintain his systems as best as possible until his body cleared the virus.

What an aggressive virus this was! Robert was receiving the best possible intensive care in the world administered twenty-four hours a day by a team of highly skilled physicians and nurses with the most up-to-date medical technologies, and he still was in imminent danger of succumbing.

Paul Farmer called or emailed me every night to check on Robert, and he even flew in from overseas to visit us and thank our team for what we were doing. Paul knew how serious the situation was, and we were all holding our breath in this standoff with the virus. Robert's parents maintained a daily vigil in the waiting room and nurses' lounge, hoping, praying, and continually thanking us for our efforts.

ONE OF THE SCARIEST episodes in my medical career occurred on Thursday evening, March 19. Robert's condition and various organ system failures were stabilizing, and we had begun to gradually taper him off his deep sedation in anticipation of ultimately taking him off the ventilator and removing his endotracheal tube. He seemed calm and tolerated tapering of the sedation very well. At around 6:00 p.m., there were two nurses in the room with Robert, and the rest of us were taking evening report in the nurses' lounge. Suddenly one of the nurses in the station banged on the window and pointed to the monitor that focused in on Robert's room. To our horror we saw that Robert had abruptly awakened, and although he had soft restraints on his arms and legs, he was flailing about trying to get out of bed. He pulled out his central intravenous catheter, and blood began to ooze onto his chest. He then yanked out the tubing that connected his endotracheal tube to the ventilator. As we all scrambled to get into our PPE to enter the room, we witnessed one of the most impressive displays of competence and bravery among medical personnel imaginable. Neil Barranta and Kim Adao were the two nurses in the room. They instinctively jumped on top of Robert and tried to pin him to the bed, getting blood all over their PPE. While pressing a towel on his bleeding intravenous site, they tried desperately to reconnect him to the ventilator at the same time that Neil was groping for the syringe that contained the sedative (Versed) to inject into Robert to knock him out. Robert was a tall, muscular guy, while Neil and Kim were no more than five feet, six inches tall. It usually takes about four to five minutes to properly don PPE. Rick Davey took charge and told Dan Chertow and Tara Palmore to dress up and go into the room with him to help Neil and Kim. It took them two minutes. Rick told Bob Danner and me to go into the nurses' station and read off the information on the monitor to them because they would not be able to read the monitor as they frantically tried to subdue Robert. Within twenty seconds of entering the room, they had successfully pinned Robert down, Neil had injected the Versed, and they had connected him back to the ventilator. The reinsertion of the intravenous line would have to wait until later. The scare was over, or so we thought. As the responding team exited the room into the anteroom to begin doffing their PPE, Neil took off his glove, threw it in the waste bin, and to his horror noticed that there was blood on his hand over a bruise and cut.

Aghast, we all stared at Neil's hand. Was this Robert's Ebola-contaminated blood that had gone through a tear in Neil's glove and infected him? God help us! There was deafening silence in the room. Someone needed to do something. Tara had the best idea. Gloved and properly dressed, she scavenged into the waste bin where Neil had deposited his gloves. She found them and filled them with water. To our enormous relief there was no breach in the glove. The blood on Neil's hand was his own, and the bruise came likely from a trauma associated with the frantic moments when he was holding down Robert. When several of us gathered around Neil in the nurses' station as he sat there staring ahead in shock and realized that he was okay and that he was not infected, there was a spontaneous group hug, and there were tears and sobs of relief from everyone in the room including me.

OVER THE NEXT SEVERAL DAYS, Robert continued to improve in every respect from his kidney and liver function to his breathing and neurological problems as the levels of Ebola virus in his blood gradually came down to a negligible level. We took him off the ventilator and removed the endotracheal tube on March 25. He gradually regained some of his strength and was able to walk with assistance around the room. I spent hours speaking with him over the next several days (he loved to talk), allowing him to express his feelings about his unique experience. He wanted to be filled in on all of the details of what had happened to him while he was unconscious and heavily sedated. When I told him, his frequent response was "Wow! Is that really what happened to me?" He told me that we were his guardian angels and, importantly, his friends. What a brave and unselfish person he was, having put his own life on the line to take care of such ill people in a faraway country. Even after what he went through, he said that if he had it to do over again, he would not hesitate.

When Robert's blood level of virus became undetectable on April 7, we took him out of isolation. On April 8, I attended an Ebola follow-up meeting in the Situation Room of the White House with President Obama and his senior staff including Denis McDonough, Susan Rice, and Lisa Monaco, among others. I briefed the president on our Ebola activities in West Africa and told him that I would be discharging Robert from the hospital within the next twenty-four hours. Obama was particularly pleased to hear this and insisted that I relay to Robert his best wishes and admiration for representing the United States so well by his brave service in Sierra Leone.

I discharged Robert the following day, April 9, 2015. It had been almost a month since I had met Robert's ambulance at the back entrance of the NIH Clinical Center in the middle of the night. Now we gave each other a warm hug, both of us with tears in our eyes, as I walked him out of the same back entrance to the car waiting to take him and his parents to the airport for the flight home. One month after he returned home, he wrote me an extraordinary letter that I will always cherish:

> *Dr. Fauci,*
>   *Would you believe that every afternoon I was in the hospital at NIH I always looked forward to receiving your visit. It's true. Every time you walked in with that distinct tenor voice and smile (behind the mask, of course), my spirits were raised. It was always a joy to speak with you and I thoroughly enjoyed our conversations. Later on when I got back [home] and had a chance to look up your*

accomplishments (and watch youtube videos of some of your
congressional hearings in the past) I was almost embarrassed that
I had spoken so casually with you. I thought maybe I should have
been more respectful or formal. And how in the world do you look so
good at your age? Please give me the secret. I'll need it someday.

All joking aside, I cannot express how much I am grateful for the
clinical care you provided during my stay at NIH. It truly was a
privilege to come there and be under the care of what, in my opinion,
are the best doctors and nurses in the world. Because of all of you, I
am alive and well today. I actually have a copy of a picture taken
while I was still intubated. In it, Dr. Chertow and you are on either
side of me, in the space suits, providing ICU care. I'll never forget
that image—it really is worth 1000 words. . . .

Truly I did not deserve the level of care you helped to provide—so
many other West African patients did not have the same privilege I
had. But nevertheless, you were by my side when it mattered most,
both with clinical acumen as well as a lighthearted demeanor that
could have taken me out of any bad mood. There's an old quote by
Hippocrates that goes like this: "It is more important to know what sort
of person has a disease than to know what sort of disease a person has." I
can honestly say that you treated me as a person, and not just a disease.
Thank you again for everything. I can never repay your kindness.

After I read Robert's letter, I could only say to myself, "What a
privilege it is to work with and care for such amazing people."

THE NUMBER OF EBOLA cases in West Africa continued to dwin-
dle, and by the fall and winter of 2015 there were virtually no new
cases with the exception of a rare outlier that did not lead to any
substantial spread. By the spring of 2016, the outbreak was declared officially over with more than twenty-eight thousand cases
globally and over eleven thousand deaths. Two people, the Texas
nurses Nina Pham and Amber Vinson, got infected while in the
United States, and several health-care workers who were infected

in West Africa received treatment in the United States for a total of eleven Ebola cases seen in the United States. The epidemic burned itself out as a result of the ultimate application of good infectious disease control practices.

No sooner did I get back to my office after saying goodbye to Robert than I received a call from one of my administrators about a "situation" that had developed with Dan Chertow. Among the team that had taken care of Robert, Dan spent as much time as anyone directly administering to him, taking more than his share of night call. Now that Robert had been discharged, Dan was exhausted, and he decided to take his wife and their child for a short vacation in the Dominican Republic. He went through all of the appropriate hoops and notifications of his intended travel including the NIH Occupational Medical Service, the State of Maryland Department of Health, the CDC, and the embassy of the Dominican Republic. However, somewhere along the way someone neglected to tell Dan that the Dominican Republic does not accept people in the country who have recently had contact with Ebola patients. When Dan landed in the Dominican Republic and was asked at passport control whether he had any contact with Ebola patients, he answered honestly that he had. When he arrived at his hotel, health officials were waiting for him, and after apologizing for what they were about to do, they escorted Dan and his family back to the airport and flew them back to Washington, D.C., at the expense of the Dominican Republic. So much for Dan's well-deserved vacation. The only thing that I could think of when they told me this was, truly, no good deed goes unpunished.

Zika and Other Surprises

Our girls were growing up, they were out of the house, and they were flourishing. Jenny was on her way to becoming a doctoral-level clinical psychologist working with troubled adolescents. Megan, who graduated from Columbia University, was pursuing her love of teaching and had become a public school teacher in New Orleans. The baby of the family, Ali, had graduated from Stanford with a degree in computer science while being one of the captains of the women's crew team. One of her many appealing qualities is her unassuming nature. She became the Pac-12 Scholar-Athlete of the Year in Women's Rowing, an accomplishment that Christine and I learned about only by happenstance when we read a Stanford news article.

Anytime my work took me to Boston, New Orleans, or San Francisco, I relished visiting with my daughters. I loved seeing their apartments, meeting their friends, and spending time with Jenny's dog, Lucca, who acted as glad to see me as I was to see her.

With the girls out of the house, Christine and I occupied ourselves pretty much the way we did before we had children—working hard and taking long walks together along the C&O Canal, my favorite place on earth. I like looking for blue herons and other birds, and I like to fish. I always feel that it would be great to have more time to do that.

Easier said than done.

We barely had enough time to catch our breath following the Ebola outbreak when another emerging infection jumped into the spotlight, this time not in faraway Africa but in our own backyard in the Americas—a virus called Zika.

Zika is a virus in the same viral family (flavivirus) as dengue, West Nile virus, and yellow fever. It is transmitted by the bite of a mosquito, usually the *Aedes aegypti* species, a notorious bad actor in the transmission of serious mosquito-borne diseases. The Zika virus was first discovered in the Ziika Forest of Uganda in 1947, hence the name Zika (the second *i* was dropped from the name). The first human cases were described in 1952 in Africa, and then the virus seemed to disappear until outbreaks occurred in Micronesia in 2007 and French Polynesia in 2013. Zika virus infections are generally very mild. Eighty percent of people have no symptoms, and the 20 percent who do have symptoms develop a rash, low-grade fever, muscle and joint aches, inflammation of the eye (conjunctivitis), and headache. The symptoms last a few days and then disappear without any serious residual consequences. Hence, the infection was felt to be "inconsequential." Not this time.

In 2015 there was a major outbreak of tens and ultimately hundreds of thousands of Zika infections in Brazil, particularly in the northeastern states of the country. Soon the disastrous nature of Zika became apparent as Brazilian obstetricians and pediatricians began noticing a dramatic increase in microcephaly in babies born to mothers who had been infected with Zika during their pregnancy. This complication had gone unnoticed in prior outbreaks due to the relatively small number of Zika infections.

Microcephaly means "small head" and results from the destruction of the developing brain of the fetus by the virus. When the fetal brain does not develop properly, the skull assumes a smaller size and shape. Babies born of mothers who were infected during pregnancy also had other brain abnormalities that did not show up as microcephaly. It was a tragic situation, and by January 2016 there were more than three thousand cases of microcephaly reported in Brazil. Because the *Aedes aegypti* mosquito was also commonly seen throughout other countries in South America and the Caribbean, including Puerto Rico, increased numbers of babies with microcephaly began to be reported from those countries. Other infections contracted during pregnancy such as rubella (German measles), chickenpox, toxoplasmosis, and cytomegalovirus have been shown to result in microcephaly of the fetus, but this was the first time that a virus transmitted by a vector, in this case a mosquito, was shown to do so.

I obviously had read about Zika in medical school, but I had never seen an actual case. Because it was a mild disease, I did not pay much attention to the prior outbreaks in Micronesia and French Polynesia. Now that large numbers of cases were being reported from Brazil with the devastating consequence of microcephaly, Zika landed squarely on my radar screen, and it was clear that NIAID would be involved in developing a vaccine for this infection.

Because millions of Americans traveled to and from these southern countries every year, the CDC came out with guidelines advising pregnant women or women who were trying to get pregnant not to travel to the involved countries. Panic set in as countless pregnant women who had already gone from the United States to the involved region feared that they might have already gotten infected and not realized it and thus their unborn babies might be at risk.

Zika fear was a different type of fear from Ebola. When pregnant women and their babies are involved, it strikes a special chord, and the possibility that we could have a Zika outbreak in the continental United States was real and frightening. To add to the problem, we have *Aedes aegypti* mosquitoes in the continental United States, particularly along the Gulf Coast in the Southern states of Florida, Alabama, Mississippi, Louisiana, and Texas.

It was inevitable that the president would get directly involved. I felt that I knew his style in responding to urgent matters fairly well by this time given our intense interactions during the Ebola saga, and I knew that he would want to stay on top of this before it became a larger problem. Sure enough, Tom Frieden and I were called to a two-hour meeting in the Situation Room on Tuesday, January 26, 2016, together with the president's top administration advisers. Tom and I emphasized to President Obama that mosquito control and avoidance were the major immediate countermeasures against Zika; however, in the long run we needed a safe and effective vaccine for the countries with major Zika issues and for American travelers to the areas with Zika activity. I promised Denis McDonough, Lisa Monaco, and the president that I would make the development of such a vaccine a high priority for NIAID. We were already well into testing vaccines for dengue and chikungunya, which were mosquito-borne viruses that had been afflicting these same regions of South America and the Caribbean for several years, so we had considerable experience in these matters.

As soon as I got back to my NIH office, I called a meeting of my senior staff and made it clear that we were initiating a "full-court press" in our Zika efforts, particularly to develop a Zika vaccine. John Mascola, who had assumed the directorship of the VRC three years earlier, and his team were already at work on a promising Zika vaccine candidate using a DNA type of vaccine. We needed to push the envelope and accelerate these efforts as well as other aspects of our Zika research agenda.

By early February 2016, we had come up with a proposed cumulative multiagency supplemental budget that we felt was necessary to adequately address the Zika challenge. It was $1.9 billion. Secretary Burwell, Tom Frieden, and I made the rounds on Capitol Hill briefing the Senate and House leadership of both parties on the evolving Zika situation and the potential threat to the continental United States and testifying at congressional hearings.

As usual I stayed out of partisan politics, but it seemed to me that the Republican-led committee was pushing back on the $1.9 billion request for Zika funds mostly because President Obama was asking for it. Whatever the reason, we did not get new funds. But we did not stop trying. On the afternoon of March 2, 2016, I went to the House side of the Capitol and met in room H-107 with the House Republican majority leader, Kevin McCarthy of California, on the Zika budget proposal. He was skeptical about the amount, but said that he would support the request if we sharply cut it back. Other Republicans wanted to go even a step further. Forget about the size of a supplement, they were talking about a "sequester" of funds, which cuts funds from our budget that have already been approved.

So, we were faced with the reality of having to address Zika as the outbreak raged, and we did not have enough money. The CDC was already heavily involved in mosquito control and disease tracking. We at NIAID were pushing toward the initial testing of a Zika vaccine. To keep the Zika efforts on track, the administration had no other choice but to move the unexpended Ebola balances to Zika, which meant pulling money away from certain ongoing Ebola follow-up studies.

It was clear in my mind that the tension and public anxiety over Zika were going to get worse rather than better. There were already hundreds of thousands of cases of Zika in South America (mostly in Brazil) and tens of thousands of cases in Puerto Rico, and there was an increasing number of "travel related" cases in the continental United States. That number would ultimately reach more than five thousand. A travel-related case is someone who either lives in or visits a country with active infections, gets infected in that country, and then travels to the United States, where the person's disease becomes evident. It was only a matter of time before a mosquito would bite an infected person who had traveled to the United States and then bite and infect someone who never left the United States. The latter would be considered a "locally transmitted" case. This specter was what was putting the American public on edge; a pregnant woman who had never left her home in the United States could contract Zika from a mosquito that had bitten a traveler. Even worse, there was concern that this would set off a chain of transmission from one person to another who had never left the country, that is, a sustained outbreak of Zika here in the United States.

On July 1, 2016, Secretary Burwell, Tom Frieden, and I again met with President Obama in the Oval Office to update him on the Zika situation. The Fourth of July congressional break was coming up and still no movement on the supplemental bill. This was truly becoming a standoff between the Democrats and the Republicans. The Republicans next proposed a budget package that would take money from the Affordable Care Act and from the Ebola account and also contained a stipulation to defund Planned Parenthood. Only in Washington, D.C., would someone link defunding health insurance, disease prevention, and women's health programs to pay to protect pregnant women from a disease that might severely damage their unborn babies. When the president's staff mentioned this to him during our White House meeting, he just rolled his eyes. The Fourth of July came and went and still no budget supplement.

THE INEVITABLE SOON HAPPENED. In early July, we began to see increasing numbers of locally transmitted cases of Zika in Florida, which led the CDC to issue travel guidance asking pregnant women to avoid travel not only to most of South America and the Caribbean but also to certain restricted areas around Miami Beach where the locally transmitted cases were occurring. This touched off a communications problem in addition to a health crisis. If the CDC was recommending that pregnant women not travel to certain areas around Miami, then what did we tell the pregnant women or women trying to get pregnant who already lived in those designated areas? The best that the CDC or anyone could do was advise such women to stay indoors in an air-conditioned room as much as possible, cover their body to the extent possible, and put insect repellent on exposed skin. We realized that this was not particularly comforting to these women, and it did little to alleviate their understandable anxiety.

The good news in early August was that we were ready to launch the phase 1 trial for the Zika vaccine developed by the NIAID VRC. The bad news in early August was that we had now run out of money from the unexpended Ebola balances. We could not just stop the Zika vaccine clinical trial, and we needed to prepare our study sites in the Caribbean and South America for the more advanced phase 2 trials that would follow right after we proved safety of the vaccine in the phase 1 trial. The CDC had also run out of money for its activities in Puerto Rico and the continental United States. Still no money from Congress for the requested supplemental budget. I was worried and frustrated that I would not be able to keep my promise of developing a Zika vaccine. We were running out of options.

Secretary Burwell was forced to do something that she clearly did not want to do. She would have to exercise her 1 percent transfer authority that allowed her to transfer up to 1 percent of an HHS agency's appropriation to another HHS agency. This meant that she would transfer $34 million from other NIH institutes such as the National Cancer Institute and the National Institute of Diabetes and Digestive and Kidney Diseases to NIAID. It was terribly difficult for those of us on both sides of the transaction to "rob Peter to pay Paul." In this case my colleagues at the NIH were Peter, and I was Paul. I was extremely uncomfortable being put in this position, especially when this all could have been avoided if Congress had acted.

THE FIGHT OVER MONEY CONTINUED. Congress returned from their summer break in early September, and the Republicans proposed a bill that the Democrats rejected because it still contained three "poison pill" riders: the money could not be used for Planned Parenthood; the money would come out of the Affordable Care Act; and the bill would lift a ban against the Confederate flag at military veteran cemeteries. One could understand and agree or not on the ideology driving the first two riders. But tacking on permission to fly the Confederate flag at military veteran cemeteries to a spending bill aimed at preventing devastating disease in babies . . . Really?

MOSQUITO-BORNE INFECTIONS such as Zika often burn themselves out, at least for a finite period of time, for a number of reasons. Paramount among these is the "saturation effect," where such a large proportion of the susceptible population has already become infected that there are relatively few susceptible people left and a degree of herd or societal immunity protects the remainder of the uninfected population. Also, spraying insecticide and larvicide to control the *Aedes aegypti* mosquito likely played an important role. Such was the case with the Zika outbreak, which burned itself out even before a vaccine was available. Nonetheless, when the final tallies from the 2015–16 outbreak were in, the impact of this disease on fetuses and newborn babies became painfully apparent. Although it was difficult to determine the precise number of cases that had occurred in the Americas because 80 percent of infections were without symptoms, it was estimated that in Brazil there were hundreds of thousands, and possibly millions, of cases of Zika infection. In Brazil alone there were close to 6,000 confirmed or suspected cases of microcephaly in babies born to mothers infected during pregnancy. An undetermined number of other babies had more subtle congenital abnormalities due to Zika infection during pregnancy. Puerto Rico had approximately 37,000 officially reported cases of Zika infection, but it was likely that there were actually more than 300,000 cases. In the continental United States there were roughly 5,300 travel-related cases and 230 locally transmitted cases, predominantly in Florida.

Working with health officials in Florida, the CDC successfully implemented mosquito-control measures that undoubtedly played a significant role in preventing any further spread of Zika in the state. Even though the number of cases had greatly diminished, we at NIAID continued our race for a Zika vaccine since almost certainly we were not finished with Zika and sooner or later it would return. By common standards of vaccine development, the initiation of a phase 1 trial in September 2016 was considered lightning speed, since the time from the sequencing of the Zika virus to the time that the vaccine went into volunteers in the phase 1 study was slightly less than four months, the fastest then on record for any vaccine. We launched the more advanced phase 2 trial in South America in March 2017. But because the outbreak had petered out and there were virtually no more cases of Zika, it was impossible to prove the efficacy of a vaccine in a phase 3 trial, which required the occurrence of active cases.

There were a number of lessons to be learned from the Zika outbreak. One of the most important for me was how detrimental to an optimal response to an infectious disease outbreak partisan politics could be. I was certain that we would experience other infectious disease outbreaks in the future. I could only hope that the specter of partisan politics would not inevitably follow.

In the summer of 2016, as Zika was winding down, it occurred to me that it had been fifty years since I had graduated from Cornell Medical School in 1966 and started my training in internal medicine at The New York Hospital–Cornell Medical Center. The intensity of my job did not leave me with much time for introspection, but as milestones often do, this one made me pause and think back on my earliest years as a physician and the path I had traveled since then.

When I was a student at Regis High School deciding that I wanted to go into medicine, I did not have a clear picture of what that meant. I just had a single image of a doctor in a white coat interacting with patients, and I believed that becoming a physician matched my interest in science and my desire to interact with and help people. By the time I completed my chief residency in internal medicine in 1972, I had been extremely well trained and knew I had a knack for clinical medicine. I loved the challenge of caring for the very sickest patients, when what was at stake was life or death. It was apparent to me that I had achieved a high degree of clinical capability when as a resident and chief resident the most experienced senior attending physicians in the hospital often sought my medical opinion on their private patients.

All my instincts to be empathetic fueled the energy to make sure that for every individual patient I gave everything I had. I felt that I balanced the cold and dispassionate application of science with my strong identification with the humanity of my patients. In addition, and I cannot explain this except to say that it comes naturally, I have what I refer to as a nonpathological form of obsessive-compulsive behavior when it comes to making sure that every aspect of my patients' care is attended to. This played out late at night before I captured the couple of hours of sleep when I was on call, where before I went off to the on-call room, I checked the settings on every ventilator, made sure every IV was open and dripping, looked at every indwelling catheter to make sure that it was performing properly, and stopped at the bedside of every one of my patients, regardless of the severity of their illness. Even as my responsibilities took me further and further from daily patient care, I never stopped thinking that what I was doing in the lab, running a large biomedical research institute, or explaining complex medical issues to the public through the media was for the benefit of individual patients.

To this day, fifty years later, when I think of my identity, it is as Tony Fauci, physician.

Passing the Baton

On October 18, 2016, President and Mrs. Obama held their last White House state dinner, this one in honor of Matteo Renzi, the prime minister of Italy. On such occasions the invitee list often includes people of the same ethnic background as the guest of honor. This guest list included people such as fashion designer Giorgio Armani, retired race car driver Mario Andretti, and actor John Turturro. Being a second-generation Italian, I was invited with Christine. Gwen Stefani (Italian American) was the entertainment and gave a knockout performance. It was a magnificent affair held under a gigantic tent outside on the South Lawn on an evening that was crystal clear and unseasonably warm (seventy-five degrees Fahrenheit) for Washington in mid-October. At the reception in the East Room prior to the sit-down dinner under the tent, as we mingled with senior members of the White House staff, there was an abiding sense of bittersweet nostalgia. For almost everyone in the room this might be the last White House state dinner that they would ever attend.

I had that feeling of imminent loss as I approached President Obama on the receiving line before the dinner. As we shook hands and he introduced me to Prime Minister Renzi, he put his arm around my shoulder and thanked me for going "through the wars" with him with the 2009 influenza pandemic, Ebola, and Zika. We joked about the countless meetings that we had together in the Situation Room as we had tackled these frightening infectious disease outbreaks.

A TERRIFIC EXAMPLE of the beauty of a democratic society where the peaceful handing over of power occurs on a regular basis with each change of administration took place on January 13, 2017, a week before the inauguration of President-elect Donald Trump. In a show of collegiality, Denis McDonough organized an exercise whereby he invited the soon-to-be-sworn-in cabinet of the Trump administration to the Eisenhower Executive Office Building adjacent to the West Wing of the White House. The purpose was to present to the incoming cabinet members potential situations such as a terror attack with bombs and bullets, a natural disaster of the magnitude of Hurricane Sandy in 2012, or a cyberattack on our country that they would likely face during their administration and give them the benefit of the eight years of experience of the Obama administration. Sylvia Burwell brought Tom Frieden, Assistant Secretary for Preparedness and Response Nicki Lurie, and me, and we discussed the perpetual threat of a new emerging infectious disease, particularly one that could have a devastating effect on the global population.

Everyone on the Trump team seemed to have a lot on their mind during that session. I hoped that at least some of them heard what we were saying.

Part Five

COVID

A Disease Like
None Other

We were about an hour into a meeting in the Situation Room on January 29, 2020, chaired by President Trump's acting chief of staff, Mick Mulvaney, discussing what appeared to be an emerging new viral illness in China. According to our sources, 7,711 people were infected and 170 had died from their disease, although reliable information from China was scarce. With several Chinese cities locked down, our group of about a dozen mostly top-level National Security Council and HHS appointees were debating how to evacuate U.S. citizens from Wuhan, China, when President Donald Trump walked in.

The first thing he did, to my great surprise, was to look right at me. "Anthony," he said, "you are really a famous guy. My good friend Lou Dobbs told me that you are one of the smartest, knowledgeable, and outstanding persons he knows." I gulped and thus began my first extended conversation with the forty-fifth U.S. president.

Dobbs, the then host of the Fox Business Network show *Lou Dobbs Tonight*, had called me that morning. I knew Lou well because he had interviewed me countless times over the past decades about public health threats—everything from HIV, anthrax, the seasonal flu, and measles to Ebola and Zika. The president wanted to meet me, Lou said. Just a few hours later, here I was with Donald Trump, a big, imposing man who filled the room. He had a New York swagger that I instantly recognized—a self-confident, back-slapping charisma that reminded me of my days in New York.

For the next twenty minutes, as we discussed the new virus that we were calling SARS-CoV-2, the president directed many of his questions my way.

Before that day, I had met President Trump only once. The previous fall, I had been one of a group invited to the Oval Office for the signing of an executive order that called for improvements to the manufacturing and distribution of flu vaccines. In the years before the signing ceremony, I sometimes wondered what it would be like if I ever were to interact with him since he shocked me on day one of his presidency with his disregard of facts such as the size of the crowd at his inauguration. His apocalyptic inaugural speech also had taken me aback, as had his aggressive disrespect for the press. But face-to-face, at that brief signing ceremony in September 2019, I had found him far more personable than I had expected from watching him on TV and reading about him in the newspaper.

After the signing ceremony ended and we were walking out, one of the president's staffers called me back into the Oval Office, where Donald Trump signed a copy of the executive order for me, the D in "Donald" oversize and looping. As I looked on, he remarked to me that he had never received a flu vaccine until he became president. As someone who is zealous about getting his annual flu shot, I was a little surprised. When I asked him why, he answered, "Well, I've never gotten the flu. Why did I need a flu shot?" I did not respond.

Now, more than four months later, in the Situation Room, as President Trump directed his comments to me, the other principal attendees and a handful of presidential advisers, sitting in the crowded spaces against the wall, seemed puzzled and were probably thinking, Who is this guy, and why is the president so interested in him?

"How fast do you think this virus will spread?" the president asked me.

"We don't know, Mr. President," I answered, "because the information we're getting from China is not entirely clear."

"Do you think we'll be able to handle this in the U.S.?" he asked.

"Well, if we do identification, isolation, and contact tracing properly, we will likely be able to handle it. But we need to be careful and learn more about this virus to be sure."

He smiled, and as he was leaving, he called out over his shoulder, "Thanks again, Anthony. We're counting on you."

Not since my first day of high school in 1954, when Father Flanagan, the assistant principal and dean of discipline at Regis High School, nicknamed me Tony, had anyone other than my parents, my sister, and Shelly Wolff ever called me Anthony.

But I was not going to correct the president of the United States.

I FIRST HEARD ABOUT a pneumonia-like virus coming out of Wuhan, China, on New Year's Day. Christine and I planned to take a brisk, four-mile walk on the C&O Canal towpath, along the Potomac River, something we had done together almost every Saturday, Sunday, and holiday since we first met thirty-seven years earlier.

Throughout the Christmas holidays, Greg Folkers, my longtime chief of staff and a human fire hose of information, emailed me updates from the CDC and other sources throughout the world on the current flu season, which was shaping up to be harder hitting than usual, especially for children. My interest was not just professional. Right before Thanksgiving, I had flown home from a medical meeting in Amsterdam, sitting for almost nine hours next to a woman with a wet, violent cough. Even standing in the back of the plane whenever the seat belt sign was off could not save me from coming down with the worst case of influenza I had ever had. And I had had my vaccination!

On January 1, 2020, I was zipping up my fleece to head outside with Christine when the phone in the kitchen rang. I picked it up to find a health reporter on the line. "Dr. Fauci," he said, "there's something strange going on in central China. I'm hearing that a bunch of people have some kind of pneumonia. I'm wondering, have you heard anything?"

I thought, He is probably referring to influenza. Or maybe this could be a return of SARS, which in 2002 and 2003 had infected about eight thousand people and killed more than 750. It had been bad, particularly in Hong Kong, but it could have been much, much worse. Thank goodness the SARS virus did not spread very efficiently from person to person. Public health officials in China, where they have a very solid infectious disease infrastructure, had been able to combat the virus by contact tracing and quarantining those who were exposed.

Someone in the press calling me at home on a holiday about a possible disease outbreak was concerning, but it was not that unusual. Reporters, who sometimes had better or at least faster ground-level sources than we did, were often the first to pick up on a new disease or situation. Nor did it automatically trigger an immediate, all-hands-on-deck response from us at NIH. These pneumonia-like cases in China might be a blip, or they might be a wave. We needed more solid information.

"I haven't heard anything," I told the reporter, "but the situation should obviously be closely monitored." And that is exactly what we did.

But monitoring was not easy, because the outbreak was a moving target from the get-go. For one thing, we had a hard time finding out what was really going on in China because doctors and scientists there appeared to be afraid to speak openly for fear of retribution by the Chinese government. One thing quickly became clear: tests were showing that this was different from influenza; it was a novel coronavirus. In the first few days of 2020, the word coming out of Wuhan—a city of eleven million—suggested that the virus did not spread easily from human to human. Bob Redfield, the director of the CDC, was already in contact with George Gao, the director of the Chinese Center for Disease Control and Prevention. During an early January phone call, Bob reported that Gao assured him the situation was under control. A subsequent phone call was very different. Gao was clearly upset, Bob said. The Chinese CDC head told him that it was bad—much, much worse than people imagined.

A full code red, with flashing lights and screaming alarms, went off in my mind during the fourth week of January when I saw photos in a newspaper that revealed the Chinese government had erected a thousand-bed prefabricated hospital over a few days. At that point, the virus was reported to have killed just twenty-five people and infected around eight hundred, according to data the Chinese had released. Time out, I thought. Why would you need that many hospital beds when fewer than a thousand people are infected? There must be a much bigger, very real problem that we are not fully aware of.

That was the moment I suspected we could be facing an unprecedented challenge, and my anxiety index took a sharp turn upward.

By the end of January, we were hearing that the cases in China were increasing by about 25 percent per day. There were now reported to be more than 9,000 people infected and 213 people dead. I was astonished to realize that the number of people infected in a single month had surpassed the original SARS total for an entire year. The United States had its first travel-related case of this novel coronavirus on January 20; a thirty-five-year-old man had returned home to Washington State, from Wuhan, with a severe cough and fever.

Because close to three million people flew into the United States from China every year at the time of the outbreak, the CDC had begun screening these passengers at several U.S. airports, scanning for fever, and asking them about symptoms such as a sore throat or a cough. We had been considering the next step for a few days: Should we recommend closing the United States to travelers from China? After weighing the pros and cons, we concluded that given China's high rate of infection, a travel ban might buy us critical time to prepare Stateside while our case numbers were still low.

On the last day of January, sequestered in the Situation Room for hours, the coronavirus task force, chosen a couple of days earlier and chaired by the HHS secretary, Alex Azar, devised a proposal to ban all foreigners who had been in China during the past fourteen days. Having reached a consensus, the entire task force plus Kellyanne Conway, counselor to the president, and other White House officials reassembled upstairs in the Roosevelt Room to hammer out how to present our recommendation to the president.

Finally, we were ushered into the Oval Office. Seated in chairs in front of the Resolute Desk, Alex Azar, Bob Redfield, and I explained the details of the proposed travel ban to the president. As in our last meeting, he posed several questions specifically to me about whether I was fully on board with the ban. "It is an imperfect process with some downsides, Mr. President, but I believe it's the best choice we have right now," I assured him.

I was relieved that the president wanted my input, because I had the sense that something large and frightening was on the horizon. The American people needed to be reassured, but they also needed to be informed about the real dangers headed our way. The White House communications team began arranging for me to appear on TV news shows. Even though this was something I had been doing regularly for decades with AIDS, anthrax, and other crises, this was different. The entire world was transfixed by this rapidly evolving outbreak and was soon to be directly affected by it.

The upshot: I became the de facto public face of the country's battle with the disease. This was good, in that I could both calm the country's anxieties and provide factual information. But it also led to the gross misperception, which only grew exponentially over time, that I was in charge of most or even all the federal government's response to the coronavirus. This would eventually make me the target of many people's frustrations and anger.

"WE DON'T KNOW what's going on with this virus coming out of China right now," I told the group assembled in the conference room down the hall from my seventh-floor office on the NIH campus. This was January 3, just forty-eight hours after the reporter had called me at home on New Year's Day. The scientists sitting around the table, led by the Vaccine Research Center director, John Mascola, and some of whom had been with me for decades, knew exactly what I was going to say next.

"We are going to need a vaccine for whatever this new virus turns out to be."

Barney Graham, a gentle giant of a man at six feet, five inches tall and one of the world's foremost vaccinologists, vowed, "Tony, get me the viral genomic sequence, and we'll get working on a vaccine in days!" His confidence was based on intellect and experience, not bravado. As skilled as he is as a scientist, he was known also for his modesty and mentorship of his students and trainees such as his brilliant young protégé Kizzmekia "Kizzy" Corbett. He was a key player in NIAID's VRC.

Vaccines comprise a "platform" and an "immunogen." The platform is the type of vaccine that delivers the immunogen to the body. The immunogen is derived from the pathogen that gets delivered to the body by the platform.

Barney had been leading a collaborative group of scientists for years within the VRC and in medical centers throughout the country. Their goal was to develop the optimal immunogens for vaccines to induce the most effective immune response against a given virus when injected into the body. The name "immunogen" comes from its function of being a generator (gen) of an immune response (immuno). Some immunogens continually change shape, making them inconsistent in their ability to induce an optimal immune response. An immunogen that continually changes is in the correct shape only part of the time. It needs to be set or fixed in the right shape to do its job. Barney and his team at the VRC, as well as two outside collaborators, Jason McLellan and Andrew Ward, figured out a way to accomplish this for some viruses by inducing certain mutations that stabilized the immunogens in the correct form. This was done for the MERS virus and, most important, for respiratory syncytial virus, or RSV, a virus that can cause serious disease and even death in infants and the elderly. The RSV vaccines currently available are derived from their work. The immunogen for the SARS-CoV-2 vaccine is the spike protein, which protrudes from the virus. Barney induced mutations in the spike protein that stabilized it in a form that made it an optimal immunogen.

The challenge for SARS-CoV-2 was to find the right "platform" or vehicle to deliver the stabilized spike protein to the body. Here is where the multiyear collaboration of the VRC with the Moderna company comes in. Barney and the VRC folks and others had been working with Moderna on a vaccine platform called mRNA. It is highly adaptable and can be ramped up quickly and modified as viruses evolve into new variants. This was a sea change from the slow and arduous classic way of influenza vaccine development that includes isolating the virus and growing it in fertilized eggs, with all the uncertainties that we had experienced over the years with influenza.

The mRNA platform technology was largely the result of research conducted over many years by Katalin Karikó and Drew Weissman, who won the Nobel Prize in 2023 for their groundbreaking research. I had been Drew's mentor when he was a trainee in my NIAID lab from 1991 to 1997, and I am not at all surprised at that accomplishment.

Even though at this point there had never been a licensed vaccine using the mRNA technology and though there remained a lot of skepticism, my VRC colleagues and I were very optimistic about it. Compared with other vaccines, the mRNA process is faster and more precise. When cells in the body make proteins, they do so by sending coding messages (m) to the complex protein-producing apparatus of the cell. The instructions in that message come from RNA, which provides the cell with the information it needs to make the correct protein. With SARS-CoV-2, the part of the virus that binds to cells in the body, particularly the nasal passages and the lungs, is the spike protein. Barney Graham and John Mascola's team, including Kizzy Corbett, merely needed to know the genomic sequence of the newly discovered SARS-CoV-2 virus to pick out the part that codes for the spike protein (the immunogen) and together with Moderna use it to make the correct mRNA. Then they would be off to the races. That is exactly what Barney meant when he made his bold claim.

Fortunately, we had to wait only a week. I received an excited phone call from Barney on Friday night, January 10, alerting me that two scientists, one from China and the other from Australia, had just uploaded the SARS-CoV-2 sequence to a public database. Barney immediately contacted a company that artificially produces or synthesizes strings of genetic code. He placed an order for the nucleotide sequence, and this lifesaving product was delivered in a small test tube packaged in a FedEx envelope. The modest charge was put on a credit card. But in a meeting in my conference room soon thereafter with John Mascola and some of my other senior staff, Barney brought up a sobering point. "Tony, if we really are going to go after this with a full-blown vaccine effort, including preclinical studies in animals and various phases of clinical trials, we're going to need a lot of money and my budget is already tight."

"Barney, don't worry about that," I instructed him. "Just let me worry about the money. I'll move things around in the current NIAID budget for now. If this thing really explodes, I promise you, I will get us more money. You just go and make your vaccine." As the group left the room, I asked John to stay for a moment. "John, I am not kidding. Pull out all the stops. I will get you what you need. If anyone can do this, your folks can."

FOR THE NEXT SEVERAL MONTHS, I bounced back and forth between the NIH and the White House, alternately sitting behind my well-worn government-issue desk at NIAID with a treetop view of suburban Maryland and perched in front of the Resolute Desk commanded by Donald Trump in the Oval Office. In early February, I was so consumed by my twin roles I had to cancel a long-planned trip with Christine to Florida to celebrate her birthday. We had been through a few epidemics together over the years; as usual she was understanding, but I still felt terrible about disappointing her.

On February 11, the World Health Organization officially designated the disease caused by the novel coronavirus as COVID-19 at the same time that the task force was working at full speed to deal with its impact. We spent several days talking about cruise ships, particularly the *Diamond Princess*, a British-flagged ship that had called at Hong Kong, Vietnam, and Taiwan and was currently docked in Yokohama, Japan. Our intense focus was what to do with the roughly four hundred mostly elderly Americans on board among a passenger manifest of several thousand.

Back at my NIAID home base, we were on target with the timeline of my primary mandate—developing a COVID vaccine. Production of vaccine and preclinical testing had started within days of the virus's genetic sequence publication. In parallel with Moderna, Pfizer and BioNTech, a German company, were on a similar fast track, using Barney's stabilized spike protein as their immunogen. The first steps toward a vaccine had been accomplished.

COVID was now spreading insidiously and relentlessly around the world. Unfortunately, in the midst of this, the country's premier public health agency, the CDC, was still suffering from many of the same issues that had hampered it previously.

The reason was more than its geographic separation from HHS central in Washington, D.C. The CDC traditionally had something of a go-it-alone perspective, generally excluding input from outside sources. To be sure, the personnel at the CDC were a group of talented and deeply committed professionals. I respected them and many were friends.

The CDC's weakness in handling COVID optimally from the start was rooted in its historical method of investigating diseases and illnesses: the syndromic approach. CDC officials traditionally track an outbreak by testing people with symptoms and then interviewing and testing those who have come into contact with the sick person. This is highly effective when, for example, there is an outbreak of a disease that is overwhelmingly spread by people with symptoms—think Ebola.

But the CDC's syndromic approach was not adequately suited to dealing with COVID, a swiftly spreading disease in which, it would later turn out, more than a substantial portion of the transmissions come from people who are asymptomatic. The CDC was slow to recognize and act on that.

Another vulnerability was the way the CDC was set up to collect data, which in fairness to them was not entirely under their control. Rather than obtaining the data firsthand, the system depended on local public health departments around the country to provide the critically needed information. The result was that CDC figures were often either incomplete, because health departments did not universally provide all the data, or out of date, because the data were not always provided in a timely fashion, thus depicting only what had happened weeks earlier, not the day before. And as the disease kept spreading, what was actually happening was always far worse than what the CDC's data were telling us at the time.

It seemed that U.S. public health officials were constantly playing catch-up. By the end of January, rather than relying on data from the CDC, we all started tracking SARS-CoV-2 through real-time statistics posted on a Johns Hopkins dashboard, which was plugged into the global information circuit. Countries such as the U.K., Israel, and South Africa were able to collect next-day numbers,

providing their public health departments with accurate information.

While my NIAID group was focused on creating vaccines and
working with pharmaceutical companies to develop treatments,
testing had always been in the CDC's portfolio. In the past, the
CDC had established an outstanding track record for quickly creating tests for diseases like Zika. With COVID, however, the system failed. Instead of immediately partnering with the diagnostic
industry, the CDC started from scratch with a test that turned out
to be defective. Then the error was compounded by not immediately collaborating with outside private laboratories to make alternative tests. Instead, the CDC tried to fix the defect itself, and
valuable time in getting adequate testing was lost during the month
of February.

Also, there were regulatory constraints on how the test could be
used. At first, the test could be used only on a "person under investigation." This meant that the person had to have an epidemiological connection to a known case—in other words, known contact or
exposure. But with an infection where you had no idea what the
connection to a known case was, this approach was inherently contradictory. I called Brian Harrison, chief of staff to Alex Azar, to
explain and, I hoped, resolve this dilemma, and he suggested that
we both talk to Azar to get the FDA and the CDC together to
loosen these constraints. It worked, but that did not solve the deeper
and pervasive problem with the initial lack of widely available tests.

Because the only way to determine how many people were infected was through testing, other public health officials and I were
advocating to flood the country with tests. Since they were hard to
come by and in many places completely unavailable, we were flying blind. Meanwhile, other countries around the world were testing hundreds of thousands of their citizens on a regular basis.

WHILE THE CDC STRUGGLED with tests and tracking, there was no mistaking the message delivered on February 25 by Nancy Messonnier. A physician and an accomplished public health official who headed the CDC's National Center for Immunization and Respiratory Diseases, she told reporters on a conference call that a pandemic in the United States was no longer a matter of *if* but *when* and that we should prepare to do things like close schools and work remotely. "Disruption to everyday life may be severe," she announced. "But these are things that people need to start thinking about now."

There is no doubt in my mind that Nancy, who was in the trenches at the CDC, did the right thing: she told Americans the truth. That is the ultimate obligation of public health officials. But not surprisingly, her statement caused a firestorm. The media erupted, the stock market plummeted by a thousand points, and President Trump was furious.

The next day, the president announced that Vice President Mike Pence would take over as the head of the White House coronavirus task force. Within days, Deborah Birx joined the team as White House COVID-19 response coordinator.

I had known Deb since she was a young army doctor working on HIV, and I had the highest respect for her. I met Mike Pence for the first time the day he ran his initial task force meeting. The soft-spoken vice president always solicited the medical opinions of the physicians on the task force: Deb Birx; Bob Redfield; the FDA commissioner, Stephen Hahn; Surgeon General Jerome Adams; and me. He listened carefully to our answers, often asking astute follow-up questions and never pretending to understand something if he did not. One day months later, while I was sitting outside his office waiting for a press briefing to start and chatting with his chief of staff, Marc Short, the vice president invited me in for a Coke. While I was in the office, I told him that this was a bit of déjà vu because I had often met with Vice President Cheney in that same office during the anthrax saga. "In fact, I have a photograph of Dick Cheney and me in these exact chairs," I said. With that, in a combination of "not to be outdone" and genuine kindness, Vice President Pence called in his photographer who took a photo of us in a similar pose. A few weeks later I received a signed print with a gracious inscription.

While many things in this White House were the same as they had always been, I also picked up on little things that indicated how differently this administration operated. Vice presidents are always publicly loyal to the president. That is part of the job. But, in my opinion, Vice President Pence sometimes overdid it. During task force meetings, he often said some version of "There are a lot of smart people around here, but we all know that the smartest person in the building is upstairs."

He was of course talking about the man sitting behind the Resolute Desk in the Oval Office.

Others joined Pence in heaping praise on Donald Trump. When the coronavirus task force held teleconferences with the governors, most of the Republicans started out by saying, "Tell the president what a great job he is doing."

I have always felt compelled to tell it like it is without being offensive. So, a couple of days after Messonnier's bombshell conference call when I got a surprise phone call from the president at 10:35 p.m., I did not flatter him. What I did do during our twenty-minute conversation about COVID-19 was to lay out the facts. I encouraged him not to underplay the seriousness of the situation. "That almost always comes back to bite you, Mr. President," I said. "If you are totally honest about what is happening with COVID, the country will respect you for it." He was courteous to me, and as we hung up, I felt satisfied that he had heard what I said.

The next day, however, he announced at a rally in Charleston, South Carolina, that COVID was the Democrats' "new hoax." This was the first, but not the last, whiplash effect that I would experience in dealing with this complex man.

WHEN COVID HIT ITALY in February, I started calling up my Italian colleagues. "Tony, we're getting overrun," they told me. "We've *never* seen anything like this before. It's absolutely terrible." I had trained some of those physician-scientists, and I knew how smart and good they were at their jobs. I also knew that the Italian health-care system is first rate. If they were telling me that COVID was a disaster in Italy, then for sure it was going to be a disaster in the United States. We would have been kidding ourselves to think that we could handle it any better than the Italians.

Deb Birx officially arrived at the White House on March 2 and was installed in an office downstairs from the Oval Office. She immediately proved to be a force of nature, getting up at 4:00 a.m. to review the latest statistics. She began every task force meeting with an update on the current number of U.S. COVID cases. On her first day, there were eighty-nine cases in the United States and six deaths.

What began to worry me at this time was community spread, and I was particularly focused on Seattle. Community spread is when there are infections in the community that are not linked to other known infections or specific exposure. My longtime colleague and close friend Dr. Larry Corey, the leader of our HIV Vaccine Trials Network, called me from Seattle on March 3 and told me that 380 people with flu-like symptoms had been screened in four emergency rooms in the Seattle area. Out of this group, four tested positive for COVID, which translates into about a 1 percent infection rate within that group. Given that the number of people who had clinically obvious infection in the Seattle area was still extremely low, 1 percent of people with documented infection in this sample of 380 people could not all have been infected from one of the very few people with obvious COVID at that time. They must have been infected by someone unaware that they were infected. That is community spread, and the 1 percent was likely the tip of an iceberg.

When I brought this information to the task force meeting, both Vice President Pence and Secretary of the Treasury Steven Mnuchin did not seem to fully appreciate the seriousness of what I was saying. In fairness to them, this was not surprising, because 1 percent sounds insignificant to the untrained ear. But I tried to explain to them that this small number reflected the situation a few weeks earlier and the real number was now probably hundreds of infections.

By this time, I was almost constantly in the media talking about the impending crisis as we saw more and more cases throughout the world that, without question, were caused by community spread. In response to questions by the press, the president hinted or declared outright that the situation was under control at the same time that I was warning of the impending disaster. Without deliberately contradicting him, I kept the message going: things would be getting worse, and indeed they did.

IN ONE OVAL OFFICE MEETING I had mentioned to President Trump that we were hard at work at the VRC in the early stages of developing a COVID vaccine. This got his attention, and he asked that I show him around the VRC. I was eager for him to meet Barney and Kizzy. On March 3, the president flew up to the NIH on Marine One, and Alex Azar and I were supposed to be waiting there to greet him. A scheduling snafu had Trump arriving before us as we raced up Wisconsin Avenue to Bethesda in Alex's car, leaving the president waiting in the holding room for several minutes. Yikes! A few more gray hairs appeared on my head imagining how upset he would be. His advance team was clearly unhappy, but Trump seemed fine. Barney and Kizzy described where we were with the vaccine. Barney told the president that within a couple of weeks, a phase 1 trial would likely begin to determine safety and to provide early indications of whether the vaccine induced an appropriate immune response.

After they made their presentation, the president asked them, "Why can't we just use the flu vaccine for this virus?" Barney said, "Well," and he picked up a 3D model of the spike protein of COVID and a 3D model of the influenza protein called hemagglutinin, and said, "Mr. President, antibodies recognize surfaces and shapes, and you can see that the shape of the influenza hemagglutinin and the COVID spike are entirely different. So, you can't use one to immunize against the other."

President Trump seemed satisfied, I thought. But it was not the first or the last time that he seemed to conflate COVID with influenza.

After the tour, the president invited Alex and me to return with him on Marine One to join him at a press conference. He took obvious delight in explaining to us the flight path from the NIH to the White House and how all air traffic to and from local airports was on hold until he landed. After landing on the South Lawn, the president asked me to explain to the press what we were doing at the NIH. He was in an upbeat mood, and all was good between us. I did not realize that not everyone in the White House shared his feeling about me.

ON MARCH 8, 2020, *60 Minutes* broadcast a segment about COVID, its first of many. In the segment after the primary show,

60 Minutes Overtime, I told the interviewer in response to a question, "Right now in the United States people should not be walking around with masks." I was not expressing solely a personal opinion; I was expressing the consensus at the time. Jerome Adams, the surgeon general, and the CDC both recommended that people not wear masks, and I was articulating that point of view. The supply of masks and other PPE was already low. If we told people to go out and buy masks such as N95 or KN95 masks, the fear was that there would be a stampede on the supply, and we would create an even greater shortage of masks needed by the health-care workers taking care of very ill COVID patients. Next, there was no clear evidence at the time that masks were effective outside the context of a health-care setting such as a hospital. Finally, although there was accumulating evidence that the virus was spread by aerosol and in large part by people without symptoms, this was not widely accepted, certainly not by the WHO.

I was not wearing a mask, nor was Christine.

Because I was the doctor whom viewers saw giving advice on *60 Minutes Overtime*, I became the public health official who very early in the pandemic instructed them to not wear a mask. Later, my words were twisted by extreme elements in an attempt to show that I and other scientists had misled the public, that we could not be trusted, and that we were flip-floppers. But the controversy over masks illustrates a fundamental misunderstanding among some about science, particularly the biological or health sciences.

People associate science with absolutes that are immutable, when in fact science is a process that continually uncovers new information. As new information evolves, the process of science allows for self-correction. The biological or health sciences are different from the physical sciences and mathematics. With mathematics, two plus two equals four today, and two plus two will equal four a thousand years from now. Not so with the biological sciences, where what we know continues to evolve and uncertainty is common. This uncertainty is magnified in the context of a deadly pandemic when there is already anxiety and suffering. With COVID, our understanding of transmissibility, severity, vulnerability of different people, and level of protection, to name a few, continually evolved, and our medical advice had to change to reflect this.

This is exactly what happened in early March with the question of whether to wear masks and how effective they were.

Right from the start in virtually every interview and TV appearance when given the opportunity, I always added the caveat that things could change, and we must be prepared for that. When additional information became available over subsequent weeks, including that there was no longer a shortage of masks; that when properly fitted and worn, quality masks did work; and that the virus was readily spread by infected people who had no symptoms, we energetically advised the public to wear masks.

MARCH 2020 WAS the month when COVID became frighteningly real to Americans. March was also when I started waking up with a jolt at 4:00 a.m. to stare at the ceiling with worry after worry going off in my head like a machine gun. Italy was locked down on March 9, and two nights later, during an Oval Office address, the president ordered that citizens from twenty-six European countries be temporarily banned from traveling to the United States. In the meantime, Deb Birx was working nonstop behind the scenes to figure out how to protect the United States even further. She formulated a layered plan of shutting down the country for at least fifteen days to see if we could "flatten the curve" of new COVID cases by limiting people's exposure. The idea was to prevent hospitals from becoming overwhelmed. I strongly supported Deb as she carefully refined a set of guidelines before taking them to the vice president. If he was convinced the plan was solid, the next step would be for him to present it to the president. All went according to Deb's well-thought-out process, and on March 16, President Trump committed to a measure that no U.S. president had ever done before, announcing a program that became known as "15 Days to Slow the Spread."

I was impressed that, although he knew there were economic considerations, the president agreed to the plan. I think Donald Trump thought that COVID would be temporary: a little time goes by, the outbreak is over, everyone goes back to work, and the election cycle can begin. He could not have imagined that the pandemic would go on for such a long time. I believe this explains why he repeatedly asked Deb, Bob, and me whether COVID resembled the flu. He desperately wanted the pandemic to disappear just as flu does at the end of the flu season.

Tragically, COVID was not the flu, and it did not vanish. Just the opposite. And so, with the ghastly reality setting in that COVID was not going to go away, Trump began to grab for an elixir that would cure this disease. Along came hydroxychloroquine. President Trump began hearing from the Fox News star Laura Ingraham and others who were touting the drug as a treatment for COVID. Hydroxychloroquine is a long-established medication that people take to prevent or treat malaria. It is also used to treat inflammatory and autoimmune diseases such as lupus and rheumatoid arthritis. Perhaps this drug would be his magic bullet, the fast way out of COVID. Soon he began touting it at our now daily press briefings. Tuning in were millions of worried Americans, hoping to put the pandemic behind them and get on with their lives.

The fact was, however, there were no clinical studies proving that this antimalarial drug would help people. And it might hurt them. The president seemed unable to grasp that anecdotes of how hydroxychloroquine might have helped some people with COVID did not translate into solid medical advice. This is when I realized that sooner or later I would have to refute him publicly.

During the early months of 2020, after a three-year hiatus following the Obama administration, I had been glad to be back working in the White House, making a difference. Then, gradually, I recognized that even though a contingent of bright and dedicated public servants filled the offices of the West Wing and the Executive Office Building, this was not the White House I had known since the Reagan administration. And the differences were going to dramatically affect the way I could do my job.

The president's overt hostility to much of the press, particularly many of the White House correspondents from a variety of outlets sitting in front of him in the Briefing Room during task force briefings, was one glaring example. At one briefing, when Peter Alexander of NBC asked what he would say to Americans frightened by the pandemic, President Trump responded, "I say that you're a terrible reporter." At another briefing, he called Jonathan Karl of ABC a "third-rate reporter." I had known Jon for years and considered him a friend, along with Jim Acosta and Kaitlan Collins, both of CNN, whom the president often verbally attacked. But even when I did not know the journalists the president insulted, I was still taken aback by his behavior. I was also concerned that my very presence at the lectern or sitting against the wall of the press room would be interpreted as acceptance on my part of his behavior.

More problematic for me was that I knew some of the things Trump was saying about the pandemic were false, and I had to push back when asked not only there at the lectern but in follow-up interviews. "Hydroxychloroquine doesn't work," I told reporters. Inevitably, they would ask me if I agreed with something Trump had said such as "Yesterday, the president said that [COVID] would just disappear like magic." I would then have to respond with the truth: "Well, that's not going to happen."

I have often been asked how I got the wherewithal to publicly contradict a president of the United States. My answer is that I harked back to my identity as a physician who has cared for thousands of patients over my long medical career. I take very seriously a statement in the first chapter of the twenty-first edition of *Harrison's Principles of Internal Medicine*, of which I have been an editor for forty years. In one section we quote from the 1950 edition of the textbook: "The patient is no mere collection of symptoms, signs, disordered functions, damaged organs, and disturbed emotions. The patient is human, fearful, and hopeful, seeking relief, help, and reassurance." Understanding this compels me to abide by the principles to always be honest; to be unafraid of saying that I do not know something; to never overpromise; to be comforting, yet realistic. When I spoke to the American public in the daily White House press conferences, I tried to act as if, metaphorically, the American public were my patient, and the principles that guided me through my medical career would have to apply.

I took no pleasure in contradicting the president of the United States. I have always had a great deal of respect for the Office of the President, and to publicly disagree with the president was unnerving at best and painful at worst. But it needed to be done. I realized I had a critical role to play, the person who showed up and told it like it was. And I not only had to tell the truth to the president; more important, I had to tell the truth to the American people; otherwise, I would compromise my own integrity and relinquish my responsibility to my patients—the American public.

At this point, with hydroxychloroquine and similar topics, I felt that I had opened the gate to go down a perilous road. But as long as reality was being distorted, I could not turn back. I leveled with the American public about the reality of the risk of COVID and calmly encouraged them to take care of themselves and minimize their risk. This feeling of responsibility toward the American public was the reason that I did not walk away from the coronavirus task force even though my closest confidants, Christine, Cliff, and Peter Staley of ACT UP fame, frequently asked me to at least consider stepping down. They feared that my association with this president, even if I objected to much of what he was saying, would taint my reputation. Much to my surprise, I became an instant hero to the millions of Americans who saw me as a physician bravely standing up for science, truth, and rational decision-making. They liked and felt reassured by this pushback against the president's ungrounded assertions. This is when people began to make donuts with my face on them and to create bobbleheads, T-shirts, candles, socks, and such with my image. I was glowingly profiled in endless articles. I felt good about being a source of comfort to the general public, and one might think that all this adulation was appealing to me. After all, one of my favorite actors, Brad Pitt, played me on *Saturday Night Live*, and people signed petitions to have me named *People* magazine's Sexiest Man Alive. But it was not appealing to me at all. As a serious seventy-nine-year-old physician and scientist who is very much a private person and who instinctively shuns attention, I felt profoundly uncomfortable.

There is a widely circulated photo of me from a White House press briefing on March 20, 2020. I put my hand to my forehead in response to a comment by the president. That day, President Trump was being especially flippant. He was standing at the podium with Secretary of State Mike Pompeo, making one provocative statement after another.

Then Trump said, "Secretary Pompeo is extremely busy, so if you have any questions for him right now could you do that because . . . I'd like him to go back to the State Department or, as they call it, the Deep State Department."

I had a moment of despair mixed with amusement. I looked to my left at the first row of reporters, where Kaitlan Collins was sitting. When our eyes met, she gave me one of those "What the . . . ?" looks. I put my hand to my forehead to hide my expression.

The problem, of course, was that while millions of Americans appreciated or admired me, a hard-core group saw me as a naysaying bureaucrat who deliberately, even maliciously, was undermining President Trump. They loved and supported the president and regarded me as the enemy.

To them, my hand to my forehead moment proved it.

This is when things began to get difficult for my family and me. The HHS Office of Inspector General monitored the dark web, and in late March they started to see a considerable amount of hostility and threats directed toward me. As a result, I was assigned a security detail. For years, AIDS had made me a target, but that was largely before social media. Back then, I used to get one to two insulting letters a month, mostly homophobic rants, sent to my office at the NIH.

This was different. Now my family and I were barraged by emails, texts, and phone calls. I was outraged that Christine, and especially our daughters, were harassed with foul language and sexually explicit messages and threatened with violence and even death. I was consumed with anger and wanted to lash out at the people who were terrifying these innocent young women.

Aside from making me incensed that my family's safety and well-being were being threatened, these direct expressions of hatred did not distract or frighten me. I did not have time for fear. I had a job to do. This goes back to my training as a physician in a busy New York City hospital. You learn to push through crises and fatigue, to not feel sorry for yourself. Doing your job was what mattered.

Physically, however, dealing with the pandemic was taking a

toll. On any given day, I was doing two to ten TV and/or radio interviews depending on the topic or crisis with a wide range of interviewers, from CNN to Fox News to the networks and PBS and NPR. I was also a frequent guest on podcasts, Instagram chats, and Zoom calls, to try to reach a wider, often younger, audience. But most of my time was spent off-screen and behind the scenes on the phone, answering questions from governors and mayors—Republican and Democratic—and with local public health officials and individual clinicians across the country. One governor might update me on the status of the COVID outbreak in their state and talk about whether things were improving or getting worse. A hospital director might use the chance to ask for more specific resources from the Feds (us) such as ventilators or more PPE. I was also able to clarify for them, when needed, a new guideline from the CDC. It was a good way for me to get a direct sense of how the outbreak was affecting individual communities and people, and for local officials and health-care professionals to make their needs known.

Mornings often meant a conference call with the WHO that segued into my daily staff meeting with my NIAID team. I was constantly in touch with the NIAID efforts in the development of a COVID vaccine, and it was not unusual when I was on the phone on one call that two or three other calls would come in. I seemed to be constantly looking for an electrical outlet to recharge my cell phone. What I could not recharge was my voice. I was talking so much that my voice developed a raspy tone that got progressively worse, only to manifest itself as a vocal cord polyp that later would have to be removed surgically. And of course I was inundated with about a thousand emails a day, many of which even with screening by my staff required my immediate attention and a personal response.

I was getting four hours of sleep a night at most, and often less.

I was not eating, nor keeping hydrated, and I was losing weight. I felt as if I were back in my medical residency days when we were on call every other night and weekend and did not leave the hospital until our patients were stable, and they were never completely stable. But that was when I was twenty-six years old, and here I was on the cusp of eighty. It took Christine to lay down the law. "You are going to bed at a decent hour, you are going to eat regular meals, and you are going to carry a water bottle," she said in a way that left no room for argument.

Keeping me up on certain nights, but it was worth it, was my close friend and confidant Peter Staley, who often called at around 10:00 to check up on me, encourage me, and provide thoughtful suggestions about issues I was facing. Peter, who had lost none of his activist intensity over the years and whose intelligence and candor I admire, was someone who I knew always had my back.

There were three other people who I knew had my back: my daughters. Three different personalities that they are, they expressed their concern and support in different ways. Ali, aged twenty-eight, in her soft but firm manner, continually advised me to take care of myself, reminding me that this was a marathon and not a sprint. She would know as she is a devoted marathon runner. Megan, aged thirty-one, the worrier, was particularly cognizant of my age. When she visited from New Orleans, she was chronically afraid of getting infected and infecting me. Before tests were available, when she flew up to Washington, she locked herself in our basement for the full fourteen days of quarantine before she came upstairs to see me. I am a passionate lover of dogs, and my eldest daughter, Jenny, thirty-four, often connected with me through her dog, Lucca, whom I deeply loved. Jenny sometimes reached out to me with photos of Lucca attached to a text message or email that had Lucca saying, "I love you, Tony" or "You got this, Tony."

During this heated period, one person at the White House continued to remain friendly to me, occasionally asking, "How are things, Anthony?"

President Trump.

I expected that he would have gotten really upset with me by this time, but he did not. I seemed to have a unique relationship with the president, at least for the time being. I attributed this to his perhaps feeling a camaraderie with me because we both grew up on the streets of New York, he in Queens, and I in Brooklyn. He might even have recognized a bit of his own New York swagger in me. Even though I was saying things he did not like, it seemed as if he did not want tension between us.

One thing that seemed to capture the president's interest were the ratings of his press briefings. After one briefing in March, the president asked me to come into his side office adjacent to the Oval Office, a room with multiple TV screens on the wall, all tuned to different news outlets. He called the Fox News personality Sean Hannity. "Hey, Sean," he said on speakerphone. "You should see the ratings we have!"

This was not a onetime occurrence. After another packed briefing in the White House Press Room, he left the podium with me and other members of the task force, and as we entered the anteroom, he looked up at the television screen and exclaimed, "Our ratings are amazing! We've got to keep doing this. We got better ratings than cable, better ratings than the networks!"

DESPITE HIS WISHFUL THINKING, two realities, both in our shared hometown of New York City, seemed to hit him hard. One involved a friend of his, Stanley Chera, a successful Brooklyn-born real estate developer who was hospitalized in late March. The president was telling a group of us gathered in the Oval Office about how he had been talking to Chera, asking him how he was doing. A few days later, President Trump called him again, and "I find he's on a ventilator," he told us. "Wow. This must really be serious." Chera died of COVID a few weeks later.

The other reality was in the images coming out of New York City in the fourth week of March. These also appeared to shake the president. By this time, it was the epicenter of COVID in the United States, and videos capturing long lines outside hospitals, the sound of endless ambulance sirens, and emergency rooms with patients on ventilators terrified the nation. There were refrigerator trucks parked outside Elmhurst Hospital, not far from the neighborhood where Donald Trump grew up. Health-care workers were storing the bodies of COVID victims in them because there were too many to fit in the hospital mortuary. More than 1,900 had now died of COVID in the United States, including 728 in New York City. It seemed at that moment President Trump really got it.

It was during these dark days that Deb, I, and the task force recommended to the president that the nation needed him to extend the fifteen-day shutdown for an additional thirty days. Deb worked out the details of the extension.

To his credit, despite a great deal of skepticism on the part of his economic advisers, the president was still listening and acted on our recommendation.

But soon, everything would change.

He Loves Me,
He Loves Me Not

It was the first Saturday in April, and once again the coronavirus task force was meeting in the Situation Room, as we had been doing every day for the past month. Vice President Pence sat at the head of the table. All of a sudden Peter Navarro, an adviser to the president on economics and trade, burst in and interrupted the discussion. He was clutching a folder of papers that he dumped on the conference table. "I hear you're saying that hydroxychloroquine doesn't work," he barked at me. "I've got a bunch of papers here that say it works. I have all the evidence in the world that hydroxychloroquine works. And by preventing people from getting it, you have blood on your hands!"

I was stunned, not only by what Navarro was saying, but by his lack of decorum. As I glanced around the crowded room and noticed how uncomfortable other people seemed, it was clear that I was not alone in this feeling. Marc Short appeared to be outright annoyed. I had witnessed heated discussions in the Situation Room, but I had never seen one person accost another—much less me—in such an aggressive manner. I was already familiar with the material in the printouts. "Excuse me, Peter," I objected. "Those papers are not properly reviewed, they're anecdotal, and they really don't prove anything."

"There you go again," Navarro shouted. I could tell by the look in his eye that he clearly disliked me. "You don't know what you're talking about. You guys have blood on your hands," he repeated. His voice still raised, he assailed me for disagreeing with the travel ban from China in late January, which was not true. I said no more. Eventually the vice president said, "Peter, I think you should take this discussion outside."

Vice President Pence's words put a stop to this particular attack, but Navarro's campaign against me was ongoing. I felt it was my responsibility to work effectively with all members of the Trump administration, but Peter made that very difficult. I think he truly believed that his Ph.D. in economics qualified him to weigh in on all matters relating to public health and medicine.

The month of April started off badly. The number of known cases and COVID-related deaths in the United States rose significantly every day. On April 1, there were 188,000 confirmed cases and 3,700 deaths. A day later, there were 215,000 confirmed cases and 4,600 deaths. Because of COVID, schools, stores, restaurants, movie theaters, malls, and theme parks had been shut down; city centers stood empty since many employees across the country were now working from home if they had not been furloughed or fired. Suddenly the president saw his roaring economy, with its bullish stock market, sputtering. I am guessing that his economic and political advisers were whispering to him, "We've got to put this virus behind us."

Christian evangelicals were a key part of the president's base, and Easter, which fell on April 12, became somewhat of an obsession with him. "We've got to get back to normal by Easter," he implored Deb and me.

I replied, "Mr. President, the virus doesn't understand Easter. I'm sorry, sir."

But the drumbeat continued. Before one press briefing, he invited Deb and me into the inner room next to the Oval Office and started saying that for me as a Roman Catholic it would be a shame if we did not celebrate the traditional Palm Sunday, Good Friday, and Easter morning services. He wanted to figure out how to do an outdoor theater-like Mass where people could stay in their cars. Deb and I needed some help here to convince him otherwise, and we got it from Hope Hicks. Hope, a counselor to Trump, did not seem to have an agenda and was known to have the president's ear. I explained my concern to her. She understood and helped us persuade the president to essentially put Easter on hold for 2020.

As the days went by and we were well into the thirty-day extension, President Trump began to sound increasingly agitated, telling us that he could not keep the country closed beyond the thirty-day extension. He went on and on, saying that this great country was being destroyed, that manufacturing would be forever ruined. He listed the names of sports commissioners who said that their sports would be wrecked if their seasons were canceled. He insisted that one way or another he was opening up the country in thirty days. At the subsequent press briefing, President Trump emphasized this repeatedly, saying, "We have to get back to work. . . . We have to open our country again. We don't want to be doing this for months and months and months."

Deb and I agreed with him 100 percent. The question was how and when to do this safely. For this reason, Deb took the lead in putting together a structured and sequentially phased plan with well-defined criteria and benchmarks for states to safely open after the thirty-day extension. The time frame would differ for each state depending on how well the infection rate was controlled and whether and when they reached the indicated benchmarks.

During all of this, the president often mixed his messages. I remember him telling me two weeks into the thirty-day period, in mid-April, "Anthony, we'll listen to you and go with the full thirty days. I know it's risky with the economy, but let's do it."

I went home that night feeling satisfied that the president was on board with the full thirty-day plan. I was sitting in my favorite leather chair drinking an IPA beer, watching TV, when I saw a commentator note Trump's tweets, "LIBERATE MINNESOTA!," "LIBERATE MICHIGAN!," and "LIBERATE VIRGINIA." This shocked me. I turned to Christine and said, "What the hell is he doing?"

In my experience, presidents typically listen to advice and do not make a decision on the spot, saying to the advisers around them that they are taking the recommendations under consideration. Only later do you learn what final decision they made. Not so with Donald Trump. At least not always. He often made up his mind as to what he was going to do while I, and others, were sitting right in front of him. But there was a parade of people in and out of the Oval Office, and after we left, the next person to meet or speak on the phone with him might well say something that changed his thinking. I believe that was how President Trump went from agreeing to abide by the thirty-day plan to "liberating" certain states.

A few days later, on April 22, I attended a task force meeting where we were briefed by William N. Bryan, acting undersecretary for science and technology at the Department of Homeland Security. Bryan explained two studies that showed how sunlight and humidity could kill the virus and substances such as isopropyl alcohol and disinfectants could be used effectively to clean nonporous surfaces.

The following day, Bryan briefed the president in the Oval Office on these studies, without Deb or me being present, and then joined him on the podium in the Briefing Room. The result was the infamous press conference where Donald Trump appeared to endorse using bleach as a way to disinfect the lungs from COVID. "Then I see the disinfectant, where it knocks it out in a minute. One minute," Trump told the White House press corps, referring to Bryan's studies. "And is there a way we can do something like that by injection inside or almost a cleaning. Because you see it gets in the lungs and it does a tremendous number on the lungs. So, it'd be interesting to check that."

I was not at that day's press briefing, but as I watched it on TV, I thought, Oh my God. Poor Deb, being onstage with the president during that musing, she must have been horrified, and given her military background it would have been very difficult for her to contradict the commander in chief, especially publicly. She looked as if she wanted to be any other place in the world but there. Sitting in front of the TV, I knew that we were going to have people who heard that from the president and would then go ahead and try it. My phone immediately exploded with texts and calls asking me to comment. I instantly realized I and other scientists had to counter this message to keep Americans from ingesting bleach, which could literally kill them. It was another example, like hydroxychloroquine, of the president's tendency to try to wish away COVID with solutions that had no scientific basis.

Because the president's off-the-cuff comments created a firestorm around the world, his staff suggested that he hold fewer press briefings going forward. I was glad that I was not going to have to spend as much time standing around waiting for the briefings to start because it was eating up valuable time I could have been spending with the task force or at NIAID doing my "day job."

The issue of masks perfectly encapsulates the contradictory messages the president issued. During the first week of April, the WHO and the CDC recommended that everyone wear a nonmedical, cloth mask because people could be spreading COVID for up to fourteen days either asymptomatically or presymptomatically. President Trump announced the new guidelines urging Americans to wear masks, then promptly added that he would not be wearing one. "So with the masks it's going to be, really, a voluntary thing," he told the American public. "You can do it, you don't have to do it. I'm choosing not to do it."

Later in the press conference, the president returned to the topic of masks, explaining, "I just don't want to wear one myself. It's a recommendation. . . . Somehow sitting in the Oval Office behind that beautiful Resolute Desk, the great Resolute Desk. I think wearing a face mask as I greet presidents, prime ministers, dictators, kings, queens. I don't know, somehow I don't see it for myself. . . . Hopefully it'll pass very quickly."

When the president made it clear he chose not to wear a mask, the whole issue of masks swiftly became politically charged: those who did not wear one were seen as supporting the president and rejecting the limitations the pandemic was placing on Americans' personal freedoms. He was not basing his decision on public health, or on the nature of COVID, or on our responsibilities to each other to remain healthy. To his followers, those who did wear them were seen as thwarting the president and willingly surrendering their liberty. The battle was joined everywhere, from supermarket aisles, bars, and political rallies to the highest levels of government. We clearly had a dual problem. It was a public health problem because we were in a public health crisis and masks helped to contain the spread of the virus and saved lives. It was also a messaging problem. I remember thinking to myself how easy it would be to get the country to voluntarily wear masks if they saw the president of the United States wearing one and how this would be the most powerful message about masks that we could give the country.

In early May, this inconsistency surrounding masking led to an awkward situation with the vice president. It started with good intentions. He wanted to come to the NIH to thank the researchers at the VRC for their work on a COVID-19 vaccine. Then Olivia Troye, one of the vice president's staffers, to her obvious discomfort informed me that Pence would not be wearing a mask. This surprised me because soon after his late April visit to the Mayo Clinic in Rochester, Minnesota, where he had refused to wear a mask despite the hospital's mask mandate, Pence admitted that this had been a mistake and he should have worn one.

Given the president's attitude, I understood why the vice president refused to wear a mask at the NIH. Although I obviously disagreed, everyone at the NIH and the White House signed off on a maskless visit by the vice president.

Not so fast. The evening before the visit, Francis Collins called me at home sounding upset. "Tony," he said, "I just looked at the email I sent to the entire NIH community that says everyone should wear a mask on campus, in every place, and at all times. We may have to disinvite the vice president, and that would be awful."

This created a tsunami of stress all over the NIH campus. Telling the sitting American vice president that he must wear a mask even though he did not want to or else he could not visit a U.S. government facility was, quite simply, inconceivable.

To everyone's relief, the vice president's chief of staff and allround reasonable and pragmatic person, Marc Short, came to the rescue. Instead of having the vice president visit the NIH, Marc suggested that John Mascola, Barney Graham, and Francis attend the task force meeting at the White House, where John and I would explain our COVID vaccine efforts. That is what we did, and although I think our presentation benefited those task force members whose expertise lay outside public health, I was disappointed that the vice president's refusal to wear a mask meant a missed opportunity to acknowledge the impressive work of the younger scientists like Kizzy Corbett and her team at the VRC.

Around the same time that the vice president's NIH visit was canceled, Katie Miller, his communications director, contracted the virus—the first of the Situation Room regulars to get infected. Because we all were routinely tested upon entering the White House, members of the task force were not wearing masks at that time. The announcement that a task force attendee had tested positive for COVID a day after testing negative punctured our false sense of security. Katie, who was ten weeks pregnant at the time, was understandably very worried about having COVID. I knew from my own experience as a husband and physician that being pregnant can be anxiety-provoking without the added stress of a virus that we still did not know enough about. I called Katie a couple of times a day and sometimes at night to check on her and offer encouragement. I was fond of Katie, who is whip-smart, all business, and extremely competent. I also gave her husband, Stephen Miller, a senior adviser to the president, guidance about the best way for him to quarantine. So far as I know, they followed my advice and all went well.

As a result of having been in the same room as Katie before we knew she was infected, I went into a modified quarantine. This meant that I got tested every day for fourteen days, wore a mask continually, and spent most of my time alone in my NIH office with the door closed or in my office at home. Luckily, I did not get infected nor, to my knowledge, did anyone else in the Situation Room. In the meantime, this modified quarantine was not all that different from what I was doing during COVID anyway. I was the director of NIAID, and I felt that it was important for me to be physically present in my office. I spent at least part of every day there, including weekends, except when I spent the entire day at the White House. Apart from Brett Rowland, my devoted security person who was with me everywhere I went, I was virtually alone on the seventh floor of Building 31. With hundreds of staff working from home, I was joined by a handful of core staff. This included my assistant Kim Barasch; my principal deputy, Hugh Auchincloss; my deputy for science management, Jill Harper; and my indispensable IT person, David Awwad, who came in every day. A few others such as my special assistant, Patty Conrad, worked mostly from home but came into the office once or twice a week. NIAID's activities in the NIH Clinical Center were fully staffed, but the institute's other business was done mostly by Zoom. This worked, but I missed very much the camaraderie that comes with interacting in person. During the modified quarantine, the White House wanted Deb, Bob, and me to appear before the U.S. Senate Committee on Health, Education, Labor, and Pensions (HELP) in person, and only after considerable back-and-forth with HHS officials did they agree that we could testify virtually. Some of the senators were physically present in the hearing room, while others participated by Zoom.

In response to a question by the Republican committee chairman, Senator Lamar Alexander of Tennessee, I said that although the development of a COVID vaccine was coming along nicely, it would not be ready to vaccinate students before the beginning of the new school year in August. Senator Alexander, before whom I had previously testified several times, later circled back to me to clarify one point: "What I thought I heard was that Dr. Fauci said that vaccines are coming as fast as they ever have, but it'll be later in the year at the earliest . . . but that doesn't mean you shouldn't go back to school. . . . Am I right, Dr. Fauci? You didn't say you shouldn't go back to school because we won't have a vaccine by the fall?"

I replied, "What I was referring to is that going back to school would be more in the realm of knowing the landscape of infection with regard to testing. . . . I did not mean to imply at all any relationship between the availability of a vaccine and treatment and our ability to go back to school." I thought that this response to Senator Alexander had underscored what I had been saying all along—that we should try to get the children back to school as quickly and as safely as possible.

But some in the press and on Twitter, as it was then called, wrongly reported that I had said that schools should not open until a vaccine was available. That is when the president told Fox Business's Maria Bartiromo, "So Anthony is a good person, a very good person—I've disagreed with him. We have to get the schools open, we have to get our country open, we have to open our country. Now we want to do it safely, but we also want to do it as quickly as possible, we can't keep going on like this. . . . I totally disagree with him on schools."

This was the first time I was aware that the president had criticized me in public, and some members of the press jumped all over this, immediately speculating about a Trump versus Fauci feud. I felt it was imperative to calm the waters immediately so that I could continue to work effectively with the president and to help the American people during this terrible pandemic, which had already claimed more than eighty thousand American lives.

I knew what I had said before the Senate committee, and I wanted President Trump to understand the truth, so I printed out the entire transcript from the HELP hearing and tabbed the parts that indicated I did *not* say "do not open the schools." On my way to show this to Marc Short, I walked past Hope Hicks's office, where she was sitting at her desk. When she noticed me walking by and asked how I was doing, I stopped in and told her I was worried about this media-driven rift. I gave the relevant pages to

Hope, who had them copied and said she would show them to the president. I hoped this would end the "feud."

The next day, May 15, I went back to the White House to attend a Rose Garden event where the president was announcing Operation Warp Speed, the bold multibillion-dollar program that aimed to accelerate the development of COVID vaccines. President Trump planned to introduce the former pharmaceutical executive Moncef Slaoui as the project's czar and General Gus Perna, who would oversee the logistics of supplying the country with vaccine doses.

Those of us who were to be on the stage with the president, which included Alex Azar, Secretary of Defense Mark Esper, Chair of the Joint Chiefs General Mark Milley, Francis Collins, Deb, and me as well as Slaoui and Perna, were waiting in the Oval Office for the president. We were all wearing masks. He walked in, caught my eye, and pulled me into the office outside the Oval where the TV was on and a commentator was giving the economic forecast. "Anthony," he said, "you are losing me trillions of fucking dollars." Then he said, "Anthony, you and I are okay. There is no problem between us. I know you better than you think, and I respect you and like you. You need to do your thing, and I need to do mine."

I felt both relieved and anxious.

Then we rejoined the group, and just as we were ready to walk out to the Rose Garden, he looked at all of us and said, "Do we really need to have those masks on? It sends the wrong signal."

"Mr. President, it would be an unforced error to take them off," I said. "The press would kill us."

"Who gives a shit about the press," Trump said. "They will try to kill us no matter what we do." Francis and Deb looked at me, and I said, "Mr. President, I will not remove my mask. I must wear it." Sounding exasperated, he said, "Okay, if you insist." Francis and Deb glanced my way, and kept their masks on. Slaoui also wore a mask.

But the president turned to the generals, Azar, and Esper and said, "You guys, take your masks off, you hear me?" The commander in chief had spoken. Their masks came off, and we all headed outside for the announcement.

After we returned to the Oval and were about to disperse, the president came over to me and said, "Anthony, we are good, right?" I replied, "We are good, Mr. President."

That moment underscored to me just how complicated our relationship was.

OPERATION WARP SPEED was a transformational program, a public-private partnership about which the Trump administration should be justly proud. It instructed pharmaceutical companies to start manufacturing COVID vaccines immediately, taking an unprecedented risk that the vaccines being tested in clinical trials might not prove to be effective. Under normal circumstances, no pharmaceutical company would ever invest hundreds of millions of dollars to produce a product before it had been proven to work. If the product had been shown not to work, they would have had to throw all this vaccine away. If, however, the vaccines did prove effective, this shortcut would mean that shots could be injected into arms much, much sooner.

Another creative aspect of Operation Warp Speed that sped up the timetable involved running with virtually no delay from one phase to the next. Usually, as with the Zika vaccine, for instance, in phase 1 the vaccine is given to several dozen people with the sole purpose of determining safety. Only after the data are collected and analyzed does one move on to phase 2, conducted in several hundred people, this time to test not just safety but also some degree of efficacy. Once again, after the data are collected and analyzed, only then does one move onto phase 3 for definitive testing of efficacy in a sample of thousands of people. This entire sequence done in the classical manner by the pharmaceutical companies usually takes several years. Operation Warp Speed got us all the necessary safety and efficacy data but dramatically sped up the process.

A couple of days after the Rose Garden event, Jared Kushner called me. It was 6:00 p.m. on a Sunday, and I think he wanted to get my thoughts on Operation Warp Speed and Moncef Slaoui. I was glad to speak with Jared because it turned out he really did not know that overseeing the development of vaccines and implementation of their clinical trials is what I and my team at NIAID had been doing for decades. In fact, the Vaccine Trials Network that I had put together in the 1980s and 1990s for HIV treatment, prevention, and vaccine research was intimately involved in the implementation of Operation Warp Speed. After explaining how this worked, I told Jared, "We are well into the clinical trials process with the COVID-19 vaccine, and we need to make sure that when new people come in to Operation Warp Speed and new teams are formed, we do not reboot each time." He agreed.

I thought Jared, who had many detractors because he was this trim, young, rich guy married to the president's daughter, had a lot of positive attributes. Although he knew very little about infectious diseases and he did not always get everything right, he had good common sense and certainly was not a villain. He was the president's roving "fix-it guy," and as far as the president was concerned, this also applied to COVID.

I sensed that Deb was very much in Jared's good graces, but it was clear to me that other people were not faring as well. For example, Jared seemed skeptical about the performance of HHS overall, but particularly the CDC and the FDA. He even suggested that he wanted to phase out the task force and focus more on the efforts of other individual agencies. This might or might not have been a useful strategy, but for sure it stirred up a sense of palace intrigue.

While it saddens me to say, part of the palace intrigue seemed directed against me. After booking me widely on the Sunday shows—*This Week*, *Face the Nation*, *Fox News Sunday*, *Meet the Press*, and *State of the Union*—a couple of months earlier in March, the White House communications team was now blocking me from most major TV news shows. This happened after the responsibility of deciding who goes on which show passed from Katie Miller to the White House press secretary, Kayleigh McEnany, who reported to Mark Meadows, Trump's new chief of staff. Once I realized what was happening, I took the opportunity to tell the vice president about how my TV appearances had been severely curtailed. Deb, who was also in the meeting, explained that she too was being shut out. Pence appeared to be surprised and said he would speak with Kayleigh, but she continued to refuse to book me on shows even when journalists implored her. I was still allowed to talk to the press if they called me but no more Sunday morning multiple appearances.

My appearances dwindled even more as Memorial Day approached and the country began to open back up. Thus, I had almost no platform to encourage optimism and patience in the American public. There was a reason I wanted television exposure: I wanted to explain that public health measures were not the enemy of reopening and that people could use public health measures like masking, testing, and social distancing to open safely.

Over the decades, I had discovered I had a knack for making science and medical issues accessible to viewers. I knew that appearing on as many TV shows as possible, although sometimes exhausting, would help me to alert people that they must be careful and reopen in a step-by-step fashion since we risked the problem of rebound. One instance when being blocked from appearing felt like a real loss came when the preliminary data from the phase 1 trial of the Moderna mRNA vaccine proved to be favorable. Barney, John, Kizzy, and I were delighted that here, at last, was some terrific news, and the fact that I could not explain this to the American public on TV profoundly frustrated me.

It was during this same period that I first experienced the brunt of the president's rage. On the evening of June 3 my cell phone rang, and the caller—the president—started screaming at me. What seemed to have angered him was my accurate remark to the editor in chief of *JAMA* (*The Journal of the American Medical Association*), Howard Bauchner, in a video interview that immunity for coronaviruses was usually six months to a year. I told Bauchner that while we did not yet know the duration of protection from a COVID vaccine, it was possible that additional booster shots would be required. In other words, unlike the measles vaccine, for example, which is a series of shots that provide lifelong immunity, the COVID vaccine might be more like the annual flu vaccine, which needs to be repeated each year. This information was wrongly reported on Twitter and in some media outlets as the COVID vaccine protecting people for only a very short time. In fact, we would ultimately learn that the vaccine protects against severe disease for a much longer period of time than it protects against infection.

It was quite a phone call. The president was irate, saying that I could not keep doing this to him. He said he loved me, but the country was in trouble, and I was making it worse. He added that the stock market went up only six hundred points in response to the positive phase 1 vaccine news and it should have gone up a thousand points and so I cost the country "one trillion fucking dollars." I have a pretty thick skin, but getting yelled at by the president of the United States, no matter how much he tells you that he loves you, is not fun. Later that evening, Katie Miller called to say that both the vice president and the president wanted her to tell me that they loved me and they were sorry about what happened. She said they also urged me to be careful when I spoke with the press because reporters were always looking for opportunities to pit me against the president.

That night, I admit that I did spend time with my in-house psychiatrist, Dr. Christine Grady, to dissect my relationship with Donald Trump. Most of my relationships are pretty even-keeled. I had been happily married to the same woman for almost four decades, and I had worked with many colleagues at the NIH—Cliff Lane, for example—for the same length of time or longer. I know I can occasionally be grumpy (just ask Christine) and, on occasion, demanding (just ask my NIAID staff). But President Trump's tendency to announce that he loved me and then scream at me on the phone—well, let's just say that I found this to be out of the ordinary. I was mystified by the president's mercurial behavior toward me but resolved not to let it throw me off my game.

By THE END OF JUNE, the president seemed increasingly ambivalent about me and my popularity with a large swath of the American public. He pointed out in a tweet that I was part of his team and enjoyed a 72 percent approval rating. Why then, he asked his vast audience, was he not also getting credit? He seemed to feel competitive with me, which puzzled me. I was not running for office against him or anyone else. I had never had an approval rating before, and it had no effect on what I did every day. What mattered to me was not whether the public embraced me but only that I could do my job and keep them healthy.

Around the same time, I had another disturbing call, this time on Zoom with my longtime ACT UP friend David Barr, who had reignited his activist passions and organized a group of health department leaders in New York City, New Orleans, Los Angeles, Washington, D.C., Seattle, and Chicago to meet with me by Zoom every couple of weeks. They had kept me updated on what was going on "in the trenches of COVID" since the third week of March. The virus was surging: more than 2 million people in the United States had contracted COVID and 122,000 had died from it. I explained to the group that to contain these increasing infections, we needed to identify, isolate, and contact trace. Their reaction was immediate and explosive: "That's not working! Contact tracing is a sham! It is done by phone, and people do not trust the government. And when tracing does occur, there is no isolation, and people go right back into multigenerational homes and infect the vulnerable."

This was the kind of uncomfortable, unvarnished, but critical boots-on-the-ground reporting that we on the task force needed to hear. I immediately knew we were in trouble if citizens were growing distrustful of the government's approach to COVID. I made it my business to go to Mark Meadows's office the next day and tell him that contact tracing and isolation were a "disaster and an abject failure." Mark clearly got what I was talking about. He promised to look into it and remarked that the CDC and its director, Bob Redfield, did not seem to be up to the task of a major pandemic, and unfortunately there was nothing he could do about that anytime soon. I defended Bob and the CDC, but I do not think that it made much of an impression on Mark, who seemed to have made up his mind.

I was equally blunt with the vice president who asked to meet alone with me before a task force meeting in mid-July. First, Pence told me he was concerned that the press was creating conflict between the president and me. Then he moved on, to his credit, asking for advice about how we were doing in terms of the pandemic. "I'll be coldly honest with you," I said. "You are losing credibility when you open press briefings by saying 'We are in a good place' in a country that has tens of thousands of new cases a day and where hospitalizations and deaths are increasing. It would be best to establish credibility first by saying we have a big problem, but we are trying to address it." I repeated myself for emphasis: "You must admit first that there is a problem and own the problem. Only then can you say we are now in a better place than we were before." He agreed and appeared grateful for my candor. I respected him for listening, but I wondered if he really heard me, or even if he did, whether he would do anything about the problem. Often, I felt my self-appointed role at the White House was being the skunk at the picnic, disturbing the peace with harsh realities.

Being a skunk was certainly better than being a punching bag. Less than a week later, my frustration level ratcheted up. The reason was Mark Meadows. I had participated in an online fireside chat for Georgetown University that happened to be picked up by CNN and other networks. I had said that in some respects the current pandemic had the potential to be comparable to the 1918 influenza pandemic in its global scope and magnitude. Meadows called Francis Collins, my administrative boss, and yelled at him about my statement, saying that I was making things sound worse than they were. Francis alerted me, and I got on the phone with Mark promising to clarify the statement on my next TV appearance, that I was talking about *potential* impact, which I believed we could contain. I apologized for what happened, and he accepted the apology. Then, the next day, he called me again saying he thought I had agreed that I would "walk [it] back" and he had not yet heard me do so.

"I was planning to wait until tomorrow when I'll be on the *NewsHour* with Judy Woodruff," I replied. My media ban did not include the *NewsHour*, at least at that point. This timing was not soon enough for Meadows, so I sent a clarification to Sanjay Gupta that he aired on CNN. I thought the matter was closed. But the next morning I got yet another angry call from Meadows saying my clarification was not strong enough. During that conversation, he also told me to back off even further with my media appearances. In effect, he was muzzling me.

If that was not galling enough, Meadows called back two hours later to say he wanted me to retract a statement he heard I had made that the incubation period for COVID was longer than fourteen days. I had no idea what he was talking about, and I told him I did not remember ever saying that. I pushed back, telling Meadows that because I had not made that statement, I had no idea how to retract it. That is when I realized that Meadows and the White House communications people were tracking my every word—and not only what I said, but what others said that I said. This made me very angry. I thought the president's chief of staff should have had more important activities to attend to during a global pandemic that was killing a lot of Americans than monitoring my media appearances in which I was trying to give the American public the unfiltered truth.

On July 14, during this back-and-forth with Meadows, *USA Today* ran an opinion piece by Peter Navarro headlined ANTHONY FAUCI HAS BEEN WRONG ABOUT EVERYTHING I HAVE INTERACTED WITH HIM ON. The op-ed was filled with falsehoods, prompting *USA Today* to publish a subsequent statement: "*Navarro's op-ed did not meet* USA Today's *fact-checking standards.*"

The day after Navarro's *USA Today* piece appeared, my cell phone rang as I was on my way to the White House. It was Presi-

dent Trump, who started off by saying that this tension of me versus him was terrible and needed to stop. He loved me, he said, as
usual, and then added that he knew we had a special relationship
and had bonded right from the beginning. He was furious about
the Navarro op-ed he told me. Then Mark Meadows apparently
walked into the room, and the president put me on speakerphone.
"I am going to tell Navarro if he says or writes one fucking word
against you, I am going to kick his fucking ass out the fucking
door. Mark, make sure Navarro understands, one more word and
he is out the fucking door, and he won't come back." I was surprised at this strong reaction because I knew that the president
also had been distancing himself from some of the things that I
was saying. Just days earlier he had told Fox News's Sean Hannity
that I was "a nice man, but he's made a lot of mistakes." Was that
outburst against Navarro just to impress upon me that he and I
were still "good"?

In fact, as I would soon learn, the Navarro piece did not occur
in a vacuum. Several reporters called to tell me that they had received what amounted to opposition research on me from someone
on the White House communications team, listing roughly a
dozen instances the White House asserted were mistakes I had
made since the start of the pandemic, with each example taken out
of context or omitting crucial information. Every reporter who
contacted me said the same thing: I've never seen anything like
this before. Leaking anonymous negative stories is standard operating procedure in Washington. But for someone in the White
House communications department to openly attack one of the
White House team was unprecedented. It was clear to me that certain elements in the White House were actively trying to discredit
me, and I could not imagine that it was being done without at least
the implicit approval of Mark Meadows and Kayleigh McEnany.

There was one communications person who seemed to be on my side: Alyssa Farah, the White House director of strategic communications and assistant to the president. Alyssa seemed almost embarrassed about what was going on. "Tony, hang in there," she said. "I am very sorry that you are going through this."

Peter Navarro never hid his antagonism toward me. He stopped me one day in the Eisenhower Executive Office Building, where we were tested routinely for COVID, and again blasted my failure to encourage people to take hydroxychloroquine, the lack of which he said was causing people to die. He would not let it go.

Perhaps he just had a thing about me. To give him the benefit of the doubt, I arranged with Cliff Lane to have Navarro present via Zoom his case on hydroxychloroquine's effectiveness to the entire NIH guidelines panel cochaired by Cliff in early August. This group was thirty-five of the top experts in infectious disease, public health, and epidemiology from all over the country. Navarro made his presentation, and uniformly they politely said, "Mr. Navarro, there's nothing there. These are anecdotes, and all the evidence indicates hydroxychloroquine doesn't work and can even cause harm."

Navarro's answer was that he valued his reading of the existing medical literature on hydroxychloroquine as much as or more than theirs. "If I am wrong, no one is harmed. If you are wrong, thousands of people die." The truth was the exact opposite. By that time, the FDA, which had given hydroxychloroquine emergency approval early in the pandemic, had revoked it on June 15, after it was found to cause heart problems and even death, not to mention proving ineffective against COVID. I had given Navarro one last chance, but he still could not accept reality.

The growing White House hostility toward me over the spring and summer seemed to trigger at least in part the overt attacks on me by right-wing media and trolls using social media platforms.

One rumor circulating on social media was that my wife, Christine, was Ghislaine Maxwell's sister; Maxwell had been the girlfriend of the infamous convicted sexual predator and financier Jeffrey Epstein. Maxwell eventually went to prison for conspiring to sexually abuse minors. Another theory making the rounds was that I was a Hillary Clinton mole specifically planted in the White House by the Democrats to destroy Trump. The most egregious examples were when two women claimed that I had sexually assaulted them. One came forward a few weeks later and admitted that she had been paid by MAGA-supporting far-right conspiracy theorists who had previously tried similar hoaxes on the former FBI director and U.S. special counsel Robert Mueller as well as the Massachusetts Democratic senator Elizabeth Warren, among others. The other woman, who claimed that she had worked at the NIH, had no record of having ever been employed there, and her other lies were equally easy to see through.

The showstopper occurred in late August. I had been absent from work for a few days because I had a benign polyp removed from one of my vocal cords. I was just getting back into the swing of things, happy to be sitting at my desk in my office at NIAID going through mail that had piled up. It was about 10:30 a.m. when I picked up a letter off one of the stacks. The envelope bore a Jacksonville, Florida, return address. It was typewritten in an unusual font but otherwise looked like the "fan mail" I got every day. Most of the time, people asked me to sign a baseball card or an index card. Occasionally, they told me they hated me.

I opened the top of the envelope with a letter opener and took out a single sheet of folded white paper. As I unfolded it, fine white powder shot up from the paper and drifted down onto my face, tie, shirt, hands, pants, desk, and chair. I instantly feared anthrax, or worse.

"Kim! Do not come in my office!" I immediately shouted to my assistant. "Go get George and Brett!"—my security detail, who were posted down the hall. They sprinted to the doorway of my office, yelling, "Don't move! Stay where you are! Don't come out because you will contaminate everything else." Following their instructions, I put the letter and envelope into a plastic bag for forensics, and George called the NIH hazmat team, who came to my office in their space suits. They had me remove all my clothes, which also went into a plastic bag, and sprayed me down with chemical foam. I thought, This is insane. There I was standing naked, being sprayed down by guys in space suits. Then they had me put on hospital scrubs with the added indignity that they were meant for someone six feet, three inches tall, and I hobbled downstairs to the locker room, where I was told to take a long shower. Afterward, I put on running shorts and a T-shirt that I had in my locker, and George Adams and Brett Rowland drove me home, where Christine and Jenny, visiting from Boston, met me at the door. Christine, calm by nature, did not show much emotion while Jenny was visibly upset. My fate hinged on a call giving me a preliminary analysis of the powder.

There were three possibilities: it was a hoax and merely a harmless powder; it was anthrax spores, and I would require four weeks of the antibiotic Cipro but would probably survive; or it was ricin and no matter what I did, I would be dead in a few days. Ricin, which is formed from the seeds of castor beans, is lethal when inhaled or injected.

Christine and our daughters were terrified that I might die. Jenny was also furious, which was probably a reflection of her fear and concern for me. Megan and Ali called multiple times asking, "Dad, are you all right? Are you all right?" They all dreaded that I might say I was starting to feel sick.

My own emotions were complicated. I felt like a complete idiot for opening what in retrospect was a suspicious letter, and I was fatalistic about the outcome. My mother died at age fifty-six; my father, at ninety-seven. At seventy-nine, I had lived a long, full, happy life of achievement. My legal papers were in order because they are always in order. As a physician, I have held the hands of many people as they died. I do not fear death. But I was not ready to leave this earth yet. Not by a long shot.

Shell-shocked, Christine, Jenny, and I did the only thing we could do: we sat in the house waiting for the preliminary report. Within a few hours an analysis determined that there was no protein in the powder, meaning that it was neither ricin nor anthrax spores. With tears in our eyes, we hugged each other. Then Christine and I grabbed our cell phones to share the news with Megan and Ali. A few days later, the FBI confirmed that the powder was something you could buy in a grocery store. The paper had a typewritten statement, "MANDATORY LOCKDOWNS... MEDICATIONS, REAP WHAT YOU SOW. ENJOY YOUR GIFT."

When my clothes were returned to me after a few weeks, I symbolically threw them away.

BY THE END OF JULY, we were witnessing about a thousand COVID deaths per day, and the toll was continuing to mount. Such a situation was unfathomable, but true. But these were not just numbers. These were people. Someone's mother, father, spouse, partner, sibling, grandparent, best friend. I knew if I focused on this reality, I would be consumed with horror and grief. My only outlet was to channel this pain into putting as much energy as possible toward my role in addressing this disaster. That was making sure our vaccine trials were well run and our drug development program in collaboration with industry was successful. Also, to use my public credibility to comfort and advise the American and global public on what they might do to stay safe during this un-precedented period.

One bright spot in this very grim summer was the start of the phase 3 trial of the Moderna mRNA vaccine to determine whether the vaccine worked. In Savannah, Georgia, at 6:45 a.m. on July 27, the first person in the trial received the Moderna mRNA vaccine. Soon, thirty thousand volunteers would get either the Moderna mRNA shot or a placebo, just 198 days after the sequence of SARS-CoV-2 was made available. The Pfizer vaccine had its own phase 3 trial and was on a similar timetable. The next question was when the results of the trials would be available and what they would show.

Later that day, a group of us met in the Oval Office to brief the president about where we stood with vaccines and drugs to treat COVID. The president was pleased that the vaccine efficacy trials had begun, but he seemed to be agitated that the pandemic was raging on. He wanted solutions that were not there. He kept push-ing us about when a medication that could either prevent, cure, or ameliorate the effects of COVID would be ready. This seemed to have reignited his obsession with hydroxychloroquine. The presi-dent retweeted a video by a group of doctors, including Stella Im-manuel, who still insisted that the antimalarial drug worked on COVID, despite the trials that had clearly refuted this. Unfortu-nately for the president, as reporters learned more about Imman-uel, they discovered that in addition to her support for the supposed curative powers of hydroxychloroquine, it was reported that she believed in demon sperm and alien DNA. The press blasted Presi-dent Trump because of this. He seemed to become even more agi-tated and walked out of a press conference upon questioning from the CNN correspondent Kaitlan Collins.

A few days later, on August 4, we were waiting in the Situation Room for a 3:00 p.m. start to what I assumed would be a routine task force meeting, but at 3:15 p.m. the usually prompt vice president still had not arrived. Finally, Marc Short came in and said the president wanted to see some of us in the Oval Office. Alex Azar, Deb Birx, Bob Redfield, Brett Giroir, who was the HHS point person for COVID tests, and I were ushered in and seated in front of the Resolute Desk. Trump glowered at us. "What the fuck are you people doing?" he demanded. "Deb, you are saying that the pandemic is now in the rural areas. First the cities, now the rural areas. Where is it now? I'm saying we have it under control, and you say it is everywhere." Next, he aimed his fire at me. At about this time he stopped calling me Anthony, which might or might not have been a good sign. "Tony, you're always contradicting me." Then it was Brett's turn: "Giroir, you say HC doesn't work," referring to hydroxychloroquine. "I took it, and many good doctors swear by it. You need to be positive!"

The president then switched topics, venting that we were seeing more cases only because we were doing more testing. The other countries looked good because they were not testing, he claimed. At that point, Kellyanne Conway jumped in to instruct us that we could say what we believed was correct, but if it contradicted the president, the White House needed to hear about it in the Oval Office or the Situation Room and not hear about it for the first time on TV.

Everyone remained silent.

Enough is enough, I said to myself. The advice my friend Jim Dickson had given me when I first became NIAID director flashed through my mind: that if I always embraced the truth, any visit to the White House might be my last because sooner or later I would have to tell the president something he did not want to hear.

This might be that moment, I thought. I took a deep breath. "Okay, Mr. President," I said, looking straight at him. "We are now in the Oval Office and so you need to hear it directly from us. Increased testing does not cause cases. When you increase testing, you will of course pick up asymptomatics whom you might not otherwise notice. However, when you have increased percent positives, increased hospitalizations, and increased deaths, that means that there are truly more cases." I could almost hear the gasps of the people in the Oval Office. The president did not respond to what I had just said, and simply moved on to the next topic.

We were a subdued group as we left, but I felt a sense of relief that I had told it like it was. Now whatever happened would happen. But I was not worried that Donald Trump would fire me. First, I did not believe that he was really angry with me, and I also had the sense that he respected people who were not afraid to stand up to him. Next, though I suspect he did not actually know this, since I was a civil servant, he could remove me from the White House, but I could not be fired as NIAID director without proving serious cause, a whole separate procedure over which he had no control.

President Trump kept me on. But later that month, he did indeed find a medical doctor who pleased him and whom he named a special assistant to the president. Scott Atlas had been a Stanford University Medical Center neuroradiologist who often appeared on Fox News commenting about the pandemic. He believed that our public health measures regarding COVID were overkill. Among his convictions were these: schools should be fully reopened because COVID was not a serious threat to children and they did not transmit the virus efficiently even if they got infected; COVID would run its course no matter what actions we took; only the symptomatic should be tested; and it was the vulnerable in nursing homes and other high-risk places who needed protection. He also thought masks were overrated and that most people should be allowed to go about their lives normally because public health restrictions were upending the economy and exacting an exorbitant social cost. Exactly what the president wanted to hear.

Atlas's public posture was very similar to that of the Great Barrington Declaration, which was an open letter from a large number of epidemiologists and public health professionals published in October 2020. It was later found that some of these signatures were fraudulent. It claimed that lockdowns and other interventions could be avoided if we focused our protection on vulnerable people such as those in nursing homes and did little else to contain the virus spread in society. The assumption was that after a few months herd immunity would be established because enough people would be infected that the outbreak would die down, thus allowing the sequestered vulnerable individuals to reenter society safely. It was a deeply flawed concept from the beginning that has since been widely discredited and shown to be incorrect in practice. Conceptually, there was no feasible way to "protect" all vulnerable people because the elderly, the obese, and the millions of people with underlying conditions form such a significant proportion of the population that they could not possibly all be sequestered. In practice, the evolution of multiple COVID variants over the years that eluded the protection of prior infection showed that herd immunity in the classic sense was not applicable to COVID. Despite the flaws in his premises, Scott Atlas continued to have outsize influence in the White House.

I had a lot of worries about the advice Scott was dispensing. Every day more people were getting sick, more hospitals were getting flooded, and more information contrary to good public health practices was coming online. People who had enthusiastically switched to remote work, taught their kids to learn online, and maintained social distancing started wearying of this new routine; it was not an easy "new normal." But we simply could not just let the virus do its thing, because people would die. Children could get infected and some got very ill, and they almost certainly played a role in community spread. A young child might not suffer, but her grandmother who lived in the same house might well die. Although the risk of hospitalization and death was heavily weighted toward the elderly, particularly those older than seventy-five years, data were also revealing that younger people were in fact dying and that people with comorbidities like obesity, hypertension, and diabetes were at greater risk of hospitalization and death no matter their age.

I also began hearing (and taking seriously) many reports about "long COVID" where both older and younger people have persistence of symptoms for extended periods of time following infection. This was commonly in the form of fatigue, but there were also reports of long-term cardiovascular and brain effects even in younger people and in patients who were never sick enough to go to the hospital.

Atlas was much more of a thorn in Deb Birx's side than in mine because he undermined her at every turn, publicly and privately. Deb felt that he was hopeless and gave up on him. She turned her efforts outside the White House, traveling extensively around the country to urge governors and local officials to abide by proper public health principles.

I tried to keep an open mind concerning Atlas mostly because the vice president and Marc Short asked me to. I called him and said, "Scott, we obviously differ in our opinions, but let us try to find common ground." After a long discussion about our differences, his response was essentially, I know you're an infectious disease guy, but I know as much about infectious disease and COVID as you do. He refused to give an inch and kept telling the president what he wanted to hear.

IN THE FALL of 2020, as the activity of the task force diminished and the White House went into full campaign mode, I was spending more time at the NIH and far less time at the White House.

But COVID was not letting up. In early October, the number of Americans who had been infected with the virus had reached 7.3 million. Among them was the president of the United States. When I heard that Hope Hicks, who was in constant proximity to Trump, had contracted COVID, I immediately feared that the president would also get sick. On October 2, he announced that he and his wife, Melania, had both tested positive.

His bout with COVID did not go smoothly. After he was hospitalized at Walter Reed National Military Medical Center, where U.S. presidents go for health care that might require hospitalization, the president called me and told me how impressed he was with the suite he was in. "Have you ever been here?" he asked. "Yes, Mr. President," I answered. "I was there in 1973 when I helped care for President Nixon, who had viral pneumonia." After commenting on my voice, which he said sounded much better following surgical removal of my vocal cord polyp, the president described his treatment, which included the Regeneron monoclonal antibody. A monoclonal antibody is an artificially produced antibody usually administered intravenously that is highly specific for a given target, in this case a part of the spike protein of SARS-CoV-2. Early clinical studies suggested that it might be an effective treatment for COVID. President Trump told me what was already being reported in the media—that he was very sick when he came into the hospital and "felt like fucking shit." But a few hours after receiving the Regeneron monoclonal antibody, he felt better than he had in years. Bottom line: he wanted me to get Regeneron monoclonal antibody emergency use approval.

I explained that the monoclonal antibody therapy was still in clinical trials. He said the most important clinical trial had been done—that is, on him, the president—which was all we needed to know. He wanted me to get back to him, and get the treatment out to millions of sick people.

"Mr. President," I told him. "This is an FDA regulatory issue, and so there is nothing I can do about it." He then said the FDA would listen to me. I did not want to argue with him, but I thought to myself that he did not seem to appreciate the complex process of drug approval. It was a friendly but strange conversation.

Mark Meadows also called me several times to ask for my advice about the president's health and when he might be able to appear in public again. I knew at this time that the White House and Trump clearly preferred Scott Atlas's advice on how to approach the pandemic. Yet because caring for patients is such a part of my identity, I felt some vindication that they were still seeking my advice, in private at least.

THE PUSH TO get a vaccine approved before the election on November 3 grew stronger and stronger. The FDA commissioner, Stephen Hahn, an oncologist from MD Anderson Cancer Center in Houston, Texas, had made some missteps early in his tenure. Given the White House push for hydroxychloroquine, he had agreed to its emergency authorization, which ultimately had to be pulled back. Next, in a press conference about the efficacy of convalescent serum he got the percent of improvement wrong, later apologizing for mistakenly exaggerating the data. After these incidents, he made it clear to the Trump administration that in terms of vaccine authorization he and his agency would not be pressured into taking scientifically incorrect action; that vaccine approvals would not be rushed just because the White House hoped that they would be approved before the election. Rather, the FDA would follow all proper procedures to make sure they were safe and effective. Steve and the FDA did their jobs well regarding decisions about the COVID vaccines.

Not only was the timing of a COVID vaccine caught in the crosshairs of the election, to my horror, I became a campaign issue as well. After Trump returned to the White House from Walter Reed, the campaign released a TV ad capturing a rare moment of the president in a mask and showing everything the administration had supposedly done to help the country through COVID. They included a clip from an interview I did in March with Fox News about the task force's efforts, saying, "I can't imagine that the government could be doing anything more." To say that my statement was taken out of context is an understatement of major proportions. I insisted—to no effect—that they stop running the ad on the grounds that I was a public health official and civil servant and that it was not my place to support one candidate over the other. On a campaign call with reporters listening in that week, Trump called me a "disaster," then later at a campaign rally claimed with zero evidence that I was a Democrat.

A few weeks later, I had what turned out to be my last conversation with President Trump. At 9:30 a.m. on Sunday, November 1, 2020, I was sitting at my desk in my office at home answering emails when my cell phone buzzed and the word "Unknown" popped up on the screen. "Please hold for a call from Air Force One," a no-nonsense voice instructed me. And then another voice came on the line. "Tony, I really like you, and you know that, but what the fuck are you doing? You really need to be positive," he said. "You constantly drop bombs on me." It was two days before Election Day, and the president was packing these last forty-eight hours full. Holding maskless rallies around the country, he was trying to slam the door shut on Joe Biden.

A couple of days earlier, I had been interviewed by the *Washington Post* reporters Josh Dawsey and Yasmeen Abutaleb, and their story had appeared on October 31. In the interview I said, "We're in for a whole lot of hurt. It's not a good situation. All the stars are aligned in the wrong place as you go into the fall and winter season, with people congregating at home indoors. You could not possibly be positioned more poorly."

By this time, the virus had infected more than 9 million Americans and killed 230,000. New daily cases were hitting record highs. But out on the campaign trail, Donald Trump insisted, "We're turning the corner, we're turning the corner, we're rounding . . . the curve. We will vanquish the virus."

"Everybody wants me to fire you," the president said to me during the call, "but I am not going to fire you, you have too illustrious a career, but you have to be positive. The country cannot stay locked down.

"You have got to give them hope," he went on. "I like you, but so many people—not only in the White House, but throughout the country—hate you because of what you are doing. I am going to win this fucking election by a landslide. Just wait and see. I always did things my way. And I always win, no matter what all these other fucking people think. And that fucker Biden. He is so fucking stupid. I am going to kick his fucking ass in this election. The smallest crowd that I had was twenty-five thousand people. Biden had five people blowing their fucking horns in their cars. Tony, you have to be positive. I do not want to keep you off TV, but when you are out there, you have to be positive."

I tried to interject, to tell him I *am* being positive when I tell people what they need to do to avoid getting sick with COVID.

The president talked over me. It was as if he were speaking to himself rather than to me.

Winding down after fifteen minutes, Donald Trump said, "Okay, Tony, I will see you in a couple of days. Take care."

Love me, love me not.

WHAT HE DID not mention was what I thought he would be most upset about. In that same interview by the *Post*, the reporters had asked me about the difference between Biden's and Trump's approaches to COVID. Trying to point out the distinction between campaigning and governing, I said that the Biden campaign "is taking it seriously from a public health perspective," while Trump as president was "looking at it from a different perspective . . . the economy and reopening the country." When the reporters read the upcoming piece back to me for accuracy, I realized that my words would likely be taken in a political context and that it sounded as if I were publicly favoring one candidate over the other. Holding on to my decades-long effort to remain apolitical, I pleaded with them to delete it. To my deep dismay, the *Post* editors stood firm. Although that statement did not seem to unduly bother the president, his loyal followers became furious at me. At a rally in Florida, the night before Election Day, the crowd chanted, "Fire Fauci! Fire Fauci!" Trump responded, "Don't tell anybody, but let me wait until a little bit after the election. I appreciate the advice." Given his unpredictability, who knew what he would do with that advice if he won. But let us just say that it did not calm my nerves when, a couple of days after the election, the former Trump adviser and right-wing extremist Steve Bannon announced on his podcast that I should be beheaded along with the FBI director and our heads put on pikes outside the White House.

On November 7, after the absentee ballots were counted, Joe Biden was declared the winner of the presidential election. It was the very next night that Albert Bourla, Pfizer's CEO, called me away from my neighbors' fire pit to inform me about the game-changing results from the Pfizer mRNA vaccine trial. I finally thought we had truly turned a corner in defeating this terrible disease.

We now had the tools; we just needed to use them.

On December 22, with the FDA's emergency approval now in place, COVID vaccines arrived at the NIH, and Alex Azar, Francis Collins, and I, along with frontline workers at the NIH, were slated to receive our first doses. With the TV cameras rolling, I pushed up the shirtsleeve on my left arm. Asked for a few words about why I was getting the vaccine, I said, "I feel extreme confidence in the safety and the efficacy of this vaccine, and I want to encourage everyone who has the opportunity to get vaccinated so we can have a veil of protection over this country."

An alcohol swab, a little pinch as the needle went in, a Band-Aid, and it was done. It was two days before my eightieth birthday, and the knowledge that millions of Americans would soon be vaccinated as I just had been was the best gift I could possibly imagine.

Illegitimi Non Carborundum

It was January 21, 2021, the first full day of Joe Biden's presidency, and I was standing at the lectern in the White House Briefing Room. "One of the things that we're going to do is to be completely transparent, open, and honest," I told members of the media and, through them, the American public. "If things go wrong, not point fingers, but to correct them. And to make everything we do be based on science and evidence. . . . [T]hat was literally a conversation I had fifteen minutes ago with the President, and he has said that multiple times." When asked how it felt to be up there at the podium, I responded, "It is somewhat of a liberating feeling."

During November and December 2020 and January 2021, in the waning days of the Trump administration, I was straddling what seemed like not just two different administrations but two parallel universes. Trump was focused on trying to hold on to the presidency while the country suffered from some of its worst days yet in terms of the pandemic.

In contrast, the Biden transition team was deep in preparation to wrestle with COVID from the moment Joe Biden was sworn in as the forty-sixth U.S. president. I was talking regularly with Ron

Klain, whom Biden had tapped to become his chief of staff and with whom I had a strong connection from our time battling Ebola during the Obama administration. Jeff Zients, who would be a counselor to the president and the White House coronavirus response coordinator together with his deputy Natalie Quillian, was checking in with me daily. Far from the hypercriticism I was used to from Trump's inner circle, these three, along with Jake Sullivan, the incoming national security adviser, were going out of their way to solicit my advice. On December 3, when I spoke for the first time with the president-elect by phone, he asked if, in addition to my job as director of NIAID, I would be his chief medical adviser, a brand-new responsibility for me.

This did not actually change anything in my portfolio. It merely clarified that when it came to medical issues related to COVID, I was his go-to person. Others remained involved, but I would be the constant in discussions about medical issues. There was no paperwork and no official position with White House personnel or the Office of Personnel Management. They just gave me an ID badge for free access around the White House and to the president.

I had spent hours with Vice President Biden in the Situation Room together with President Obama as we tackled the influenza pandemic of 2009, Ebola, and Zika. I knew him to be a no-nonsense person guided by integrity and empathy who stayed in the background as most vice presidents do. But today, he clearly was in charge.

I said yes on the spot.

Under President Biden the White House COVID-19 Response Team, largely made up of physicians and public health professionals, was dedicated full-time to dealing with COVID, and it was immediately evident that the issues would be openly debated. Led by Jeff Zients with Natalie Quillian's able assistance, the core team included two old friends. Rochelle Walensky was the new CDC director, chosen at my strong recommendation. I had known Rochelle for twenty years, since the time she finished her training in Boston and went on to be chief of the Division of Infectious Diseases at Massachusetts General Hospital. Vivek Murthy was Biden's surgeon general, the same post he had held with distinction under Obama. It was during those years that I got to know and deeply respect him. I was excited about working with them as well as with other members of the team, including Bechara Choucair, a veteran health official from Kaiser Foundation Health Plan; Andy Slavitt, who brought his experience as acting administrator of the Centers for Medicare and Medicaid Services during the Obama administration; Cyrus Shahpar, who provided us with the daily deluge of data; my old friend David Kessler, former FDA commissioner and now chief science officer for the team; and Marcella Nunez-Smith, our equity expert from Yale School of Medicine. We had our own communications team led by Courtney Rowe, Kevin Munoz, Ben Wakana, Kate Berner, Ian Sams, and Mariel Saez, among others. They became thoroughly familiar with the nuts and bolts of the pandemic issues and were a pleasure to work with. No opposition research directed at me with this group.

The new president wanted to know what the COVID trouble spots were and how best to address them. The United States had been setting disastrous COVID records, with a death toll topping 400,000. Although the rising cases were beginning to plateau, new daily infections remained high—more than 4,000 Americans were dying of COVID each day—and hospitalizations were still up, with medical facilities in some parts of the country at risk of running out of beds.

At Jeff's insistence, the response team met with President Biden every few days in the Oval Office so that he could hear from each of us directly. And most of the time, instead of holding forth behind the Resolute Desk, President Biden sat in a chair in front of the fireplace facing the room, while we sat on couches nearby. It was a small detail, but it reflected that he was actively inviting back-and-forth discussion. Some of these discussions involved the rollout of vaccines. There were some hurdles early on in getting the vaccines to those who wanted them and having them available to be evenly distributed. But we finally got it right, and by the end of the administration's first hundred days, 200 million doses had been distributed, double President Biden's promise of 100 million doses in arms by April 30.

THROUGHOUT THE SPRING, while the White House had returned to its pre-Trump normal, I had the unsettling realization that the political divide in the country had not closed. If anything, with Donald Trump out of office, it had gotten worse, and this was directly affecting me. I had testified before Congress hundreds of times during my career—perhaps more than anyone else in the history of the country, given my more than half a century at the NIH—and I usually enjoyed the give-and-take with House members and senators. I was always well prepared for hearings, which required a written statement and a five-minute oral opening statement. In addition, there were hours of reviewing briefing materials and rehearsing with my team of legislative affairs staff, my deputies, our scientific program directors, and the ever-valuable Cliff Lane and Greg Folkers. On the morning of March 18 as I put on my dark gray suit and navy blue polka-dot tie to head to a Senate Health, Education, Labor, and Pensions Committee hearing on Capitol Hill, I anticipated that all would go smoothly.

Unfortunately, that did not turn out to be the case. As more and more Americans got vaccinated, some people were beginning to lose patience with public health protocols such as mask wearing, and of course some had objected to them even before vaccines became available. In Florida, for example, Governor Ron DeSantis had recently signed a state law that gave him the power to block local authorities from putting in place protective measures such as mask and vaccine mandates. This, while more than 535,000 people in the United States had died of COVID, with the toll continuing to climb every day.

In this context, Senator Rand Paul fired at me: "If you've had a vaccine and you're wearing two masks, isn't that theater?" And a few minutes later: "You're defying everything we know about immunity by telling people to wear masks who have been vaccinated." There was a tinge of aggression in his voice that startled me.

"Well, let me just state for the record that masks are not theater," I responded, trying to bring a degree of civility to the conversation. "Masks are protective."

Senator Paul interrupted me, saying, "If you have immunity, they are theater. . . . You're wearing a mask to give comfort to others. You're not wearing a mask because of any science."

"I totally disagree with you," I replied. I was trying to explain that with the recent emergence of new variants and uncertainty over the durability of protection against infection we simply did not know the level of protective immunity people had, regardless of whether they had gotten COVID or had been vaccinated. The basis of my message was that it was best to play it safe, particularly for vulnerable people such as the elderly and those with underlying conditions. But it was clear that we were not going to come to an agreement here.

A month later, at another hearing I clashed with the Republican representative Jim Jordan of Ohio. He was pressuring me to give him definitive metrics as to when Americans could get their "liberty and freedoms back." "When is the time? When is the time?" he demanded.

"I look at it as a public health measure to prevent people from dying and going to the hospital," I responded.

"You don't think Americans' liberties have been threatened in the last year, Dr. Fauci? They've been assaulted," he insisted, listing among his grievances the fact that some Americans were not able to attend church in person, to assemble, or to petition the government. Aggressively drilling me without giving me a chance to answer, he went on to say that people who disagreed with me had been censored. I told him that he was making this personal. "We're not talking about liberties," I said. "We're talking about a pandemic that has killed 560,000 Americans."

In the car on my way back to the NIH from the hearing, I was thinking that even though Jordan had attacked me, I could understand where he was coming from. I was not locking down the country; I had no power to do so, even though he said I had. That was a local decision based on the level of infection in a given community. But that did not change the fact that people were frustrated. Jim Jordan figured that someone needed to be scolded, and he decided that this was me. I had been frustrated myself at times. I had celebrated my eightieth birthday without my three daughters, who could not travel, and on a Zoom call with a few close friends. Christine could not see her ninety-seven-year-old mother, who was in an extended care facility. It was tough, but the virus could not care less. But by this time, things were changing. Governors, mayors, and local political leaders were "opening up" at the rate and to the extent that they saw fit.

Even though the country was starting to look ahead, I was back in Trump's sights. At a Mar-a-Lago donor retreat for the Republican National Committee, he sharply criticized me, declaring that I was "full of crap." And then he mocked how I threw a baseball. In July 2020, I had thrown out the opening day pitch at Nationals Park in Washington, D.C., that to my chagrin was nowhere near the strike zone—in fact it was not even near home plate—and Trump had ridiculed me more than once for this somewhat embarrassing moment. I thought this kind of taunt made him sound more like a middle school bully than a former U.S. president, but it was indicative of the vitriol toward me on the part of far-right Republicans. Representative Marjorie Taylor Greene of Georgia piled on, introducing legislation to fire me. "Dr. Fauci was not elected by the American people. He was not chosen to guide our economy. He was not chosen to rule over parents and their children's education," Greene said. "But yet, Dr. Fauci very much controlled our lives for the past year."

I had no idea what she was talking about regarding me. What "control" was she referring to? I had no power to mandate or control anything. Guide the economy? This was pure fantasy. And of course, Congress had no authority to fire me. But this narrative that I was restraining the American public as opposed to doing my job to save lives had taken hold of the Republican base and was being widely promoted. As much as I wanted to keep politics out of this public health crisis, I was increasingly being made a very convenient symbol of and receptacle for COVID-related anger and resentment on the part of the far right. I was never particularly popular with the extremists in the Republican Party during the Trump administration, but now that Biden was president, the hostility toward me had gotten considerably worse.

THE IRONY FOR ME was that the CDC was inadvertently giving the extreme right additional fodder to work with. By May 2021, the agency's guideline that people should wear masks outdoors seemed excessively strict even in my view. I was on NBC's *Today* when Savannah Guthrie pushed me on how inflexible this was for children in camp. Would kids playing outside in ninety-degree weather really have to be masked? she asked. I did not want to be publicly critical of the CDC, but I had to admit that the guidelines were "conservative," at best. I had expressed my concerns to the CDC leadership during our response team meetings, but the rank and file stuck to their recommendations longer than I would have liked.

Luckily, Rochelle Walensky ultimately got the agency to change the guideline to read that a vaccinated person could go without a mask indoors and outdoors.

Nevertheless, the MAGA Republican attacks on me continued to accelerate. On one side, I was now working for a president whom I found to be deeply empathetic to the unthinkable suffering and loss of life that COVID had caused. His administration vigorously defended me and gave me a great deal of support and freedom to express myself. I also was getting a lot of love from the public. On a walk one evening through our neighborhood and onto the American University campus, Christine and I ran into a small group of students who were relaxing in the quadrangle. A few recognized me and started squealing and laughing and asking for selfies; requests granted. This attracted dozens and dozens more students who gathered around me and wished me well. Then, as Christine and I walked home, we passed our favorite restaurant, where outdoor diners were sitting enjoying their meals on a balmy spring night. Everyone stood, gave me a round of applause, and shouted, "Thanks for keeping us safe."

This moved me, and it also bolstered my spirits, especially in light of everything else that was going on. Because, on the other side, I was constantly battling an angry barrage of disinformation spearheaded by extreme-right Republicans in Congress who were using attacks on me to show their loyalty to Trump and who were hell-bent on discrediting not just me but also Biden and the Democrats, as well as established principles of public health. It did not escape me that with few exceptions there were no Bush-era

Republicans, whom I had known and worked with so well, left to represent the party. Always in the background loomed a virus that would not go away and was not behaving in ways that the best scientists in the world could ever have anticipated.

SPEAKING FROM THE SOUTH LAWN of the White House on Independence Day 2021, President Biden struck an optimistic tone: "This year, the Fourth of July is a day of special celebration, for we are emerging from the darkness of years; a year of pandemic and isolation; a year of pain, fear, and heartbreaking loss. . . . Two hundred and forty-five years ago, we declared our independence from a distant king. Today, we're closer than ever to declaring our independence from a deadly virus. That's not to say the battle against COVID-19 is over. We've got a lot more work to do."

It was important that he included those caveats because it turned out that the latter part of his statement was much closer to what occurred. Just as we thought we were reining COVID in, a new strain—the Delta variant—was starting to circulate. By mid-month, Delta had become the dominant strain of COVID, and cases had risen dramatically nationwide. It was also becoming clearer to me and my colleagues that immunity wanes after only a few months, and I was more and more convinced that we would need booster shots. The appearance of variants that elude the protection afforded by vaccine or prior infection within a given outbreak was unprecedented. And we were about to see a lot more of this.

Meanwhile, the attacks on me came daily. Starting in April 2021, in addition to getting FOIA (Freedom of Information Act) requests from media organizations, I was also getting them from the Republican National Committee, individual Republican members of Congress, and right-wing organizations for tens of thousands of my emails. The latter were obviously digging for something that would discredit me. When nothing was found, they just made up stories with no evidence whatsoever to back them up.

The smear campaign soon boiled over into conspiracy theories. One of the most appalling examples of this was the allegation, without a shred of evidence, that an NIAID grant to the Eco-Health Alliance (EHA) with a sub-grant to the Wuhan Institute of Virology (WIV) in China funded research that caused the COVID pandemic.

At a May 11 Senate HELP Committee hearing, Senator Rand Paul fed the conspiracy theory, which he amped up further at the subsequent HELP hearing on July 20. Now Paul was essentially holding me personally responsible for the creation of the virus that caused the COVID pandemic, saying, "You're trying to obscure responsibility for four million people dying around the world from a pandemic." He went on: "We don't know that [SARS-CoV-2] didn't come from the lab, but all the evidence is pointing that it came from the lab, and there will be responsibility for those who funded the lab, including yourself."

I was shocked and incensed by this totally inappropriate accusation.

We knew the molecular makeup of the viruses that had been studied and reported on under the EHA sub-award to the WIV, and we knew the molecular makeup of SARS-CoV-2, and the WIV viruses were very different. I responded, "If you look at the viruses that were used in the experiments that were given in the annual reports that were published in the literature, it is molecularly impossible [for them to become SARS-CoV-2]."

Interrupting me repeatedly, Paul continued: "We're saying they are gain-of-function viruses, because they were animal viruses that became more transmissible in humans, and you funded it. And you won't admit the truth."

I repeated what I had said at the May 11 hearing that the sub-award to WIV did not fund gain-of-function (GoF) research, and I said, "And you are implying that what we did was responsible for the deaths of individual[s]. I totally resent that." And then I added, "If anyone is lying here, Senator, it is you."

I harbored no disrespect for Senator Paul, and it is uncharacter-istic of me to respond to anyone so strongly, especially a senator, given my respect for the institutions of government including the legislative branch. To explain the context of this back-and-forth and why I responded so forcefully to Senator Paul's accusation, I need to give a bit of background. It is important to look at estab-lished facts.

The New York City–based EHA is one of the leading authori-ties in the world on the study of the emergence of infectious diseases. The NIH provided a five-year grant to them in 2014 (renewed in 2019). The grant application underwent a rigorous peer-review process by top non-NIH scientists. EHA provided a sub-award of that grant to the WIV for approximately $600,000 over five years, or about $120,000 per year. This was out of an an-nual NIAID budget of about $5 billion. As might be expected, since NIAID funds thousands of grants, I had no knowledge of this grant until after the COVID outbreak. It funded research that investigated the risk of coronavirus emergence from bats by study-ing the human-animal interface in nature to understand what drives spillover to humans and how this affects viral emergence. The goal was to help prepare for the possibility of another corona-virus outbreak.

No portion of the grant was aimed at increasing the transmissi-bility of any viruses. Yet in keeping with his anti-China policy, when President Trump heard about the grant in spring 2020, he ordered it to be canceled, implying that the virus might have come from the WIV even though there was no evidence to support this.

Senator Paul and others were now arguing that the research conducted under the sub-award to the WIV constituted what is known as gain-of-function research. "Gain of function" is a generic term that has been the source of more confusion than enlightenment. In microbiology it means to provide to a virus or other microbe a function it does not naturally have. GoF is an essential tool in the field of microbiology, with many benefits. For example, in the development and preparation of most influenza vaccines, the virus from which the vaccine is derived gains function by our deliberately inducing mutations in the virus that allow it to grow more efficiently in eggs. In this way, enough virus can be produced to expeditiously develop the vaccine.

GoF has gotten a bad name recently because many assume that it inherently implies dangerous research and results in the creation and propagation of pathogens that can escape from the lab and do harm in the world. Under certain circumstances, and these are uncommon, when GoF research that carries some risk must be done because a question important to the public health must be answered, the research must be done in a strictly regulated manner by trained individuals to ensure nothing like that can happen. This type of research is referred to as GoF research of concern.

Because there had been much confusion as to exactly what GoF research of concern is and what guardrails should be established for its conduct, a three-year moratorium on experiments that might constitute GoF research of concern was put into place from 2014 to 2017. That period was devoted to determining a practical framework for defining and regulating GoF research of concern and establishing criteria that would trigger additional scrutiny for certain experiments. This three-year deliberative process involved the National Science Advisory Board for Biosecurity (NSABB), the National Academies of Sciences, Engineering, and Medicine, and multiple risk-benefit assessment conferences.

This led the White House Office of Science and Technology Policy to issue on January 9, 2017, guidance for HHS to develop review mechanisms for oversight of the study of pathogens of pandemic potential. This process was referred to as Potential Pandemic Pathogen Care and Oversight (P3CO).

According to the P3CO framework, the operative definition of GoF research of concern is the "enhancement" of the function of pathogens of pandemic potential. This specifically refers to the experimental enhancement of a pathogen's transmissibility (ability to spread from person to person) and/or pathogenesis (ability to cause severe disease).

The P3CO framework states, "A potential pandemic pathogen (PPP) is a pathogen that satisfies both of the following: 1) It is likely highly transmissible and likely capable of wide and uncontrollable spread in human populations; and 2) It is likely highly virulent and likely to cause significant morbidity and/or mortality in humans." The framework further states, "An enhanced PPP is defined as a PPP resulting from the enhancement of the transmissibility and/or virulence of a pathogen. Enhanced PPPs do not include naturally occurring pathogens that are circulating in or have been recovered from nature, regardless of their pandemic potential."

The viruses studied under the NIAID-funded EHA sub-award to WIV had never been shown to infect humans, much less to cause high transmissibility or significant morbidity and mortality in humans. The grant funded research to examine bat viruses that had been obtained from the wild (local woods and caves) to study whether they had the potential to infect cells with human receptors and mice that expressed human receptors for bat spike proteins and thus could evolve to actually infect humans and cause a pandemic. The purpose of the studies was to better prepare us for a potential future pandemic. In addition, the studies included measuring antibodies to the bat viruses (sero-surveillance) among various groups of people who might have come into contact with the bat viruses in order to determine if there were human behaviors such as occupations that increased the risks of exposure to and infection with these bat viruses.

Moreover, even if those viruses had previously been shown to infect humans, for which there was no evidence, the design of the experiments was not to enhance transmissibility or pathogenesis in humans or any other species, nor were the anticipated outcomes of these experiments expected to alter those attributes. Therefore, according to the P3CO framework, which was then the operative definition of GoF research of concern, those experiments clearly were not GoF research of concern. Senator Paul was using a different definition of GoF research, and not the operative definition of GoF research of concern as established under the P3CO framework. These facts formed the basis of my response to him on July 20, 2021, and I stand by these facts today. If at a future date it is determined by the NSABB or other advisory bodies to modify the P3CO framework and/or broaden the operative definition of GoF research of concern, then I am certain that the NIH will comply with those changes.

Senator Paul also did not seem to fully appreciate an important virological fact. Any card-carrying virologist would tell you that the molecular makeup of the bat viruses studied at the WIV under the NIAID/EHA grant was genetically so different from SARS-CoV-2 that they could not possibly be the source of SARS-CoV-2. This fact led the NIH director, Francis Collins, an internationally renowned geneticist, to publish on the NIH website the following statement: "Analysis of published genomic data and other documents from the grantee demonstrate that the naturally occurring bat coronaviruses studied under the NIH grant are genetically far distant from SARS-CoV-2 and could not possibly have caused the

COVID-19 pandemic. Any claims to the contrary are demonstrably false."

As it stands, the origin of SARS-CoV-2 remains uncertain, and there are still heated discussions over whether it was the result of a "lab leak" or was a natural spillover from an animal reservoir to humans, as could have occurred in the Huanan wet market of Wuhan, where exotic animals were brought in for sale. As for the lab leak hypothesis, the most commonly discussed scenario is that Chinese scientists were working on viruses from the wild that accidentally infected one of them and then spread outside the lab to cause the COVID pandemic. We in the United States cannot account for all the research that takes place in Wuhan or in the rest of China. That is why, as I have often stated publicly, we must keep an open mind to the origin of COVID, as I do.

Keeping an open mind about both possibilities does not mean that one cannot have an opinion. Possibility does not necessarily mean equal probability. Although U.S. intelligence agencies are not uniform in their opinion about COVID's origin, the majority favor a natural occurrence. Importantly, experienced evolutionary virologists throughout the world, while acknowledging the lack of definitive proof, have published in the peer-reviewed scientific literature their belief, based on geospatial information from the Huanan wet market in Wuhan as well as on epidemiological and virological data, that the virus emerged as a natural spillover from infected animals brought illegally into the market.

Precedent also carries some weight. About 75 percent of all new, emerging infectious diseases result from a spillover of a pathogen, usually a virus, from an animal reservoir to humans. Importantly, this includes the original SARS outbreak in 2002–3, which has been shown to have resulted from a natural spillover from a bat to a civet cat to humans.

If and when the origin of COVID is definitively proven, I and my public health colleagues will accept this conclusion.

A WEEK AFTER the July 20 HELP hearing, a fifty-six-year-old man was arrested (and later convicted) for having sent my family and me threatening emails that said we would be "dragged into the street, beaten to death, and set on fire" and telling me to blow my "own fucking brains out." Obviously, this terrified Christine and our daughters and angered me greatly. I've been getting hate mail of one kind or another for almost my entire career, but this new threat reinforced the continued need for me to have a security detail.

Brett Rowland and his team of special agents had accompanied me everywhere since early 2020. Brett spent the day in a room adjacent to my NIH office when I was there, and evenings found him in a van outside our house; he became part of our daily life and a good friend. A native of Florida, Brett is of medium height, strong build, with a kind face and has a great sense of humor but is not someone you would want to mess with. We felt safe under his calm but determined watch.

We loved Brett and were profoundly grateful to him and his team, but of course the reality was that Christine and I did not want to be in this situation to begin with. No doubt, these threats were a result of the lies and conspiracy theories being spread about me: that I was responsible for creating the virus and that I personally took away people's liberties by shutting down the country and overwhelming them with mandates. I think it's safe to assume that the people who were lying about me and those who believed the lies for the most part were among the people who believed that the 2020 presidential election was stolen and that the January 6 attack on the Capitol either was justified or was a harmless demonstration. It was sinking in for me that although I was being attacked directly, this normalization and ready acceptance of lies and the prevalence of belief in conspiracy theories in a broader sense were part of an assault on our very democracy, and I was considerably more worried about the country than about myself.

As the conspiracy theorists continued to wage their political campaign, the Biden administration's response to COVID continued full speed. We had realized that the vaccines' protective power waned over time, and studies, particularly in Israel, showed that the third dose diminished breakthrough symptomatic infections and dramatically reduced hospitalizations.

The question was, Who exactly should get a booster shot? Should it be limited to elderly Americans and the immune compromised, or should it be universally available to everyone who had qualified for the initial doses? To me, it should be the latter. I believed—and still do—that given the fact that the vaccine had been proven safe in billions of people throughout the world with only very rare adverse events, infections with mild to moderate disease as well as those with severe disease should be prevented wherever possible in everyone. This was not only because illness disrupts individuals and society but because even a mild case can lead to long COVID, a condition we are still learning about. Adding to the debate over the summer about distributing booster shots was the concern that the developing world still did not have enough vaccine for their initial doses, despite the fact that the United States was leading the way to distribute vaccine to these countries.

On August 11, 2021, I got a call from President Biden. Jeff Zients had been briefing him about the issues surrounding booster shots, and he wanted to talk to me directly. The president listened attentively to my opinion, and as always, I was impressed with his focus on details. A few weeks later, I met with him in the Oval Office to go over the speech he planned to deliver the next day. As we talked, I was struck again by his empathy. "Doc," he said, "I am really concerned about the terrible impact of this pandemic on Americans. This is so important, and we have got to get it right." Some of the pandemic measures were ending, with varying consequences. For example, the COVID moratorium on evictions by landlords for tenants who could not pay their rent, which the Biden administration had extended for several additional months, had recently expired. As he talked about it, I could see that the potential hurt this might cause those who were already struggling weighed on him. He hoped his speech would resonate in a divided country, instilling a sense of optimism while also cautioning Americans that moving forward would be more difficult unless more people got vaccinated. It was clear that his primary concern was the safety of the American public.

Two weeks later, the initial boosters were rolled out to people sixty-five and older, adults with underlying conditions, and front-line workers. I felt good about the progress we had made, but I was still hoping that the FDA and the CDC would eventually expand eligibility for boosters to all adults. On the international front, the administration announced it would be donating an additional 500 million doses of the Pfizer vaccine to the developing world.

But in the split-screen world in which I lived, the far right had found a new line of attack on me: an animal rights group released a report alleging that I had directed NIH funding to be used for cruel testing on beagle puppies. The freshman representative Madison Cawthorn, a Republican from North Carolina, gave a speech on the House floor calling me a "demon doctor" and demanding to know "why the hell Americans are funding the torture of puppies in Africa." Donald Trump Jr. was selling T-shirts emblazoned with messages like "Fauci Kills Puppies." You really cannot make this stuff up! Though, of course, they did. These off-the-wall accusations were particularly bothersome to me for two reasons. NIH-funded research that involves animals is conducted under strict guidelines for the use and care of laboratory animals, and I am a passionate animal lover, especially of dogs.

In the midst of this lunacy, my cell phone rang. It was a familiar and welcome voice on the line: Barack Obama. The former president asked me how I was holding up under this onslaught of lies. "I'm concerned about you, Tony," he said. "You are a civilian, and you should not have to put up with this nonsense. As a politician, I'm used to this, but you have done nothing but serve the American public and the world for decades." The conversation was just what I needed, and I hung up feeling much better.

Late one evening in early November, I received another encouraging call, this one from Albert Bourla. "Tony, tomorrow morning, we will announce extremely favorable results for Paxlovid." He was referring to a much-anticipated antiviral treatment for adults who contract COVID. Paxlovid can keep a mild or moderate case from progressing to one that requires hospitalization. This was great news; a true breakthrough. Bourla's announcement was followed by more good news a couple of weeks later, when the FDA authorized Pfizer and Moderna booster shots for everyone aged eighteen and older. Delta variant cases were declining, and for the first time since Albert's phone call a year earlier about the unexpectedly high efficacy rate of the Pfizer vaccine, I felt that we had developed an arsenal to effectively battle the virus. I approached Thanksgiving, which fell on November 25 that year, feeling especially grateful.

CHRISTINE WAS JUST PULLING our turkey out of the oven when I got a text message from Jeff Zients that said check your email. He had forwarded an email from Moderna's CEO, Stéphane Bancel, alerting Jeff to a highly transmissible new COVID variant in South Africa that was widely infecting vaccinated people and those who had recovered from Delta. The new variant's name: Omicron.

Oh my God, I thought. Here we go again.

I spent the next day in my kitchen on a Zoom call with South African colleagues. Providing us with data in real time, they gave us a good sense of the variant's course. The virus was spreading rapidly. What was not yet clear was how sick people would get from Omicron.

Jeff arranged for a conference call with Ron Klain, Jake Sullivan, and President Biden, who was spending the Thanksgiving holiday with his family on Nantucket. I described the medical and public health situation to the president, and we discussed the question of blocking travel from South Africa and neighboring countries. The U.K. had already done so. The president decided that we needed to take swift action and that he would make a public announcement about flight bans shortly—just as the holiday season was getting under way. I knew the restrictions were the right thing to do, because they might buy us a little time to prepare. But travel bans wreak havoc economically and socially on the affected countries, and it seemed like a classic case of no good deed goes unpunished. I felt terrible that this was the outcome after the South Africans had notified us immediately and had been completely transparent about Omicron.

Even before Omicron's arrival, all of us on the coronavirus response team were worried about the low rates of COVID vaccinations and boosters among certain pockets of the population. Jeff had arranged for me to make a surprise visit just after Thanksgiving to promote the safety record of COVID shots in Anacostia, a predominantly Black Washington, D.C., neighborhood, where vaccination rates lagged behind the rest of the District. As I walked into the gym at Kimball Elementary School, I was joined by another unannounced guest. Barack Obama's presence created a palpable buzz, and I thought to myself that he was as reassuring to families there as he had been to me on the phone a month earlier.

The two of us had a great time together making the rounds from one vaccination booth to the next, handing out stickers, and posing for photos. When the event ended and we were getting in our cars, the former president and I gave each other a big hug. "I love you, my friend," I said. "Love you back, man," he replied, and then gave me some parting advice: "Don't let the bastards wear you down, Tony." I knew that phrase well. It was the same advice my Jesuit Latin teachers at Regis High School often gave me when I felt particularly hassled: "Illegitimi non carborundum."

A couple of weeks later, I received some relatively good news about Omicron from our South African colleagues: it seemed that it may not be as dangerous a disease as the Delta variant. Perhaps vaccinations and prior infections had created a degree of background immunity. What's more, the South Africans told us that even two doses of an mRNA vaccine seemed fairly protective against hospitalization.

With global cases exceeding 266 million and deaths topping 5 million, it felt more urgent than ever to get vaccines into the arms of people in low- and middle-income countries, especially in southern Africa. Given the United States' current budget constraints and its divided politics, we could not hope to undertake anything nearly as ambitious as what PEPFAR did for HIV/AIDS in the developing world. But in the spirit of taking that kind of sweeping action, I invited a group to my house for dinner to talk about how we could overcome chronic inequity, this time to fight COVID. Besides Christine and Jeff, those in attendance were Samantha Power, an old friend from the Obama administration, where she served as UN ambassador, and who was now USAID administrator, and David Kessler, who had taken over vaccine distribution under Biden. I had known David for many years dating back to working together during the George H. W. Bush and Bill Clinton administrations. Also at our dining table were some of my longtime HIV activist friends, including Peter Staley and David Barr. Their passion for equity did not stop with HIV. Two newbies to the activist movement, James Krellenstein and Zain Rizvi, rounded out the group. The mix of high-level Biden officials who had to operate within accepted government channels and street-smart, seasoned advocates who were impatient and somewhat intolerant of political roadblocks made for a lively discussion. The meeting fortified our commitment to provide increased amounts of vaccines for developing countries, although even this effort did not completely eliminate the inequity of vaccine availability.

As December progressed, we were consumed by Omicron's phenomenally rapid spread; the number of infected people was doubling every three days. Seated at the long table in the White House's Roosevelt Room to brief President Biden and Vice President Kamala Harris, I had to deliver the painful truth that the data we were seeing pointed to a massive upsurge of cases as we got deeper into the winter. I could tell by the look on Biden's face that he was concerned. "Doc, this sounds serious," he said, then asked a question he already knew the answer to. Was it more important now than ever to get vaccines and boosters to people? "Absolutely, Mr. President," I answered.

Notwithstanding Omicron, it was still the Christmas season, and both Christine and I wanted to try to create a festive mood. With all three of our daughters back home for a visit—Jenny from Boston, Megan from New Orleans, and Ali from San Francisco—I decided to do something unusual for me. When it comes to cooking, I am a two-trick pony. I know how to make only two dishes: The first is rigatoni and sausages. But let me tell you, my second dish, timpano, is a showstopper. It is a combination of ziti, mozzarella, ricotta cheese, sweet Italian sausage, garlic, and marinara sauce all encased in dough—en croûte—in a deep pot to resemble a drum, hence its name. I first learned about it in 1996 when Christine and I saw the movie *Big Night*, starring Stanley Tucci and Tony Shalhoub as two brothers running a struggling Italian restaurant in New Jersey in the 1950s. It became a family tradition for me to make the dish once a year while our daughters were growing up. It is an afternoon-long undertaking, but it is not hard if you follow the steps. This one worked so well that I took a few photos of it, and on a whim I emailed Stanley Tucci, whom I did not know but whose contact information I was able to find. I felt he might appreciate that I used his movie recipe for my family's Christmas feast, and I wanted to thank him for the inspiration. To my delight, he emailed back a warm note saying, "How you manage to do what you do . . . and STILL have the energy to make a timpano is beyond me!" I was flattered and proud, but what I did not tell him was that this was my first venture into the kitchen since the pandemic had started. I took special enjoyment in these light moments, because there were so many sobering ones.

Good news was coming from other fronts as well. On Christmas Eve, President Biden announced that he would be lifting the travel restrictions on southern African countries in a week. I had been pushing for the White House to end these from the moment it became apparent Omicron was ricocheting around the world and that we would not be able to stave it off here, with or without travel bans.

But this positive development was followed by a chilling report, on December 30, that there had been another credible threat on my life. A twenty-five-year-old grocery store employee had been arrested in Iowa and charged after making threats against former U.S. presidents, Facebook cofounder Mark Zuckerberg, and me as part of a plan to "combat evil demons in the White House." Stopped for a traffic violation, he was found to have an AR-15 rifle, loaded magazines, boxes of ammunition, and body armor in his car, and his GPS showed that he was bound for Washington, D.C. Once again, the COVID crisis was both global and personal, and I knew I had to learn to cope, both for myself and for my family, with the reality that I would continue to be a reviled symbol for extremists and a target for the crazies.

On New Year's Eve, the country was again under a COVID cloud. The United States was registering about 400,000 new cases a day, and thousands of flights were canceled because the crews were ill. Christine's mother had just died the day before after an extended illness, and we canceled our traditional New Year's Eve dinner. Alone in our home together, Christine and I drank our glasses of prosecco, watched the ball in Times Square drop, shared a prolonged hug and a kiss, and called 2021 a wrap.

JANUARY 1, 2022, marked the start of the world's third year grappling with COVID. The country experienced a tsunami of cases— peaking at more than one million in one day alone. Hospital systems were being greatly stressed, and I was warning that we should not be complacent because the sheer volume of infections might override the diminished severity of the variant. Strictly speaking, we had not yet turned the corner, but as the month was coming to a close, cases started to plateau and then come down just as we had seen happen in South Africa a few weeks earlier.

Although it was clear that Omicron seemed to seek out everyone, vaccinated and unvaccinated alike, the saving grace was that vaccinated and boosted people had a very low chance of having a severe outcome. The data showing the difference between vaccinated and boosted versus unvaccinated with regard to hospitalizations and deaths were stunning. We learned that there was a forty to fifty times greater chance of dying from COVID if you were unvaccinated compared with a vaccinated and boosted person. And yet only 62 percent of the U.S. population had received all the recommended COVID shots, meaning we were not on track to reach the 70 percent threshold by midyear that public health experts considered an adequately vaccinated country. I found this statistic truly disturbing.

On Sunday, January 23, anti-vaxxers led by Robert F. Kennedy Jr. held a rally in Washington, D.C., marching from the Washington Monument to the Lincoln Memorial. Kennedy had had me in his sights for a while, and had written a book in which he accused me of being in bed with the pharmaceutical industry in my dangerous quest to get people vaccinated. Francis Collins and I along with others at the NIH had met with Kennedy in 2017 at Jared Kushner's request so that he could report back to President Trump, since Kennedy had been pushing the administration to be appointed head of a commission on vaccine safety. At our meeting, Kennedy had gone on for more than an hour about the dangers of vaccines including the relationship between the vaccine preservative thimerosal and autism, making points that were clearly inaccurate. It was a painful discussion in which he distorted the literature and denied evidence widely accepted by the scientific community. Now, in his Lincoln Memorial speech before a crowd of thousands, including members of the white supremacist group the Proud Boys, Kennedy likened U.S. vaccine policies to Nazi Germany. All of us in the administration were on high alert. Brett Rowland, in charge of my security detail, slept in our guest room that night for fear that demonstrators would show up at my house. Fortunately, all was quiet.

A couple of months later that would not be the case. A group of about twenty demonstrators came to our house early one afternoon with bullhorns, shouting, "Fauci, you are a murderer!" Some of our neighbors gathered around them and told them to "get the hell out of here," with one neighbor on the verge of a fistfight with one of them. Christine and I were at our offices at the NIH along with Brett and my security detail. Brett called his contacts at the D.C. Metropolitan Police Department. As soon as squad cars showed up on the scene, the crowd dispersed. By the time we got home, everyone was long gone. But my deep disappointment and even anger at the ongoing anti-vax movement—despite the avalanche of evidence that COVID vaccines were safe and lifesaving—did not subside.

I totally understand why, in light of historical health injustices and current health-care inequities, there might be reluctance among some people of color to get vaccinated. For this reason, I, Francis Collins, and people on my staff had spent nights and weekends on Zoom eighteen months earlier with the directors of the Moderna and Johnson & Johnson vaccine clinical trials. We wanted to make absolutely sure that there was an equitable number of people of color in the trials. It was paramount that when the trials ended, we could prove the vaccines were safe and effective in *everybody*. Indeed, we did prove this, but there was still vaccine hesitancy, which we were now working hard to overcome.

At the request of the White House, I did a walking tour through Washington, D.C.'s largely Black Ward 8 neighborhood with D.C.'s mayor, Muriel Bowser. We went door-to-door and street-to-street answering people's questions and encouraging them to get vaccinated. I also did an interview with the filmmaker and fellow Brooklynite Spike Lee for his HBO documentary *NYC Epicenters 9/11–2021½*, about how September 11, COVID, and other events had affected New York. The health equity authority Marcella Nunez-Smith from the White House COVID-19 Response Team and I did a virtual town hall with the rap artist LL Cool J called "Is the Vaccine Safe for Us?" I also did an interview with the hip-hop star Lil Wayne on his podcast. I accompanied First Lady Jill Biden to New York to visit the COVID vaccination clinic at the Abyssinian Baptist Church in Harlem. "I am very well aware that historically the medical community has not treated you well," I said to the people I met there. "We all know about Tuskegee"—the forty-year study in Alabama that initially involved 600 Black men, including 399 with syphilis who were left untreated even after treatment became widely available, a clear violation of medical ethics—"and we should be ashamed. But that is history, and this is now. This is something different. These vaccines are designed to save everybody, you and me."

However, while I had deep empathy for these communities of color, I had little tolerance for the dominant anti-vaccine movement led by conspiracy theorists who were determined to derail the work of scientists and physicians. There was not a scintilla of truth in the stories they were wielding. The misinformation and disinformation surrounding vaccines had its modern origin with the British physician Andrew Wakefield, who published a paper in the scientific journal *Lancet* in 1998 claiming that the measles vaccine was responsible for autism. This claim was based on fraudulent data that resulted in Dr. Wakefield losing his medical license in the U.K. in 2010. The lies surrounding the COVID vaccines included the idea that thousands were dying immediately after getting a COVID vaccine and that Bill Gates was behind a plot to put microchips in the vaccines that would track vaccinated people's movements. Although I respect the right of people to choose, the active disparaging of vaccines based on untruths and distortions of safety data was causing people who would otherwise have been vaccinated to shun this lifesaving intervention, leading to avoidable disease, hospitalizations, and even death. This violated every principle of medicine and public health that I had lived by since I took the Hippocratic oath when I was twenty-five years old.

And some of these same people were fueling outlandish stories about me, even wilder than the puppy-torturing one. One was about my supposed endorsement of a plan to abolish the Second Amendment, which came out of nowhere as pure paranoid fantasy because I have never given this a thought. Some GOP candidates in their primaries continued to mount vicious attacks against me, making up absurd conspiracy theories and proclaiming that if elected, they would prosecute me and put me in jail. "Fire Fauci" had become a convenient campaign slogan and a kind of code for a panoply of extremist proposals. More and more FOIAs were coming in from the usual far-right organizations and from the Republican National Committee, now demanding not just my emails but my calendar entries and phone records as well as all of Christine's. In March, after Russia had invaded Ukraine, a Republican member of Congress in discussing his theory of deaths caused by the COVID vaccines referred to "crimes against humanity" by me, the CDC, and the federal government. Then a bunch of pro-Russian conspiracy peddlers claimed that Moscow's air strikes in Ukraine were aimed to destroy bioweapon-manufacturing labs where I was said to be creating a COVID-19 sequel. Welcome to my dystopian nightmare.

On a day-to-day basis, what kept me going was unwavering support from a handful of very close friends and, importantly, Christine. My spirits were also buoyed by encouraging words from unexpected sources. At a social event in Washington, the former president Bill Clinton came up to me and put his hand on my shoulder. "I was always grateful to you for your hard work, and never more grateful than to see you try to talk common sense in the middle of nonsense. I'm amazed to see you still standing after all you have been through," he said. "Hang in there, Tony."

JEFF ZIENTS HAD BECOME a trusted confidant and friend. Not only were we colleagues but we also lived just a few city blocks apart, and Jeff frequently asked me to go for a walk or came over to my house to unwind from the high-stress nature of our COVID-related jobs. I didn't think anything of it when he called me late one night in mid-March 2022 and invited himself for coffee at 7:00 a.m. the next day. Sitting at my kitchen table, Jeff told me that he would be stepping down from his role as COVID response coordinator, a position he had held for the last fourteen months, which was longer than he had originally planned. He said the timing coincided with the stabilization of the pandemic. We had come out of the acute phase of the Omicron variant, and hospitalization and deaths were leveling off at a relatively low number. I knew that my public health colleague Ashish Jha, dean of the Brown University School of Public Health, the person Jeff had recommended to President Biden to replace him, was an excellent choice, but I was sad to see my dear friend leave his post.

Before Jeff left my house that morning, he asked me if I had thought about stepping down myself. "Well," I said, "that's a good question. I have been thinking seriously about it for some time." Jeff was aware that I had planned to stay at NIAID to see the country through COVID, but now we both knew that there would not be a clear end to this pandemic. We had started to adapt to the realization that we would likely have to somehow live indefinitely with COVID and that Omicron-derivative variants would continue to emerge. One, BA.2, already had. Vaccinations had clearly been shown to protect against severe disease but not necessarily as well against infection. The fact that the virus would continue to spread meant that it would not disappear. With this understanding, our mindset was shifting from pandemic to endemic, a disease that has become established at a relatively fixed and usually low level. We were hopeful that in the future we could keep the virus at a very low level of controlled infection and hospitalization.

"Don't wait too long to make a decision, Tony," Jeff said. We hugged each other goodbye, as we always do, even though I would likely see him later that day.

As Jeff walked down the walkway from my front door, I started thinking about what the country and the world had been through over the past two years and what lessons we had learned.

There are different vantage points from which to evaluate our response to COVID. I look at how well, or not, we prepared for and responded to COVID as comprising two separate but sometimes overlapping "buckets": the scientific bucket and the public health bucket. The scientific preparedness and response to COVID were about as good as it gets. It was a model of public-private partnership. We developed a safe and highly effective vaccine with unprecedented speed (less than eleven months from the time the offending pathogen was identified). This accomplishment resulted from decades of investment in basic and clinical biomedical research. The payoff was that millions of lives were saved. The same holds true for the years of prior research, mostly with HIV, which led to the targeted design of effective antiviral drugs for COVID as well as the development of an array of monoclonal antibodies to prevent and treat COVID. The lesson here is clear. We must sustain this critical investment in the biomedical and health sciences and continue to nurture collaborations between the public and the private sectors.

The situation was much more complicated in the arena of the public health response to COVID. The United States, the richest country in the world, had many more deaths per capita than we should have had. The reasons for this are complex. First, over many years we had let our public health infrastructure become a low priority. A system that was already stressed was pushed to the breaking point when plunged into a historic pandemic outbreak. Lack of sufficient support, including financial, had led to an attrition in the numbers of local public health professionals, and these vacancies could not be adequately filled as COVID struck. Nationwide, the system itself was antiquated with some local departments still relying on fax machines rather than online communications. This dangerously impaired the federal government's ability to assist in the emergency efforts of many local communities and kept it from potentially providing them with additional needed resources.

The considerable degree of disparity in access to adequate health care likely led to avoidable deaths. Persons in lower income brackets including minorities often had sparse access to regular health care, and were even more delayed getting into the health-care system upon getting infected, all of which led to a poorer health outcome—increased risk of more severe illness and death. In addition, there was a notable disparity between communities in access to lifesaving vaccines and the availability of physicians willing to prescribe antiviral drugs.

Also, the percentage of people in the United States with underlying conditions that make it more likely to have a severe outcome from COVID leading to hospitalization and death is higher than in many countries. This is especially true of the prevalence of obesity, which is one of the most important predictors of a severe outcome. Also, the elderly were at much higher risk of hospitalization and death from COVID, and the average age in the United States was significantly higher than that in many other countries.

Adding to the problem was our lack of access to real-time data on the dynamics of the outbreak and the emergence of new variants, requiring us to rely on other countries for this information. Critical on-the-ground information was not readily available to the federal government. Federal authorities were often late in receiving important data and anecdotal evidence that could inform important policy decisions. Contact tracing, which had been life-saving in other countries, was for the most part ineffective due to this lack of a robust local health-care system.

The public expected definitive answers leading to immutable guidelines and recommendations. But this was impossible in a rapidly evolving situation. Moreover, as new and sometimes contradictory information unfolded, the CDC often lacked clarity in its communication, a situation that its own internal review revealed. This intensified an already growing skepticism and distrust of science and scientists. Complicating matters was the fact that we were dealing with a moving target in an ideologically divided country, with implications for policy and behavior, as different state leaders took widely different approaches to controlling the pandemic and guarding public health.

Federal and local public health officials including me; school officials; and federal, state, and local political leaders are often asked whether we would have done anything differently than we did. Of course, we would have. If we knew in the first months what we know now, many things would have been done differently. In addition, we should have made it clearer from the beginning to a deeply concerned public that we knew very little about this virus and that we should expect the unexpected because the virus was rewriting the history of pandemic outbreaks. We learned, for example, that aerosol transmission of infection was important, and asymptomatic spread of virus played a much greater role in transmission than originally appreciated. This knowledge clearly would have influenced earlier recommendations for mask wearing, social distancing, and ventilation. We did not fully appreciate the difference between absolute protection against infection versus protection against severe disease in someone who got infected. As it turned out, protective immunity against infection was far less effective than that against severe disease. A better understanding of this, particularly in the Omicron era, would have avoided some of the confusion about what vaccines can and cannot do. And the transient nature of protection from infection following vaccination and/or prior infection turned upside down the classic concept of herd immunity and was a strong argument for booster shots.

One can look upon a devastating global pandemic as similar to being at war, in this case with a virus as the enemy. Under these warlike circumstances, it is best that all involved parties work together and in synergy and not as a house divided. Extending the war metaphor, it was as if our army were constantly at odds with our navy instead of concentrating all our efforts against the common enemy. The country was divided about masking, and during the first year the messages from the top were quite confusing. Political leaders disagreed on social restrictions and on vaccines, interventions that were clearly shown to save millions of lives. Unfortunately, the acceptance of public health measures such as vaccinations was highly politicized as exemplified by the fact that there were fewer vaccinations and more hospitalizations and deaths in states that are predominantly Republican versus states that are predominantly Democratic. Furthermore, our overall uptake of vaccines was less than most developed nations and even less than some low- and middle-income countries. That should never have happened and likely would not have happened had the right tone been set by the highest levels of government for the promotion of proper public health principles and practices right from the start of the outbreak.

All these weaknesses in our public health response to COVID were profoundly compounded by one of the true enemies of public health: the spread of egregious misinformation and disinformation enabled by the internet and social media that unfortunately remains with us today.

OVER THE MONTHS of April and May 2022, I had intense, one-on-one conversations about retirement with my innermost circle: Christine, Cliff Lane, Peter Staley, and Stewart Simonson. "I want to teach and interact with young people while I have a lot of gas left in my tank," I told each of them. Cliff, always calm and measured, said, "Tony, you've saved millions of lives. It's time for you to enjoy your own life." Peter, a straight talker, told me, "Do it! Get out. There is never a perfect time to leave, but this is as good as it is going to get." Stewart, my old friend from the George W. Bush days, who was very upset about the attacks on me by the far right, said, "Tony, you don't deserve this crap. Leave!"

While we walked one Sunday morning, Christine said, "It's totally your decision, Tony. You know I'll support you whatever you do."

"Well, do you *think* I should step down?" I asked.

Her response was immediate and unequivocal: "Yes!"

By mid-April, I had made up my mind, even though I cannot say that I had fully embraced my decision yet. Now I had to decide when to make the announcement. And on this question Jeff weighed in heavily. He stopped by my house with bagels or croissants and encouraging words every couple of weeks. His philosophy was, When you delay implementing a decision that you have already made, nothing good ever happens.

In mid-June, I flew to Worcester, Massachusetts, where my undergraduate alma mater, the College of the Holy Cross, was rededicating the science buildings in my honor: the Anthony S. Fauci Integrated Science Complex. The event coincided with my sixtieth college reunion, and I was looking forward to seeing some of my former classmates. The day was even better than I expected. Bob Cousy, a 1950 Holy Cross grad who became a beloved Hall of Fame point guard for the Boston Celtics, joined me for the naming ceremony. The Cooz, my idol during my basketball days at Regis High School, is someone who became a friend years after his time on the courts. Later, I walked across campus to the reunion. I put on a mask, as I always did in indoor public settings, when I looked into the reception hall where about fifty of my classmates were milling about and chatting. It was a welcome scene, but there was one problem: no one was wearing a mask. I did not know what to do.

I thought to myself that if I kept my mask on, I might make some people feel uncomfortable. Ever since the spring of 2020, I had rarely faced this dilemma in Washington, D.C., because typically at social gatherings we were masked and required to test in advance. But by the spring of 2022, maskless events were becoming more and more commonplace and, of course, we'd all started hugging each other again after two years of social distancing. Still, I was "Dr. Fauci," and I had to do a quick calculation—one that I know many Americans were familiar with: Do I take off my mask? Just then, I saw my old buddy Jim Mulvihill, who had earned a dental degree from Harvard after Holy Cross and later headed the University of Connecticut Health Center. Hell, I thought, and quickly stuffed my mask into my pocket. I was a little nervous. I was fully aware that I was taking a risk, but my split-second decision was based on the fact that I intended to be in there for only a few minutes. I gave Jim a bear hug, and then I did the same with Jack Fellin, who in my day was Holy Cross's star football wide receiver, and several other class of 1962 alumni. I flew home masked and feeling grateful for these encounters.

Three days later, I had a bit of a scratchy throat, which I attributed to the dry air from Washington, D.C.'s ubiquitous air-conditioning that time of year. But by the next morning, the scratchiness had turned into a mild sore throat with a bit of muscle achiness, and out of an abundance of caution I took a rapid COVID test. To my horror, a minute later, a dark band popped up indicating I was positive. "Christine," I said timidly, putting on a mask as I walked into the kitchen, "you're not going to believe this." I had had to occasionally deliver bad news to seven U.S. presidents as part of my job, but this moment was more difficult. In fact, it was excruciating.

"Oh my God. What are we going to do now?" she asked.

The problem was not just that I was sick. It was that our daughter Megan was getting married five days later in New Orleans, and I was set to walk her down the aisle. I was devastated that I would have to miss this milestone, and along with a worsening sore throat and achiness I was furious that I had brought this on myself. Christine and I together called Megan, and Megan was terrific—she was way more concerned about me than her—but I knew in my heart that she was crushed. Christine eased some of the disappointment we all felt by FaceTiming me throughout the ceremony and reception so that although I did not get to do the traditional father-daughter dance, I still got to see Megan as a stunning and happy bride.

I later learned from a molecular analysis done at the NIH that I was infected with the Omicron variant BA.2.12.1. This came as no surprise because it was the dominant variant, accounting for 64.2 percent of U.S. cases at that time. My physician started me on Paxlovid, and it was a real advantage to have a wife who had trained as a nurse taking personal care of me. I had one tough night and then started to feel better once the third dose of Paxlovid kicked in. My diagnosis was well covered by the mainstream media, and I was also the butt of a couple of late-night comedians' jokes. I had to laugh at Trevor Noah's comment: "Dr. Fauci has COVID, which feels a little like finding out Smokey the Bear got trapped in a forest fire." I also found to be healing the texts and emails that I received from all over the world wishing me a speedy recovery.

I was thrilled on June 20 when I tested negative. My elation was short-lived. I rebounded and tested positive four days after finishing my five days of Paxlovid. Despite this minor setback, I was thoroughly convinced that Paxlovid did its job, keeping my eighty-one-year-old body out of the hospital and my symptoms not much to write home about.

Then, a month later on July 21, President Biden got COVID. Although his symptoms were mild, I spoke every morning and evening with Dr. Kevin O'Connor, Biden's personal physician at the White House, about every step in the president's treatment regimen, which as the media reported included Paxlovid. It was always a privilege for me to be consulted on a president's care, but these interactions meant even more to me because I found Kevin to be both an excellent physician and a thoroughly likable guy. I knew that with him on the job President Biden was in the best possible hands.

My BOUT WITH COVID did not provide me with immunity against continual attacks by the usual suspects. This was on display on August 9, when I threw out the first pitch in Seattle at the Mariners versus New York Yankees baseball game. Even as I got a prolonged standing ovation from almost all of the forty-five thousand people in T-Mobile Park, there were about six people on the side booing. As I had come to expect, the following day the headline above a video on the website of a conservative-leaning newspaper was FAUCI BOOED BEFORE THROWING FIRST PITCH AT MARINERS V. YANKEES GAME. Sometimes you just cannot win.

Although in this case, I sort of felt that I had. After my errant throw back in 2020 at Nationals Park, this time I redeemed my record somewhat when I was able to get the ball basically over home plate (high and inside) and into the glove of the Mariners' manager, Scott Servais. It was a powerful moment for the young boy in me, whose fantasy was a blazing career at shortstop with the New York Yankees.

Meanwhile, my real career was at a turning point. I was nervous when I met with Ron Klain in his West Wing office on the morning of August 16, 2022. I had no idea how he would react to what I planned to tell him: that I had decided to step down from all of my current positions including chief medical adviser to the president. Based on his wide experience in government, Jeff had counseled me to not be surprised if Ron tried to persuade me to stay on. I said to Ron, "I will make the announcement publicly next week, and I will step down sometime this December." Instead of pushing back, Ron said that although it was his instinct to ask me to stay, he would be embarrassed to try to get me to change my mind about something I had obviously thought about for some time and "that you deserve." After reminiscing for a few minutes about our work together on Ebola under President Obama, Ron told me he would arrange a phone conversation so that I could tell President Biden the news myself.

That call came about twenty-four hours later. "Hi, Joe here," the president said when I answered my phone. I thanked him and said that working with him over the past two years was a highlight of my career. "Doc, you are the best. You have saved a lot of lives, and it has been my great pleasure working with you," he said. I was flattered, and I really could not have asked for a warmer send-off.

The following Monday, August 22, I publicly announced my plan to step down and, as I said, "pursue the next chapter of my career." Speaking with the NIH logo behind me, I said, "I hope to be remembered as someone who gave my all 24-7, and left it all on the field."

Predictably, the response to my announcement reflected the divisions in the country in the same way so much else had in the past two years. Along with phone calls and letters from former presidents, vice presidents, and members of Congress, and thank-yous for my public service from people all over the world, a few MAGA politicians were not as gracious. "Don't let the door hit you on the way out, Dr. Fauci," one said. Others vowed to have me investigated and "thrown in jail" for imaginary crimes, whatever they were, whether I retired or not.

As I rounded the turn into my last few months on the job, one source of concern was that our COVID numbers seemed to hit more or less of a plateau, trending only slightly downward. I wanted to do a last push for vaccinations. For months, producers of *The Late Show with Stephen Colbert* had been asking me to be on the show. I was a big fan of Colbert, and I also had a few things in common with his father, who had graduated from Holy Cross and worked at NIAID for a time. But I kept declining these invitations because my team and I felt strongly that it was inappropriate for me to make light of COVID in any way. Then we hit on a two-birds-one-stone idea: the latest booster had just been released, and I could go on and talk about it.

"Have you had it yet?" Colbert asked me on air.

"I haven't had it yet. I'm due for it," I said.

"We have a drugstore down the street. Do you want to go get the booster right now?"

"Can we? If we can, let's do it!"

With that, we walked out of the studio onto Manhattan's West Fifty-third Street and down the block to the Walgreens pharmacy. On the way, Stephen asked me because we were in New York City to say a few phrases in my best Brooklyn accent, so I happily obliged. "Fuhgetaboutit," I belted out.

When we got inside the store, he cupped his hand to his mouth and said, "Let me know if you need some condoms. I'll ask for you." The TV audience loved it. Then we stopped in the Halloween candy and costume aisle, where he handed me a headband with kitten ears, insisted I put it on, and had me say into the camera, "Don't forget to get your booster." I felt ridiculous, but I was also having the time of my life.

After I got my shot, Stephen produced a gigantic lollipop and told people to head to vaccines.gov to find boosters near them. It was a good way to promote boosters without being heavy-handed, and as I told Stephen on air, "It was worth the trip."

That was not my last chance to talk to the American public about vaccines before I stepped down. On November 22, the White House comms team of Press Secretary Karine Jean-Pierre and Kevin Munoz, who led the White House's COVID-19 messaging, arranged for me to be part of their press briefing. Standing at the lectern, I could not help but think about how many times I had been in this same spot, through HIV, anthrax, pandemic influenza, Ebola, Zika, and then COVID. As emotional as I felt, I wanted to make a graceful exit and decided that this moment was ripe for a public health message. "Please for your own safety, for that of your family, get your updated COVID-19 shot as soon as you're eligible, to protect yourself, your family, and your community."

There was no looking back now.

NIAID AND THE NIH wanted to throw a big bash for me, but I opted instead for a no-bells-and-whistles, carrots-and-hummus affair on the top floor of a campus building. The room was filled with colleagues who felt like family after all our years together. Cliff Lane; Francis Collins; my old pal John Gallin; the acting NIH director, Larry Tabak, another longtime friend; and my dear Christine got up to make a few affectionate remarks. The emphasis here was on "few," because I insisted that no one go on for longer than three minutes so that we could spend more time shaking hands and giving hugs and less time speechifying. I had the last word. I had written out my thoughts and hoped I would get through them without choking up. But when I thanked Christine, I had to stop briefly to contain myself. Even though the ceremony was exactly what I hoped for, there was no getting around the fact that my heart was a little heavy as I went around the room saying goodbye.

A few nights later, Peter Staley, David Barr, Mark Harrington, and some of my other friends from the activist community hosted a dinner in my honor at a downtown D.C. restaurant. We talked about our encounters in the early days of HIV/AIDS when we seemed to be on different sides—I, in the government, and they, protesting the government—and were just realizing that we were trying to achieve similar goals.

Then it was time for me to pack up my office, which was not easy. I of course had amassed a lot of books and photos, but that wasn't what I was sentimental about. The small yucca plant that Christine had given me for my office when I became NIAID director in 1984 had practically taken over the space. I had a psychological connection to the plant, believing that if it survived, I would survive. Over the years the plant grew so big that I attached it at various points across the ceiling with bungee cords. Now we could not get it out of the room intact, but I refused to leave my loyal office mate behind. We brought in a horticulturist to cut it up and plant the pieces in pots, a couple of which I brought home to start anew and others I gave to some of my favorite people at the NIH. I also presented one as a thank-you to Brett Rowland, who took it with him back to his home base in Florida. Finally, on January 4, 2023, I walked down the long hall from my office, headed to the lobby, and went through the front door that I had come in and left from thousands of times. As I got into the car, I turned and took one last look at my building, a building that had been my second home for almost forty years as NIAID director and which in that instant was no longer my building. Seeing the concrete overhang, I pictured a young Peter Staley being dragged off by the police to be arrested during the massive May 1990 ACT UP protest.

It was only as I closed the car door and drove away, reversing the route I had taken in 1968, at age twenty-seven, that I began to grasp the depth and breadth of what I had experienced over those past fifty-four years. I had followed my instincts, my curiosity, my passion for science and medicine. I took risks, and I was not intimidated by the challenges, discouraged by the failures, or self-congratulatory about the triumphs. I had decided back then to embark on a career in infectious diseases and immunology with little idea of what that would ultimately mean. I expected a fulfilling but quiet and predictable life conducting research and treating patients. Then came HIV and AIDS in 1981 when I made the decision to change the direction of my career. AIDS brought me into a world filled with suffering and death. I assumed the dual role of a physician-scientist and a domestic and global leader as NIAID director in the battle against HIV/AIDS. I am immensely proud that I was part of the group that enabled people with HIV to live normal lives. I was honored to serve seven U.S. presidents during outbreaks of pandemic influenza, Ebola, and Zika as well as the anthrax and smallpox threats. I am grateful to President George W. Bush, who gave me the opportunity to play a role in the creation of PEPFAR, one of the most important lifesaving global health initiatives in history.

The last three years of my career were consumed by the most devastating global pandemic in a hundred years, culminating my half-century journey in public service. At every point in that journey, I have done everything I possibly could in my many roles to promote sound public health practices aimed at saving lives.

As I drove out on to Wisconsin Avenue heading back to my house in Washington, D.C., I could only think to myself, "This has been quite a ride, and I am a really lucky guy."

Epilogue

So many things have happened over my eighty-three years, and I have tried to recount in this memoir the experiences that reflect who I am. This book is not meant to be an exhaustive chronicle of AIDS, pandemic influenza, Ebola, COVID-19, and other infectious diseases; instead, I set out to provide context, both personal and historical, for the major events I took part in or observed over my almost sixty years as a physician, scientist, science administrator, and public health official.

But I also believe there is a bigger theme here: at its heart, my story is about what it means to devote one's life to public service.

It has not always been an easy life. It comes with long hours, missing out on personal and family time, an enormous burden of responsibility, and considerable anxiety and stress and, at times, opposition and even hostility. It often requires putting aside personal fears to fulfill one's mandate, and it demands rising to occasions that others might choose to avoid. But it can be a deeply purposeful and rewarding experience, one that centers on taking care of people and working toward the common good.

My parents instilled in me a conviction that helping others

could be a meaningful way of life. This conviction was strengthened during my years in high school and college under the Jesuit priests whose mantra is service to others. In my case, the vehicle for this has always been science and medicine. Yet when I first came to Washington, D.C., from New York City as a fellow at the National Institute of Allergy and Infectious Diseases, I did not know that this calling would take me where it has: to the very center of the catastrophic AIDS epidemic; to helping protect the country from potential bioterrorism threats such as anthrax and smallpox; to combating outbreaks such as influenza, measles, Ebola, and Zika; and of course to contending with the COVID-19 pandemic. My career placed me at the center of crises where I confronted death all around me. These crises also allowed me to participate in and occasionally contribute to breakthroughs that saved countless lives.

Nor could I predict that I would work with so many White House occupants, Republicans and Democrats; testify before Congress hundreds of times; and forge lasting friendships with people of different nationalities and political beliefs. And after a career of remaining determinedly nonpolitical, I certainly could not anticipate that I would become a political lightning rod—a figure who represents hope to so many and evil to some. Beyond my control, I became a symbol of the profound divisiveness in our country.

This brings me to the issue of my now being one of the most recognizable people in the country. The positive aspect of this is that I can touch so many people in a way that helps to preserve or improve their health. But it is one thing to go on TV and deliver public health messages to millions of people where I need only to look into a camera and my impact can be felt. It is an entirely different feeling to walk down the street or into a restaurant or the post office and have most people know who I am. It is this complete loss of privacy for someone who is fundamentally a private person that can be unnerving. This is one of the many ways that COVID has affected me and my family.

As I write this in the winter of 2024, COVID still lingers among us. This disease will not be eradicated and is not likely to be eliminated from certain geographic areas. But we can all see that the dire situation that gripped the nation and the world beginning in the winter of 2020 is behind us. Thanks to vaccines and treatments, most of us are going about our lives as we did before COVID. While I recognize with a heavy heart the cost of the pandemic in terms of lives lost, ongoing health concerns for those with long COVID, and the economic and social upheaval so many people experienced, I am deeply grateful for the scientific and public health progress we have made.

Still, as exceptional and even unique as COVID and this period in our collective history seem to us, unfortunately it was not. The entire history of humanity has been marked by plagues and devastation, and new pandemics will certainly emerge in the future. This is why it is so critical to prepare for the unpredictable, or, as I have often said, expect the unexpected.

At times, I am deeply disturbed about the state of our society. But it is not so much about an impending public health disaster. It is about the crisis of truth in my country and to some extent throughout the world, which has the potential to make these disasters so much worse. We are living in an era in which information that is patently untrue gets repeated enough times that it becomes part of our everyday dialogue and starts to sound true and in a time in which lies are normalized and people invent their own set of facts. We have seen complete fabrications become some people's accepted reality.

This is not a new paradigm. Propaganda—turning words and ideas into weapons—no doubt started thousands of years ago, and we have seen it used to devastating effect many times within the life span of this country as well as over the course of world history. We have seen how easy it is to undermine the foundations of our democracy and of the social order. What is new is the dizzying pace at which information gets disseminated and amplified on the internet and through social media, disorienting and dividing us as a nation.

These divisions did not come out of nowhere, and they will not go away overnight, because they are set in the minds of so many people. It is why I am putting my hope in the young people I encounter around the country and the world.

Which brings me to the next chapter in my life. When I decided to step down from my position as director of NIAID, I asked myself what I could do over the next few years while I am still filled with passion and energy and blessed with good health. The answer came to me quickly and clearly: to share my experiences with the world and particularly the younger generation where I might serve as an example and hopefully an inspiration for some to pursue a life serving others not only in the field of medicine and science but in any of a number of career paths that one might choose. This was my main motivation in writing this memoir.

It was also the reason I was delighted to accept the offer of Georgetown's president, Jack DeGioia, to become a Distinguished University Professor at the School of Medicine and the McCourt School of Public Policy, where I can have daily contact with the bright and inquisitive minds on the Georgetown campus.

In the year since I stepped down as NIAID director, I have had the opportunity to lecture and engage in fireside chats and moderated discussions throughout the country. What became even more clear to me was something I already knew: that the diversity in our country in its myriad forms—geographic, economic, cultural, racial, ethnic, and political—makes us an attractive and great country. It is when this diversity gives way to divisiveness that society suffers.

I have always been a cautious optimist, and I hope that the better angels in all of us, who tell us that we are more alike than different, will prevail and lead to a spirit of civility and respect for each other.

In the coming years, I look forward with a great deal of enthusiasm to spending more time with the love of my life, my wife, Christine Grady, and as much time as possible with my three adult daughters, who are pursuing their own lives and careers. I have recently become a grandfather for the first time, and I can already understand why people want to spend so much time with their grandchildren. I hope this book also will serve as a historical account written by someone who actively participated in historic events.

Finally, I hope it will serve as my way of speaking to the people whom I love the most—my family: my wife, Christine; my daughters, Jenny, Megan, and Ali; my granddaughter, Lina; and grandchildren to come—about the trials, tribulations, and mostly the rewards experienced by someone who gave it his all.

ACKNOWLEDGMENTS

This book is the story of my life through my more than eight decades on this planet. I have been blessed by my association with a number of people who have made this story possible either indirectly through their impact on my life or directly by their encouragement and input into this book. It would be impossible to recognize everyone by name who touched my life during these eighty-three years. Here are a few of them, and I apologize for not naming them all.

My journey in public service was inspired by my parents, Stephen and Eugenia, who taught me the importance of helping others beginning in my early childhood. I thank my sister, Denise, and her late husband, Jack Scorce, and their family whose support never faltered over the years. I was fortunate to have been educated by Dominican nuns at Our Lady of Guadalupe elementary school in Brooklyn. They always expected more of me, which fed into my need to continually do better. I give profound thanks to the Jesuit priests and priests in training and the lay faculty at Regis High School in Manhattan and the College of the Holy Cross in Worcester, Massachusetts, who nurtured in me the concept of and desire for serving others. I cannot overestimate this positive impact on me.

I thank my professors, the attending physicians, and fellow trainees at Cornell University Medical College (now Weill Cornell) and The New York Hospital–Cornell Medical Center, who provided the environment that fostered my love of medicine and who helped teach me the science and art of patient care. Many of my extraordinarily talented classmates at Cornell remain friends to this day.

I spent fifty-four years at the National Institute of Allergy and Infectious Diseases at the National Institutes of Health, my professional home and the setting for most of this memoir. It would be impossible to adequately thank the large number of people who were mentors to me, my mentees, and the other administrators, physicians, nurses, and health-care personnel with whom I worked closely and learned from. You know who you are, and for those no longer with us, your families and friends know. I am in debt to the many members of my lab, the Laboratory of Immunoregulation, who were integral to any and all of my scientific accomplishments. I give specific thanks to the late Sheldon M. "Shelly" Wolff, who recruited me to NIAID. Shelly became one of my closest friends, and I learned more from him than from any other individual physician-scientist, not only about medicine and science but about the importance of asking critical questions. Of course, I thank my late dear friend and principal deputy Jim Hill, my relationship with whom I describe in great detail in this memoir. I also thank the late James F. Dickson III, M.D., for his friendship and sage advice on how to navigate the complexities of the White House. I thank Dr. Jack Whitescarver and the late Dr. Richard Krause for their unflinching support of me. I thank Dr. Henry Masur for being part of the original NIAID AIDS team with me and Cliff Lane.

Among my colleagues at NIAID, I would like to single out a few who stood by me through tribulations and triumphs and without whom I could not have achieved what I did. John Gallin and his wife, Elaine, have been Christine's and my closest friends for decades and served as reliable sounding boards. I could not have performed as effectively as director and chief of a research laboratory without having the immensely scientifically and clinically talented Cliff Lane, my colleague, dear friend, and trusted confidant, by my side. Greg Folkers, unselfish, loyal, and a man of the utmost integrity, helped me wear my multiple hats by serving as a walking encyclopedia of valuable information. I thank my late principal deputy John LaMontagne, who opened my eyes to the dangers of emerging infectious diseases, and his successor, the steadfast Hugh Auchincloss. I thank Jill

Harper, my most recent deputy director for science management. I thank my former deputy director for science management John Mc-Gowan and my former executive officer Mike Goldrich for teaching me how to navigate government bureaucracy. I thank the NIAID division directors who served during my tenure, particularly Jack Killen, Carl Dieffenbach, Carole Heilman, Emily Erbelding, Dan Rotrosen, Kathy Zoon, Steve Holland, Matthew Fenton, Gary Nabel, and John Mascola together with their talented staffs, as well as the several division directors who preceded them over my almost forty years as NIAID director. I also thank the many talented individuals who served as assistants and advisors in my immediate director's office. I thank the many NIAID office directors and their talented staffs, especially Courtney Billet, director of communications and government relations, and her amazing staff who served me so well over many stressful years. A special thanks to Laurie Doepel for her sharp editorial eye.

I am grateful to Patty Conrad, my special assistant extraordinaire, my wonderful assistant Kim Barasch, and their talented predecessors who served my office over the years. After I left the NIH, Jenn Kuzmuk took the baton as my indispensable special assistant. A very special thanks to my talented and totally reliable IT person, David Awwad.

I thank the many hundreds of patients whom I took care of directly or consulted on at the NIH Clinical Center over my more than half a century at this extraordinary facility. It was a privilege to care for them, and they taught me so much about medicine and about humanity.

I could not have asked for better colleagues than the directors of the twenty-six other institutes and centers at the NIH. While I was NIAID director, I was fortunate to serve under five permanent and five acting (interim) directors. Among these uniformly brilliant individuals, some became good friends, including the late James B. Wyngaarden, who appointed me as NIAID director, the late Ruth Kirschstein, Elias Zerhouni, Harold Varmus, Francis Collins, and Larry Tabak.

As I describe in this memoir, I had the privilege of serving seven presidents of the United States, their vice presidents, their immediate staffs, and members of their cabinets. I want to thank them for an honor that I could never have conceived of as I took the Hippocratic oath in 1966.

I particularly want to thank people at the Department of Health and Human Services who became my friends and continued to support and encourage me long after they moved on. I am indebted to the following HHS secretaries as well as their staffs: the late Louis Sullivan, Donna Shalala, Tommy Thompson, Michael Leavitt, Kathleen Sebelius, Sylvia Burwell, Alex Azar, and Xavier Becerra. I am particularly grateful to Donna Shalala, Tommy Thompson, and Sylvia Burwell for their enduring friendship and to Sylvia for choosing me as one of three speakers to celebrate the hanging of her portrait in the Hubert H. Humphrey Building. I am especially indebted to Stewart Simonson, who was assistant secretary for preparedness and response under Tommy Thompson and who became a close family friend and trusted confidant, always providing sound advice.

Others who served in various administrations deserve special thanks for their friendship, encouragement, and assistance, particularly those involved in the creation of PEPFAR. I thank Mark Dybul, Josh Bolten, Gary Edson, Jay Lefkowitz, Kristen Silverberg, Margaret Spellings, and the late Michael Gerson. I also want to thank Secretaries of State Condoleezza Rice and the late Colin Powell for their help with PEPFAR. The latter also gave me important tips in writing this memoir. I thank Bono for his encouragement and friendship. I thank Vice President Dick Cheney and his chief of staff Lewis "Scooter" Libby for trusting and helping me put together the post-9/11 biodefense plan. I thank Ron Klain for his guidance during Ebola in the Obama administration and his leadership as chief of staff during the Biden administration. Special thanks to my dear friend Susan Rice, who served in multiple roles in both the Obama and the Biden administrations. I also thank Denis McDonough, whom I first met when he was a staffer for Senator Tom Daschle more than twenty years ago. He has been a friend and supporter during his multiple roles in the Obama and Biden administrations. I thank Lisa Monaco, who was so supportive during the Ebola and Zika crises during the Obama administration and who went on to serve in the Biden administration. I thank Hillary Clinton, who was helpful to and supportive of me during various public health challenges in her multiple roles as first lady, senator, and secretary of state. I thank all the leaders and members of the coronavirus task force during the Trump administration, particularly Deb Birx, who has been a friend and colleague for decades, as well as the other physicians on the task force, Jerome Adams, Bob Redfield, and Stephen Hahn. I also thank Marc Short, Katie Miller, Olivia Troye, and Alyssa Farah Griffin for their support during difficult times. I thank the Biden COVID-19 Response Team, including Ashish Jha, Lisa Barclay, Vivek Murthy, Rochelle Walensky, David Kessler, Marcella Nunez-Smith, Bechara Choucair, Cyrus Shahpar, Andy Slavitt, Natalie Quillian, Courtney Rowe, Ben Wakana, Kevin Munoz, and Kate Berner, among others.

A very special thanks to the immensely talented and universally admired Jeff Zients, with whom I worked daily during his tenure as the coordinator of the COVID-19 Response Team. I got to know Jeff when he was at the National Economic Council and OMB during the Obama administration. Jeff and his wife, Mary, have become cherished friends. He closely advised me on important career decisions during my last two years at the NIH.

I thank the large number of my colleagues and other friends, some of whom were in government for a period, for their support and friendship. Special thanks to the long line of CDC directors, together with their talented and dedicated personnel, alongside whom I had the privilege of serving for so many years. I also point out the late Paul Farmer, Hilary Marston, Tom Frieden, Bill Gates, Larry Corey, Bart Haynes, Rob Califf, Bob Seder, Julie Gerberding, Giuseppe Pantaleo, David Morens, Lorenzo Moretta, Margaret (Peggy) Hamburg, and Eric Goosby. I thank the late Rob Stein and Ellen Perry for their years of friendship and support. I am grateful for the love and support of Christine's family, including her late parents, John and Barbara Grady, and her four siblings, Joanne, Barbara, Jack, and Bob, and their families. I thank Neal Katyal, David Schertler, Danny Onorato, Drs. Alec Whyte, Theodore Li, David Hellmann, Stephen Yang, and Andrew Lerner for their advice and care.

I thank the many members of the AIDS activist community for pushing me to do better and for their unflinching support over the past few years. Particular thanks to my close friend and comrade in arms, Peter Staley, as well as to David Barr, Mark Harrington, Gregg

Gonsalves, Lawrence (Bopper) Deyton, and the late Marty Delaney and Larry Kramer.

Over my almost forty years as NIAID director, I had the privilege of testifying before the U.S. House of Representatives and the U.S. Senate literally hundreds of times and have encountered many fine people in both bodies, many of whom became friends. I thank them.

I believe strongly in the importance of the press, the legitimate press, that is, which is integral to our democracy. Over the past forty years, I have had the opportunity to work with some of the finest print, TV, radio, and digital journalists, many of whom have become friends. There are so many of them that I hesitate to single out only a few, but you know who you are.

Special gratitude goes to my security details. The HHS security team included, among others, Brett Rowland, George Adams, and Andre Jacobs. I am profoundly grateful to Brett, who spent three years with us and became a treasured friend. Shawn Larson and Urbino "Benny" Martinez led the U.S. Marshals Service team. I extend my deepest thanks to them for keeping me and my family safe.

With the encouragement of many of the people mentioned above, I began writing my memoir full-time after stepping down as director of NIAID. I had been working on drafts nights, weekends, and holidays at home for years. I needed to find out if the book was going in the right direction. One person among several stands out as a critical figure in my pushing forward with the project. That was Rick Atkinson, an old friend and two-time Pulitzer Prize winner, once for journalism at *The Kansas City Times* and again for history as the author of *An Army at Dawn: The War in North Africa, 1942–1943*. Rick was the first person to read the manuscript. I will be forever grateful to him for his literary suggestions as well as his friendship and generosity.

I had known the attorney Bob Barnett for more than twenty years, mostly through Washington, D.C., social events. I also know his wife, Rita Braver, who interviewed me several times as a CBS News correspondent. Almost every time we met, Bob reminded me to see him when I was ready to step down from the NIH and write a book. And so, when I was ready to take the plunge, I contacted Bob, and that was one of the best decisions that I have ever made. Bob guided me through the process of writing a book proposal and choosing a publisher. But more than that, he was available on a moment's notice to help me negotiate other career decisions such as joining the faculty at Georgetown University. Bob has become a dear friend and confidante.

I thank Dr. John "Jack" DeGioia, president of Georgetown University, who visited me at the NIH years ago and suggested that I join the Georgetown faculty after I stepped down from NIAID, whenever that would be. Soon after my retirement, he offered me a position as Distinguished University Professor with a joint appointment in the School of Medicine and the McCourt School of Public Policy. I accepted with great enthusiasm. He graciously allowed me the time to finish my book even as he welcomed me into the outstanding Georgetown academic community. I thank Jack for his kindness and flexibility.

I thank Brian Tart, president and publisher of Viking, for taking me and my project on. I thank my extremely talented and tough editor, Wendy Wolf. She pushed and pushed, getting me to cut stories that I loved and people I wanted to include. "You may love it," she stated firmly, "but your reader does not really care. Cut it." After I stopped grumbling about her under my breath, I realized that she was correct. This book is considerably better because of her input.

I was not planning to have a "collaborator" to help me line edit the 80 percent of the book that I had already written and write with me the 20 percent that needed to be completed. Bob Barnett and a close friend, Liz Whisnant, persuaded me to engage a collaborator. Enter Linda Kulman, a former journalist and experienced wordsmith. Bringing on Linda is one of the best decisions I made about the book. Besides being extremely talented and knowledgeable, she was great fun to work with. She made the sometimes-tedious task of going over every line of the book together (more than once) actually enjoyable, and I wound up with a new good friend.

I thank the people who generously took the time to read what I have written. My wife, Christine Grady, an excellent writer herself, read the entire manuscript carefully and made several critical suggestions, all of which I followed closely. Cliff Lane, who lived through much of the story with me, offered excellent recommendations for which I am grateful. Greg Folkers, who helped edit almost every scientific and policy paper I have written and almost every lecture I have given over the decades, applied the same sharp eye to my memoir. Peter Staley read the chapter on HIV activism and made valuable suggestions.

My daughters, Jenny, Megan, and Ali, read the chapter on the family ("La Famiglia") and reminded me of moments I had forgotten. I am particularly appreciative of Jenny's very precise pen. I thank my daughters, whose unconditional love never prevented them from telling me an inconvenient truth that I might not like to hear. It has made me a better father and person.

Finally, I thank Christine, the love of my life and my inspiration. She has been my partner, my adviser, my gentle critic, and my best friend. The hundreds of hours I put into this book took away from our time together, but her only reaction was encouragement.

Please scan the following code or go to the URL beneath it for the endnotes to this title.

https://sites.prh.com/oncall